vanDam. NY @tlas

In celebration of the city's Centennial, VanDam
presents the first innovation in urban cartography
in 50 years. Here's what they say about VanDam:

"...A sophisticated resource..." **NEW YORK TIMES**

*"The best innovation in map design since the globe
was flattened onto paper!"* **DIVERSION MAGAZINE**

"...For savvy travelers..." **PLAYBOY**

"Ingenious... A magical series..." **TRAVEL & LEISURE**

Vent, applaud, criticize and respond: www.vandam.com.

NY @tlas

Centennial Edition

While the area of today's New York had been settled by the Manates for millennia, it was first settled by the Dutch in 1626. The City of New York, incorporating the five boroughs of the Bronx, Brooklyn, Manhattan, Queens and Staten Island, is a more recent invention and dates back only to 1898.

NY@tlas organizes the metropolis into three easily accessible parts:

Basics: neighborhoods, hospitals, schools, streets, and the like.

Top 100: the best in dining, attractions, architecture, hotels, performing arts, nightlife, shopping, sports, natural resources, theatre, education & more.

Histories: Ten diagrammatic spreads illustrate how NYC has shaped global pop culture.

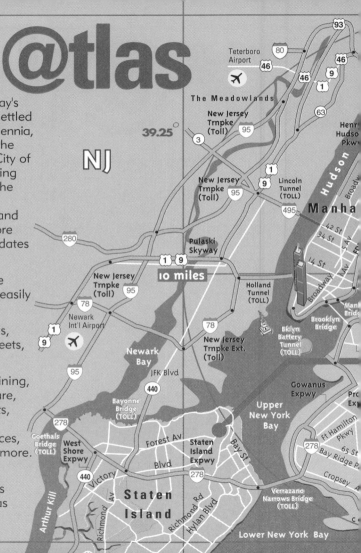

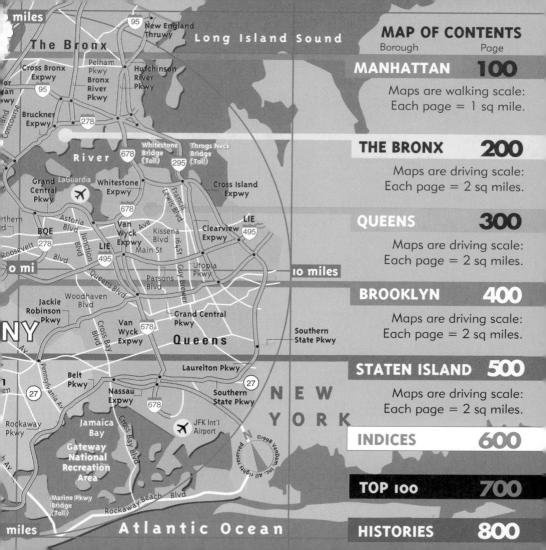

The Bronx

Long Island Sound

New England Thruway

95

Pelham Pkwy

Cross Bronx Expwy

95

Bronx River Pkwy

Hutchinson River Pkwy

Bruckner Expwy

278

River

678

Whitestone Bridge (Toll)

Throgs Neck Bridge (Toll)

295

Grand Central Pkwy

LaGuardia

Whitestone Expwy

Cross Island Expwy

Astoria Blvd

Francis Lewis Blvd

BQE

278

Junction Blvd

Van Wyck Expwy

Kissena Blvd

Clearview Expwy

LIE

495

Roosevelt

LIE

495

Main St

164 St

Guy Brewer

Utopia Pkwy

10 miles

Queens Blvd

Parsons Blvd

Grand Central Pkwy

Jackie Robinson Pkwy

Woodhaven Blvd

Van Wyck Expwy

678

Queens

Southern State Pkwy

Cross Bay Blvd

NY

Belt Pkwy

Laurelton Pkwy

Pennsylvania Av

27

Nassau Expwy

678

Southern State Pkwy

27

N E W

Rockaway Pkwy

Jamaica Bay

Cross Bay Blvd

JFK Int'l Airport

©1998 VanDam, Inc. All rights reserved

Y O R K

Gateway National Recreation Area

Marine Pkwy Bridge (Toll)

Rockaway Beach Blvd

miles

Atlantic Ocean

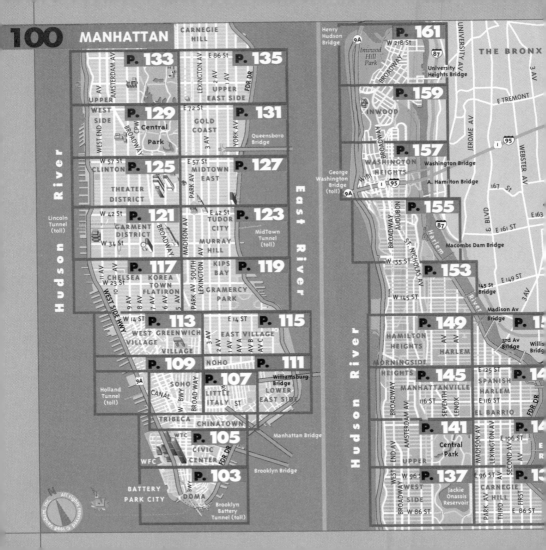

MANHATTAN

CARNEGIE HILL

P. 133

LEXINGTON AV   E 86 St   **P. 135**

AMSTERDAM AV

UPPER

2 AV   FDR DR

UPPER EAST SIDE

WEST SIDE   **P. 129**

E 72 St   **P. 131**

WEST END   Central Park

GOLD COAST

BROADWAY   CPW

YORK AV   3 AV

Queensboro Bridge

W 57 St   **P. 125**   E 57 St   **P. 127**

CLINTON

MIDTOWN EAST

THEATER DISTRICT

PARK AV

W 42 St   **P. 121**

E 42 St   **P. 123**

GARMENT DISTRICT

BROADWAY

TUDOR CITY

W 34 St

MADISON AV   SOUTH

MURRAY HILL

MidTown Tunnel (toll)

Lincoln Tunnel (toll)

P. 117

KIPS BAY   **P. 119**

11 AV   AV

CHELSEA   KOREA TOWN

W 23 St

FLATIRON

9 AV   8 AV

7 AV   6 AV   5 AV

LEXINGTON   PARK AV SOUTH

GRAMERCY PARK

W 14 St   **P. 113**

E 14 St   **P. 115**

WEST VILLAGE   GREENWICH VILLAGE

3 AV   2 AV   1 AV

AV A   AV B   AV C   AV D

EAST VILLAGE

P. 109   NOHO   **P. 111**

9A

SOHO   **P. 107**

CANAL   W. BWY   BROADWAY

Williamsburg Bridge

Holland Tunnel (toll)

LITTLE ITALY   St

LOWER EAST SIDE

TRIBECA

CHINATOWN

WTC   **P. 105**

CIVIC CENTER

FDR DR

WFC

Manhattan Bridge

Brooklyn Bridge

BWY   **P. 103**

BATTERY PARK CITY   DUMA

Brooklyn Battery Tunnel (toll)

N   ALL RIGHTS   © 1998 VAN DAM, INC.

Henry Hudson Bridge

P. 161

9A   W 218 St

UNIVERSITY AV

Inwood Hill Park

87

THE BRONX

BROADWAY

University Heights Bridge

3 AV

E TREMONT

P. 159

INWOOD

JEROME AV

95

BROADWAY

P. 157

WASHINGTON HEIGHTS   Washington Bridge

WEBSTER AV

George Washington Bridge (toll)

W 181   I   95

A. Hamilton Bridge

167 St

9A

P. 155

BROADWAY   AUDUBON

87

ST NICHOLAS AV

E 163

3 BLVD   E 161 ST

W 155 St

Harlem   Macombs Dam Bridge

River

P. 153

W 145 St

145 St Bridge

E 149 ST

3 AV

Madison Av Bridge

Hudson River

P. 149

P. 15_

HAMILTON HEIGHTS

AV   AV

HARLEM

3rd Av Bridge   Willis Bridg_

MORNINGSIDE HEIGHTS

P. 145

E 125 ST

P. 14_

SPANISH HARLEM

BROADWAY

AMSTERDAM AV

116 ST

SEVENTH   LENOX

E 116 ST

FDR DR

MANHATTANVILLE

EL BARRIO

P. 141

MADISON AV   LEXINGTON AV

E 106 ST

P. 14_

END AV   AMSTERDAM AV

Central Park

FIRST   SECOND AV   AV

WEST   W 96 St   **P. 137**

UPPER

E 96 ST   AV

P. 1__

WEST SIDE

BROADWAY   BROADWAY

Jackie Onassis Reservoir

W 86 ST

CARNEGIE HILL

PARK AV   THIRD

FIRST   AV

E 86 ST

Manhattan's Best

his is the ultimate vertical city
here "the Culture of Congestion"
les.

entral Park is the city's
rand public square. Treasured
y locals and visitors alike, it is
e locus for play, pastoral love,
orse—back riding, jogging,
irding, biking, rollerblading &
cnics. Its Metropolitan Opera
nd Philharmonic concerts in
e summer and the NY Marathon
November are living proof of
w the uniquely American
uman experiment can work. **129A**

ainbow Room Uniquely NY!
eserve for dinner and dancing in
e clouds. The "Fred & Ginger"
t is an Art Deco stunner as is the
2 prix fixe. The best views are
om the Promenade Bar. 30 Rock.
aza, 65th fl, 212-632-5100. **126A**

orld Financial Center

merica's most successful urban
velopment of the 1980s opened
e city to the Hudson & reinvented
wntown as a destination.
hiffing the breezes on the
planade, one is tempted to forsake
e country for the city. The free
ening mambo and guajira
ncerts in the summer have made
eat strides in unwelding
rtherners at the hip. **104C**

The Metropolitan Museum of Art

Covering five millennia, this is the
world's encyclopedia of the arts
with collections too numerous to
list. Favorites include the Rockefeller
wing, the Egyptian galleries and
the Lehman Wing. Allow for more
than one visit to drink in the views
of Central Park from the Roof Terrace
Bar. 5 Av ⊘ 82 St, 212-535-7710. **133B**

Lever House This classic of
Corbusian modernism marked the
beginning of what has become a
virtual museum of modern
architecture on Park Avenue. **126B**

TriBeCa Once the poor cousin
of SoHo,TriBeCa (Triangle below
Canal St) is now the rich Hollywood
uncle. Robert de Niro's Tribeca Grill,
Drew Nieporent's Montrachet and
Nobu as well as Chanterelle and
Bouley Bakery are the temples of
haute cuisine downtown.
Yes, that's JFK Jr. at the bar.
(Check top 100 Dining for
details). **106C**

Chrysler Building

Despite recent plans to turn
it into a hotel, William Van Alen's
classic Deco tower remains the
pièce de resistance of
1930s American skyscraper
design. 405 Lexington Av,
212-682-3070. **126C**

Manhattan Stats
Population:
1.4 million
Area: 24 sq miles

Chrysler Building
by William Van Alen

Lever House
by Gordon Bunschaft

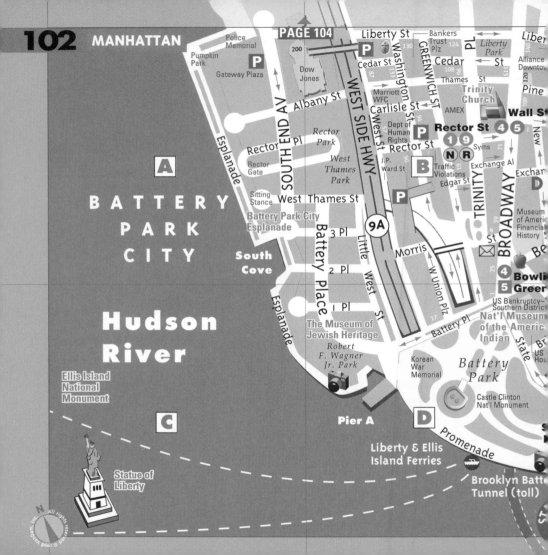

PAGE 104

Police
Memorial

Pumpkin
Park

Liberty St

Bankers
Trust Plz 124

Liber

P

Cedar St

Washington St

GREENWICH ST

Cedar

St

Liberty
Park

Alliance
Downtov

Gateway Plaza

200

Dow
Jones

Albany St

108

130

133

87

Thames St

Trinity
Church

Pine

SOUTH END AV

Marriott
WFC

Carlisle St

AMEX

Wall St

WEST SIDE HWY

West St

Dept of
Human
Rights

Rector St 4 5

Esplanade

Rector St

Rector
Park

P

1 9

N R

Syms

71

New

Rector
Gate

West
Thames
Park

J.P.
Ward St

Rector St

TRINITY

Exchange Al

Exchar

D

BATTERY
PARK
CITY

Sitting
Stance

West Thames St

B

Traffic
Violations

Edgar St

BROADWAY

39

Museum
of Americ
Financial
History

Battery Park City
Esplanade

P

Be

South
Cove

3 Pl

9A

Morris

W Union Plz

25

Bowli
Greer

Battery Place

2 Pl

Little West St

4 5

Esplanade

1 Pl

17

US Bankruptcy–
Southern Distric

Hudson
River

The Museum of
Jewish Heritage

Robert
F. Wagner
Jr. Park

Battery Pl

Korean
War
Memorial

Battery
Park

Nat'l Museum
of the Americ
Indian

Ellis Island
National
Monument

C

Castle Clinton
Nat'l Monument

Br
US Hou

Pier A

D

Promenade

S

Statue of
Liberty

Liberty & Ellis
Island Ferries

Brooklyn Batt
Tunnel (toll)

N

QUEENS

START WALK

BROOKLYN

Maiden St

Platt St

Gold St

John St

Fletcher St

Louise
Nevelson Plz

Fortis

Chase
Manhattan
Plaza

Legion
Memorial Sq

Pearl

US Life

Maiden Ln

Cedar St

William St

Federal
Hall, Heritage
Trails

Bank
of NY

J P
Morgan

Continental
Center

WALL

Skyscraper
Museum

St

Hanover St

Water St

Front

ST

FDR DRIVE

South St

NYHRC

A

Hanover
Sq

Gouverneur Ln

William St

P

Mill La

S William St

Coenties Al

Pearl

Old Slip

P

Fraunces
Tavern
Museum

Goldman
Sachs

**Broad
St**

Coenties
Slip
Jeanette Park

J

M

Z

1 NY
Plaza

P

Moore St

NYHRC

N

R

Whitehall St

Peter Minuit Plaza

C

1 **9**

Staten
Island
Ferry

Vietnam Veterans
Memorial Plaza

1

Wall St
Heliport

Governors
Island
Ferry

Staten
Island
Ferry

Weehawken
Port Liberté,
Jersey City
Ferries

South
Street
Seaport
Ferry

17

16

B

Yankee
Clipper

14

13

Wall
Street
Ferry

11

Floating
Hospital

9

LaGuardia
Shuttle

Brooklyn Army
Terminal &
Atlantic Highlands,
Highlands Ferries

PAGE 406

1 MILE= 1.6 KMS

East **D**
River

END 20 MINS

1 MILE= 1.6 KMS

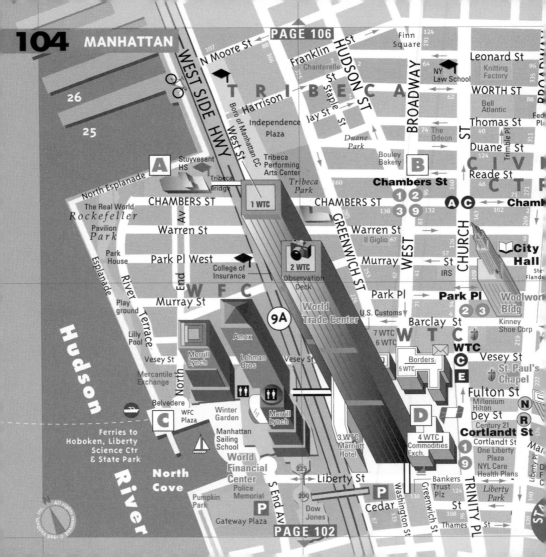

PAGE 106

Finn Square

Leonard St

Knitting Factory

WORTH ST

Bell Atlantic

Thomas St

NY Law School

N Moore St

Franklin St

Chanterelle

HUDSON ST

Staple St

BROADWAY

T R I B E C A

Harrison

Independence Plaza

Jay St

Staple St

Duane Park

The Odeon

Duane St

Trimble Pl

Fed'l Pl

WEST SIDE HWY

Boro of Manhattan CC

WEST ST

Bouley Bakery

B

CIVI

CTR

Stuyvesant HS

A

Tribeca Bridge

CHAMBERS ST

Tribeca Performing Arts Center

Tribeca Park

Chambers St

Reade St

Chamb

North Esplanade

1 WTC

CHAMBERS ST

1 2

A C

9

The Real World

Rockefeller Park

Pavilion

Warren St

Warren St

Il Giglio

WEST

CHURCH

City Hall

Park House

Esplanade

River Terrace

Park Pl West

College of Insurance

End Av

2 WTC

Observation Deck

Murray St

IRS

Ste Flande

Play ground

Murray St

W F C

Park Pl

Park Pl

2 3

Woolwor Bldg

Lilly Pool

9A

World Trade Center

U.S. Customs

Barclay St

Kinney Shoe Corp

Hudson River

Vesey St

North

Amex

7 WTC 6 WTC

W T C

WTC

Vesey St

C

St Paul's Chapel

Mercantile Exchange

Merrill Lynch

Lehman Bros

Vesey St

Borders

5 WTC

E

Fulton St

Millenium Hilton

Dey St

N

Belvedere

C

WFC Plaza

Winter Garden

Merrill Lynch

D

Century 21

R

Ferries to Hoboken, Liberty Science Ctr & State Park

Manhattan Sailing School

4 WTC Commodities Exch.

Cortlandt St

1 9

Cortlandt St

One Liberty Plaza

NYL Care Health Plans

World Financial Center

Police Memorial

3 WTC Marriott Hotel

Washington St

Greenwich St

Bankers Trust Plz

Liberty

North Cove

S End Av

225

Liberty St

Liberty Park

Pumpkin Park

P

Dow Jones

200

P

Cedar

Bankers Trust Plz

St

Gateway Plaza

PAGE 102

Thames St

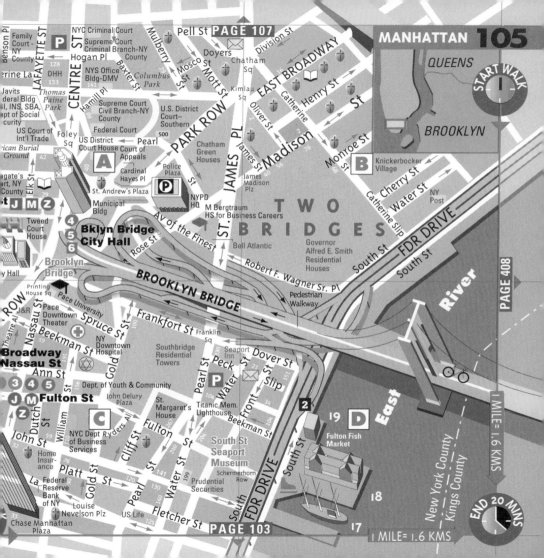

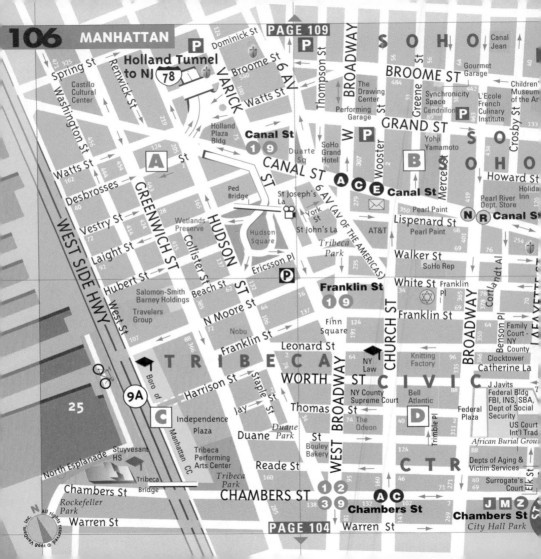

PAGE 109

PAGE 104

PAGE 112

W 10 St

Weehawken St

Christopher St

St Luke's-in-the-Field

Wings
The
Archive

HUDSON ST

Barrow St

GREENWICH ST

West St

Morton St

Leroy St

Printing
House
Fitness &
Racquet

B FedEx

Clarkson St

560 Wash.

WEST HOUSTON St

Saate
Saate
Turne
Corp

A

St. John's
Bldg

UPS
Terminal

Washington St

46

45

42

P

9A

Port
Authority

40

Hudson River

Ear
Ca
Cu
Ce

CAN

WESTSIDE HWY

C

78 Holland Tunnel to NJ

34

D

Watts

32

De

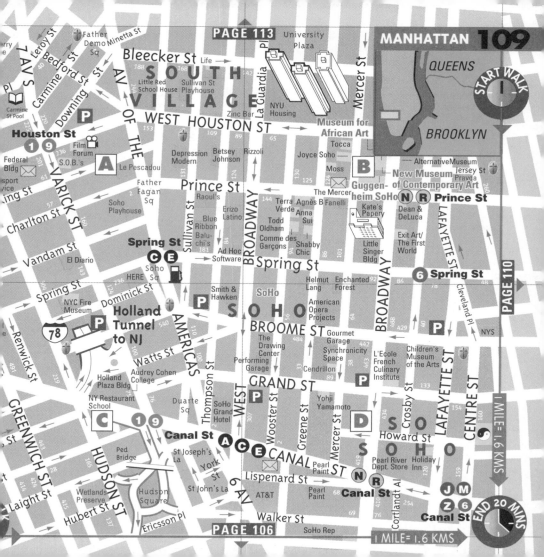

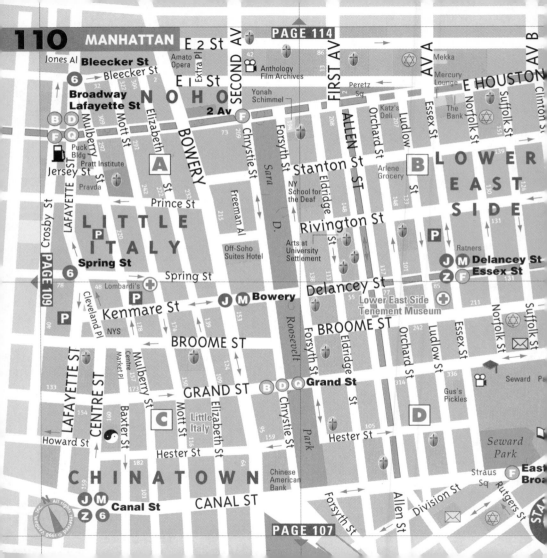

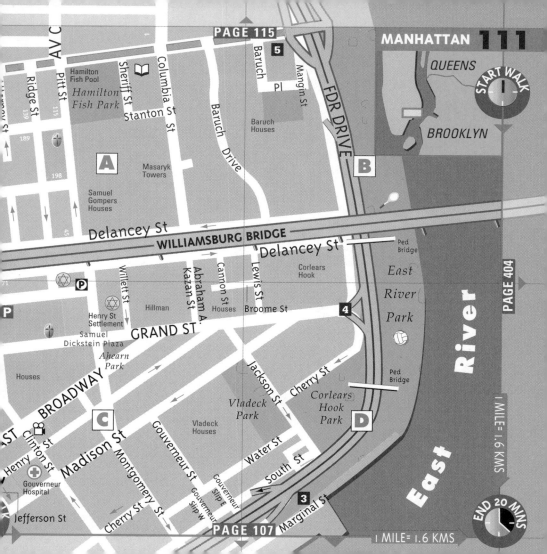

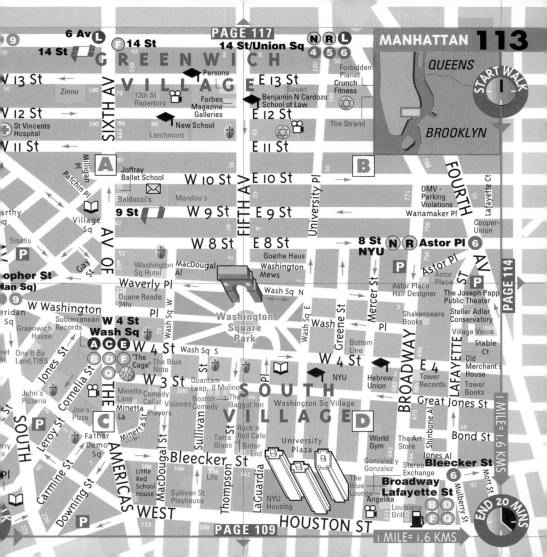

PAGE 118

E 14 St

L 1 Av

Variety Arts 106

Kiel's

92

CSC Rep 142

100

Agrotikon 50

NY Eye & Ear Infirmary

300

213

219

444

500

210

E 13 St

246

Ukrainian Museum

192

Detour 356

198

448

500

550

196

E 12 St

Webster Hall

Stuyvesant Al

242 Iso

Angelica Kitchen

P

Brownies

500

546

67

NY Central Art Supply

124

St Mark's Book Shop

Lafayette Ct

232

Dancespace at St Mark's Church–in–the–Bowery

A

E 11 St

Izzy Bar Standard

B

500

Tompkins Sq

548

162

FOURTH AV

98

128

145

Wanamaker Pl

115

Hasaki Coney Island High

2 Av Deli

Theater for the New City PS 122

Russian & Turkish Baths

Alt. Coffee

134

129

Tompkins Square Park

Around the Clock

138

E 10 St

E 9 St

Stuyvesant St

147

756

746

St Mark's Book Shop

Astor Pl

6 Astor Pl

Jules

P

Alphabets

EAST

Cooper-Union

McSorley's

119

Orpheum

Pearl Theater Co

115

Saint Mark's Pl

VILLAGE

Astor Wines & Liquors

P

THIRD AV

E 7 St

Astor Pl

The Joseph Papp Public Theater

Taras Shevchenko Pl

36

104

48

86

University of the Streets

100

Pyramid Club

95

ALPHA

YWCA

2

Stella Adler Conservatory

E 6 St

Opaline

74

CIT

Audobon Society

Village Voice

200

87

E 5 St

Village View Houses

59

550

56

Stable Ct

Cooper Sq

NY Theater Workshop

300

185

Old Merchant's House

44

Duo

La MaMa E.T.C.

130

138

First Houses

180

242

AV A

AV B

Fez

684

Bowery Bar

86

53

Little Rickie

50

42

Brisas la Caribe

Great

Jones St

E 4 St

SECOND AV

FIRST AV

670

Jean Cocteau Rep

19

Bouwerie Lane Theater

C

E 3 St

Internet Cafe

D

Nuyorican Poets Cafe

Bond St

NOHO

E 2 St

86

Shinbone Al

644

Jones Al

Bleecker St

Amato Opera

Extra Pl

13

Anthology Film Archives

Mekka

225

SoHo B & B

6

BOWERY

Mott St

Elizabeth St

CBGB

E 1 St

Peretz Sq

Mercury Lounge

Crosby St

Broadway Lafayette St

22

Yonah Schimmel

Orchard St

Ludlow St

207

Essex St

The Bank

Norfolk St

151

Suffolk St

B D

F C

2 Av

F

EAST

HOUSTON ST

73

208

PAGE 110

PAGE 113

6

QUEENS

START WALK

BROOKLYN

213

700

199

700

198

P

654

740

Jacob Riis Houses

650

162

P A

Szold Pl

147

East River Park

East

B

394

145

700

448

134

650

126

700

Jacob Riis Houses

B St

FDR

107

90

E T

90

77

ixth & B

60

700
301

752
41

Lillian Wald Houses

300
33

360

AV C

AV D

1

C

5

D

River

Baruch

Mangin St

Attorney St

Ridge St

139

Pitt St

115

Hamilton Fish Pool

Hamilton Fish Park

Sheriff St

Columbia St

Baruch Dr

Baruch Pl

DRIVE

Stanton St

Baruch Houses

1 MILE= 1.6 KMS

END 20 MINS

1 MILE= 1.6 KMS

PAGE 120

W 29 St

W 28 St

Tunnel

W 27 St

W 26 St

W 25 St

W 24 St

W 23 ST

W 22 St

W 21 St

W 20 St

W 19 St

W 18 St

W 17 St

W 16 St

W 15 St

W 14 ST

TWELFTH AV

ELEVENTH AV

WEST SIDE HWY

9A

Hudson River

67

66

A

64

63 Great Hudson Sailing Center

Outdoor In-Line Roller Rinks

62 Ice Rinks

Sports Super Store

61

Basketball Volleyball

Chelsea Piers

60 Batting Practice

Golf Driving Range

C

59

58

57

US Postal Service

Chelsea Park

Elliott Houses

Chelsea Houses

B

London Terrace

DOT Towaway

Empire Diner

WPA

Dia Center for the Arts

GALLERY ROW

W E C H E E

The Kitchen
The Roxy

P

TENTH AV

D DEA

Prince Lumber

P

VanDam Bldg

The Cooler

PAGE 112

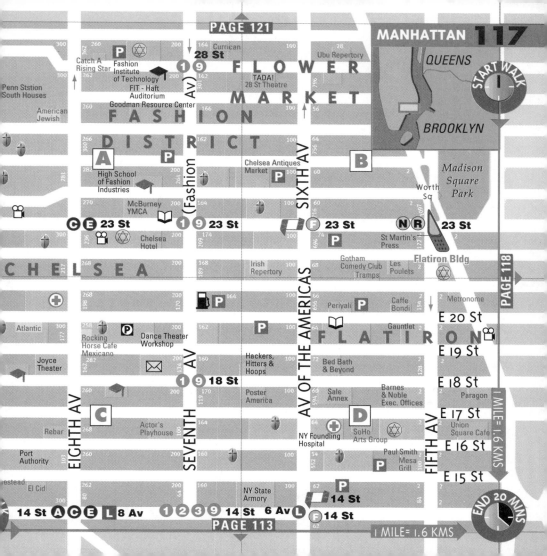

PAGE 121

QUEENS

START WALK

BROOKLYN

Catch A Rising Star

Fashion Institute of Technology

FIT - Haft Auditorium

Goodman Resource Center

Penn Ststion South Houses

American Jewish

Ubu Repertory

28 St

Currican

TADA! 28 St Theatre

F L O W E R

M A R K E T

F A S H I O N

D I S T R I C T

A

B

High School of Fashion Industries

Chelsea Antiques Market

Madison Square Park

Worth Sq

(Fashion AV)

SIXTH AV

McBurney YMCA

23 St

23 St

23 St

N **R** 23 St

Chelsea Hotel

St Martin's Press

C H E L S E A

Irish Repertory

Gotham Comedy Club Tramps

Les Poulets

Flatiron Bldg

PAGE 118

Caffe Bondi

Metronome

E 20 St

Periyali

Gauntlet

AV OF THE AMERICAS

F L A T I R O N

Atlantic

Rocking Horse Cafe Mexicano

Dance Theater Workshop

Hackers, Hitters & Hoops

Bed Bath & Beyond

E 19 St

E 18 St

Joyce Theater

18 St

SEVENTH AV

Poster America

Sale Annex

Barnes & Noble Exec. Offices

Paragon

C

Actor's Playhouse

NY Foundling Hospital

D

SoHo Arts Group

E 17 St

Union Square Cafe

Rebar

EIGHTH AV

Port Authority

Paul Smith

Mesa Grill

FIFTH AV

E 16 St

E 15 St

El Cid

estead

NY State Armory

1 MILE= 1.6 KMS

14 St **A** **C** **E** **L** 8 Av **1** **2** **3** **9** 14 St 6 Av **L** **F** 14 St

PAGE 113

END 20 MINS

1 MILE= 1.6 KMS

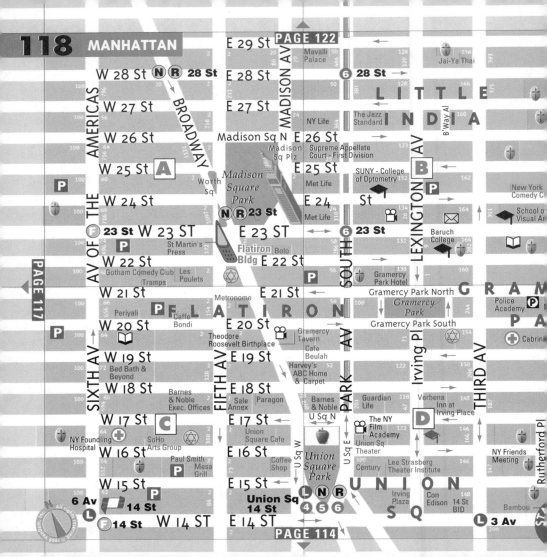

PAGE 122
PAGE 117
PAGE 114

E 29 St

W 28 St (N)(R) 28 St   E 28 St   (6) 28 St

W 27 St   E 27 St

W 26 St   Madison Sq N   E 26 St

W 25 St   A   E 25 St

W 24 St   E 24 St

(F) 23 St   W 23 ST   E 23 ST   (6) 23 St

W 22 St   E 22 St

W 21 St   E 21 St

FLATIRON

W 20 St   E 20 St

W 19 St   E 19 St

W 18 St   E 18 St

W 17 St   C   E 17 St

W 16 St   E 16 St

W 15 St   E 15 St

6 Av   14 St

(F) 14 St   W 14 ST   E 14 ST

LITTLE INDIA

Mavalli Palace
Jai-Ya Thai
NY Life
The Jazz Standard
B'way Al
Madison Sq Plz
Supreme Appellate Court - First Division
Met Life
SUNY - College of Optometry
Worth Sq
Madison Square Park
Met Life
New York Comedy C
School o' Visual Ar
Baruch College
B
P

St Martin's Press
Flatiron Bldg   Bolo
Gotham Comedy Club   Les Poulets
Tramps
Gramercy Park Hotel

Metronome
Periyali
Caffe Bondi
Theodore Roosevelt Birthplace
Gramercy Tavern
Cafe Beulah
Gramercy Park North
Gramercy Park
Gramercy Park South
Police Academy
Cabrini

Bed Bath & Beyond
Barnes & Noble Exec. Offices
Harvey's ABC Home & Carpet
Guardian Life
Verbena
Inn at Irving Place
Sale Annex   Paragon
Barnes & Noble
D
NY Foundling Hospital
SoHo Arts Group
Paul Smith   Mesa Grill
Union Square Cafe
The NY Film Academy
Union Sq Theater
NY Friends Meeting
Coffee Shop
Union Square Park
Lee Strasberg Theater Institute
Century
Irving Plaza
Con Edison   14 St BID
Bambou
3 Av

UNION SQ

Union Sq
14 St
(L)(N)(R)
(4)(5)(6)

GRAMERCY PARK

AMERICAS
BROADWAY
MADISON AV
LEXINGTON AV
AV OF THE
SIXTH AV
FIFTH AV
PARK AV SOUTH
PARK AV
IRVING PL
THIRD AV
U SQ W
U SQ E
U Sq N
Rutherford Pl

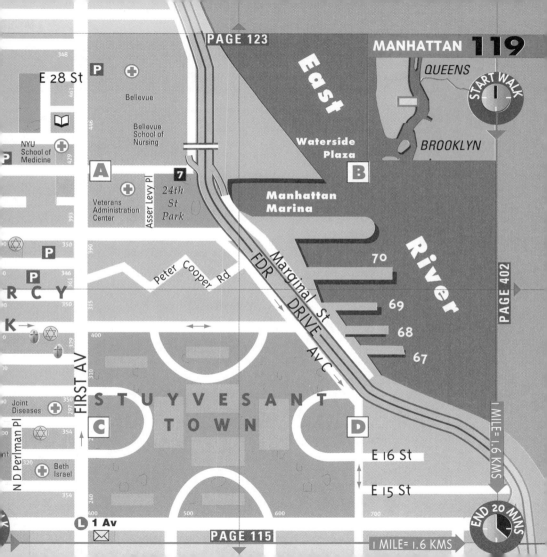

Circle Line

Lincoln Tunnel to NJ Meadowlands; Giants Stadium; Continental Airline Arena

NY Waterway

A

81

78

76

73

72

Hudson River

30 St Heliport

C

WEST SIDE HIGHWAY

9A

9A

TWELFTH AV

ELEVENTH AV

TENTH AV

W 44 PAGE 124 St →

W 43 St

W 42 ST

W 41 St

Greyhound-Trailways Bus Lines

W 40 St →

To NJ 495

W 39 St

DOT Towaway Lot

Javits Convention Center

W 38 St →

W 37 St ←

W 36 St →

W 35 St ←

P

W 34 ST ←→

W 33 St ←

W 32 St ←→

W 31 St

W 30 St

PAGE 116 W 29 St

Market Diner

Patents 521 W. 43rd

Martin Kaufman

Signature

Fed Ex

Cardinal Stepinac Pl

Lincoln

Galvin Av

Tunnel

P

B

D

Actors Studio

Westside Theater

Judith Anderson, Harold Clurman

Douglas Fairbanks

Playwrights Horizons

P

Theater R

John Houseman

Nat Horne

Chez Josephine

Samu Beck

CUNY Hunter College

Parking Ramp

DYER AV

The Original Improv

Lincoln Tunnel Entrance

ST4

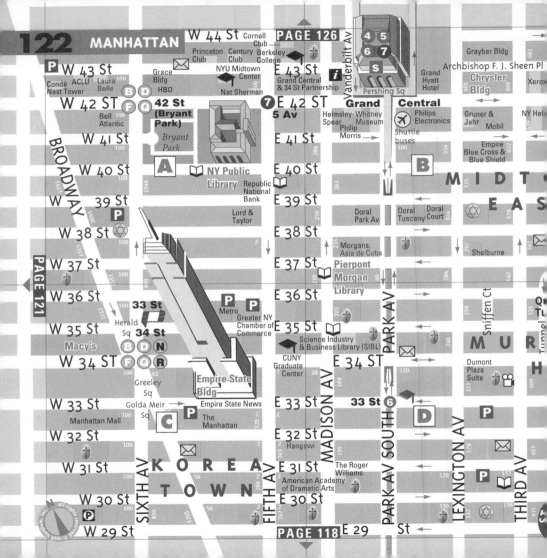

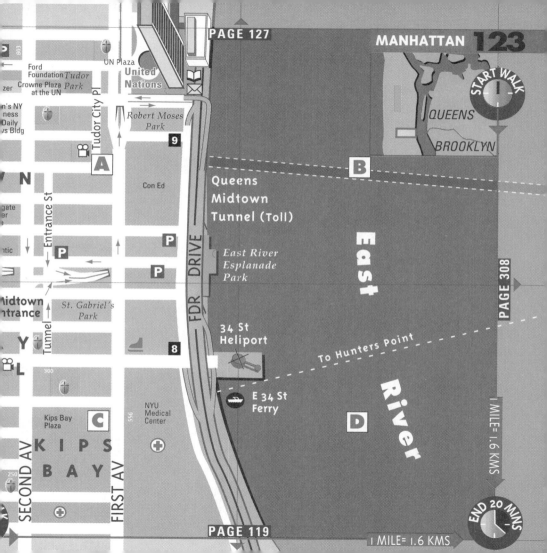

PAGE 127

Ford Foundation
Crowne Plaza at the UN

'zer

n's NY
ness
Daily
vs Bldg

UN Plaza
United Nations

Tudor City Pl

Tudor Park

Robert Moses Park

9

A

Con Ed

START WALK

QUEENS

BROOKLYN

B

Queens Midtown Tunnel (Toll)

E a s t

FDR DRIVE

Entrance St

gate
er

ntic

P

P

East River Esplanade Park

P

Midtown
ntrance

St. Gabriel's Park

Tunnel

Y

L

34 St Heliport

8

To Hunters Point

R i v e r

PAGE 308

1 MILE= 1.6 KMS

E 34 St Ferry

D

Kips Bay Plaza

C

NYU Medical Center

SECOND AV

FIRST AV

K I P S

B A Y

END 20 MINS

1 MILE= 1.6 KMS

Copacabana **PAGE 128**

W 57 ST John Jay College

CBS

Days Inn Looking Glass

W 56 St

HS Environmental Studies

W 55 St

Theater Four

W 54 St

AT & T **B**

De Witt Clinton Park

W 53 St

Ensemble Studio Theatre

9A

A

NYC Convention Pier

W 52 St

Irish Arts Center

(W.C. Handy Pl)

St Clare's Hospital

Hudson

W 51 St

C L I N T O N

W 50 St

T H E A

River

HS of Graphic Communication Arts

D I S T

W 49 St

W 48 St

Hell's Kitchen Park

Intrepid Sea-Air-Space Museum

W 47 St

W 46 St

Pan Asian Theater
Repertory

W 45 St **D**

C

W 44 St

New Dramatist

Market Diner

Patents 521 W. 43rd

Actors Studio

Westside Theater

W 43 St

Judith Anderson, Harold Clurman

Douglas Fairbanks

Playwrights Horizons

Circle Line

W 42 ST Theater Row Nat

PAGE 120 Kaufman Signature 500 John Houseman Horne Samuel Beckett

WEST SIDE HWY

TWELFTH AV

ELEVENTH AV

TENTH AV

NINTH AV

96 95 94 93 92 90 86 84 83 81

600 600 600 600 600 600 600 600 600 600

500 500 500 500 500 500 500 500 500 500

400 400 400 400 400 400 400 400

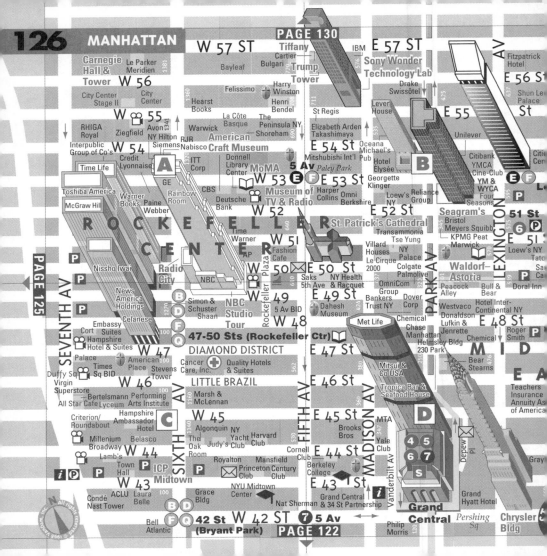

START WALK

QUEENS

BROOKLYN

E 57 ST

E 56 ST

Sutton Pl S

P

E 55 St

E 54 St

B

Il Nido

1066

1006

985

A

Casa Brasil

(Swing St)

11

E 53 St

River

on Av/3 Av

984

945

E 52 St

FDR DRIVE

T U R T L E

Peter Detmold Park

en es k

Pickwick Arms

Zarela

m

B A Y

889

E 51 St

E 50 St

Beekman Pl

th & lensky & Grill

1003

923

FIRST AV

333

Beekman Tower

Chin Chin

E 49 St

Mitchell Pl

902

MacArthur Plaza

E 48 St

803

PAGE 308

W N

P

Japan Society

10

Peace Garden

Vanderbilt YMCA

E 47 St

Dag Hammar-skjold Plz

U.N. Plaza

Peace Statue

East

T

P

Sparks

E 46 St

863

Marichu

1 MILE = 1.6 KMS

C

E 45 St

D

Palm

SECOND AV

Regal UN Plaza Hotel

Palm Too

E 44 St

803

P

E 43 St

Ford Foundation

Tudor Park

Tudor City Pl

END 20 MINS

Xerox

Pfizer

Crowne Plaza at the UN

United Nations

E 42 ST

LK

1 MILE= 1.6 KMS

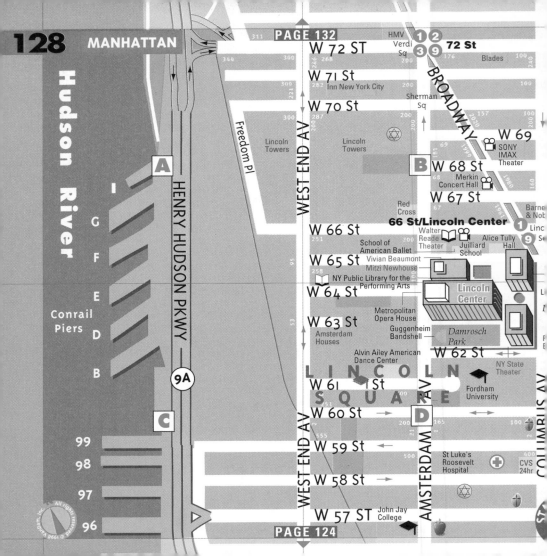

Hudson River

PAGE 132

HMV

72 St

W 72 ST

Verdi Sq

Blades

311

Broadway

W 71 ST

Inn New York City

Freedom Pl

W 70 ST

Sherman Sq

WEST END AV

Lincoln Towers

Lincoln Towers

SONY IMAX Theater

W 69

A

HENRY HUDSON PKWY

B

W 68 St

Merkin Concert Hall

I

G

W 67 St

Barnes & Nob

F

Red Cross

E

66 St/Lincoln Center

Linc

Conrail Piers

Walter Reade Theater

School of American Ballet

Juilliard School

Alice Tully Hall

Se

D

W 65 St

Vivian Beaumont

Mitzi Newhouse

B

NY Public Library for the Performing Arts

Lincoln Center

W 64 St

Metropolitan Opera House

9A

W 63 St

Amsterdam Houses

Guggenheim Bandshell

Damrosch Park

C

Alvin Ailey American Dance Center

W 62 St

NY State Theater

L I N C O L N

W 61 St

Fordham University

S Q U A R E

COLUMBUS AV

AMSTERDAM AV

99

W 60 St

D

98

555

W 59 St

97

St Luke's Roosevelt Hospital

CVS 24hr

W 58 St

96

John Jay College

W 57 ST

PAGE 124

72 St

Strawberry Fields

Cherry Hill

START WALK

QUEENS

BROOKLYN

Terrace Drive

Naumburg Bandshell

Rumsey Playfield

Central Park

Bowling Green

Mineral Springs Concessions

Singer Lilac Walk

Café Des Artistes

CENTRAL PARK WEST

Central Park

Sheep Meadows

The Mall

Roller Skating

Literary Walk

East Drive

E 68 St

E 67 St

E 66 St

Balto

E 65 St

Armani

Tavern on the Green w/the Chestnut Room

65 St Transverse

Ballplayers Houses

The Carousel

The Dairy

India House

Chase Manhattan

PAGE 130

West Drive

Heckscher Ballfields

Chess & Checkers House

Chess Rock

Cat Rock

Central Park Zoo Wildlife Conservation Center

The Arsenal

E 64 St

Berwind Mansion

NY Society for Ethical Culture

YMCA

W 63 St

Rat Rock

Heckscher Playground

Wollman Mem. Rink

FIFTH AV

E 63 St

Post House Arcadia

E 62 St

Helmsley-Carlton House

Umpire Rock

Puppet House

Center Drive

MADISON AV

The Mayflower Hotel

Trump Int'l Hotel & Tower

Hallett Nature Sanctuary

Gapstow Bridge

5 Av

N R

E 61 St

The Pierre

Barneys NY

NYIT

Merchant's Gate

Columbus Cir

Maine Memorial

Cop Cot

Simon Bolivar Statue

The Pond

E 60 St

Grand Army Plz

Sherry-Netherland

A C 1

B D 9

Columbus Circle 59 St

CENTRAL PARK SOUTH

The Plaza Hotel

Pulitzer Fountain

Estee Lauder G M Vidal Sassoon Bldg

E 59 St

NY Coliseum

Universal News

Coliseum Books

Le Bar Bat

Hard Rock Cafe

Nikko Essex House

Les Célébrités

Westin Central Park South

St Moritz

Wyndham

9 W 57

FAO Schwarz

E 58 St

Warner Bros Studio Store

Bergdorf Goodman

Van Cleef & Arpels

E 57 ST

END 20 MINS

N R 57 St

SEVENTH AV

AV OF THE AMERICAS

Q 57 St

PAGE 125

1 MILE = 1.6 KMS

1 MILE = 1.6 KMS

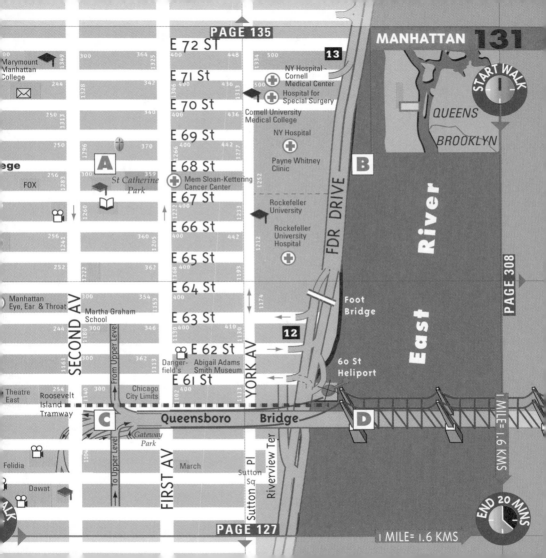

START WALK

QUEENS

BROOKLYN

13

NY Hospital - Cornell Medical Center

Hospital for Special Surgery

Cornell University Medical College

NY Hospital

Payne Whitney Clinic

Rockefeller University

Rockefeller University Hospital

Mem Sloan-Kettering Cancer Center

St Catherine Park

A

B

Marymount Manhattan College

FOX

ege

E 72 ST

E 71 St

E 70 St

E 69 St

E 68 St

E 67 St

E 66 St

E 65 St

E 64 St

E 63 St

E 62 St

E 61 St

East River

FDR DRIVE

YORK AV

SECOND AV

FIRST AV

Manhattan Eye, Ear & Throat

Martha Graham School

Danger-field's

Abigail Adams Smith Museum

Theatre East

Roosevelt Island Tramway

Chicago City Limits

Felidia

Dawat

Gateway Park

March

Sutton Pl

Sutton Sq

Riverview Ter

Foot Bridge

60 St Heliport

From Upper Level

To Upper Level

12

C

D

Queensboro Bridge

1 MILE= 1.6 KMS

END 20 MINS

1 MILE= 1.6 KMS

86 St Ⓑ Ⓒ

PAGE 137

85 St Transverse

Central Park Precinct Ⓟ

Ross Pinetum

South Gatehouse

QUEENS

START WALK

BROOKLYN

Ⓐ

The Great Lawn

Cleopatra's Needle

Bridle Path

Ⓑ

Metropolitan Museum of Art

Goethe House

E 82 St

Frank E. Campbell Funeral Chapel

E 81 St

The Stanhope

E 80 St

81 St
Museum of
ural History

Hayden
Planetarium
ax

Ⓑ
Ⓒ

Delacorte Theatre

Henry Luce Nature Observatory

Shakespeare Garden

Belvedere Castle

Turtle Pond

West Drive

East Drive

(Museum Mile)

MADISON AV

PAGE 134

E 79 ST

an Museum
ral History

Swedish Cottage

79 St Transverse

Winter Drive

Cedar Hill

French Embassy

James B Duke House

E 78 St

NY Historical
Society

The Mark

E 77 St

Central
Park

Levin Playground

ntral Park West
St Historic Dist

Alice in Wonderland Statue

E 76 St

Harkness House

Daniel Surrey

San Remo Bldg

 Ⓒ

Ladies Pavilion

The Ramble

The Lake

Boathouse Cafe

Loeb Boathouse

Kerbs Mem. Model Boathouse

Conservatory Water

E 75 St

FIFTH AV

1 MILE = 1.6 KMS

Whitney Museum
of American Art

E 74

The
Dakota

Ⓑ
Ⓒ

72 St

Bow Bridge

Strawberry Fields

Cherry Hill

Wagner's Cove

Bethesda Fountain

Bethesda Terrace

Hans Christian Andersen Statue

Pilgrim Hill

E 73 St

END 20 MINS

E 72 ST

PAGE 129

1 MILE = 1.6 KMS

85 St Transverse

PAGE 138

The YIVO Institute for Jewish Research

86 S
4 5

E 86 ST

48   78   1021   100   128
1165   1163

Central Park Precinct

P

Ross Pinetum

South Gatehouse

E 85 St

38   74   132
1130   1000   1248
1030   35

Ancient Playground

E 84 St

1140   132
                            1223

The Great Lawn

A

Metropolitan Museum of Art

E 83 St

28   72   132
960   1210
2   39

Goethe House

B

Bridle Path

Cleopatra's Needle

E 82 St

Frank E. Campbell Funeral Chapel

1075   72   100   136
941   1195

Delacorte Theatre

E 81 St

The Stanhope

2   36   64   126
916   1164
30

Lewis Spencer Morris House

Henry Luce Nature Observatory, Shakespeare Garden

Turtle Pond

Belvedere Castle

E 80 St

40   76   142
1033   903

Junior League of the City of NY

Swedish Cottage

79 St Transverse

E 79 ST

2

PAGE 133

Winter Drive

West Drive

Cedar Hill

East Drive

French Embassy

82   100   142
878   1120
2   39

Central

James B Duke House

E 78 St

The Mark

72   138
993   863   1163

Park

Levin Playground

E 77 St

6

Ladies Pavillion

Alice in Wonderland Statue

The Carlyle
Cafe Carlyle w/Bemelman's Bar

Lenox Hill Hospital

50   86
840
950

The Ramble

C

Kerbs Mem. Model Boathouse

E 76 St

Harkness House

Daniel Surrey

D

Whitney Museum of American Art

The Lake

The Boathouse
Cafe

Loeb Boathouse

Conservatory Water

E 75 St

2   24   56
921

24   100   136
2

MADISON AV

LEXINGTON AV

Bow Bridge

Hans Christian Andersen Statue

E 74 St

39   58   142
785

FIFTH AV

PARK AV

Pilgrim Hill

E 73 St

34   68   140
760   1060

Cherry Hill

Bethesda Fountain

Bethesda Terrace

Wagner's Cove

E 72 ST

Madison Av BID

Ralph Lauren

64   100   140

PAGE 130

START WALK

QUEENS

BROOKLYN

Dalton Gym

U P P E R

E A S T

S I D E

E 86 ST

Henderson Pl

E 85 St

E 84 St

E 83 St

E 82 St

Gracie Ter

E 81 St

The Gracie Inn

E 80 St

East End Av

E 79 ST

East River

PAGE 309

E 78 St

Cherokee Pl

E 77 St

John Jay Park

E 76 St

Gracie Square Hospital

E 75 St

FDR DRIVE

D

E 74 St

THIRD AV

SECOND AV

FIRST AV

YORK AV

E 73 St

13

E 72 ST

Marymount Manhattan College

END 20 MINS

1 MILE = 1.6 KMS

1 MILE = 1.6 KMS

A

B

C

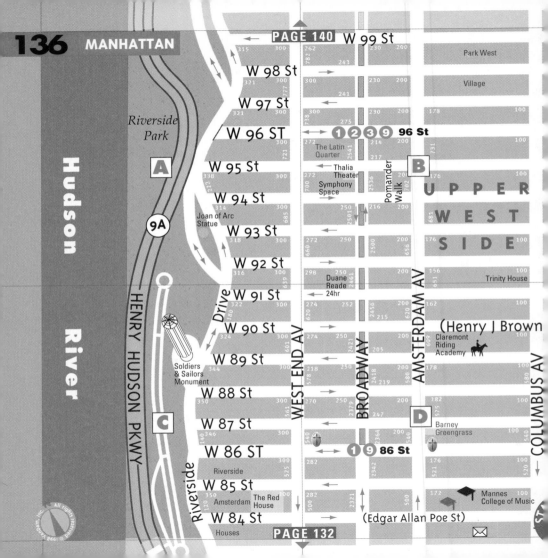

Hudson River

Riverside Park

Henry Hudson Pkwy

Drive

Riverside Drive

← PAGE 140

W 99 St
W 98 St
W 97 St
W 96 ST
W 95 St
W 94 St
W 93 St
W 92 St
W 91 St
W 90 St
W 89 St
W 88 St
W 87 St
W 86 ST
W 85 St
W 84 St

WEST END AV
BROADWAY
AMSTERDAM AV
COLUMBUS AV

A
B
C
D
9A

Park West Village

U P P E R
W E S T
S I D E

The Latin Quarter

Thalia Theater

Symphony Space

Pomander Walk

Joan of Arc Statue

Duane Reade
24hr

Soldiers & Sailors Monument

Trinity House

(Henry J Brown
Claremont Riding Academy

Barney Greengrass

Riverside

Amsterdam
The Red House

Houses

Mannes College of Music

(Edgar Allan Poe St)

① ② ③ ⑨ 96 St

① ⑨ 86 St

PAGE 132 ▼

East Meadow

North Meadow
Security Center

START WALK

QUEENS

BROOKLYN

East Drive

97 St

Transverse

96 St Ⓑ Ⓒ

C e n t r a l

A

Tennis Courts

P a r k

B

E 95 St

ICP Uptown

E 94 St

FIFTH AV

MADISON AV

.5 mi

.25 mi

E 93 St

Jewish
Museum

E 92 St

North
Gatehouse

Bridle
Path

West Drive

Jackie

E 91 St

Cooper–Hewitt
Museum

PAGE 138

Onassis

.75 mi

Fred Lebow
Running Track

START
FINISH

E 90 St

National Academy
Museum NY Road
Runners Club
Fred Lebow Pl

Reservoir

Claremont
Stables

1.5 mi

Solomon R
Guggenheim
Museum E 88

1 mi

C

D

1.25 mi

(Museum Mile)

East Drive

1 MILE = 1.6 KMS

E 87 St

The YIVO Institute
for Jewish Research

86 St Ⓑ Ⓒ

85 St Transverse

South
Gatehouse

E 86 ST

Central
Park Precinct
Ⓟ

Ross
Pinetum

Fred Lebow
Running Track

E 85 St

Ancient
Playground

E 84 St

END 20 MINS

1 MILE = 1.6 KMS

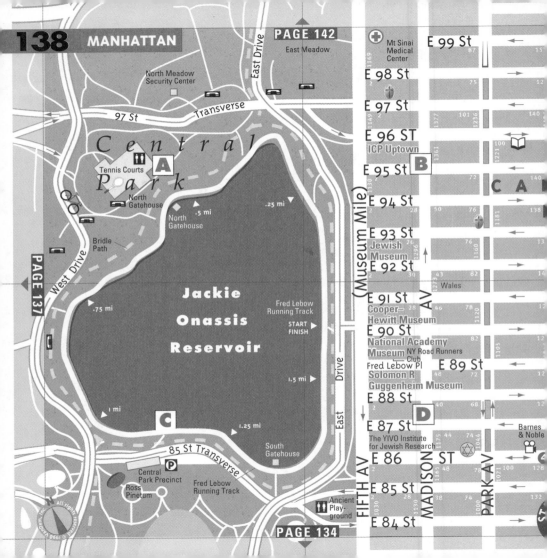

PAGE 142
East Meadow

North Meadow Security Center

97 St   Transverse

C e n t r a l

Tennis Courts **A**

P a r k

North Gatehouse

North Gatehouse

.5 mi   .25 mi

Bridle Path

West Drive

.75 mi

Jackie

Onassis

Reservoir

Fred Lebow Running Track

START FINISH

1.5 mi

1 mi

1.25 mi

C

East Drive

South Gatehouse

85 St Transverse

Central Park Precinct

Ross Pinetum

Fred Lebow Running Track

Ancient Playground

PAGE 134

PAGE 137

East Drive

Mt Sinai Medical Center

E 99 St   87   15

E 98 St   75   12

E 97 St   1016

E 96 ST   100
ICP Uptown   1361   1221   140

E 95 St   **B**   72

C A
140

E 94 St   28 50 76   1181   138

E 93 St   76   13
Jewish Museum   1296   1160

E 92 St   30 43 82   14

Wales

E 91 St   28 46 78 1120 12
Cooper– Hewitt Museum

E 90 St   82   1105
National Academy Museum NY Road Runners Club,
Fred Lebow Pl   E 89 St   12
48 72

Solomon R Guggenheim Museum

E 88 St   2 40 68   12
D

E 87 St   1175   44   74 1044
The YIVO Institute for Jewish Research

Barnes & Noble

FIFTH AV

E 86   **MADISON**   **ST**
1165 48   PARK AV   1021 100 128

E 85 St   1150 38 74   132
930

E 84 St

(Museum Mile)

FIFTH AV

© 1998 VARMAP INC. All rights reserved

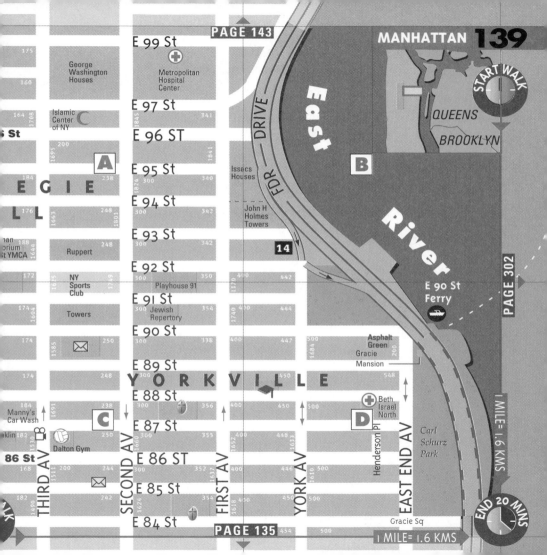

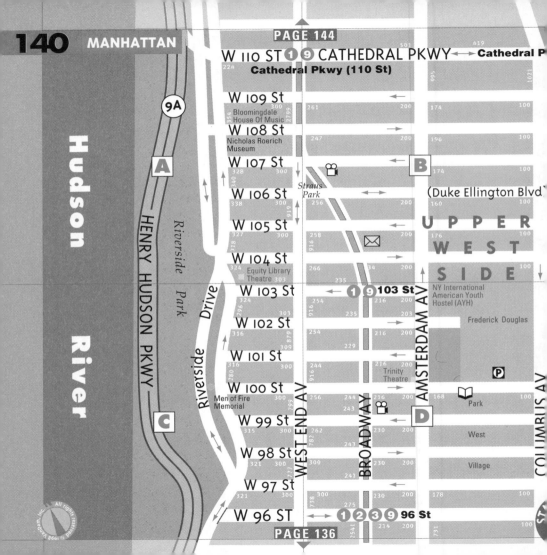

PAGE 144

W 110 ST ① ⑨ **CATHEDRAL PKWY** ← → **Cathedral P**
Cathedral Pkwy (110 St)

Hudson River

HENRY HUDSON PKWY

Riverside Park

Riverside Drive

9A

A

C

W 109 St
Bloomingdale House Of Music

W 108 St
Nicholas Roerich Museum

W 107 St

Straus Park

W 106 St

W 105 St

W 104 St
Equity Library Theatre

W 103 St ← ① ⑨ **103 St**

W 102 St

W 101 St

W 100 St

Men of Fire Memorial

W 99 St

W 98 St

W 97 St

W 96 ST ← → ① ② ③ ⑨ **96 St**

B

(Duke Ellington Blvd

U P P E R

W E S T

S I D E

NY International American Youth Hostel (AYH)

Frederick Douglas

Trinity Theatre

D

Park

West

Village

WEST END AV

BROADWAY

AMSTERDAM AV

COLUMBUS AV

PAGE 136

START WALK

QUEENS

BROOKLYN

CENTRAL PARK NORTH ② ③

110 St) B C
348
Douglass
Circle

East

Blockhouse No. 1

Duck
Island

Harlem
Meer

Charles A. Dana
Discovery Center

Drive

West

Nutter's
Battery Site

McGowan's
Pass

A

Lasker Rink
& Pool

Fort Clinton
Site

B

E 107 St
48

E 106 ST
26 1550

Drive

Huddlestone
Bridge

Great Hill

Fort
Fish
Site

Fort
Fish
Site

Conservatory
Garden

The Mount

El Museo
del Barrio

E 105 St

E 104 St
Museum of
the City of NY

The
Loch

Ravine

C e n t r a l

NY Academy
of Medicine

E 103 St

103 St B C

The
Pool

P a r k

E 102 St
22

E 101 St
20

MANHATTAN AV

CENTRAL PARK WEST

FIFTH AV

MADISON AV

Park
West

Village

Bridle
Path

North Meadow

North Meadow
Security Center

97 St Transverse

C

D

East Meadow

Mt. Sinai
Medical
Center

1189

1169

E 98 St

E 97 St

1149

END 20 MINS

96 St B C
2

Tennis Courts PAGE 137

1 MILE = 1.6 KMS

1 MILE = 1.6 KMS

E 96 ST

PAGE 142

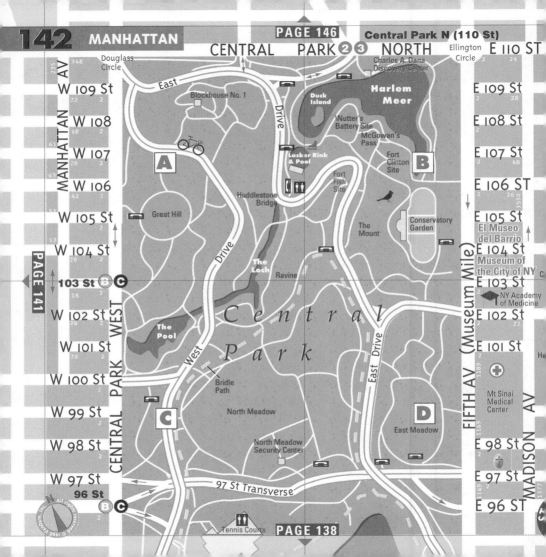

PAGE 146
PAGE 141
PAGE 138

Central Park N (110 St)

CENTRAL PARK ❷❸ NORTH

Ellington Circle

E 110 ST

Douglass Circle

East

Drive

Blockhouse No. 1

Charles A. Dana Discovery Center

W 109 St — E 109 St

Duck Island

Harlem Meer

W 108 — E 108 St

Nutter's Battery Site

McGowan's Pass

W 107 — E 107 St

Fort Clinton Site

A

Lasker Rink & Pool

B

W 106 — E 106 ST

Huddlestone Bridge

Fort Fish Site

W 105 St — E 105 St

El Museo del Barrio

Great Hill

The Mount

Conservatory Garden

W 104 St — E 104 St

Museum of the City of NY

The Loch

Ravine

E 103 St

103 St ❻ C — NY Academy of Medicine

W 102 St — E 102 St

Central

FIFTH AV (Museum Mile)

The Pool

W 101 St — E 101 St

Park

W 100 St — Bridle Path

West

Drive

East Drive

Mt Sinai Medical Center

North Meadow

C — W 99 St

D

East Meadow

W 98 St — E 98 St

North Meadow Security Center

W 97 St — E 97 St

97 St Transverse

96 St ❷ C — E 96 ST

MADISON AV

Tennis Courts

CENTRAL PARK WEST

MANHATTAN AV

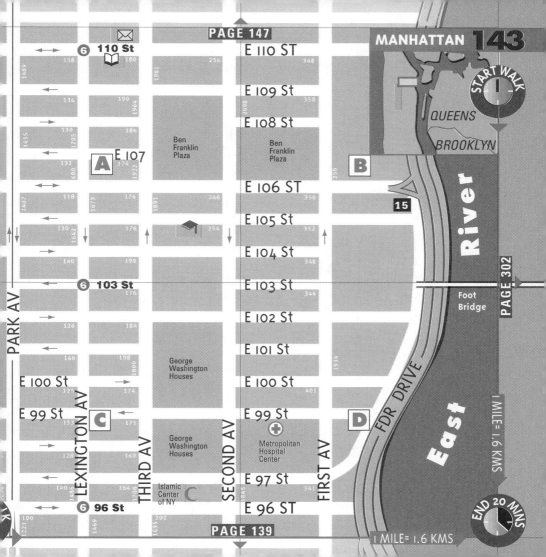

PAGE 147

START WALK

QUEENS

BROOKLYN

River

East

PARK AV

⊠

6 110 St

138   180

256   348

E 110 ST

1489

E 109 St

136   190   1964   2098   350

E 108 St

130   186   1705   1964

Ben Franklin Plaza

Ben Franklin Plaza

1455   680   132   174   1922

A E 107

B

E 106 ST

118   176   1891   246   350   250

1407

E 105 St

130   1642   176   254   352

E 104 St

140   190   348

6 103 St

176   E 103 St   344

15

E 102 St

126   184

E 101 St

140   198   1800

George Washington Houses

E 100 St   401

E 100 St   125   174

1934

LEXINGTON AV

THIRD AV

SECOND AV

FIRST AV

FDR DRIVE

E 99 St

C   153   175

D

George Washington Houses

Metropolitan Hospital Center

Foot Bridge

PAGE 302

1 MILE= 1.6 KMS

126   160

E 97 St

140   164   1845   341

Islamic Center of NY

6 96 St

1469

200   1695

E 96 ST

END 20 MINS

100   1221

1 MILE= 1.6 KMS

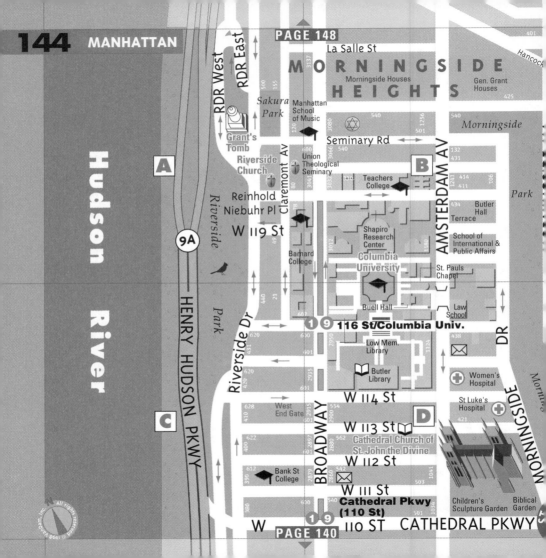

PAGE 148

Hudson River

RDR West
RDR East

La Salle St

M O R N I N G S I D E
H E I G H T S

Morningside Houses

Gen. Grant
Houses

401

Hancock

Sakura Park

Manhattan
School
of Music

Morningside

Seminary Rd

A

Grant's
Tomb

Riverside
Church

Union
Theological
Seminary

Riverside

Claremont Av

Teachers
College

B

AMSTERDAM AV

Park

Reinhold
Niebuhr Pl

Butler
Hall
Terrace

Park

W 119 St

9A

Shapiro
Research
Center

School of
International &
Public Affairs

Barnard
College

**Columbia
University**

St. Pauls
Chapel

Riverside Dr

Buell Hall

Law
School

1 9 116 St/Columbia Univ.

Low Mem.
Library

Henry Hudson Pkwy

C

Butler
Library

Women's
Hospital

DR

W 114 St

MORNINGSIDE

Morning...

West
End Gate

BROADWAY

W 113 St

D

St Luke's
Hospital

Bank St
College

Cathedral Church of
St. John the Divine

W 112 St

W 111 St

**Cathedral Pkwy
(110 St)**

Children's
Sculpture Garden

Biblical
Garden

1 9

W **PAGE 140** 110 ST CATHEDRAL PKWY

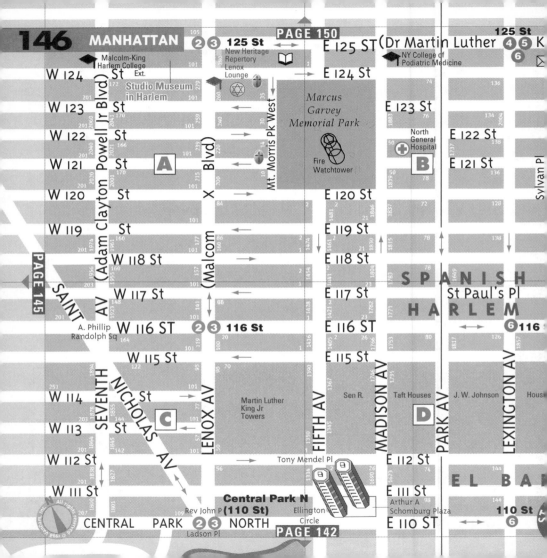

125 St

E 125 ST (Dr Martin Luther ④ ⑤ K ⑥

W 124 St
Malcolm-King Harlem College Ext.
New Heritage Repertory
Lenox Lounge
E 124 St

NY College of Podiatric Medicine

Studio Museum in Harlem

W 123 St

Marcus Garvey Memorial Park

E 123 St

W 122 St

E 122 St

North General Hospital

W 121 St   **A**   **B**   E 121 St

X Blvd)

Fire Watchtower

W 120 St

E 120 St

Mt. Morris Pk West

W 119 St

E 119 St

W 118 St

E 118 St

S P A N I S H

PAGE 145

SAINT NICHOLAS AV

W 117 St

E 117 St

St Paul's Pl

H A R L E M

A. Phillip Randolph Sq
W 116 ST ② ③ **116 St**

E 116 ST

⑥ **116**

W 115 St

E 115 St

SEVENTH

St

W 114   **C**
Martin Luther King Jr Towers

FIFTH AV

Sen R.

MADISON AV

Taft Houses

J. W. Johnson

Housi

W 113 St

PARK AV

D

LEXINGTON AV

W 112 St

Tony Mendel Pl

E 112 St

E L   B A

W 111 St

E 111 St

Central Park N

Rev John P **(110 St)**
Ellington Circle

Arthur A Schomburg Plaza

110 St

⑥

E 110 ST

(Adam Clayton Powell Jr Blvd)

(Malcom

LENOX AV

Sylvan Pl

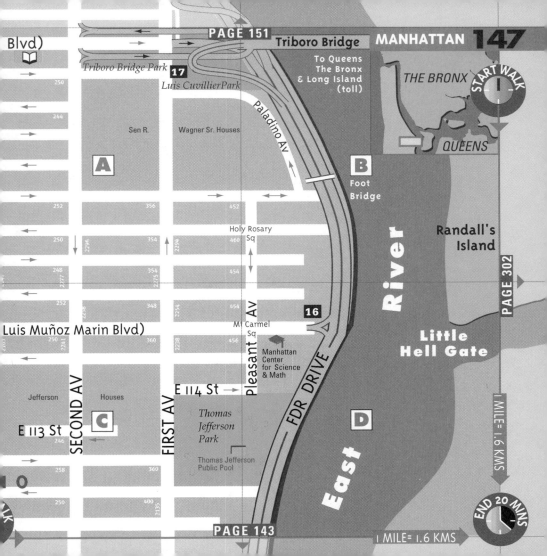

Blvd)

Triboro Bridge

MANHATTAN 147

Triboro Bridge Park 17

Luis Cuvillier Park

Sen R.

Wagner Sr. Houses

Paladino Av

To Queens
The Bronx
& Long Island
(toll)

THE BRONX

START WALK

QUEENS

A

B
Foot
Bridge

River

Randall's
Island

250

244

250

252

356

452

2296

354

2294

460

Holy Rosary
Sq

250

2177

248

354

2175

454

PAGE 302

252

2273

348

2254

454

16

Luis Muñoz Marin Blvd)

2203

2241

250

2241

360

2238

456

Mt Carmel
Sq

Manhattan
Center
for Science
& Math

Little
Hell Gate

Pleasant Av

FDR DRIVE

1 MILE= 1.6 KMS

Jefferson

Houses

SECOND AV

FIRST AV

E 114 St

E 113 St

246

Thomas
Jefferson
Park

Thomas Jefferson
Public Pool

D

East

258

360

250

400

2135

END 20 MINS

1 MILE= 1.6 KMS

North River
Water Pollution
Control Plant (Below)

Riverbank
State Park

Running
Track

9A

Ped
Bridge

A

Hudson River

HENRY HUDSON PKWY

Riverside Dr

TWELFTH AV

PAGE 152

W 140 St

W 139 St

W 138 St

W 137 St   1 9 **137 St**
                City College

W 136 St

W 135 ST (Shona Bailey Pl)

W 134 St

Montefiore
Sq

Hamilton Pl

A. Philip
Randolph
Campus HS

Shepard
Hall

CUNY
North Campus

Admin.
Building

North
Academic
Center

Robert E.
Marshak
Building

B

Aaron
Davis
Hall

CONVENT AV

M A N H A T T A N V I L L E   City
                                Coll
                                CUN

W 133 St

W 132 St
Fairway

W 131 St

W 130 St

St Clair Pl

12

C

Riverside Dr West
RDR East
Riverside Dr

Claremont Av

Tiemann Pl

BROADWAY

Old B'way

Manhattanville
Houses

Old B'way

Sheltering Arms Park

125 St
1 9 (Dr Martin Luther King Jr Blvd)

Gen. Grant
Houses

La Salle St

AMSTERDAM AV

Convent

CONVENT AV

Sou
Cam

W 129 St

D

P

W 128 St

W 127 St

W 126 St

Gen. Grant
Houses

Roosevelt
Sq

H

PAGE 144

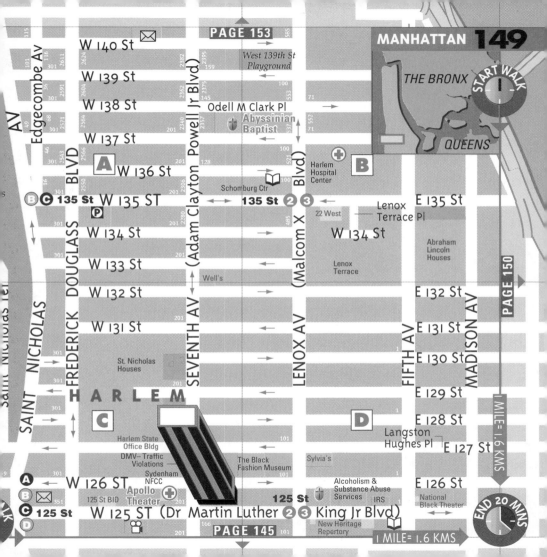

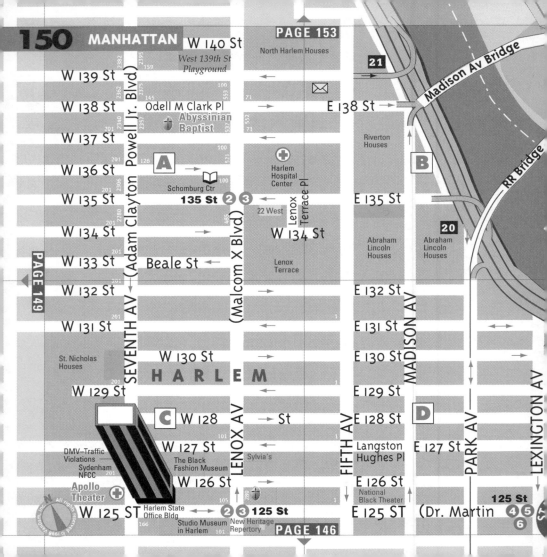

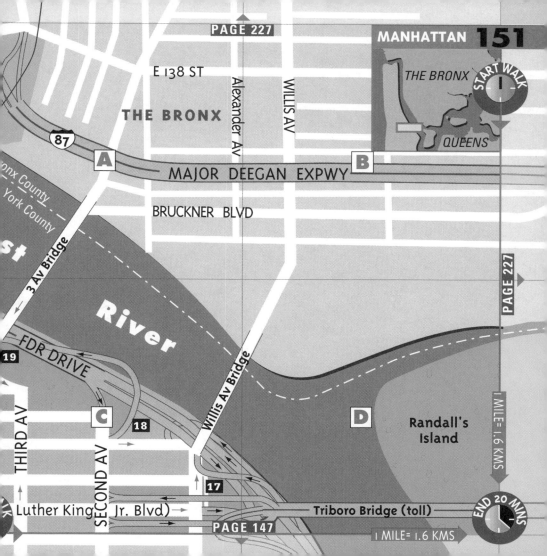

MANHATTAN **151**

THE BRONX

START WALK
1

QUEENS

E 138 ST

Alexander Av

WILLIS AV

THE BRONX

87

A

B

MAJOR DEEGAN EXPWY

BRUCKNER BLVD

3 Av Bridge

onx County
York County

River

st

FDR DRIVE

19

Willis Av Bridge

PAGE 227

THIRD AV

C

18

SECOND AV

D

Randall's
Island

1 MILE = 1.6 KMS

17

Luther King Jr. Blvd)

Triboro Bridge (toll)

END 20 MINS

PAGE 147

1 MILE = 1.6 KMS

PAGE 154

13

W 159 St

W 158 St

Edward M
Morgan Pl

157 St

W 157 St

W 156 St

American
Numismatic
Society
AudubonTer
American
Academy &
National Institute
of Arts & Letters

Boricua
College

The Hispanic
Society of
America

W 155 ST

A B C 155 St

Highbridge
Park

Trinity

Church of
the Intercession

B

Cemetery

W 154 St

AMSTERDAM AV

Hudson

River

A

C

HENRY HUDSON PKWY

Riverside Dr W

9A

North River
Water Pollution
Control Plant (Below)

Ped
Bridge

Carousel

Picnic
Area

Amphi-
theater

Cultural
Center

*Riverbank
State
Park*

Indoor
Pools

Running
Track

BROADWAY

W 153 St

W 152 St

W 151 St

W 150 St

W 149 St

HAMILTON

W 148 St

HEIGHTS

W 147 St

W 146 St

145 St

1 9 W 145 ST

W 144 St

D

W 143 St

W 142 St

W 141 St

W 140 St

Riverside Dr

DanceTheatre
of Harlem

P

St Nick's

Alexander
Hamilton
Sq

Hamilton Pl

Hamilton
Grange

CONVENT AV

Plaza'd

PAGE 148

N

© 1998 VistaMap Inc. All rights reserved

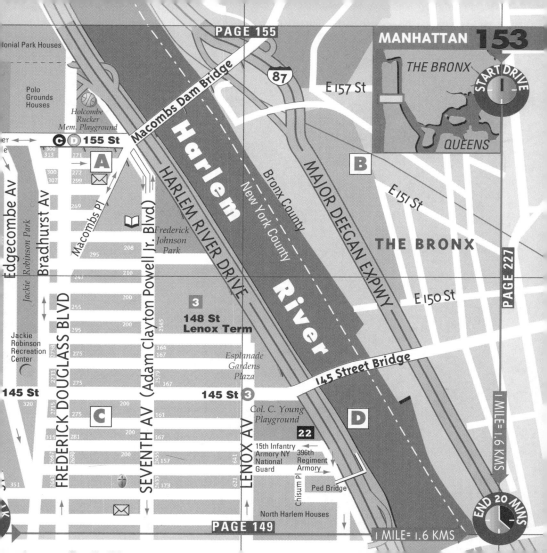

MANHATTAN **153**

THE BRONX

E 157 St

START DRIVE

QUEENS

lonial Park Houses

Polo
Grounds
Houses

Holcombe
Rucker
Mem. Playground

er ←→
e

C D 155 St

Macombs Dam Bridge

I 87

Harlem

HARLEM RIVER DRIVE

A

Macombs Pl

Edgecombe Av

Bradhurst Av

Jackie Robinson Park

Frederick
Johnson
Park

Bronx County

New York County

B

E 151 St

THE BRONX

MAJOR DEEGAN EXPWY

River

E 150 St

PAGE 227

FREDERICK DOUGLASS BLVD

Jackie
Robinson
Recreation
Center

145 St

3

**148 St
Lenox Term**

SEVENTH AV (Adam Clayton Powell Jr. Blvd)

Esplanade
Gardens
Plaza

145 St 3

C

145 Street Bridge

D

Col. C. Young
Playground

22

LENOX AV

15th Infantry
Armory NY
National
Guard

396th
Regiment
Armory

Chisum Pl

Ped Bridge

END 20 MINS

North Harlem Houses

I MILE= 1.6 KMS

I MILE= 1.6 KMS

167 St
E 4 167 St

THE BRONX

START WALK 1

QUEENS

SEDGEWICK AV

MAJOR DEEGAN EXPWY

Dr Martin Luther King Jr Blvd

Union Pl

W 167

W Av

Woodycrest Av

Nelson Av

Ogden Av

Shakespeare Av

Cromwell Av

McClellan St

John Mullaly Park

A

W 166 St

B

Anderson Av

THE BRONX

W 165 St

E 165 St

River Av

Gerard Av

Walton Av

GRAND CONCOURSE & BLVD

W 164 St

E 164 St

Summit Av

Ped Bridge

W 163 St

Macombs

Joyce Kilmer Park

PAGE 221

W 162

87

New York County

Bronx County

JEROME AV

E 162 St

Dam Park

W 161 St

E 161 ST

161 St
Yankee Stadium
C D 4

Babe Ruth Plaza

Lou Gehrig Plaza

6

Macomb's Dam Bridge Approach

Ruppert Pl

Borough Hall

River

5

Yankee Stadium

D E 158 St

1 MILE = 1.6 KMS

ouses

C

Macombs Dam Bridge

E 157 St

Franz S Sigel Park

END 20 MINS

Holcombe Rucker Memorial Playground

ads rs

C D 155 St

1 MILE= 1.6 KMS

PAGE 158

Hudson River

A

Fort Washington Park

HENRY HUDSON PKWY

RIVERSIDE DRIVE

9A

Chittenden Av

Riverside Dr

Cabrini

Alex Rose Pl

Pinehurst Av

Bennett Park

B

Ⓐ 190 St

W 190 St

Overlook Ter

Bennett Av

BROADWAY

Wadsworth Ter

Gorman Memorial Park

W 186 St

W A S H

W 185 St

W 183 St

Magaw Pl

Col. R.

9

Ⓐ 181 St

FT

Plaza Lafayette

Blvd

TRANS MAN

WASHINGTON AV

Bus Terminal

BROADWAY

S Pinehurst Av

C George Washington Bridge

9 I 95

1A

D

Haven

J. Wood Wright Park

Ⓐ 175 St

(toll)
To NJ

W 172 St

W 171 St

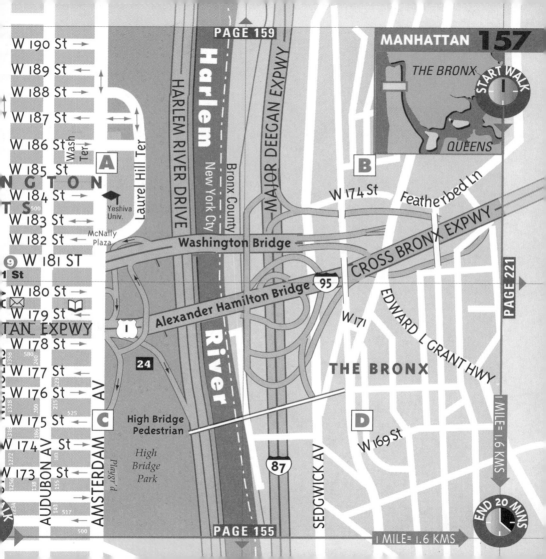

THE BRONX

START WALK

QUEENS

W 190 St →
W 189 St ←
W 188 St →
W 187 St ←
W 186 St →
Wash Ter
W 185 St →

A

N G T O N

W 184 St →
500
W 183 St ←
McNally Plaza
W 182 St ←
9 W 181 ST
1 St

Yeshiva Univ.

Harlem

HARLEM RIVER DRIVE

New York City

Bronx County

MAJOR DEEGAN EXPWY

Laurel Hill Ter

W 174 St

Featherbed Ln

B

CROSS BRONX EXPWY

Washington Bridge

W 180 St →
W 179 St ←
TAN EXPWY
W 178 St →

I

24

Alexander Hamilton Bridge

95

W 171

EDWARD L GRANT HWY

W 177 St ←
580 240
W 176 St →
215 200
W 175 St →
525

C

AMSTERDAM AV

High Bridge Pedestrian

River

THE BRONX

D

W 169 St

W 174 St ←
W 173 St ←

AUDUBON AV

Pudge' pl

High Bridge Park

87

SEDGWICK AV

1 MILE = 1.6 KMS

1 MILE= 1.6 KMS

END 20 MINS

Inwood Hill Park

Dyckman Marina

Dyckman Fields

Bolton Rd

Payson Av

Beak St

Seaman Av

Cumming St

Cooper

DYCKMAN

H. HUDSON PKWY

Staff St

Dyckman (200 St)

Henshaw St

W. Tigne Triangle

Thayer

A

B

17

Playgr'd

The Cloisters

BROADWAY

Arden

9A

Margaret

Corbin Dr

Dongan Pl

SHERM

St

P

Ellwo

9A

16

Fort Tryon Park

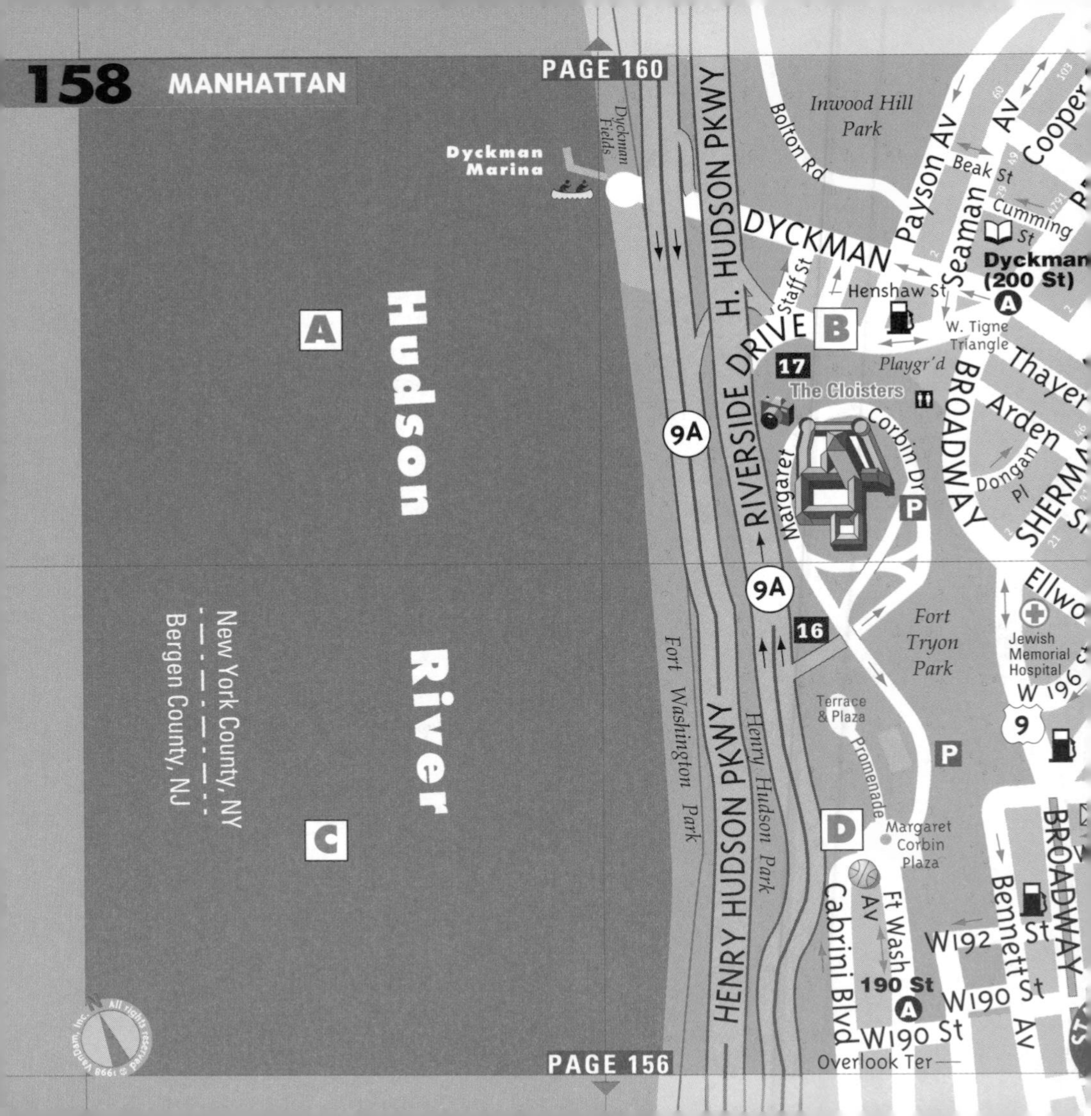

Jewish Memorial Hospital

W 196

9

Hudson River

Fort Washington Park

Terrace & Plaza

Henry Hudson Park

Promenade

P

New York County, NY
— · — · — · —
Bergen County, NJ

C

D

Margaret Corbin Plaza

BROADWAY

HENRY HUDSON PKWY

Ft Wash Av

Cabrini Blvd

Bennett St

W192

W 196

190 St

W190 St

Overlook Ter

Av

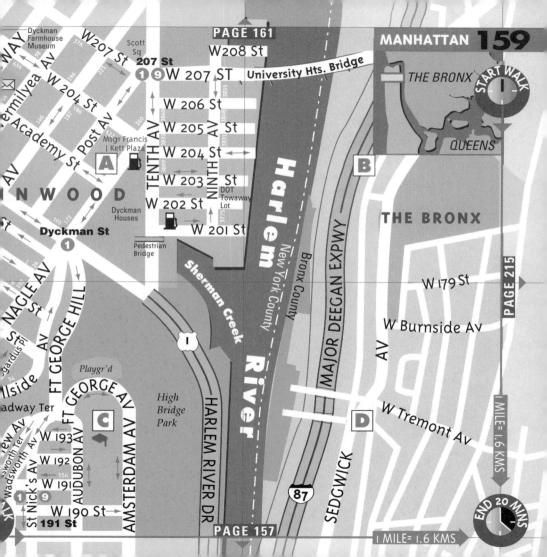

THE BRONX

START WALK

QUEENS

THE BRONX

Dyckman Farmhouse Museum

W 207 St

Scott Sq

207 St
① ⑨ W 207 ST

University Hts. Bridge

Vermilyea Av

W 204 St

Post Av

Academy St

W 206 St

W 205 AV St

Msgr Francis J Kett Plaza

A

W 204 St

W 203 St

TENTH AV

NINTH AV

DOT Towaway Lot

I N W O O D

Dyckman Houses

W 202 St

Dyckman St
①

W 201 St

Pedestrian Bridge

Harlem

New York County

Bronx County

MAJOR DEEGAN EXPWY

B

W 179 St

PAGE 215

W Burnside Av

NAGLE AV

Sherman Creek

FT GEORGE HILL

Bogardus Pl

I

AV

Hillside

Broadway Ter

FT GEORGE AV

Playgr'd

High Bridge Park

HARLEM RIVER DR

SEDGWICK AV

W Tremont Av

D

1 MILE = 1.6 KMS

New Av

Wadsworth Ter

C

Wadsworth Av

St Nick's Av

W 193 St

W 192 St

AUDUBON AV

AMSTERDAM AV

W 191 St

① ⑨

W 190 St

191 St

87

END 20 MINS

1 MILE = 1.6 KMS

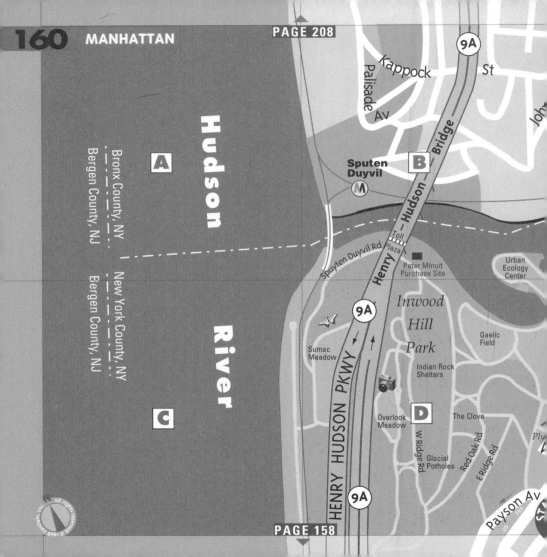

PAGE 208

9A

Kappock St

Joh

Palisade Av

Hudson

A

Bronx County, NY
Bergen County, NJ

Sputen Duyvil
M

B

Hudson Bridge

River

Spuyten Duyvil Rd

Henry

New York County, NY
Bergen County, NJ

C

Toll Plaza

Peter Minuit
Purchase Site

Urban
Ecology
Center

*Inwood
Hill
Park*

9A

Sumac
Meadow

Gaelic
Field

Indian Rock
Shelters

Overlook
Meadow

D

The Clove

W Ridge Rd

Glacial
Potholes

Red Oak Rd

E Ridge Rd

Ply

HENRY HUDSON PKWY

9A

Payson Av

PAGE 158

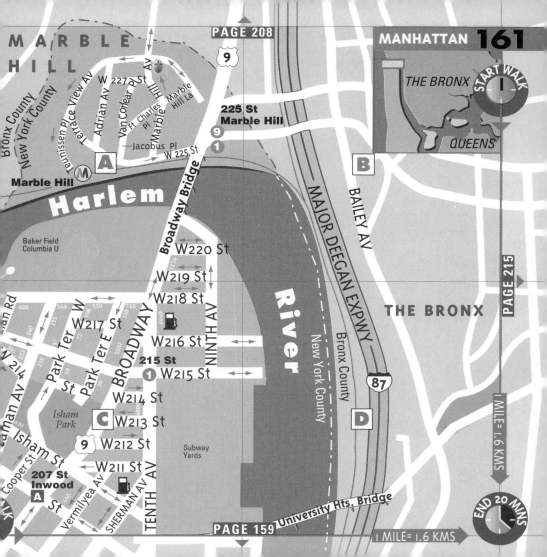

MARBLE
HILL

Bronx County
New York County

Teunissen Place
Terrace View Av
W 227 St
Adrian Av
Van Corlear Pl
Ft Charles Pl
Marble Hill Av
Marble Hill La

9
PAGE 208

225 St
Marble Hill

Jacobus Pl
W 225 St

9
1

Marble Hill
M
A

THE BRONX
START WALK
1
QUEENS

Harlem

B

BAILEY AV

MAJOR DEEGAN EXPWY

Baker Field
Columbia U

Broadway Bridge

W 220 St

W 219 St

W 218 St

574

W 217 St

600
564
530
510
240
251
257
537
507
72
Park Ter W
Park Ter E

BROADWAY

NINTH AV

W 216 St

215 St
1
W 215 St

W 214 St

River

New York County

Bronx County

THE BRONX

PAGE 215

Isham
Park

C
W 213 St

9
W 212 St

W 211 St

W 214
630
St
Cooper St
Isham St
man Rd

207 St
Inwood
A

Vermilyea Av
SHERMAN AV
TENTH AV

Subway
Yards

87

D

1 MILE = 1.6 KMS

END 20 MINS

PAGE 159
University Hts. Bridge

1 MILE = 1.6 KMS

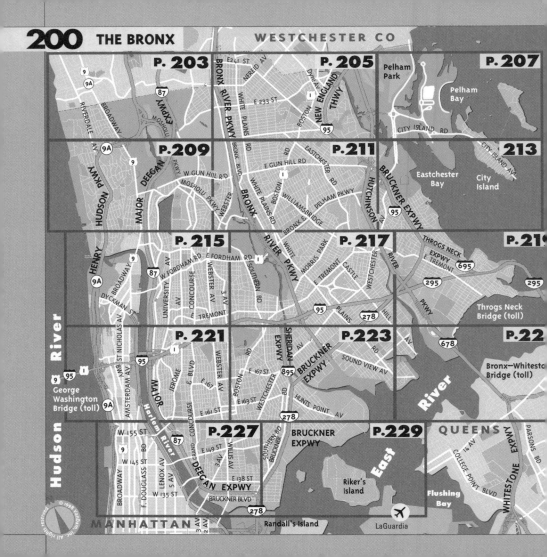

Best of the Bronx

Though geographically part of the US mainland, the Bronx joins NYC's other boroughs as a trendsetter in many areas of pop culture. Hip Hop and homeboys originated from here to take the universe by rhyme.

Bronx Zoo/Int'l Wildlife Conservation Park

One of the world's best parks and greatest research institutions with programs on five continents. Bronx River Pkwy @ Fordham Rd, 718-367-1010. **216A**

Jimmy's Bronx

For the serious Mambo crowd this gargantuan disco-cum-restaurant is the G spot on Thursday nights. 281 W Fordham Road, 718-329-2000. **214B**

Wave Hill

Anybody in search of a robber baron mansion on the Hudson should do themselves the favor and visit. Yes, this is the Bronx. 675 W 252 St, 718-549-3200. **208A**

Yankee Stadium

Arguably America's premier sports franchise, the Bronx Bombers got their start in Manhattan as the Highlanders. 161 St & River Av, 718-760-6200. **221C**

NY Botanical Garden

A renowned leader in conservation and, following its most recent renovation, the most stunning glass palace this side of Kew Gardens, England. Its four rainforest habitats alone are worth the visit. 200 St @ Southern Blvd, 718-817-8705. **216A**

Enid A. Haupt Conservatory restored in 1978 by Edward Larrabee Barnes

Le Refuge Bed & Breakfast

Gourmands the world over flock to Pierre Saint-Denis's eight-room sea captain's house on Eastchester Bay. Unique to the Bronx, there is no better place for breakfast. Lunch, however, should be enjoyed at Pierre's restaurant, Le Refuge, on Manhattan's Upper East Side. 620 City Island Av, 718-885-2478. **213B**

Bronx Stats:
Population:
1.2 million

Area:
43 sq miles

Hudson River

Ferry

A

RIVERDALE AV

BROADWAY

B

RADFORD ST

VALENTINE LA

9A

Delafield Pl

St. Spencer

W 263

W 262

Pl

St

Liebig Av

Delafield Av

Fieldston Rd

Tyndall Av

Spence

Westchester County
Bronx County

College of
Mt St Vincent

W 261 St

W 260

6100

D

550

RIVERDALE AV

400

750

M **Mt St
Vincent**

W 259

Judaica
Museum

Independence Av

Sigma
Pl

Arlington Av

Netherland Av

Mosh

C

Palisade Av

Bronx County, NY
Bergen County, NJ

W 256 St

5600

22

© 1996 Vernon Inc. All rights reserved

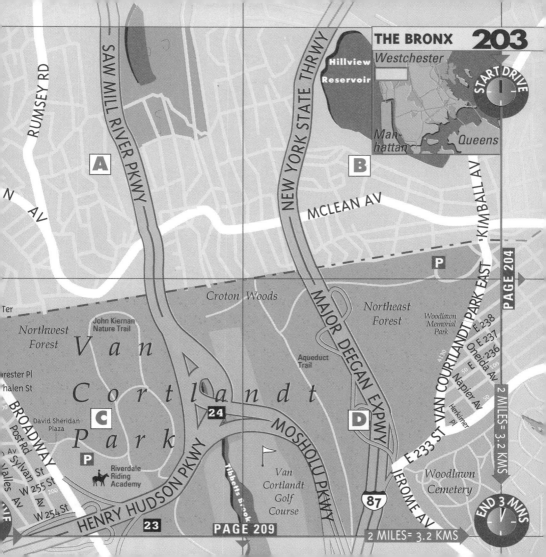

RUMSEY RD

SAW MILL RIVER PKWY

N AV

A

NEW YORK STATE THRWY

Hillview Reservoir

Westchester

Man-hattan Queens

START DRIVE

B

MCLEAN AV

KIMBALL AV

P

PAGE 204

Croton Woods

Northeast Forest

Woodlawn Memorial Park

E 238

E 237

Oneida Av

Ter

Northwest Forest

John Kiernan Nature Trail

V a n

Aqueduct Trail

MAJOR DEECAN EXPWY

VAN COURTLANDT PARK EAST

Napier Av

2 MILES = 3.2 KMS

rester Pl
halen St

C o r t l a n d t

D

E 233 ST

Herkimer Pl

BROADWAY

Post Rd

David Sheridan Plaza

C

P a r k

24

Riverdale Riding Academy

MOSHOLU PKWY

Woodlawn Cemetery

Av
Sylvan
Valles
St
AV

W 255 St

W 254 St

HENRY HUDSON PKWY

Tibbetts Brook

Van Cortlandt Golf Course

JEROME AV

87

END 3 MINS

23

PAGE 209

2 MILES= 3.2 KMS

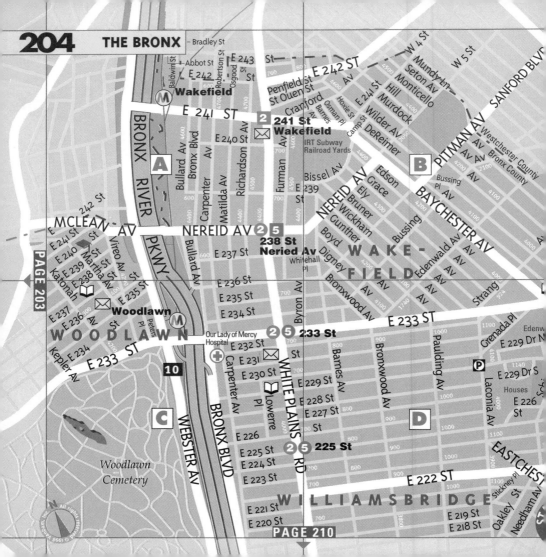

Bradley St

Baldwin St
Abbot St
E 242 St
E 243 St
Penfield St
St Ouen
Osgood St
Robertson St
W 4 St
W 5 St

Wakefield

SANFORD BLVD

Mundy Ln
Seton Av
Monticello
Hill
Murdock
E 244 St
Wilder Av
DeReimer

Cranford
Osman Pl
Hoxie St
Barnes
Camp St

E 241 ST

2 **241 St**
Wakefield

IRT Subway
Railroad Yards

PITMAN AV

Westchester County
Bronx County

Bullard Av
Bronx Blvd
Carpenter Av
Matilda Av
Richardson Av
Furman Av
E 240 St

E 239 St

Bissel

A

B

Bussing Pl Av

BAYCHESTER AV

BRONX RIVER

Edson
Grace
Ely
Bruner
Wickham
Gunther
Boyd Digney
Whitehall Pl
Bronxwood Av

Bussing Av

242 St

MCLEAN AV

E 241 St
E 240 St
Katonah
Vireo Av
Martha Av
E 239 St
E 238 St
E 235 St
E 236 St
E 237

NEREID AV 2 5

238 St
Neried Av

W A K E-
F I E L D

Edenwald Av
Av
Av
Av
Av

Strang

E 237 St
E 236 St
E 235 St
E 234 St

Bullard Av

E 237 St
E 236 St

Byron Av

W O O D L A W N

Woodlawn

Peters Pl

BRONX RIVER PKWY

E 233 ST

Kepler Av
E 234

Woodlawn

Our Lady of Mercy
Hospital
E 232 St

2 5 **233 St**

E 233 ST

Barnes Av

Bronxwood Av

Paulding Av

Grenada Pl
E 229 Dr N

Edenw

10

E 231
E 230 St
Carpenter Av
Lowerre Pl

WHITE PLAINS RD

E 229 St
E 228 St
E 227 St
St
E 226

P
E 229 Dr S
Houses
Laconia Av
E 226 St

C

WEBSTER AV

BRONX BLVD

E 225 St
E 224 St
E 223 St

2 5 **225 St**

D

E 222 ST

EASTCHEST

Woodlawn
Cemetery

E 221 St
E 220 St

W I L L I A M S B R I D G E

E 219 St
E 218 St

Oakley St
Needham Av
Stickney St

PAGE 203

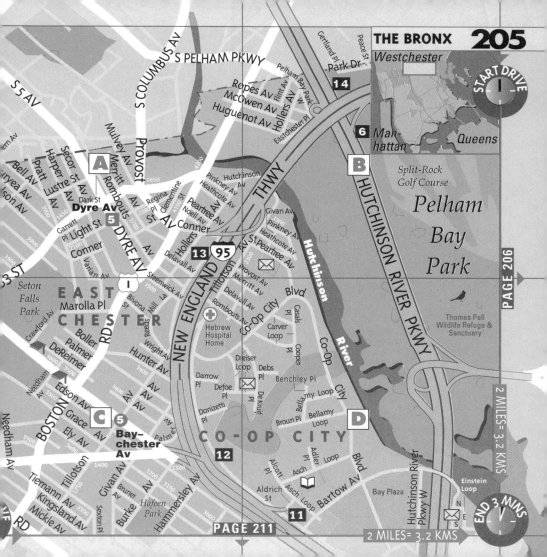

S 5 AV

S COLUMBUS AV

S PELHAM PKWY

Westchester

Manhattan

Queens

Ropes Av

McOwen Av

Huguenot Av

Hollers Av

Flint Av

Pelham Bay Park

Gerland Pl

Peace St

Park Dr

14

6

Split-Rock
Golf Course

*Pelham
Bay
Park*

B

Mulvey Av

Provost

Secor Av

Harper Av

Bell Av

Pratt Av

Lustre St

yrea Av

son Av

A

Merritt Av

Rombouts Av

Dark St

Dyre Av

Regina Pl

Clementine St

Peartree Pl

Conner

Noell Av

Pinkney Av

Hutchinson Av

Heathcote Av

Eastchester Pl

THWY

Givan Av

Pinkney Av

Heathcote Av

Garrett
Pl

Light St

5

Conner

Varian Av

DYRE AV

Hollers

Delavall Av

13

95

Peartree Av

St

St

Provost Av

Merritt

Hutchinson

River

HUTCHINSON RIVER PKWY

Thomas Pell
Wildlife Refuge &
Sanctuary

1

Steenwick Av

Bivona

Reeds Mill

*Seton
Falls
Park*

**E A S T
C H E S T E R**

Marolla Pl

Crawford Av

Boller
Palmer
DeReimer

Hunter Av

Wright Av

Rombouts Av

BOSTON RD

Tillotson Av

NEW ENGLAND

Hebrew
Hospital
Home

Delavall Av

CO-OP
City

Blvd

Casals
Pl

Carver
Loop

Cooper
Pl

Co-Op

City

Needham
Av

Edson Av

Grace Av

Ely Av

C

5

**Bay–
chester
Av**

Givan Av

Bruner
Av

Burke

Sexton Pl

Hammersley Av

Hafeen
Park

Tiemann Av

Kingsland Av

Mickle Av

NF RD

Needham

Darrow
Pl

Defoe
Pl

Donizetti

Dreiser
Loop

Debs
Pl

De Kruif
Pl

Benchley Pl

Bellamy Loop

Bellamy
Loop

Broun Pl

D

C O - O P   C I T Y

12

Alcott
Pl

Asch
Loop

Adler
Pl

Loop

Palme

Aldrich
St

Asch

Bartow Av

Blvd

Bay Plaza

Hutchinson River
Pkwy W

Einstein
Loop

11

2 MILES= 3.2 KMS

2 MILES= 3.2 KMS

2 MILES = 3.2 KMS

PAGE 206

START DRIVE

END 3 MINS

N
W   E
S

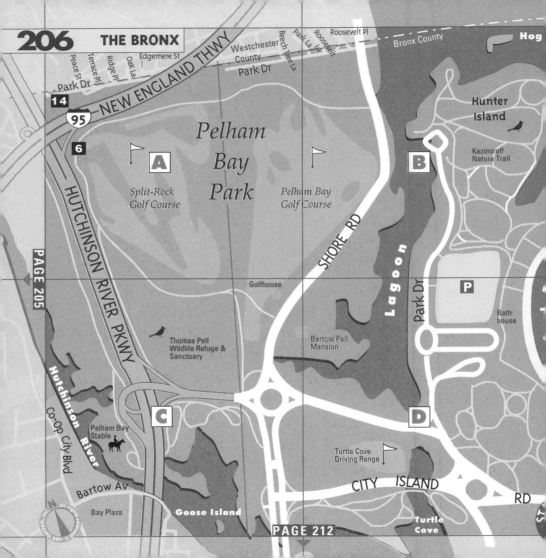

Middle Reef

East
Nonations

South
Nonations

Westchester

Man-
hattan

Queens

START DRIVE

A

B

Twin
Island

mental

The Blauzes

elham

ay

Chimney Sweeps Islands

(Pelham Bay Park)

High
Island

Hart
Island

Long Island Sound

Rat
Island

Green
Flats

D

2 MILES= 3.2 KMS

C

Footbridge

Terrace St

King St

Bridge St

Sutherland St

Av

Kilroe St

Cross St

Minnieford Av

Beach St

Bowne St

Kirby St

**City
Island**

Ferry

END 3 MINS

Le Refuge
Northwind
Undersea Institute

City
Island Bridge

PAGE 213

2 MILES= 3.2 KMS

208 THE BRONX

PAGE 202

22 **9A** **23** **9**

Hudson River

Ferry

A

C

Bronx County, NY
Bergen County, NJ

Dyckman
Marina

Riverdale Ⓜ

W 255 St
Palisade Av
Ladd Rd
W 254 St
Hudson River Rd
Rivercrest Rd
Blackstone Av
St Arlington Av
W 252 St
Netherland Av
RIVERDALE AV
Mosholu Av

W 255 St
W 253 St
Fieldston Rd
Lake View Pl
W 252 St
Fieldston Ter
Post Rd
W 251 St

F I E L D S T O N

Grosvenor
Coolidge Rd
Iselin Av
Delafield Av
Fieldston Rd
Indian Rd
Waldo Av
College Rd
Greystone
W 246 St
W 245 St
Livingston Av
Manhattan Rd
Cayuga Av
St
Post Rd

B

W 250 St
W 249
Henry Hudson Pkwy E

Sycamore Av
Independence Av (Bingham Rd)
Hudson Av

Wave
Hill

21

W 248 St
W 247 St
Alderbrook Rd
Ploughman's Bush
Dodge-wood Rd
Delafield La
Hudson Pkwy W
Independence

College Pkwy
W 242 St
Greystone St
Dash Pl
Waldo Av
Gaelic Park
W 240 St
W 238 St
238

Manhatta
College

Riverdale Park

R I V E R D A L E

Palisade Av
Douglas Av Ter
Hudson Manor Ter
W 246
W 239 St
Blackstone Pl
Blackstone Av

20

W 238 St
W 237 St
W 236 St
Ped Bridge
W 235 St

Hill Tower
Park

Tulfan Ter
Riverdale
Fieldston
W 238
Cambridge Av
Oxford Av
Johnson Av
Netherland Av
Arlington
HUDSON

Irwin Av
W 236
W 234
W 232 St

D

K I N G S B R I D G

Ewen Park
W 231 St
W 230
W 230

River Rd
W 232 St
Independence Av
Pl
W 231 St
Palisade Av

19

9A

Fairfield Av
Arlington Av
ton Av

Irwin Av
Johnson Av

Schervier
Frances
Home

Henry Hudson Mem Park
Independence Av
Scenic
Kappock St

W 227 St

HENRY

S P U Y T E N
D U Y V I L

Johnson

PAGE 214

© 1998 Vandam, Inc. All rights reserved

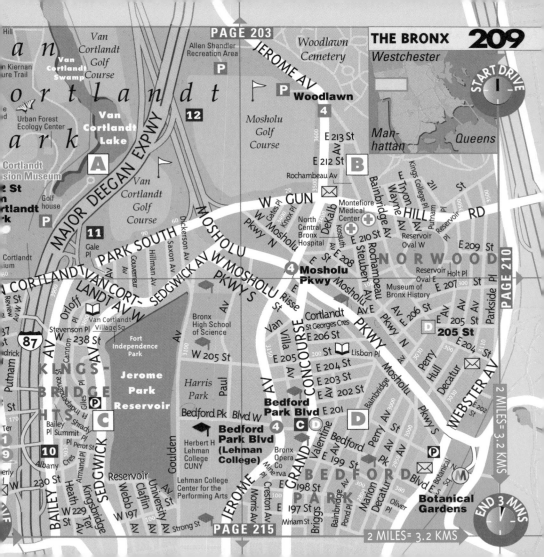

START DRIVE

Hill

a n

Van Cortlandt Golf Course

n Kiernan ure Trail

Van Cortlandt Swamp

o r t l a n d t

Woodlawn Cemetery

Allen Shandler Recreation Area

JEROME AV

P

Urban Forest Ecology Center

Van Cortlandt Lake

12

P

Woodlawn

Mosholu Golf Course

Man-hattan

Queens

a r k

Cortlandt sion Museum

A

Van Cortlandt Golf Course

MAJOR DEEGAN EXPWY

4

E 213 St

E 212 St

B

: St n rtlandt rk

Golf house

Rochambeau Av

Montefiore Medical Center

E Tryon Pl Wayne Av

Kings College Pl

211

Putnam

Reservoir Pl

RD

P

11

Gale Pl

PARK SOUTH

Dickerson Av

Saxon Av

W GUN

W Gates Pl

Knox Pl

W Mosholu

DeKalb

North Central Bronx Hospital

Kossuth

E 210 St

Bainbridge Av

Steuben Av

Rochambeau Av E

Reservoir Oval W

HILL

E 209 St

N O R W O O D

Cortlandt ium

CORTLANDT VANCORT-LANDT AV

Orloff Av

Stevenson Pl

Hillman Av

Gouverneur

SEDGWICK AV

W MOSHOLU

PKWY S

Risse St

Van Villa Av

Mosholu

4 Mosholu Pkwy

Reservoir Oval E

Holt Pl

PAGE 210

37

87

Cannon Pl

238 St

Van Cortlandt Village Sq

Fort Independence Park

Bronx High School of Science

Cortlandt Av

St Georges Cres

E 206 St

Museum of Bronx History

E 207 St

MOSHOLU

PKWY N

D

E 206 St

E 205 St

205 St

E 204 St

ndrick

Putnam

KINGS-

W 205 St

Harris Park

Paul Av

E 205 St

Lisbon Pl

E 204 St

E 203 St

E 202 St

Bainbridge Av

PKWY S

Perry Av

Hull Av

Decatur Av

WEBSTER AV

2 MILES = 3.2 KMS

St

BRIDGE

Giles Pl

Jerome Park Reservoir

GRAND

E 202 St

202

St

Ter

HTS

Bailey
Pl Summit

Shrady Pl

Perot St

C

Bedford Pk Blvd W

Bedford Park Blvd

E 201

E Concourse

C

D

Bedford

Perry Av

Marion Av

P

1

10

Albany

Reservoir

Goulden Av

Herbert H Lehman College CUNY

4 Bedford Park Blvd (Lehman College)

Bronx Opera Co

Valentine Av

Bedford Pk

Decatur Av

Oliver Pl

Botanical

M

9

230 St

BAILEY AV

Kingsbridge Ter

Heath Av

Webb Av

University Av

Claflin Av

W 197

Lehman College Center for the Performing Arts

Minerva Pl

E 199 St

E 198 St

Creston Av

Morris Av

Briggs Av

Bainbridge Av

Pond Pl

B E D F O R D

P A R K

Oliver Pl

Botanical Gardens

END 3 MINS

erly

W 229 St

Strong St

197 St

Miriam St

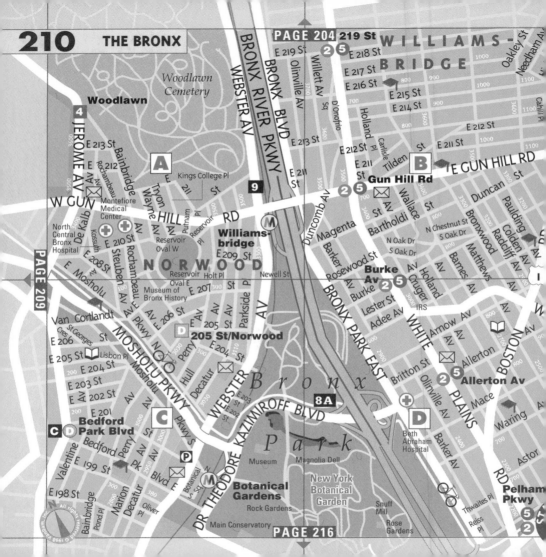

Westchester

Man-
hattan

Queens

START DRIVE

Corsa
Sexton
Pl
EASTCHESTER
Av
Kingsland Av
Tiemann Av
Hafeen
Park
Bruner Av
Wickham Av
Gunther Av
BAY
CHESTER
Baychester
I-95

ton
Seymour Gl
Fish Av
Av
Givan
Av
Mickle Av
Hammersley
Av
Fox Ter
Deyo St
Adee Av
Arnow Av
Ely Av
Bartow Av
Allerton Av

Wilson Av
Bouck Av
Pearsall Av
RD
Knapp St

E GUN HILL RD

Eastchester
Gardens Park

Gun
Hill Rd

A

Givan
Square
O'Neill

Schorr Pl
Bantam
Pl

E GUN HILL RD

B

1900
Ely Av

9

Bouck Av
Throop Av
Tenbroeck Av
Pearsall Av
Hering Av
Yates Av
onia Av

De Witt Pl
Sexton Pl
Fenton
Seymour Av
Fish Av
Young Av
Wilson Av
De Witt Pl
Morgan Av

Hawthorne St
Fielding St

Westervelt Av
Lodovick Av
Tiemann Av
Kingsland Av
Wickham Av
Gunther Av
Lodovick Av

Delanoy Av
Bruner Av

Demeyer St
Vance St
Erskine Pl

8C

Pelham Bay
General
Hospital

Stedman

Mickle
Woodhull Av

EASTCHESTER RD

HUTCHINSON RIVER PKWY

Pelham Pkwy S
E 197 St
E 196 St
E 195 St
E 194 St

Hobart Av

PAGE 212

2 MILES = 3.2 KMS

BRIDGE RD

Esplanade
Stell Pl

North

PELHAM

PKWY

Wilkinson Av
Mulford Av

Hutchinson River

elham
wy
ouses

and

Rhinelander Av
Stillwell St
McDonald St
Seminole St

WEST-
CHESTER
HTS

Bassett Av

Mildred Pl

Esplanade
South

Pelham
Pkwy

Jacobi
Medical
Center

Hutchinson River Pkwy W

Laurie Av

New York
Institution
for the
Blind

C

Van
Hosen Av
Choctaw Pl
Pawnee Pl
Pinchot Pl
Wilkinson

D

Bronx
Psychiatric
Center

Hutchinson River Pkwy E

Ulpin Pl

2 MILES = 3.2 KMS

BRONX

Parkway

Naragansett

Tenbroeck Av
Seminole

Lakewood

Loomis
St

Parkway

Hering Av
Yates Av

Newport
Av

Ives St
Calvary
Hospital

McAlpin Av
Chesbrough Av
St Raymond Av

Waters Pl

END 3 MINS

Pelham
Matthews Av
Barnes Av
Muliner Av

Esplanade
Lydig
Av

WILLIAMSBRIDGE

Tomlinson Av
Haight Av
Lurting Av
Hone Av

Woodmansten Pl

Paulding Av

Neill Av

MORRIS PARK AV

Albert Einstein
College of
Medicine

Waters Av

Blondell
Av

5
Morris Park

2 MILES = 3.2 KMS

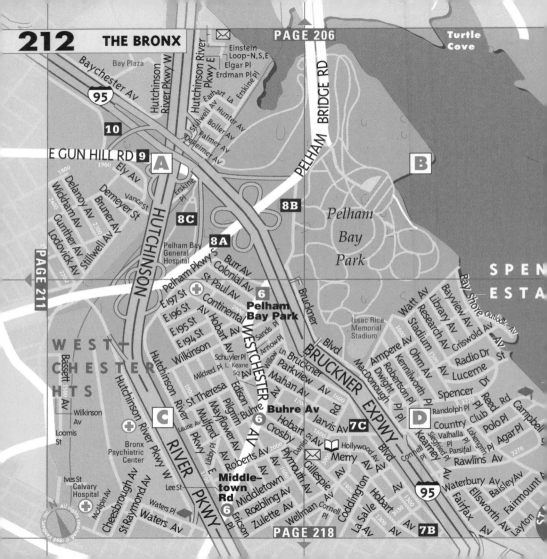

PAGE 206

Turtle Cove

Baychester Av

Bay Plaza

95

10

9 E GUN HILL RD A

Hutchinson River Pkwy W

Hutchinson River Pkwy E

✉ Einstein
Loop-N,S,E
Elgar Pl
Erdman Pl

Earhart La.
Erskine Pl
Stillwell Av
Hunter Av
Boller Av
Palmer Av
Edenwald Av
Erskine Pl

PELHAM BRIDGE RD

B

Ely Av
Demeyer St
vancest

Delanoy Av
Wickham Av
Bruner Av
Gunther Av
Stillwell Av
Lodovick Av

HUTCHINSON

8C

8B

Pelham
Bay
Park

SPEN
ESTA

PAGE 211

Pelham Bay
General Hospital

8A

Pelham Pkwy S
Burr Av
Colonial Av
St Paul Av

6

Bruckner

Issac Rice
Memorial
Stadium

Bay Shore Outlook Av

WEST
CHESTER
HTS

Bassett Av

E 197 St
E 196 St
E 195 St
E 194 St
Wilkinson

Continental
Hobart Av

WESTCHESTER

Pelham
Bay Park

Sands Av

Watt Av
Bayview Av
Library Av
Research Av
Griswold Av
Stadium
Ohm Av
Radio Dr
Luceme
St

Wilkinson
Av

Loomis
St

Hutchinson River

Schuyler Pl
Mildred Pl
L. Keane
Sq

Willow Ln
Arrow Pl
Parkview Av

Bruckner

BRUCKNER EXPWY

Ampere Av
Kennworth Pl
Dwight Pl
Robertson Pl
MacDonough Pl

Spencer Dr
Reed
Rd

Bronx
Psychiatric
Center

St Theresa
Pilgrim
Mulford
Edison
Buhre

AV

6

Mahan Av

Buhre Av

Hobart St

Blvd

Randolph Pl
Country Club
Rd
Polo Pl
Campbell

RIVER

C

Laurie Av
Mayflower Av
Libby Av

Crosby

Jarvis Av

7C

Valhalla Pl
Loheng'n Pl
Siegfried Pl
Cornell Pl
Parsifal

Agar Pl

Ives St
Calvary Hospital

McAlpin Av

Wilkinson Av

PKWY

Roberts Av

Middle-
town
Rd

6

Middletown

Plymouth Av
Gillespie

Cornell
Pl

✉ Merry

Hollywood Av

Merry Av

Kearney Av

Rawlins Av

D

Waterbury Av
Baisley Av
Ellsworth Av
Fairmount Av

Lee St
Cheesbrough Av
St Raymond Av

Waters Pl
Waters Av

Ericson
Pl

Roebling Av
Zulette Av

Wellman

Coddington Av

La Salle Av

Hobart Av

95

7B

Fairfax Av
Layton
St

PAGE 218

© 1993 Vision, Inc. All rights reserved

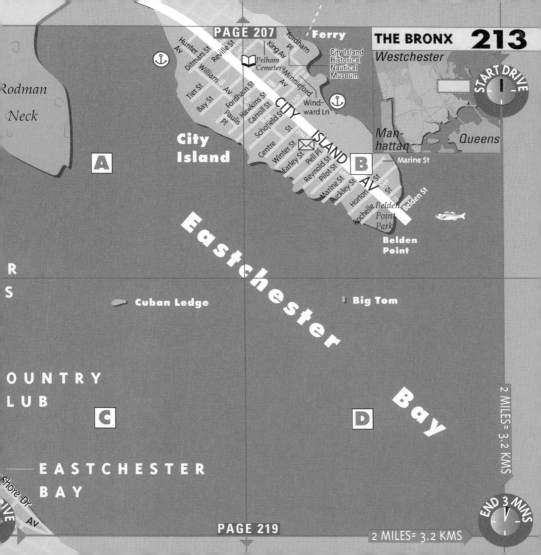

PAGE 207

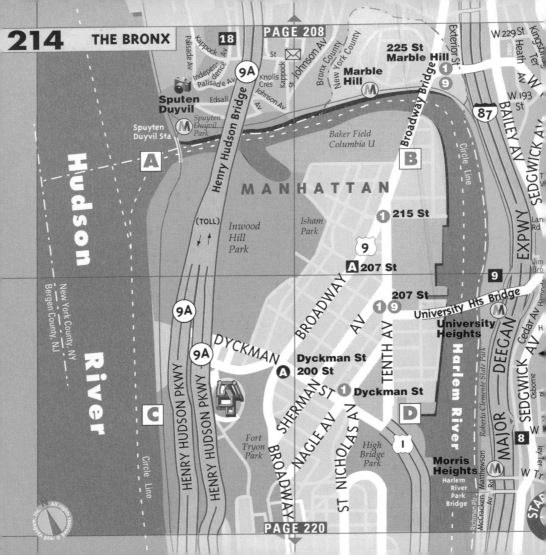

18

Palisade Av

Kappock Av

St

Johnson Av

9A

225 St Marble Hill

Exterior St

W 229 St

Kingsbridge Ter

Heath

Av

Independence Av

Palisade Av

Knolls Cres

Kappock St

Johnson Av

Bronx County
New York County

Marble Hill

M

1
9

W 193 St

BAILEY AV

SEDGWICK

87

Sputen Duyvil

Edsall

Spuyten Duyvil Park

M

Spuyten Duyvil Sta

Henry Hudson Bridge

Broadway Bridge

Baker Field Columbia U

Circle Line

EXPWY

Lan Rd

A

B

M A N H A T T A N

Vim Bro

Hudson

(TOLL)

Inwood Hill Park

Isham Park

1
215 St

9

A
207 St

9

River

New York County, NY
Bergen County, NJ

9A

207 St

1
9

University Hts Bridge

University Heights

M

Cedar Av

H

DEEGAN

Hammond

9A

DYCKMAN

A

**Dyckman St
200 St**

BROADWAY

AV

TENTH AV

D

Harlem River

Roberto Clemente State Park

SEDGWICK AV

Osborne

HENRY HUDSON PKWY

HENRY HUDSON PKWY

C

SHERMAN ST

NAGLE AV

1
Dyckman St

MAJOR

8

Fort Tryon Park

ST NICHOLAS AV

High Bridge Park

I

Morris Heights

M

W Tr

Circle Line

BROADWAY

Harlem River Park Bridge

Richman Plz

McCracken

Av

Matthewson

Rd

STA

N

All Rights Reserved

© 1994 Vignelli Inc.

PAGE 209

Queens

Man-
hattan

W 197 St
Strong St
W 195 St
Couldn
Eames Pl
SBRIDGE RD
Barn Hill Square
verans

UNIVERSITY AV
Devoe Ter
Father Zeiser
enroe Park

N FORDHAM RD

Aqueduct

ghts

UNIVERSITY
TS

Andrews Ter
mx mmunity lege
o St

ide Av
179 St

Harrison Av
W TREMONT

t Av
Macomb's Rd

Creston Av
Morris Av
E 197 St
Miriam St
E 196 St
Kingsbridge Armory
Kingsbridge Rd
4 E KINGS- C D
En Foco E 193 St
Edgar St
St James Park
W 192 St
E 192
Briggs
Bainbridge Av
E 194 St
Poe Pl Dorothea Pl
Poe Allan Poe Cottage
Coles La

Decatur Av
Pond Av
E 193 St

WEBSTER AV

Fordham
M Fordham Plaza
Fordham Library Center

A W 191 St
Fordham Rd
E 190 St C D
Monroe College
4 **Fordham Rd**
Walton Av
Morris Av
Creston Av

FORDHAM
CONCOURSE

W 184 St North St
Evelyn Pl
E 183 St
Field Pl
Valentine Av
Tiebout Av
Elm Pl
E 187 St
E 186 St
E 185 St
E 184 St
E 183 St
Union Hospital
Cyrus Pl
I

E FORDHAM RD
Fordham University
E 191 St
Emmet St
Washington Av
Hoffman
Lorillard
Arthur Av
Hughes
St
Belmont Av
Cambreleng Av
Beaumont Av
Crotona Av

SOUTHERN BLVD
E 189
Columbus Square
E 188
Mario's
Belmont Italian American Playhouse
Crescent Av
E 186 St
E 185 St
E 183 St
Grote St

W 183 St 4 **183 St**
Buchanan Pl
W 182 St
Clinton Pl Cameron Pl
W 181 St E 181 St
W 180 St
Davidson Av
JEROME AV
GRAND

E 182 St C D **182 St/ 183 St**
Ryer Av
P Crames Square
Folin
E 180 St
E 182 Fletcher Pl St
Park Av
E 181 St
E 180 St
WEBSTER AV
Arthur Murphy Square
Oak Tree Pl
Quarry Rd
Adams
Bassford Av
Bathgate Av
St Barnabas Hospital for Chronic Diseases

E Grote St
182 St
Garden St
Arthur Av
Clinton Av
Prospect Av
EAST TREMONT
Oakland Pl

PAGE 216
2 MILES = 3.2 KMS

Burnside Av
4 BURNSIDE AV
C E 179
E 178 St
Echo Pl
Devanney Square
Bush St
Julius J Richman Mem Park
O'Brien Square I
E 179 St
Alden Pl
E 178 St
THIRD AV
Lafontaine Av
Monterey Av
D

C D **Tremont Av**
Kingsland Pl
E 177 St
Mount Hope Pl
Morris Av
Topping Av
Monroe Av
Anthony Av
TREMONT
Prospect Pl
Carter Av
M **Tremont**
E 176 St
E 175 St
Ittner St
E 174 St
95 CROSS BRONX EXPWY
E 175
Crotona Park N
Crotona Park
Crotona Av
END 3 MINS
V

Morton Pl
Unknown Soldier Plaza
W 177 St
4 **176 St**
E 176 St
Henwood Pl
Weeks Av
Eastburn Av

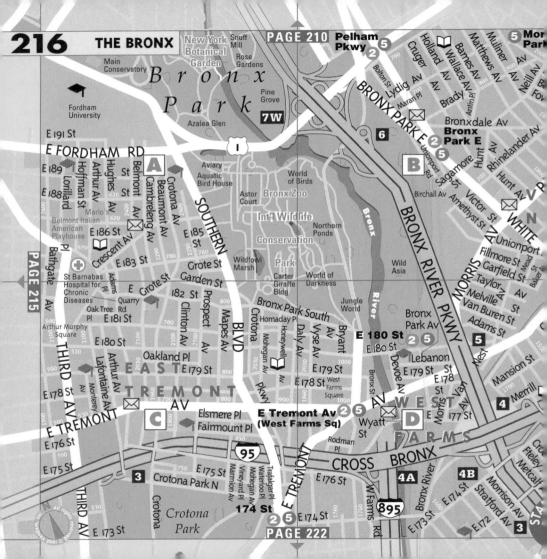

START DRIVE

Manhattan

Queens

St Raymond's Cemetery

MORRIS PARK AV

Hone Av
Lurting
Haight
Av
Paulding Av
Hone Av
Neill Av

MORRIS PARK

WESTCHESTER

Poplar St
Jarrett Pl
Waters Av
Fink Av
Ponton Av
Roberts Av
Halpern Av
Tan Pl

Silver St
Lane Av
Westchester Square
Dock St
Kirk St
Ferris Av

E TREMONT
Benson
Roselle Av
Lurting Av
Montgomery Pl
Hone Av
Paulding

Overing St
Marvin
Frisby Av
Commerce Av
Peters Av

6 Westchester Sq
E Tremont Av

A

Bronxdale Av
Pierce Av
Nest Av
Sacket
Poplar
Seddon St
Lyvere
Fuller St
Buck St
Maday St
Dorsey
Hubbell St
Rowland
St Raymond
Tratman Av

Westchester Hospital

Butler Pl
Rowe St
Herschell St
Halsey St

B

Halsey St
Seabury Av

6 **Zerega Av**

6B
Graff Av

CASTLE HILL AV

Van

E TREMONT AV
Purdy St

DMV
Purdy St
Elm
Dr
Hawthorne
Dr
Pine Dr
Dogwood
Dr

Parker Av
Steams
Odell
St Raymond
Glebe Av
Glover St
Doris St
Lyon Av
Glebe Av

Butler
St
6 **Zerega Av**

Waterbury Av
Zerega Av
Havemeyer Av

Commerce Av

Westchester

PAGE 218

Laurel
Dr

Metropolitan Oval

PARK-

Manning St
Starling Av

6 **Castle Hill Av**

Newbold Av
Ellis Av
Gleason

5B

6A

Brush Av

Creek

UNIONPORT

CHESTER

METROPOLITAN

Archer Rd
East Av
West Av
Wood Rd

Monsignor A. Scanlon Square

Parkchester Rd

Benedict Av
Pugsley Av

WESTCHESTER

95

UNION-PORT

PLAINS RD
Archer St

McGraw
Virginia
Wood Av

Hugh J Grant Circle

Blvd

Av
Av
Blvd

Lafayette Av
Virgil Av

CASTLE HILL AV

EXPWY

5A

Powell Av
Haviland Av
Watson Av
Blackrock Av
Chatterton Av
Bruckner

6 **E 177 St
Parkchester**

St Lawrence
Commonwealth Av
Westdale Av

C

Taylor Av
Leland Av
Thieriot Av
Beach Av

WHITE PLAINS RD

Virginia Av
Underhill Av

278

D

Bruckner
Quimby Av
Story Av
Hermany Av
Olmstead Av
Turnbull Av

Cincinnatus Av

6 **St Law-
rence Av**

Bronxdale Houses

BRUCKNER
EXPWY

Homer Av
Seward Av

Castle Hill Houses

END 3 MINS

BRUCKNER

PAGE 223

2 MILES= 3.2 KMS

2 MILES= 3.2 KMS

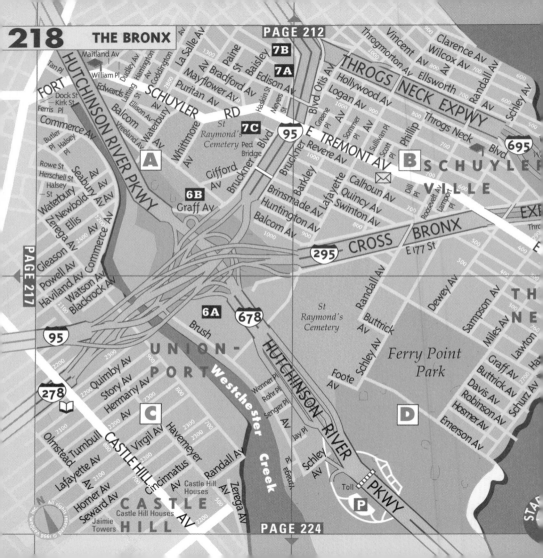

PAGE 212

7B

7A

Maitland Av

FORT SCHUYLER

HUTCHINSON RIVER PKWY

Tan Pl
Dock St
Kirk St
Ferris Pl

Commerce Av

Butler Pl
Halsey Pl

Rowe St
Herschell St
Halsey — St

Waterbury Av
Newbold Av
Zerega Av
Ellis

Gleason
Powell Av
Haviland Av
Watson Av
Blackrock Av

95

278

PAGE 217

William Pl
Edwards Av
Latting
Harrington
Dudley Av
Coddington
Ellison Av
Vreeland Av
Waterbury

La Salle Av

Paine St
Bradford Av
Mayflower Av
Puritan Av

Baisley

Edison Av

Haskin St
Meyers St

1300

Balcom

Seabury Av

Whittmore Av

SCHUYLER RD

St Raymond's Cemetery

7C

Gifford Av

Bruckner Blvd

6B

Graff Av

Brush

1000

Ped Bridge

1000

B

95

E TREMONT AV

Blvd Otis Av
Hollywood Av
Logan Av

Greene

Sommer

Sullivan Pl
Scott St

Revere Av

Barkley

Lafayette Av

Brinsmade Av

Huntington Av

Balcom Av

900

800

Calhoun Av

Quincy Av

Swinton Av

THROGS NECK EXPWY

Throgmorton Av
Vincent Av
Ellsworth
Wilcox Av
Clarence Av

Randall Av

Schley Av

THROGS NECK

Throgs Neck Blvd

695

Phillip

Dill

SCHUYLER VILLE

Roosevelt Av
Lampart Pl

700

EX

Thro

295

CROSS BRONX

E 177 St

500

400

Randall Av

Buttrick Av

Dewey Av

Sampson Av

Miles Av

Lawton

THE NE

6A

678

UNION-PORT

Westchester Creek

Quimby Av
Story Av
Hermany Av

2300
2300
800
2300
2300

2200

Wenner Pl
Rohr Pl
Senger Pl

Jay Pl

C

Olmstead Av
Turnbull
Lafayette Av
Homer Av
Seward Av

Virgil Av
Havemeyer
Cincinnatus
AV
Randall Av
Zerega Av

2100
2100
800
2200
2300

Castle Hill Houses

Castle Hill Houses

Jaimie Towers

CASTLE HILL AV

CASTLE HILL

PAGE 224

St Raymond's Cemetery

Ferry Point Park

Foote Av

Schley Av

D

Schley Av

HUTCHINSON RIVER

Toll
P
PKWY

Graff Av
Buttrick Av
Davis Av
Robinson Av
Hosmer Av
Emerson Av

Schurz Av
Lawton
Ha

STA

N

EDGEWATER
PARK
Creek PARK

Long Island Sound

Westchester

Man-
hattan

Queens

START DRIVE

A

B

C

D

Locust
Point

Toll
Plaza

4 Av
2 Av
Center St
Main Av
Stevens Av
Harding Av
Miles Av
1 St Av
3 Av
5 Av
7 Av
9 St Av
Dock
Edge
App
Sound View Dr.

4 St
3 St
2 St
1 St
2 Av
3 Av
4 Av
5 Av
6 Av
7 Av
Pennyfield Av
Meagher Av

Wissman Av
Longstreet Av
Blair Av
Reynolds Av
Prentiss Av

Chaffee Av
Hatting Pl
Clemson Pl
Giegerich Pl
Tierney Pl
E 177 St

Epwy Throgs
Hollywood
gan Av
Keamey Av
Ext
Prentiss Av
Pennyfield
Reynolds Av
Longstreet Av

Neck Blvd
Schurz Av
Mullan
Chaffee Pl
Hatting Pl
Clemson Pl
Giegerich Pl
Tierney Pl

Milton Av
Halpin Pl
N.Poplar Av
Oak Av
Maple Av
Sunset Tr
Plaza Pl
Holly Pl
Acorn Pl
Beech Pl
Cedar Pl
Daisy Pl
Elm Pl
Fern Pl
Geranium Pl
Hazel Pl
Ivy Pl
Jasmine Pl
 Mitchell Pl
Dave Pl
Egan Pl
Alan Pl
Bevy Pl
Castor Pl
Schuyler Ter

295

State University
of New York
Maritime College

MONT AV
GS AV
Collis Pl
Catalpa Pl
Balsam Pl
Linden
Aster Av

Magnolia Pl
Indian Ter

Sound View
Ter

East River

THROGS NECK EXPWY

Bronx County
Queens County

2 MILES= 3.2 KMS

END 3 MINS

2 MILES= 3.2 KMS

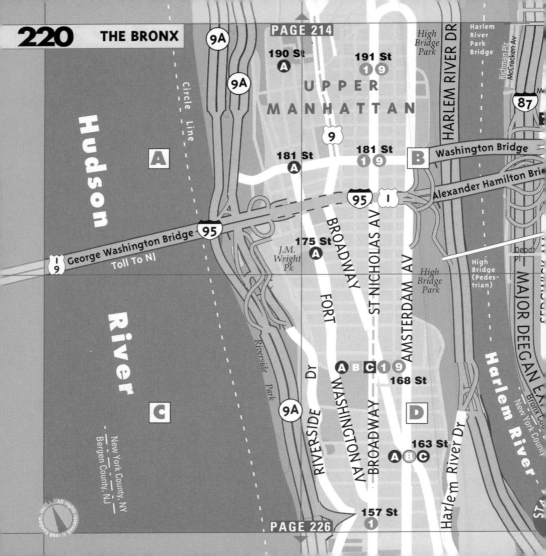

9A

PAGE 214

190 St
Ⓐ

191 St
①⑨

U P P E R

M A N H A T T A N

High Bridge Park

HARLEM RIVER DR

Harlem River Park Bridge

Richman Plz
McCracken Av

87

9A

⑨

181 St
Ⓐ

181 St
①⑨

Ⓑ Washington Bridge

95 Ⓘ

Alexander Hamilton Bri

High Bridge Park

Hudson

Circle Line

Ⓐ

Ⓘ⑨ George Washington Bridge

95

Toll To NJ

175 St
Ⓐ

J.M. Wright Pk

BROADWAY

ST NICHOLAS AV

AMSTERDAM AV

High Bridge (Pedestrian)

Depot Pl

MAJOR DEEGAN EX

River

Riverside Park

Riverside Dr

FORT

WASHINGTON AV

BROADWAY

Ⓐ Ⓑ Ⓒ ①⑨

168 St

Ⓓ

9A

Ⓒ

New York County, NY
Bergen County, NJ

163 St
Ⓐ Ⓑ Ⓒ

157 St
①

Harlem River Dr

Harlem River

Bronx Cou
New York County

© 1998 VistA, Inc. All rights reserved.

PAGE 226

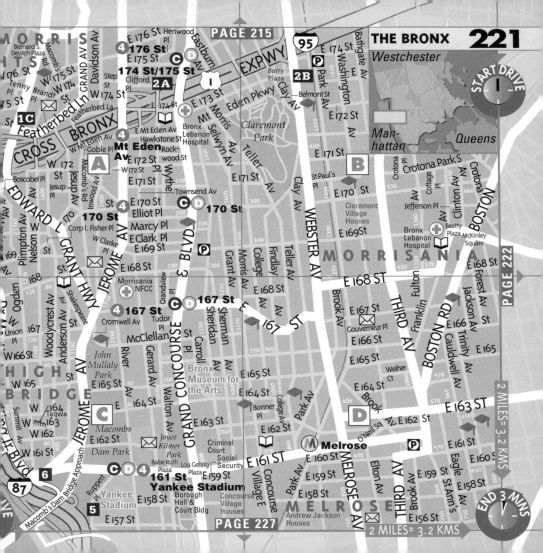

START DRIVE

MORRIS HTS
Bernard S. Deutch Plaza
Macomb's Rd
W 175 St
176 St
Tenny Brandt Pl
W 174 St
75 St
St

1C

Macomb's Rd
Davidson Av
GRAND AV
Henwood Pl
E 176 St
176 St
174 St/175 St
Eastburn Av
Clifford Pl
2A
Step St

CROSS
BRONX
Featherbed La
Goble Pl
Featherbed La
W Mt Eden Av
E Mt Eden Av
Hawkstone St
Rockwood St
E 173 St
E 174 St
Morris Av
Selwyn Av
Eden Pkwy
Clay Av
95
E 174 St
Washington Av
Bathgate Av
Park Av
Belmont St
2B
E 172 St
Barry Plaza

EDWARD L GRANT HWY
EXPWY
I
Bronx Lebanon Hospital
Claremont Park
Crotona Park S
Crotona Av
Cottage Av
Clinton Av
BOSTON

Mt Eden Av
4
E 172 St
W 172 St
E 171 St
Wythe Av
Townsend Av
Teller Av
Clay Av
St Paul's Pl
E 170 St
A
E 171 St
B
Jefferson Pl

170 St
4
Elliot Pl
Marcy Pl
E Clark Pl
E 169 St
C D
170 St
E BLVD
Grant Av
Morris Av
College Av
Findlay Av
Webster Av
Claremont Village Houses
E 169 St
Beatty Plaza
Bronx Lebanon Hospital
McKinley Square
Manhattan
Queens

Plimpton Av
Nelson Av
JEROME AV
W Clarke Pl
E 168 St
Morrisania NFCC
Grandview
167 St
4
C D
E 168 ST
MORRISANIA
Forest Av
Jackson Av
PAGE 222

Ogden Av
Shakespeare Av
Cromwell Av
Tudor Pl
McClellan St
Carroll Pl
Sherman Av
Sheridan Av
E 167 St
E 167 ST
Gouverneur Pl
Brook Av
THIRD AV
Franklin Av
Fulton Av
E 166 St
Trinity Av
Cauldwell Av
E 165 St

Union Pl
W 166 St
River Av
Gerard Av
John Mullaly Park
E 165 St
Walton Av
Bronx Museum for the Arts
College Av
E 165 St
Weiher Ct
Brook Av
E 164 St

HIGH BRIDGE
W 164 Taqwa
W 163
W 162
Macombs
E 162 St
C
Gerard Av
E 164 St
Bonner Pl
College Av
Park Av
E 163 St
E 163 ST
D
E 162 St

Summit Av
Joyce Kilmer Park
Babe Ruth Plaza
Lou Gehrig Plaza
Grand Concourse
Criminal Court Social Security
Concourse Village E
E 161 ST
Melrose
M
Park Av
Melrose Av
Elton Av
Eagle Av
St Ann's Av
E 161 St
E 160 St
E 159 St

6
87
Ruppert Pl
C D 4
161 St Yankee Stadium
Yankee Stadium
5
E 158 St
E 157 St
Borough Hall & Court Bldg
E 159 St
Concourse Village Houses
Andrew Jackson Houses
MELROSE
THIRD AV
Brook Av
E 158 St
E 156 St

PAGE 227

2 MILES = 3.2 KMS

2 MILES = 3.2 KMS

END 3 MINS

PAGE 216

PAGE 221

PAGE 227

Crotona Park N

Crotona
Park

174 St
175 St
D
C
2A

174 St
2 5

E 174 St
Bathgate Av
Washington
THIRD AV
173 St
E 173 St
Crotona Park E
Suburban Pl
Seabury Pl
Minford Pl

E 174 St

Barry
Plaza

Park Av
2B

Belmont St
Bathgate
Industrial
Park

Fulton Av

Crotona

Louis Nine

Charlotte St
Southern Blvd

E 172 St

Drain

E Mt Eden Av
Hawkstone St
Rockwood St

Eden Pkwy
Mt Morris Av
Selwyn Av

Clay Av

E 173 St

Claremont
Park

E 172 St
Claremont

Pkwy

RD
BOSTON

Jennings
Blvd

St

E 172 St
Pl
E 171 St
Wythe

Teller Av

A

E 171 St

St Paul's
Pl

Crotona Park S

Crotona Av
Clinton Av

Stebbins Av
Bristow St

Chisholm St
Prospect

Vyse

960

Hoe St

2 5
Freem
St
Home Av

Townsend Av

E 170 St
Elliot Pl

C D
170 St

Clay Av

E 170 St

Claremont
Village
Houses

E 169 St

Jefferson Pl

Bronx
Lebanon
Hospital

Cottage

Crotona
Pl

Beatty
Av

MORRISANIA

Freeman St

Intervale Av

Simpson St

E 167

Marcy Pl
E Clark St
E 169 St

Ritter
Pl

McKinley
Square

E 169 ST

Lyman Pl

Latkin
Square

BLVD

P

College Av

Findlay Av

Teller Av

WEBSTER AV

E 168 ST

E 168 St

Brook Av

Home
Av

Forest Av

E 167 St

Kelly St

Tiffany St

Fox St

2

Grandview
Pl

167 St
C D

Morris Av

Grant Av

E 167
ST

E 167 St
Gouverneur Pl

E 166 St

Jackson Av

Franklin

BOSTON RD

Trinton Av

Union Av

Hall Pl

Rev James
A Polite

Rogers
Pl

Intervale

CHESTER

Tudor
Pl
McClellan
St

Sherman Av
Sheridan Av

Carroll
Pl

E 167

E 166 St

Cauldwell Av

Trinity Av

E 165 St

2 5 Interv

Gerard Av

Bronx
Museum
for the Arts

E 165 St

E 164 St

College Av

Park Av

E 164 St

Weiher
Ct

Brook Av

E 163 ST
D

E 162
St

E 162
St

Av

Hewitt
Pl

GRAND CONCOURSE

C

E 163 St
Bonner Pl

E 162 St

O'Neill St

NY Founding
Hospital

E 161 St

E 161 St
Prospect
Av
2 5

Longwood Av

Walton Av

Lou Gehrig
Plaza

M Melrose

P

E 160 St

Eagle Av

Macy
Pl

Kelly St

Beck St

Babe Ruth
Plaza

161 St
Yankee Stadium
Borough
Hall

E 159 St

Concourse
Village E

MELROSE

E 161 ST

Park Av

Concourse
Village Houses

E 159 St

Andrew Jackson
Houses

MELROSE AV

E 160 St

E 158 St

Elton Av

THIRD AV

E 159 St

St Ann's Av

Brook Av

E 158 St

E 156 St

WEST

Leggett Av

Dawson St

STA

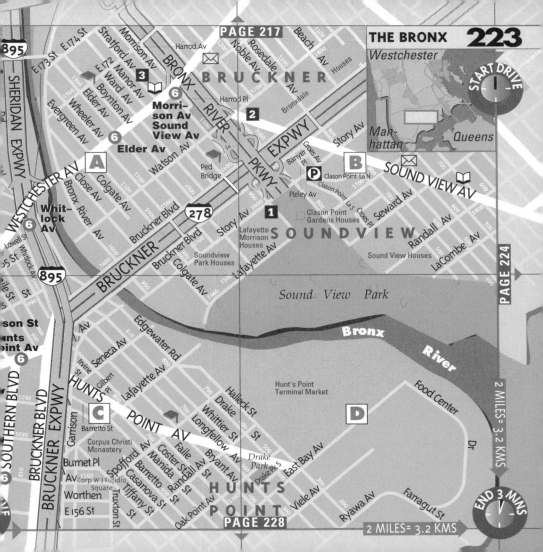

Westchester

START DRIVE

Man-hattan

Queens

SHERIDAN EXPWY

895

E 174 St

E 173 St

Stratford Av

Morrison Av

Harrod Av

BRUCKNER

ROSEDALE

Noble Av

Beach Av

Houses

B R U C K N E R

E 172 St

Manor Av

Ward Av

Boynton Av

Elder Av

3

Harrod Pl

Bronxdale

Wheeler Av

Evergreen Av

RIVER

6

2

Story Av

Morri-son Av Sound View Av

6

EXPWY

Cross St

Elder Av

Watson Av

PKWY

Banyer Pl

WESTCHESTER AV

A

Colgate Av

Bronx River Av

Close Av

Ped Bridge

P Clason Point La N

B

Clason Point La S Cross Pl

SOUND VIEW AV

Seward Av

Randall Av

LaCombe Av

Whit-lock Av

Bruckner Blvd

278

Story Av

Ffeley Av

Clason Point Gardens Houses

Lowell St

Whitlock Av

Bruckner Blvd

1

S O U N D V I E W

PAGE 224

St

895

Colgate Av

Soundview Park Houses

Lafayette Morrison Houses

Lafayette Av

Sound View Houses

B R U C K N E R

son St

nts oint Av

6

Sound View Park

Bronx

River

Av

Edgewater Rd

Seneca Av

Irvine St

Gilbert Pl

Lafayette Av

Halleck St

Hunt's Point Terminal Market

Food Center

SOUTHERN BLVD

HUNTS

Drake St

Whittier St

D

BRUCKNER BLVD

BRUCKNER EXPWY

C

Garrison

Barretto St

POINT AV

Longfellow Av

Bryant Av

Drake Park

Dr

Corpus Christi Monastery

Faile

Coster St

Drake St S

East Bay Av

Bumet Pl

Spofford Av

Manida St

Randall St

Av

Corp W J Fujidio

Barretto St

Casanova St

H U N T S

Worthen

Square

Tiffany St

Oak Point Av

Viele Av

Ryawa Av

Farragut St

E 156 St

Truxton St

P O I N T

END 3 MINS

2 MILES= 3.2 KMS

2 MILES = 3.2 KMS

BRUCKNER

3

Morrison Av
Sound View Av

6 Elder Av

2

BRONX RIVER PKWY

BRUCKNER EXPWY

A

Ped Bridge

1

Story Av

Lafayette Morrison Houses

Soundview Park Houses

Colgate Av

Lafayette Av

E 172
Manor Av
Ward Av
Boynton Av
Elder Av
Wheeler Av
Evergreen Av
Colgate Av
Close Av
Watson Av

Noble Av
Rosedale Av
Harrod Pl
Bronxdale

Houses
278
Story Av
Leland Av
Thieriot Av
Taylor Av

James Monroe Houses

Banyer Av
Cross Av

SOUND VIEW AV

Clason Point La N
 Freley Av
Clason Point Gardens Houses
Clason Point La S Cross Pl

P

Turnbull Av
Lafayette Av
Pugsley Av
Homer Av
Seward A
Jaimie
Towe

Stickball Blvd
Park

WHITE PLAINS

Bolton Av
Underhill Av

B

LAC

Ra
Ca

SOUNDVIEW

Sound View Houses

Patterson Av

Sound View Park

Bronx River

Seneca Av
Edgewater Rd
Gilbert Pl
Lafayette Av
Whittier St
Longfellow Av
Drake St
Halleck St

HUNTS POINT AV

C

Corpus Christi Monastery

Spofford Av
Coster St
Faile St
Bryant Av
Randall Av
Manida St
Barretto St
Casanova St
Tiffany St
Oak Point Av

HUNTS POINT

Hunt's Point Terminal Market

Drake Park
Drake Park S

East Bay Av
Viele Av

Ryawa Av

Food Center

D

Dr

Farragut St

Hunts Point

STA

Westchester

START DRIVE

Man-
hattan

Queens

Castle Hill
Houses
Castle Hill Houses

CASTLE
HILL

Zerega Av

Effingham Av

Tumeur Av

CASTLE HILL AV

Howe Av

Torry Av

Olmstead Av

Norton Av

Screvin Av

AV

Barrett

Hart St

A

Pugsley's
Creek Park

Pugsley's Creek

David Av

Betts Av

Husson Av

Pugsley Av

Stephens Av

Newman Av

Castle Hill
Park

**Clason's
Point**

Neptune Ct

Neptune Ct

Neptune La

Fleet Ct

Admiral La

Sunset Blvd

ell Av

Bronx River Av

*Ferry
Point
Park*

678

B

Bronx–Whitestone Bridge

River

*Francis
Lewis
Park*

5 Av

PAGE 306

2 MILES = 3.2 KMS

**CLASONS
POINT**

C

East

Bronx County
Queens County

D

**Powell's
Cove**

Powell's Cove Blvd

5 Av

6 Av

QUEENS

135 St

END 3 MINS

2 MILES = 3.2 KMS

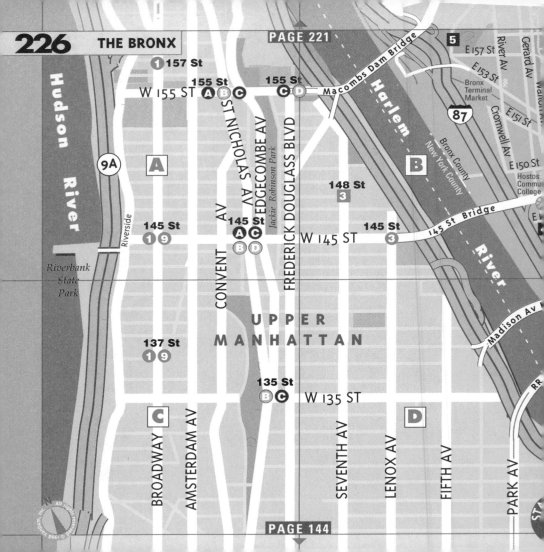

PAGE 221

Hudson River

Riverside

Riverbank State Park

9A

A

1 157 St

155 St **A** **B** **C**
W 155 ST

155 St **C** **D**
Macombs Dam Bridge

5 E 157 St

River Av

Gerard Av

E 153 St

Bronx Terminal Market

87

E 151 St

Cromwell Av

Walton

Harlem

Bronx County
New York County

E 150 St

Hostos Communi College

B

148 St **3**

ST NICHOLAS AV

EDGECOMBE AV

Jackie Robinson Park

FREDERICK DOUGLASS BLVD

145 St **1** **9**

145 St **A** **C**
B **D**

W 145 ST

145 St **3**

145 St **3**

145 St Bridge

E

River

Madison Av

CONVENT AV

U P P E R
M A N H A T T A N

137 St **1** **9**

135 St **B** **C**
W 135 ST

C

BROADWAY

AMSTERDAM AV

SEVENTH AV

LENOX AV

FIFTH AV

D

PARK AV

RR

ST

N

© 1998 VELCOM, INC. ALL RIGHTS RESERVED

PAGE 144

Westchester

Man-
hattan

Queens

START DRIVE

MELROSE

Concourse
Village Houses

Concourse
Village Houses

Andrew Jackson
Houses

E 156 St

E 156 St

155 St
154 St

E 153 St

Melrose
Houses

E 153 St

E 152 St

E 151 St

Park Av

Courtlandt Av

MELROSE AV

THIRD AV

Brook

Rae St

E 152 St

Cauldwell Av

St Ann's Av

Eagle Av

Westchester Av

E 155 St

Tinton Av

E 152 St

E 151 St

E 150 St

Wales Av

Jackson Av

Pontiac Pl

Concord Av

2 **5**
**Jackson
Av**

A

**149 St
Grand Concourse**

2 **5**

**3 Av
149 St**

R. Clemente
Plaza

E 148 St

E 147 St

Bergen

College Av

E 149 ST

E 147 St

Jackson Av

St Mary's
Park

B

Samuel
Gompers

St Ann's Av

Austin Pl

DOT
Towaway

**E 143 St
St Mary's
St**

Lincoln
Medical &
Mental Health
Center

E 146 St

E 145 St

E 144 St

E 143 St

E 142 St

E 141 St

WILLIS AV

Brook Av

E 144 St

E 142 St

St Mary's

Powers Av

Cypress Av

E 142 St

Crimmins Av

Beech Ter
Oak Ter
Tem

6

278

E 149 St

PAGE 228

2 MILES = 3.2 KMS

stos
reforming
ts Center

E 144 St

E 143 St

E 142 St

E 140 St

St W

Morris Av

THIRD AV

Lester
Patterson
Houses

138 St

140 St

E 141 St

MOTT

E 140 St

E 141 St

E /139 St

E /140 St

Bruckner Expwy

E 138 St

E 137 St

E 135 St

Walnut Av

Locust Av

5

6

**138 St
3 Av**

Canal Pl

Canal
Rider

GRAND

5

Alexander Av

Lincoln Av

HAVEN

E 138 ST **6**

John P.
Mitchell
Houses

2 E 136 St

E 135 St

Brown

Brook Av

E 138 ST

Brook Av

6

**Cypress
Av**

6

Mill Brook Houses

1

Beekman Av

P O R T

M O R R I S

E 136 St

E 135 St

E 134 St

E 133 St

E 132 St

Willow Av

3

3 Av Bridge

Willis Av Bridge

MAJOR

E 134 St

C

P

Av

BRUCKNER

E 132 St

DEEGAN

EXPWY

BLVD

St Ann's Pl

Cypress Pl

Harlem River

D

Intermodal Railroad Yard

END 3 MINS

Randall's
Island

278

PAGE 302

2 MILES = 3.2 KMS

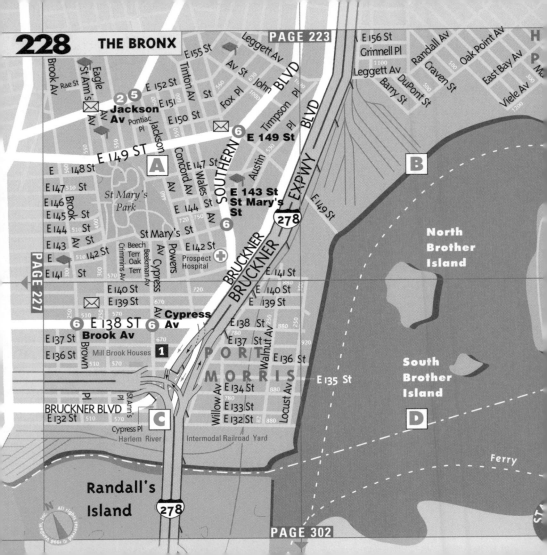

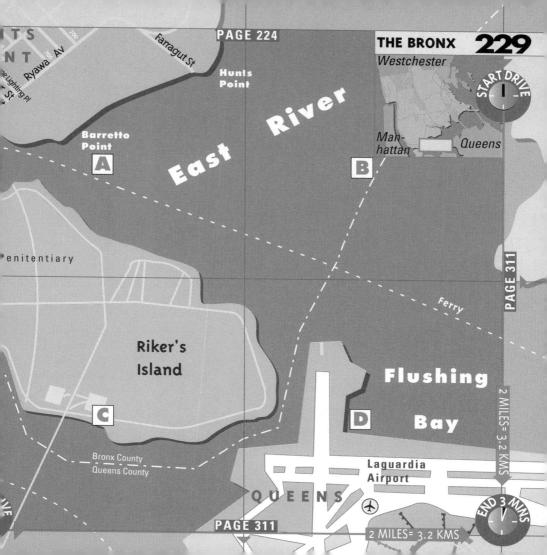

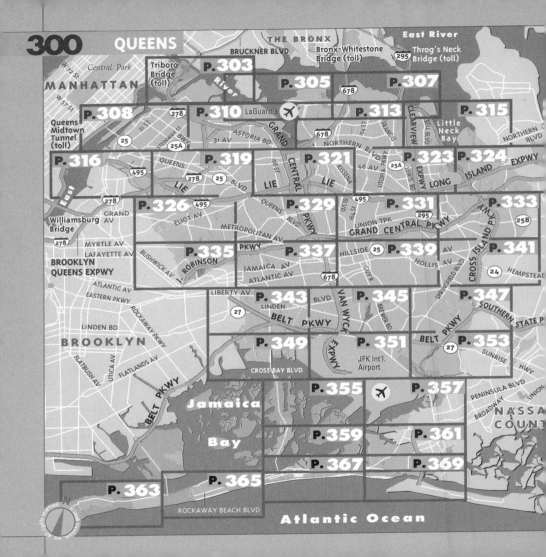

e Best of Queens

is conglomeration of towns, villages,
d utopian real estate developments
the most diverse community on earth.
er 175 languages are spoken in NYC's
gest borough. Among its 1.9 million
sidents are the largest populations
Greeks outside Athens, Dominicans
tside Santo Domingo, and Colombians
tside Bogotá. Its cultural attractions
e world renowned.

merican Museum of the loving Image

ffs of TV, film, digital imaging
chnology, and pop-art rejoice in
s splendid resource. Its "Behind
e Scenes" is a hands-on, interactive
aypen for would-be image makers.
must-see on the culture map of NYC.
-01 35 Av (36 St), Astoria,
8-784-0077. **309C**

ater's Edge

ectacular views of Manhattan
mplement the elegant setting and
lendid seafood. 44th Dr ⊅ East River,
8-482-0033. **308C**

amaica Bay Wildlife Refuge

rders-in-the-know treasure these vast
dal wetlands and uplands to see over
o different species of birds. The annual
ristmas count is a NYC ritual.
aily 8:30AM–5PM. Cross Bay Blvd ⊅
oadchannel. 718-318-4300. **358B**

Flushing Meadows–Corona Park

Created for the 1939 World's Fair,
this park is a celebration of city
impressario Bob Moses's vision
of the city beautiful. It is also
the center of culture in Queens.
Is it possible that Walt Disney was
inspired by the 1965 World's Fair
in creating a permanent one at
Walt Disney World? **320D**

Queens Museum of Art

In addition to its excellent art and
photography exhibits, the museum
showcases "The Panorama of NYC,"
the world's largest architectural
scale model. A revelation for anyone
fascinated by how the map becomes
the model. 718-592-5555. **320D**

NY Hall of Science

Over 150 interactive exhibits
covering light, color and quantum
physics make this **the** hands-on
science and technology center of NYC.
718-699-0005. **320B**

Shea Stadium

This arena is filled with history—
from bringing the National League
back to the city to winning the
World Series in '69. 126th St ⊅
Roosevelt Av. 718-507-8499.
320B

Queens Stats:
Population:
1.9 million

Area:
112.1 sq miles

THE US OPEN IS AN ANNUAL RITE

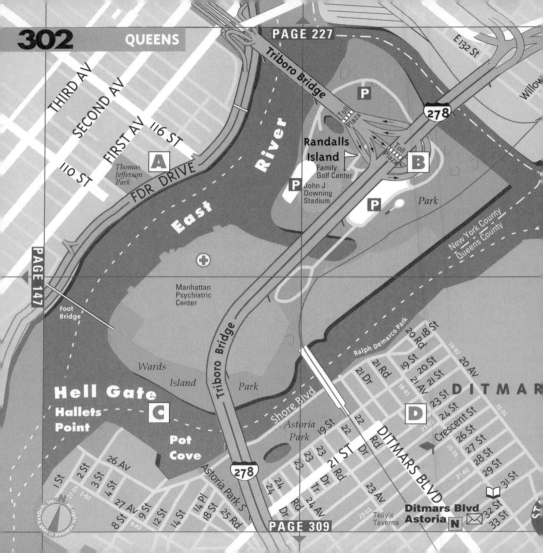

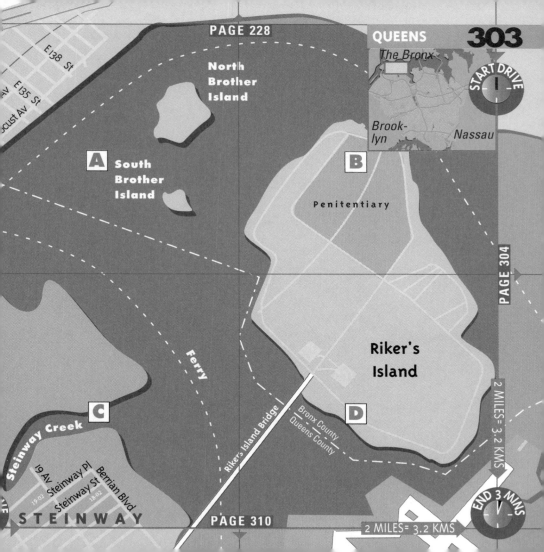

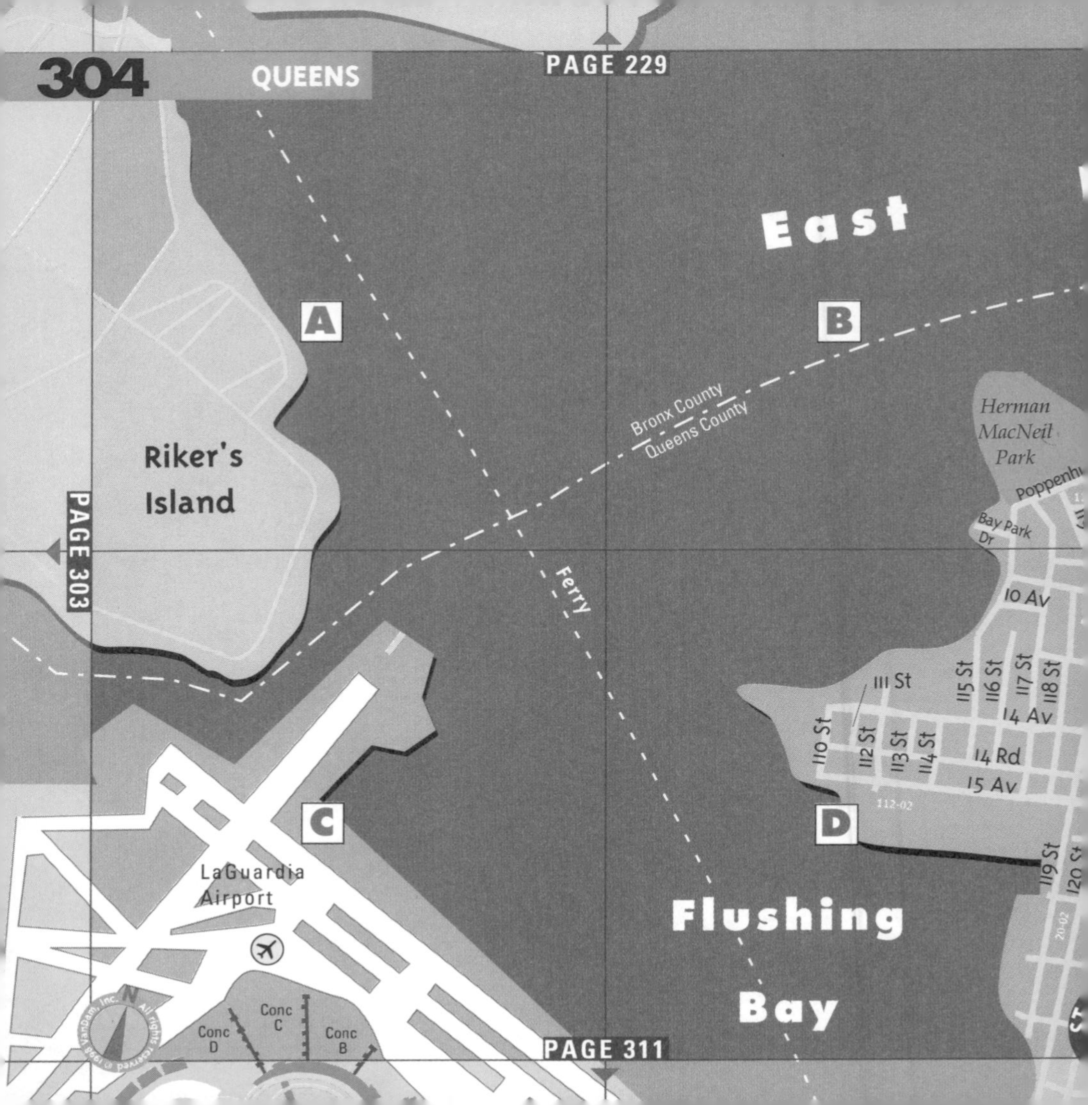

PAGE 229

PAGE 303

East

A

B

Bronx County
Queens County

Herman
MacNeil
Park

Poppenhu

Bay Park
Dr

Riker's
Island

Ferry

10 Av

111 St

115 St
116 St
117 St
118 St

14 Av

110 St

112 St

113 St
114 St

14 Rd

15 Av

112-02

C

D

119 St

120 St

2n92

LaGuardia
Airport

Flushing

Bay

N

Conc
D

Conc
C

Conc
B

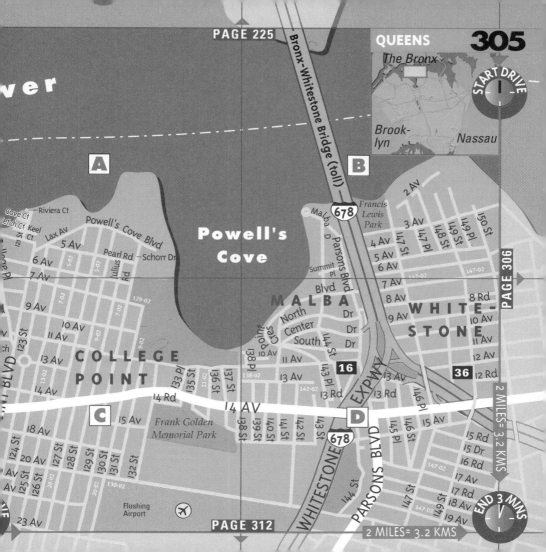

The Bronx

START DRIVE

Brook-lyn

Nassau

Bronx-Whitestone Bridge (toll)

A

B

Cove Ct — Riviera Ct

tch La Keel Ct

121 St

Lax Av

Powell's Cove Blvd

5 Av

Pearl Rd — Schorr Dr

Julius Rd

6 Av

5-02

7 Av

5-03

Francis Lewis Park

678

2 Av

3 Av

147 St

148 St

149 St

149 Pl

150 St

Malba Dr

4 Av

5 Av

6 Av

147-02

Parsons Blvd

Summit Pl

7 Av

8 Av

147-02

Powell's Cove

9 Av

7-02

10 Av

7-02

11 Av

9-02

Blvd

MALBA

North Center South

Dr

Dr

Dr

8 Rd

10 Av

11 Av

12 Av

WHITE-STONE

129-02

COLLEGE

POINT

123 St

13 Av

13-02

14 Av

Point Cres

10 Av

138 Pl

11 Av

13 Av

138-02

142-02

144 St

143 Pl

143 Rd

16

13 Av

13 Rd

36

12 Rd

146 St

C

15 Av

133 Pl

135 St

136 St

137 St

121-02

Frank Golden Memorial Park

14 Rd

138 St

139 St

140 St

141 St

142 St

14 AV

13 Rd

D

678

EXPWY

13 Av

13 Rd

15 Av

145 Pl

PARSONS BLVD

15 Av

15 Rd

15 Dr

16 Rd

17 Av

18 Av

124 St

20 Av

125 Av

126 St

127 St

128 St

129 St

130 St

131 St

132 St

20-02

130-02

18 Av

Flushing Airport

23 Av

144 St

WHITESTONE

17 Rd

147-02

145 Pl

146 St

147 St

17 Av

17 Rd

18 Av

19 Av

147-02

END 3 MINS

2 MILES = 3.2 KMS

PAGE 306

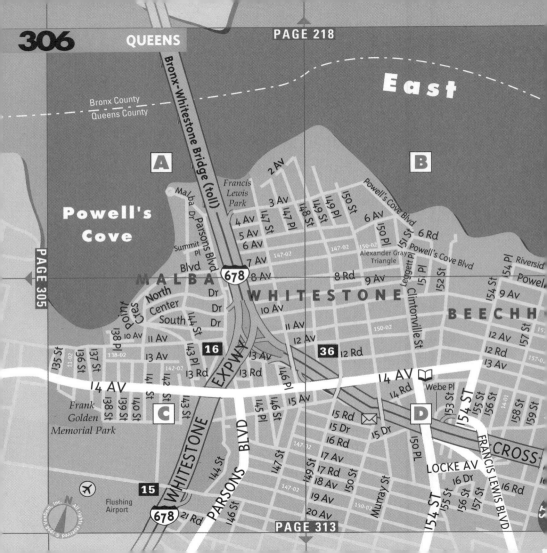

PAGE 218

A

B

Bronx-Whitestone Bridge (toll)

Bronx County
Queens County

East

Powell's Cove

PAGE 305

Francis Lewis Park

Malba Dr
Parsons Blvd
Summit Pl

2 AV
3 AV
4 AV
5 AV
6 AV
7 AV
8 AV

147 St
147 Pl
148 St
149 St
149 Pl
150 St
150 Pl

Powell's Cove Blvd

6 AV
6 Rd

147-02
147-02
150-02

Alexander Gray Triangle

Clintonville St
152 St

154 Pl
Riversid
Powel

M A L B A
678

Blvd
North Center South
Point Cres
Dr Dr Dr
144 St

8 Rd
9 AV

W H I T E S T O N E

9 AV
154 St

B E E C H H

150-02

138 Pl
10 AV
11 AV
13 AV

143 Pl

EXPWY

16

10 AV
11 AV
12 AV

13 AV
13 Rd

146 Pl

36

12 Rd

157 St

12 AV
12 Rd
13 AV

135 St
136 St
137 St

142-02

13 Rd
13 Rd

157-0

138-02

14 AV

140 St
139 St
138 St

143 St

WHITESTONE

144 St

147 St
149 St

147-12

14 AV

14 Rd

Webe Pl

D

15 Dr

153 St
155 St
151 St

140

C

145 St
146 Pl

15 AV

15 Rd
15 Dr
16 Rd

150 St

150 Pl

✉

FRANCIS
154 ST

CROSS

Frank Golden Memorial Park

PARSONS BLVD

17 AV
17 Rd
18 AV
19 AV
20 AV

150-02

Murray St

LOCKE AV

154 St
155 St
157 St
156 St

16 Dr
16 Rd

158 St
159 St

✈
Flushing Airport

15
678

146 St

21 Rd

147-02

©1994 Hagstrom Map Company, Inc. All rights reserved

N

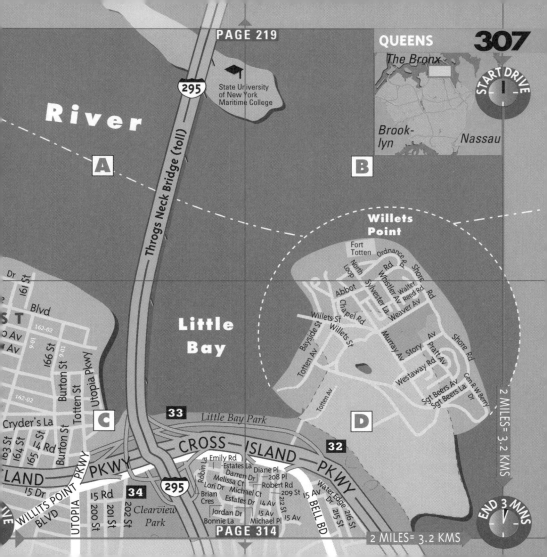

The Bronx

Brook-lyn

Nassau

START DRIVE

River

295

State University
of New York
Maritime College

A

B

Throgs Neck Bridge (toll)

Willets
Point

Fort
Totten

Ordnance Rd

Shore Rd

North
Loop

Rd

Whistler Av

Walter
Reed Rd

Abbot

Sylvester La

Weaver Av

Chapel Rd

Little
Bay

Willets St

Willets St

Bayside St

Murray Av

Story Av

Pratt Av

Shore Rd

Westaway Rd

Totten Av

Gen R W Berry

Sgt Beers Av

Totten Av

Sgt Beers La Dr

C

D

Dr

161 St

Blvd

162-02

9-01

166 St

Burton St

9-01

Utopia Pkwy

162-02

Cryder's La

163 St

164 St

165

14 Rd

Burton St

Totten St

33

Little Bay Park

32

2 MILES = 3.2 KMS

CROSS—ISLAND

PKWY

WILLITS POINT

PKWY

PKWY

295

Emily Rd

Robin La

Estates La

Darren Dr

Diane Pl

Melissa Ct

208 Pl

Lori Dr

Michael Ct

Robert Rd

Brian
Cres

Esfates Dr

209 St

212 St

Water Ridge Dr

15 AV

216 St

215 St

BELL BD

LAND

15 Dr

34

15 Rd

200 St

201 St

202 St

Clearview
Park

Jordan Dr

Bonnie La

14 Av

15 Av

15 Av

Michael Pl

15 Av

END 3 MINS

2 MILES= 3.2 KMS

E 75 St

E 65 St

FDR DRIVE

THIRD AV

SECOND AV

FIRST AV

E 72 ST

NY Hospital Cornell Medical Center

Rockefeller University Hospital

A

Coler Memorial Hospital

New York County
Queens County

Hallet Cove

Socr
Scul
Park

Isamu Noguchi Garden Museum

West channel

River Rd

B

Rainey Park

33 Rd

13 St

E 60 St

YORK AV

60 St Heliport

Main St

Correction Hospital

Roosevelt Is. Bridge

9 St

10 St

11 St

12 St

P

Ravenswood

P

E 57 ST

E 59 St

Roosevelt Island

S

Roosevelt Island Tramway

East Channel

Queensboro Bridge

West Rd

East Rd

Goldwater Memorial Hospital

City Hospital

C

Queens Bridge Park

VERNON BLVD

35 AV

36 AV

Houses

37 Av

21 ST

38 Av

39 Av

36 Av

Queensbridge

40 Av

13 St

41 Av

41 Rd

8 01

21 St (Queensbridge)

22 St

23 St

24 St

27 St

LON
CITY

Houses

9 St

10 St

11 St

43 Av

S

D

Crescent St

30 St

N 39

Fila Sports Club

Water's Edge

Roosevelt Island

43 Rd

44 Av

44 Rd

44 Dr

45 Av

45 Rd

46 Av

46 Rd

47 Av

Queens Plaza

25

41 Rd

42 Rd

Club Broadway

28 Av

29 Rd

40 St

N

E **F**

Queensboro Plaza

7

N

E **F**

Queens

G **R** **Plaza**

E **F**

23 St (Ely Av)

Hunter St

PAGE 131

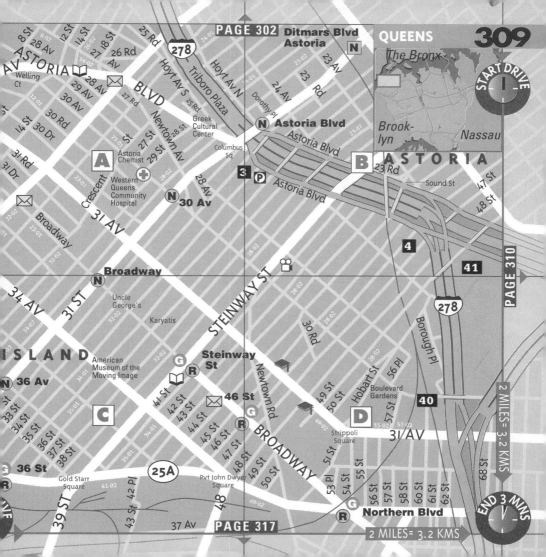

QUEENS

Ditmars Blvd
Astoria

The Bronx

N

START DRIVE
1

Brook-
lyn

Nassau

ASTORIA

8 St
28 St
12 St
14 St
18 St

25 Rd

26 Rd

Hoyt Av N
Hoyt Av S

24 Av

23 Av

23 Rd

24 Av

ASTORIA AV

Welling
Ct

28 Av

27
Av

Triboro Plaza

Dorothy Pl

28 Av

29 Av

30 Av

Newtown Av

Greek
Cultural
Center

N Astoria Blvd

Astoria Blvd

30 Av

30 Rd

27 Rd

B

23 Rd

ASTORIA

Sound St

47 St

30 Dr

14 St

Columbus
Sq

3

P

Astoria Blvd

48 St

31 Rd

A

Astoria
Chemist

29 St

28 St

31 Dr

Western
Queens
Community
Hospital

28 Av

N 30 Av

Crescent

Broadway

31 AV

4

41

Broadway

N

31 ST

Uncle
George's

STEINWAY ST

278

PAGE 310

34 AV

Karyatis

30 Rd

2 MILES = 3.2 KMS

ISLAND

American
Museum of the
Moving Image

G

Steinway
St

R

Newtown Rd

56 Pl

56 St

Borough Pl

40

N 36 Av

33 St
34 St
35 St
36 St
37 St
38 St

C

41 St
42 St
43 St

44 St
45 St
46 St

46 St

G
R

49 St
50 St

Hobart St
57 St

Boulevard
Gardens

D

31 AV

57 St

68 St

G 36 St

25A

55-01

BROADWAY

Strippoli
Square

G
R

Gold Starr
Square

41-02

42 Pl

43 St

48

Pvt John Dwyer
Square

48 St
49 St
50 St

51 Pl

53 Pl
54 St

55 St

56 St
57 St
58 St
60 St
61 St
62 St

39 ST

37 Av

PAGE 317

G
R Northern Blvd

END 3 MINS

2 MILES = 3.2 KMS

PAGE 303

N

STEINWAY

Ditmars Blvd
Astoria

35 St
36 St
37 St
38 St

Steinway St

23 AV

23-02

DITMARS

STEINWAY ST

20 Rd

41 St
42 St
43 St
45 St
46 St
47 St
48 St
49 St

Hazen St

20 Av

21 Av

Berrian Blvd
42-01

19 AV

19-02

Rikers Island Bridge

Bowery Bay

A

ASTORIA

23 Rd

Sound St

19 Rd

19 Dr

19-02

B

General Aviation Terminal

P Delta Shuttle/
#6 Marine Air Terminal

43 St
44 St
45 St
46 St
47 St
48 St
49 St
50 St

28-02

N Astoria Blvd

S Astoria Blvd

20-02

20-02

BLVD

20-02

P
#7
Marine Terminal Rd

P
#7

DITMARS

GRAND C

BLVD

6

4

41

St. Michael's Cemetery

Borough Pl

278

Queens Chamber

83-02

College of Aeronautics

ASTORIA BLVD

5

90 Pl

90-02

24 Rd

30-02

Capt Christoph
O'Sullivan Pla

⊠

39

Bulova

Boody St

20-02

75-02

30-02

82 ST

30 Av

D

EAS

56 Pl

Hobart St

57 St

Boulevard Gardens

55-02

57-02

40

C

30-02

71-02

31 AV

⊠

E L M

Strippoli Square

54 St
55 St
56 St
57 St
58 St
60 St
61 St
62 St

68 St
69 St
70 St
71 St
72 St
73 St
74 St
75 St
76 St
77 St
78 St
79 St
80 St
81 St

32 Av

83 St
84 St
85 St
86 St
87 St
88 St
89 St
90 St
91 St
92 St

ST

38

25A

PAGE 319

NORTHERN BLVD

PAGE 309

© 1994 Hagstrom Map, Inc.
All rights Reserved

F l u s h i n g

B a y

The Bronx

Brooklyn

Nassau

La Guardia Airport

✈

Conc C
Conc D
Conc B
Conc A

A

B

✉

P #1

P #2

P #3

P #4

P #5

P #6

US Air Shuttle Terminal

Delta Terminal

121 St

25 Rd

Graham Ct

123 St

27 Av

28 Av

29 Av

30 Av

31 Av

31 Rd

122 St

123 St

124 St

125 St

COLLEGE PT BLVD

PAGE 312

CENTRAL PKWY
I-94

22 Dr

7

LaGuardia Marriott

23 Rd

Crown Plaza LaGuardia

23 Av

24 AV

25 Av

103 St

Jackson Mill Rd

23-02
23-07
24-02

98-02

Ericson St
Gillmore St
Humphreys St
McIntosh St

25 Av

27 Av

29 Av

31 Av

Butler St
Curtis St
Buell St
Couch Pl

C

Keamey St

Liev Barclay Square

96 St
97 St
98 St
99 St
100 St
101 St
102 St
103 St
104 St
105 St
106 St
107 St
108 St
109 St
110 St
111 St

ELMHURST

Jackson Mill Rd

DITMARS BLVD

101 ST

D

World's Fair Marina

3

2

1

126 Pl

13

8

PAGE 320

2 MILES = 3.2 KMS

2 MILES = 3.2 KMS

END 3 MINS

QUEENS ✉

PAGE 305

14 Av
15 AV
14 AV
14 Rd
13

136
137

142-02
13

14 AV

138 St
139 St
140 St
141 St
142 St
143 St

15 AV
18 Av

15 Av

Frank Golden Memorial Park

119 St
120 St
121 St

COLLEGE POINT BLVD

123 St
124 St

20 Av
20-07

127 St
128 St

21 Av
22 Av
23 Av

125 St
126 St

129 St
130 St
131 St
132 St

130-02

A

B

15

67

21 Av
22 Av
22 Rd

143 St
144 St
145 St

WHITESTONE EXPWY

✈ *Flushing Airport*

25 Av
25 Rd

Graham Ct

25 Av
25 Rd

127-07

Flushing Bay

27 Av

26 Av

124-02

28 Av

NY Times Plant

141 St

UNION ST

29 Av

30 Av

Ulmer St

Higgins St

28 Rd

Mitchell Gardens

139-02

137 St
138 St
139 St

📖

144 St
145 Pl
145 St

31 Av

123 St
124 St

125-02

College Point Industrial Park

DOT Towaway ⓟ

14

133 St

Traffic Violations DMV

140 St

✉

143

145 St
145 Pl
145 St
146 St

31 Rd
125 St

31 Rd

31 Dr

BA

LINDEN HILL

C

D

32 Av

33 Av

143

Stratton St

31 Rd

33 Av
34 Av
34 Rd

33 Av
34 Av

127-02

145 St
145 Pl
146 St

World's Fair Marina

Harper St

Higgins St

Downing St

Miller

Farrington St

Leavitt St

33 Av
34 Av

Linneaus Pl

Latimer Pl

13

Collins Pl

Prince St

MAIN ST

35 Av

➕ *Flushing Hospital Medical Center (N Div)*

William Prince Bridge

678

King Rd

36 Av

Carlton Pl

Flushing Town Hall

NORTHERN BLVD

Congressman Rosenthal Av

ST

PAGE 311

PAGE 321

The Bronx

START DRIVE

Brook-lyn

Nassau

13 Rd

146 Pl

145 Pl

15 Av

145 Pl

36

14 AV

CROSS

14 Rd

CLINTONVILLE

Webe Pl

153 St

154 St

157-02

12 Rd

160 St

13 Rd

14 Av

155 St

156 St

157 St

158 St

159 St

Cryder's La

161 St

162 St

163 St

15 Rd

15 Dr

15 Dr

16 Rd

17 Av

17 Rd

150 PL

ISLAND

LOCKE AV

16 Dr

16 Rd

16 Av

PKW

16-01

16 Av

18 Av

19 Av

147-02

A

20 Av

20 Rd

150-02

Ryan Ct

147 St

149 St

147-02

21 Av

22 Av

23 Av

24 Av

150 St

Murray St

150-03

155 St

155 St

157 St

16 Dr

18 Av

Clintonville St

154 ST

Larry Muss
Memorial
Square

B

WILLETS POINT BLVD

Clearview
Gardens

166-02

163-02

166-02

163-02

17 Av

19 Av

200 St

201 St

202 St

Clearview Park

170-01

WILLETS POINT BLVD

148 St

Memorial Field
of Flushing

150-02

Murray La

24 Rd

25 Av

25 Dr

26 Av

27 Av

28 Av

29 Av

157 St

157-0?

157-02

160 St

22-07

163 St

161-02

FRANCIS

163-07

166 St

166-02

169-02

UTOPIA PKWY

171-0?

21 Av

22 Av

23 Av

24 Av

24 Rd

169 St

26 Av

27 Av

203 St

E AV

P. R. Bayer
Square

C

Bowne
Park

29 AV

BAYSIDE LA

D

29 Av

169-02

LEWIS

28 Av

29 Av

28-02

150 St

Murray La

Murray St

152 St

153 St

155 St

156 St

158 St

159 St

29-01

161 St

162 St

164 St

165 St

33 Av

32 Av

168 St

33-01

30 Av

32
Rd

32 Av

Jordan St

200 Av

Henry T
Triangle

33 Rd

M U R R A Y

H I L L

148 St

149 St

149 Pl

35 Av

167 St

170 St

171 St

172 St

BLVD

END 3 MINS

DE AV

38 AV

25A

2 MILES = 3.2 KMS

2 MILES = 3.2 KMS

QUEENS

PAGE 307

Little Bay

155 St
156 St
157 St
158 St
159 St
12 Rd
14 Av
162-02
13 Av
TotTen St
Utopia Pkwy
Totten Av

33

32

160 St
161 St
162 St
163 St
164 St
165 St
166 St
14 Av
Cryder's La
Burton
14 Rd

15 Dr

Emily Rd
Robin
Estates La
Darren Dr
Diane Pl
208 Pl
Melissa Ct
Lori Dr Michael Ct
Robert Rd
Brian Cres
Esfates Dr
14 Av

Water Edge
216 St
215 St
Dr

157 St
16 Rd
16 Av
166-01
16 Rd
17 Av
17 Rd
18 Av
19 Av
20 Av

A

15 Rd
200 St
201 St
202 St
15 Rd

34

Clearview Park

I-295

B

Jordan Dr
Bonnie La
15 Rd
Michael Pl
Jordan Ct
15 Av

208 St
16 Av
15 Dr
209 St
212 St
BELL BLVD

17 Av
18 Av
23 Av
23 Rd
215-02

Larry Muss Memorial Square
Clearview Gardens
166-02
163-02
20 Rd
21 Av
166-02
17 Av
19 Av

**B A Y
T E R R A C E**

PAGE 313
Clintonville St
FRANCIS
163-02
23 Av
24 Av
24 Rd
25 Av
25 Dr
160 St
163 St
166 St
169 St
22 Av
166-02
21 Av
169-02
22 Av
23 Av
24 Av
24 Rd
169-02

Clearview Golf Course

207 Rd
203 St
204 St
205 St
206 St
23 Av
Corp Kennedy St
211 St
23
Av

Bay Terrace Shopping Center

24 A
215-
27
26

6B

26 Av
27 Av
162 St
164 St
165 St
168 St
LEWIS
BAYSIDE LA
166 St
170 St
171 St
172 St
169-02
26 Av
27 Av
28 Av
28 Av

C

27 Av
27 Av
203
28-02
26 Av
28 Av

27 Av
28 Rd
210 St
211 St
212 St
213 St
210 Pl
29 Av
209 Pl

D

St
Ho
Ch
214 St
32

CLEARVIEW EXPWY

29 Av
29 Av
30 Av
Henry T Triangle
32 Av (Vista Av)
32 Rd
Jordan St
200 St
201 St
202 St
203 St
30 Av
28
Rd
205-02
32-02
33 Av
204 St
205 St
209 St
208 St
33 Av
33 Rd
34 Av
34 Rd
213 St
24 St
33 Av
33 Rd
34 Av
34 Rd

PAGE 323

6A

STA

The Bronx

Brook-lyn

Nassau

START DRIVE

A

B

BAYVIEW AV

Little

Neck

Bay

Nassau County
Queens County

G R E A T

N E C K

E S T A T E S

ISLAND

Neck Blvd

PKWY

216 St

31 Rd

218 St

C

John
Golden
Park

Crocheron
Park

Bayview Av

Kenmore Rd

Knollwood Av

Richmond Rd

Shore Rd

Warwick Av

Grosvenor St

East Dr

Beverly Rd

Westmoreland Pl

Marinette St

Udall's Cove
Park

D O U G L A S

D M A N O R

Little Neck Pkwy

34 Av 255 St

37 Av

Brookside St

Douglas Rd

38 Av 38 AV

Av

254 39 AV

St 39 Rd

4 Av

**Little
Neck**

2 MILES = 3.2 KMS

END 3 MINS

Hollywood Av

Manor Rd

West Dr

Center Dr

Arleigh Rd

Park La

Ridge
Forest Rd

Ardsley Rd

Oak La

Bayshore Rd

36 Av

Melrose La

Bay Dr

Cedar La

237-02

PAGE 324

38 Rd

2 MILES = 3.2 KMS

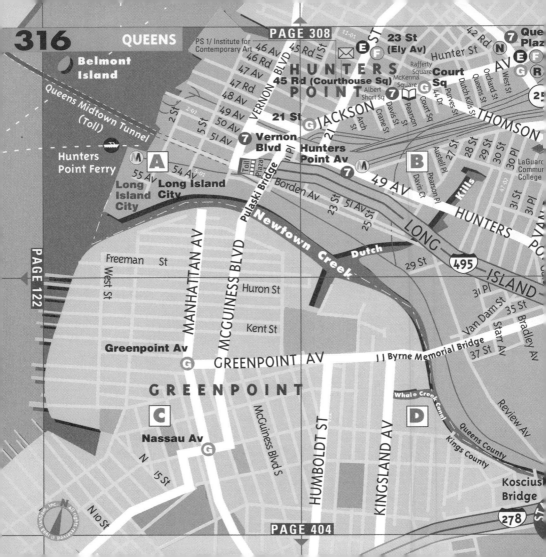

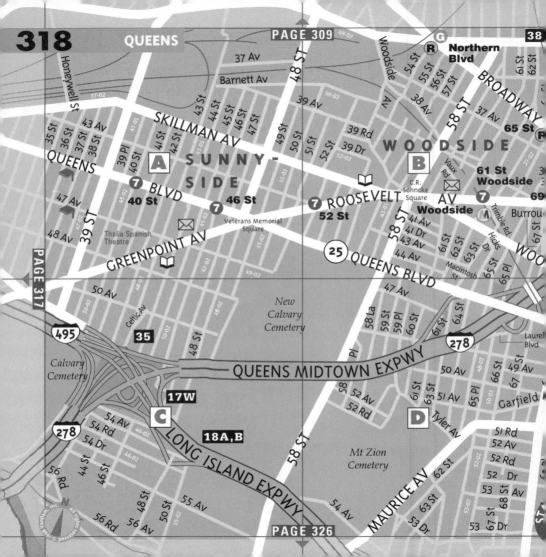

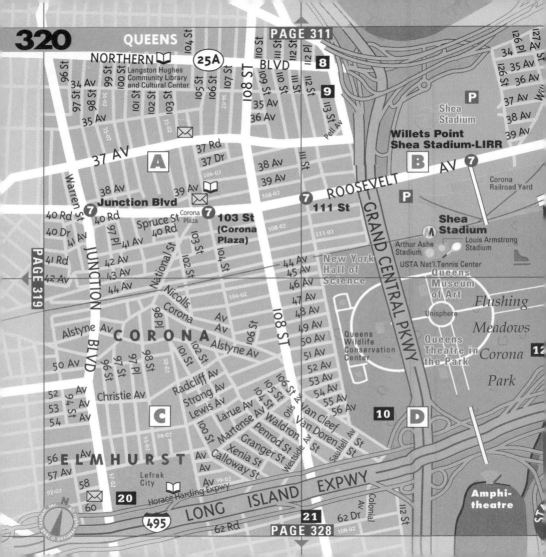

QUEENS

NORTHERN

Langston Hughes
Community Library
and Cultural Center

25A

BLVD

8

96 St
97 St
98 St
99 St
100 St
34 Av
35 Av
101 St
102 St
103 St

104 St
105 St
106 St
107 St

108 ST

109 St
110 St
111 St
112 St
112 Pl

110 St
111 St

35 Av
36 Av

9

113 St
Pell Av

37 AV

37 Rd
37 Dr

A

38 Av
39 Av

104-02

B

Shea
Stadium

P

126 St
127 St
34 Av
126 Av
35 Av
36 Av
37 Av
38 Av
39 Av

Willets Point
Shea Stadium-LIRR

38 Av
Junction Blvd

39 Av

Corona
Plaza

7

7

103 St
(Corona
Plaza)

Warren St

40 Rd
40 Dr

40 Rd

7

Spruce St
40 Rd

97 Pl
41 Av

38 Av
39 Av

108-02

7 ROOSEVELT AV

111 St

P

Shea
Stadium

M

7

Corona
Railroad Yard

41 Rd
42 Av

41 St
42 Av
43 Av
44 Av

JUNCTION BLVD

National St

98 St
97 Pl
101 St
102 St
103 St

104 St

108-02

104-02

108 ST

111-02

44 Av
45 Av
46 Av

New York
Hall of
Science

Arthur Ashe
Stadium

Louis Armstrong
Stadium

USTA Nat'l.Tennis Center

Queens
Museum
of Art

PAGE 319

Nicolls
Corona

98 St

C O R O N A

Alstyne Av

47 Av
48 Av
49 Av

GRAND CENTRAL PKWY

Unisphere

Flushing

Meadows

Alstyne Av

50 Av

52 Av
53 Av
54 St

94 St
96 St
97 St
97 Pl
98 St

101 St
102 St

Radcliff Av
Strong Av
Lewis Av

Christie Av

C

100 St

106 St

Alstyne Av

50 Av
51 Av
52 Av
53 Av
54 Av
55 Av
56 Av

Queens
Wildlife
Conservation
Center

Queens
Theatre in
the Park

Corona

Park

12

98-02

104-02
105 St
104 St

Larue Av
Marlense Av
Waldron St
Penrod St
Granger St
Xenia St
Calloway St

Otis Av
Van Cleef Av
Van Doren St
Sautell Av

Westside Av

10

D

56 Av
57 Av

E L M H U R S T Av

58

60

92-02

57-02

N

20

Lefrak
City

Horace Harding Expwy

99-02

Av
Av
Av

62 Dr
62 Rd

LONG ISLAND EXPWY

112 St
Av
Colonial

Amphi-
theatre

495

21

PAGE 311

PAGE 328

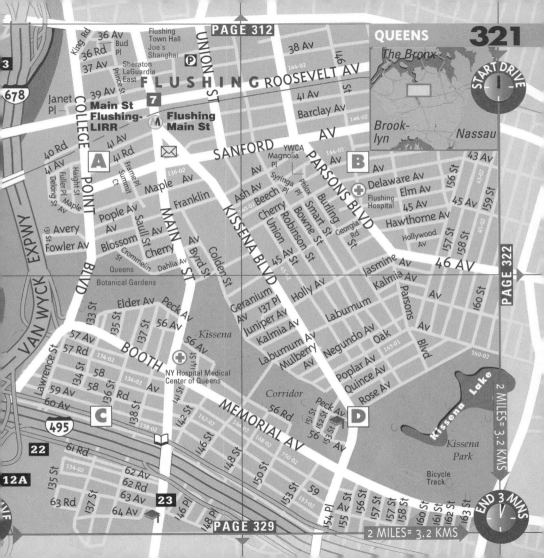

QUEENS

PAGE 315

Regatta Pl

233 Pl

38 Dr

West Dr

38 Dr

39 Av

Hillcrest Av

38 Dr

Cherry St

40 Av

41 Av

41 Rd

233 St

234 St

39 Rd

40 Av

41 Av

Willow Dr

Willow Av

Depew Av

Depew Av

235 St

242 St

42 Av

243 St

43 Av

248 St

249 St

250 St

LITTLE N

38 Av

37 Av

39 Av

222 St

223 St

223 Rd

38 St

217 St

218 St

219 St

220 St

215 St

215 Pl

214 Pl

216 St

40 Av

41 Av

41 Av

41 Rd

42 Av

Douglaston

Ⓜ

DOUGLASTON

247 St

42 Av

43 Av

214 Pl

215 St

43 Av

43 Av

44 Av

Douglaston Pkwy

Cary Pl

247 St

LITTLE

NECK

Alameda Av

245 St

244 St

Camb

Van 7

A

31

25A

Golden Bear ▽

B

233 St

233 St

233 St

234 St

241 St

Rushmore

Carolina Rd

Barrows Ct

51 Av

52 A

51

Redfield St

52 St

240 Pl

240 St

241 St

Pkwy

Thornhill

51

54

NORTHERN BLVD

📖 Ⓟ

215 St

215 Pl

216 St

217 St

218 St

219 St

220 St

220 Pl

46 Av

46-02

Maryland Rd

Hanford St

Oakland Lake

47 Av

47 Rd

217-02

48 AV

Birmington Pkwy

Garland Dr

Enfield Pl

Horatio

Kenilworth Dr

232 St

231 St

50 Pkwy

49 Rd

Hoxie Dr

East Hampton Blvd

CROSS ISLAND PKWY

Alley Pond Park

Alley Creek

Alley Pond Environmental Center

30N

◀ PAGE 323

Dermody Square

49 Av

50 Av

51 Av

Queensborough Community College

53 Av

54 Av

56 AV

228 St

229 St

230 St

53 Av

56 Rd

56 St

231 St

56 Rd

231 St

31

30N

53 Av

BELL BLVD

SPRINGFIELD

Cloverdale Blvd

56 Rd

57 Av

57 Rd

230-02

57 Av

58 Av

58 Rd

58 St

244 St

244-02

C

213 St

214 St

215 St

217 St

218 St

219 St

220 St

56-02

58-02

223 St

224 St

225 St

226 St

57 Av

59 AV

29

Horace Harding Expwy

Cloverdale Blvd

58 Rd

D

Horac

EXPWY

DOUGLASTON PKWY

30

65 Av

66 Av

67 Av

68 Av

69 Av

70 Av

242 St

242 St

212 St

495

LONG ISLAND

30S

W ALLEY RD

228 St

229 St

230 St

231 St

232 St

233 St

BLVD

219-07

✉

64 Av

65 Av

224 St

Cloverdale Blvd

64-02

67 Av

Decadon Pond

N

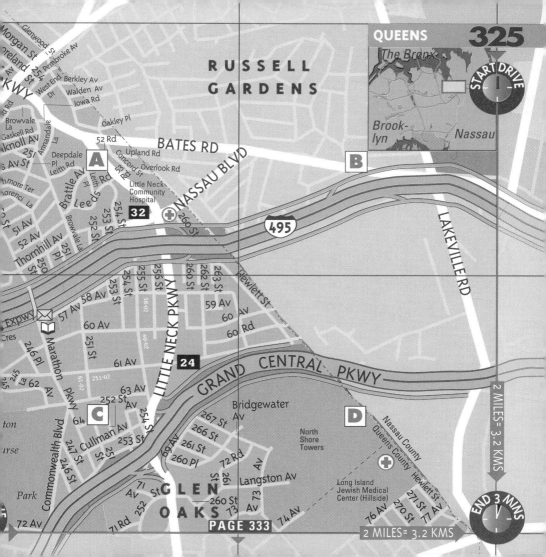

The Bronx

Brook-lyn

Nassau

START DRIVE

R U S S E L L
G A R D E N S

Glenwood St

Morgan St

reland St

PKWY

West End
Dr
Berkley Av
Walden Av
Iowa Rd
Pembroke Av

Browvale
La
Gaskell Rd
Knoll Av

25

S Av St

Oakley Pl

52 Rd

BATES RD

NASSAU BLVD

Deepdale
Pl
Leith Rd

A

Upland Rd

Overlook Rd

Brattle Av

Leeds Rd

Leith Rd

Concord St

53 St

Little Neck
Community
Hospital

32

260 St

more Ter

orenci La

51 Av

52 Av

Thornhill Av

250
St

251
Pl

Browvale La

252 St

253 St

254 St

255 St

256 St

260 St

262 St

263 St

Hewlett St

B

495

LAKEVILLE RD

Expwy

Cres

57 Av

58 Av

60 Av

251 St

251
Pl

253 St

254 St

38-02

59 Av

60 Av

60 Rd

24

LITTLE NECK PKWY

61 Av

63 Av

64
Av

Marathon

246 Pl

245
St

62
Av

pkwy

251-02

60-02

252 St

254 St

C

Cullman Av

253 St

25
St

Bridgewater
Av

267 St

266 St

261 St

260 Pl

GRAND CENTRAL PKWY

North
Shore
Towers

D

Nassau County

Queens County

Hewlett St

Commonwealth Blvd

247 St

246 St

ton

urse

Park

72 Av

71
Av

71 Rd

252

71
Av

260 St

73
Av

259 Av

261 St

261
St

72 Rd

Langston Av

73
Av

74 Av

GLEN
OAKS

Long Island
Jewish Medical
Center (Hillside)

76 Av

270 St

271 St

77
St

2 MILES= 3.2 KMS

END 3 MINS

PAGE 333

2 MILES= 3.2 KMS

PAGE 318

PAGE 405

Maspeth Creek

Galasso Pl

MASPETH

55 Av
55 Rd
55 Dr
54 Av

Melvina Pl

MAURICE AV

Maurice Park

Clinton Av
Claran Ct
Jay Av
Hull Av
Hamilton Pl

56 Av
56 Rd
56 Dr

Perry Av
Ramsen Pl

GRAND

58 Av
Brown Pl

57 Rd
58 Av
57 Dr
58 Rd

MASPETH AV

58 Dr
59 Av

58 Dr
58 St
57 St
59 Av

64 St
63 St
62 St
65 St

58 Rd
59 Av

Mt Olivet Cemetery

GRAND AV

FLUSHING AV

54 St
55 St
57 St
56 St

59 Rd
59 Dr
59 St

60 Av
60 Rd
60 Dr
60 Ct

60 La
60
61 St

Mt Olivet

65 St

ELIOT AV

Nurge Av
Arnold Av
53 St
54 St
54 Pl
55

Andrews Av
56 St
62 Av

62 Av
63 St
65 St
64 St
Cres

METROPOLITAN AV

62
62 Rd

Ahawith Cemetery

Rene Ct
Amory Ct

Tonsor St

Linden Hill Cemetery
Grover Cleveland Park

Ricard St

Butler Av

Bleecker St

60 Pl
60 St

FRESH POND RD

Admiral Av
65 La
65 Pl

Onderdonk Av
Queens County
Kings County
Charlotte

Troutman St
Starr St
Willoughby Av
Suydam Av
Hart St
Dekalb Av
Woodward
Cemetery

Stockholm St
Stanhope St

Himrod St
Harman St
Greene St
Grandview
Bleecker St
Menahan St

Forest Av

Grove St
Linden St
Gates Av

Traffic Av

64 St
Fremont St

RIDGEWOOD

St John's Rd

AV
Fairview

Palmetto St
Woodbine St
Madison

St. Nicholas Av
Cypress Av
Seneca Av

57 Av
56 Rd
56 Av
48 St
50 St
55

55 Av
58 St

55 Rd
55 Dr

54 Av

53 St
63 St
53 Dr
53 Av

55
56 Ter
56 St

59 Pl
59 St

56 Av
56
56 Rd
56 Dr

58 St
57 St
Rust
57 Pl
57 St

58 Pl
58 Av
58 Rd

49 Pl
47 St
48 St
58 Rd
Page Pl

A

B

C

D

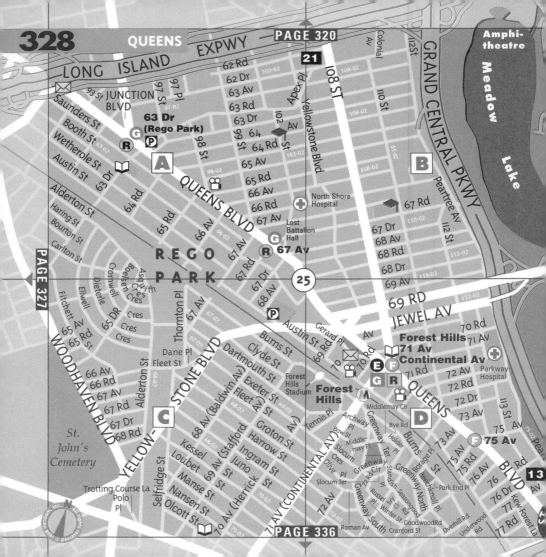

328

LONG ISLAND EXPWY

QUEENS EXPWY

PAGE 320

21

Amphi-theatre

Meadow Lake

Colonial Av

112 St

GRAND CENTRAL PKWY

93 St JUNCTION BLVD
97 Pl
97 St
97-02

62 Rd
62 Dr
63 Av
63 Rd
63 Dr

Apex Pl

Yellowstone Blvd

108 ST

110 St

108-02

Saunders St
Booth St
Wetherole St
Austin St

63 Dr
(Rego Park)

G
R
P

A

98 St
96 St
99 St
64

64 Rd

102 Av
102 St

A

65-02

B

108-02

108-02

Peartree Av
112 St

63 Dr

64 Rd
65 St

66 Av
66-02

65 Av
65 Rd
66 Av
66 Rd
67 Av

67 Rd

North Shore Hospital

67 Dr

Alderton St

Haring St
Bourton St
Carlton St

64 Rd

65 St

QUEENS BLVD

Lost Battalion Hall

G
R 67 Av

67 Dr
68 Av
68 Rd

68 Dr

110-02

112 St

112-02

R E G O

P A R K

Asquith Cres
Boelsen Cres
65 Cres

Cromwell

67 Rd

67 St

67 Dr

25

69 Av

69 RD

110-02

112-02

PAGE 327

Dieterle
Ellwell
Fitchett

65 DR
65 St

Cres
Cres
Cres

Thornton Pl

67 Av
67-02

68 Av

P

Austin St Rd

Gerard Pl

Av

70 Rd

JEWEL AV

70 Rd

71 Av

65 Av
65 Rd

66 Av
66 Rd
67 Av
67 Rd
67 Dr
68 Rd

Dane Pl
Fleet St

Alderton St
68-02

Burns St

Clyde St
Dartmouth St

Exeter St
Fleet St

68 Av (Baldwin)

Forest Hills Stadium

Av

69 St Rd

70 St

Forest Hills
71 Av
Continental Av

E F
G R

Forest Hills

71 Rd

72 Av
72 Rd
72 Dr
73 Av

Parkway Hospital

113 St

WOODHAVEN BLVD

YELLOW-STONE BLVD

C

St. John's Cemetery

Selfridge St

Kessel St
Loubet St
Manse St
Nansen St
Olcott St

68 Av (Stafford)
68-02

69 St

Groton St
Harrow St
Ingram St
Juno St

70 Av (Herrick)
70-02

Tennis Pl

70 AV (CONTINENTAL AV)

M

Archway Pl
Bow Pl
Slocum Cres
Olive Pl

Slocum Ter

72 Av
72-02

Middlemay Cir

Greenway Ter
Greenway North
Greenway Cir

Greenway South

Bye Rd
Holder Pl

Middle-may Pl

D

Standish Rd
72 Rd
Russel Pl
Winter St
Goodwood Rd
Cranford St

Burns

Borage Pl
Seasongood Rd

73 Av

Beechknoll Pl
Park End Pl

Roman Av

75 Av
75 Rd
76 Av
76

F 75 Av

75 Rd

76 Dr
Kew Forest Rd

76

Overhill Rd
Underwood Rd

77 Rd

75-02

BLVD

13

Trotting Course La
Polo Pl

PAGE 336

QUEENS

The Bronx

START DRIVE

Brook-lyn

Nassau

63 Rd
137 St
63 Av
64 Av

23

146 Pl

64 Rd

148 Pl
149 Pl

MAIN ST

Reeves Av

153-02

155 St
156 St
154 Pl

495

Mount Hebron

Cemetery

Queens College CUNY

CUNY Law

Golden Center for the Performing Arts

64 Av

65 Av

Gravett Rd

Louis Armstrong Archives

A

Melbourne Av

68 Av

68 Rd

160 St

Electchester

162 St

165 St
166 St

B

Pomonok Housing

162 Houses

161 St

164 St

141 St

68 Dr

136 St

138 St

139 St

140 St

69 Av

69 Rd

KISSENA BLVD

Parsons Blvd

69 Av

167 St

Jewel Av

11

152 St

153 St

156-02

161-02

71 Av

JEWEL AV

137 St

136 St

70 Av

70 Rd

71 Av

147-02

Vleigh Pl

147 St

Dana Garden

156 St

P

71-02

73-02

PAGE 330

EXPWY

Park Dr E

71 Rd

72 Av

141 St

Aguilar Av

K E W

160-02

162-02

73 Av

75 Av

72 Rd

72 Cres

139 St

141-02

72 Rd

72 Dr

73 Av

75 Av

180-02

G A R D E N S

75 Rd

76 Av

73 Ter

137 St

136 St

73-02

75 Rd

76 Av

75 Rd

76 Av

H I L L S

160-02

164-02

2 MILES= 3.2 KMS

C

77 Av

141 Pl

77 Av

77 Rd

150 St

153 St

PARSONS BLVD

160 St

162 St

160-02

164-02

D

78 Av

138 St

141 St

78 Av

78 Rd

150-02

152 St

154-02

St Joseph's Hospital

160 St

162 St

81 Av

165 St
166 St

167 St

678

10

78 Rd

78 Dr

Vleigh Pl

141-02

79 Av

146 St

149 St

150 St

152 St

154 St

159 St

160 St

161 St

164 Pl

81-02

UNION TPK

ow ke

14

15

MAIN ST

Charter Rd

Goethals Av

END 3 MINS

2 MILES= 3.2 KMS

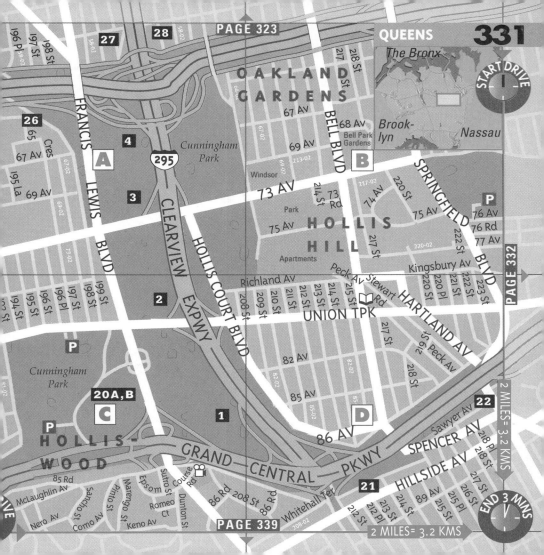

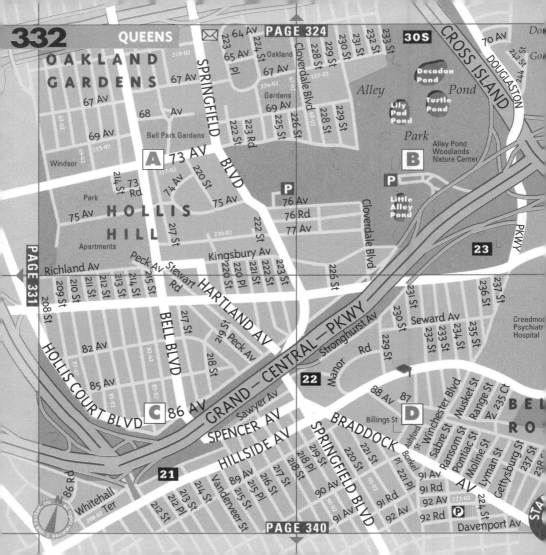

PAGE 324

30S

CROSS ISLAND

70 AV

242 St

44 Av

Don

Gou

OAKLAND GARDENS

64 AV

223 St

224 St

65 AV

65 PI

Oakland

Cloverdale Blvd

228 St

229 St

230 St

231 St

232 St

233 St

219-02

67 Av

67 AV

Gardens

69 AV

226 St

228 St

229 St

DOUGLASTON

67 Av

67 AV

68 Av

SPRINGFIELD

224-02

227-02

Alley

Pond

Decadon
Pond

Turtle
Pond

Lily
Pad
Pond

213-02

69 Av

Bell Park Gardens

69-02

222 St

223 Rd

223 St

225 St

226 St

228 St

Park

Alley Pond
Woodlands
Nature Center

B

Windsor

A

73 AV

BLVD

217-02

P

Little
Alley
Pond

214 St

73
Rd

73 Rd

74 Av

220 St

75 Av

76 AV

P

PKWY

HOLLIS

75 Av

222 St

76 Rd

77 Av

Cloverdale Blvd

23

HILL

217 St

230-02

Kingsbury Av

222 St

220 PI

221 St

223 St

226 St

Apartments

Peck Av

Stewart Rd

HARTLAND AV

222 St

220 St

Richland Av

208 St

209 St

210 St

211 St

212 St

213 St

214 St

215 St

231 St

230 St

232 St

233 St

234 St

235 St

236 St

237 St

PAGE 331

BELL BLVD

217 St

Peck Av

85-02

GRAND — CENTRAL — PKWY

Stronghurst Av

Seward Av

229 St

Manor

Rd

Creedmoor
Psychiatric
Hospital

82 Av

82-02

218 St

22

87

88 Av

HOLLIS COURT BLVD

85 Av

85-02

C

86 AV

Sawyer Av

SPENCER AV

BRADDOCK

Billings St

D

Ashford St

Borkel

Winchester Blvd

Sabre St

Ransom St

Pontiac St

Moline St

Musket St

Range St

235 Ct

Lyman St

Gettysburg St

237 St

BEL

RO

HILLSIDE AV

SPRINGFIELD BLVD

86 Rd

21

Whitehall Ter

208-02

212 St

213 St

214 St

212 PI

215 St

Vanderveer St

89 Av

215 PI

216 St

217 St

218 St

218 PI

219 St

221 St

220 St

90 Av

91 Av

221 PI

92-02

91 Rd

91 Av

91 Rd

92 Av

222-02

92 Av

92 Rd

P

224 St

AV

Davenport Av

STA

PAGE 340

The Bronx

Brooklyn

Nassau

START DRIVE

71 Av   252 St   73

71 Rd   **G L E N**   73 Av

72 Av   **O A K S**   260 St

73 Rd

265 St

264 St

263 St

Av

St

Long Island
Jewish Medical
Center (Hillside)

Park

72 Av

73 Av

243 St

244 St

Queens
Children's
Hospital

Queens County
Farm Museum

74

75

79 Av

79-01

79-02

B

267 St (Castlewood St)

268 St

269 St

LANGDALE ST

29

COMMONWEALTH BLVD

Elkmont Av

Shiloh Av

76
Av
77 Cres

247-02

255 St

UNION TPK

80 Av

80-02

80-01

79-02

80-02

80-02

81-01

81-02

266 St

265 St

264 St

80 Rd

249 St

248 St

81 Av

250 St

252 St

254 St

255 St

256 St

257 St

258 St

259 St

260 St

261 St

262 St

263 St

80-02

28B

247 St

246 St

251 St

82 Av

82-01

82-02

82-02

82-02

82-02

83-02

F L O R A L

P A R K

PKWY

LITTLE NECK

243 St

82-02

82 Av

82
82
Rd
Dr

83 Av

83-02

83 Rd

83-02

83-02

83-02

28A

83 Av

240 St

241 St

242 St

25B

84 Rd
Dr

84

85 Av

HILLSIDE AV

84 Rd

84

85 Av

85-02

85-02

E Williston Av

85 Av

D

85 Rd

86

86 Rd

87 Av

241 St

C

Av

85 Av

86 Av

86-02

86-02

86-02

Queens County
Nassau County

F L O R A L

88 Av

242 St

87 Av

247 St

Commonwealth Blvd

87 Av

87-02

87-02

87 Rd

87 Dr

87 Ter
87 Rd

P A R K

C E N T E R

END 3 MINS

88 Av
88 Rd
88 Dr
89 Av

2 MILES = 3.2 KMS

2 MILES = 3.2 KMS

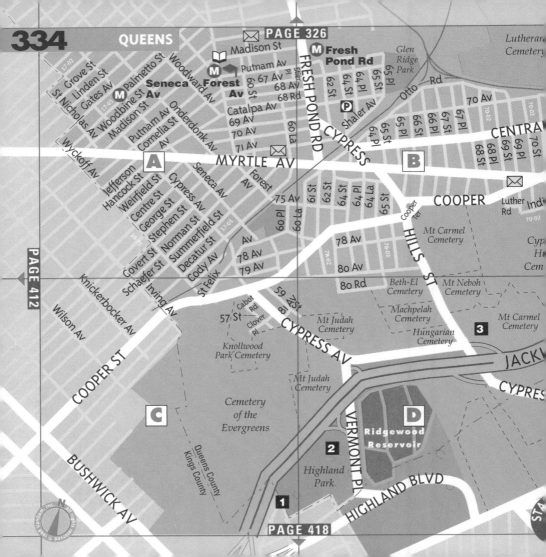

PAGE 326

Madison St

M Fresh
Pond Rd

Glen
Ridge
Park

Rd

Lutheran
Cemetery

Grove St
Linden St
Gates Av
St Nicholas Av
Woodbine St

17-02

Palmetto St
Putnam Av
Madison St

Woodward Av

M
Putnam Av
67 Av

Seneca
Av

Forest
Av

68 Av
68 Rd

Fresh Pond

62 St
64 St
65 St
65 St

Otto

70 Av

70-02

Putnam Av
Cornelia
Av

Onderdonk Av

Catalpa Av
69 Av
70 Av
71 Av

60 La

M
Shaler Av

P

64 St
65 St
66 St
67 St
67 Pl

65 St
66 St

CENTRA

Wyckoff Av

17-03

A

Jefferson
Hancock St
Weirfield St
Centre St
George St
Stephen St

Seneca Av

Cypress Av

Forest Av

MYRTLE AV

FRESH POND RD

CYPRESS

68 St
69 St
68 Pl
69 Pl
70 Pl
70 St

B

COOPER

Luther
Rd

Indi

70-02

Cyp
Hi
Cem

75 Av
60 Pl
60 La

61 St
62 St
64 St
64 Pl
64 La
65 St

Cooper Ter

Covert St
Schaefer St
Summerfield St
Norman St
Decatur St
Cody Av
St Felix

78 Av

80 Av

80 Rd

78-02

HILLS ST

Mt Carmel
Cemetery

Mt Neboh
Cemetery

Mt Carmel
Cemetery

3

Wilson Av

Knickerbocker Av

Irving Av

17-01

Cabot Rd

Clover Pl

57 St

59 St

25 St

81

CYPRESS AV

Beth-El
Cemetery

Machpelah
Cemetery

Hungarian
Cemetery

Mt Judah
Cemetery

Knollwood
Park Cemetery

Mt Judah
Cemetery

JACK

CYPRESS

COOPER ST

C

Cemetery
of the
Evergreens

Queens County
Kings County

Mt Judah
Cemetery

2

1

D

Ridgewood
Reservoir

VERMONT PL

Highland
Park

HIGHLAND BLVD

ST

BUSHWICK AV

N

1997 Hagstrom Map Company, Inc.

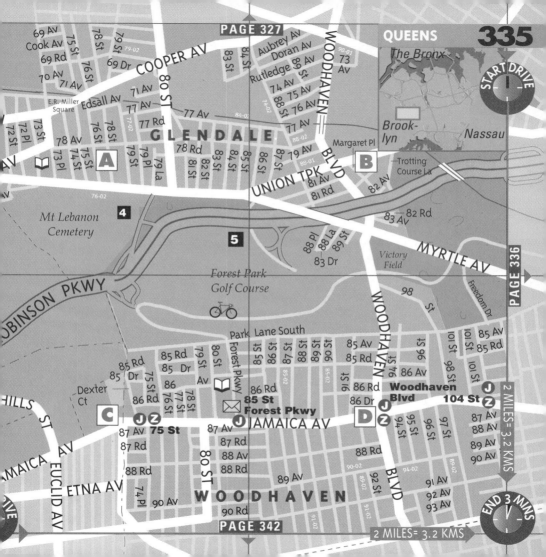

The Bronx

Brook-lyn

Nassau

START DRIVE

69 Av
Cook Av
69 Rd
70 Av
71 Av
75 St
78 St
79 St
76 St
69 Dr

COOPER AV
80 ST

73 St
72 Pl
72 St
73 St
E.R. Miller Square
Edsall Av
71 Av
77 Av
77 Av
83 St
84 St

Aubrey Av
Doran Av
Rutledge Av
74 Av
88 Av
75 Av
76 Av

WOODHAVEN BLVD
73 Av

78 Av
76 St
78 St
77 Rd
79 St

GLENDALE
78 Rd
79 St
79 Pl
81 St
82 St
83 St
84 St
85 St
86 St
87 St
79 Av
77 Rd

Margaret Pl
UNION TPK
81 St
81 Rd
82 Av
82 Rd
83 Av

Trotting Course La

A
B

76-02
4
5

Mt Lebanon Cemetery

ROBINSON PKWY

Forest Park Golf Course

88 Pl
88 La
89 St
83 Dr

Victory Field

MYRTLE AV
PAGE 336
98 St
Freedom Dr

Park Lane South

85 Rd
85 Dr
85 Rd
85 Dr
86
85 St
80 St
79 St
Forest Pkwy
85 St
86 St
87 St
88 St
90 St
85 Av
85 Av
86 Av
85 Av
85 Rd
101 St
101 St
98 St
96 St

Dexter Ct
85 St
75 St
76 St
77 St
78 St
86 Rd
86 Rd
86 Rd
86 Dr
91 St
96 St
94 St
Woodhaven Blvd
104 St

C
D
J Z
J Z
J Z
J Z

87 Av
75 St
87 Rd
87 Av
87 Rd
88 Av
88 Rd
JAMAICA AV
85 St
Forest Pkwy

88 Rd
87 Av
88 Av
95 St
96 St
97 St
87 Av
88 Av
89 Av
90 Av

ETNA AV
EUCLID AV
JAMAICA AV
HILLS ST

74 Pl
90 Av
80 ST
89 Av
90 Rd

WOODHAVEN
88 Rd
92 St
BLVD
91 Av
92 Av
93 Av

END 3 MINS

2 MILES = 3.2 KMS
2 MILES= 3.2 KMS

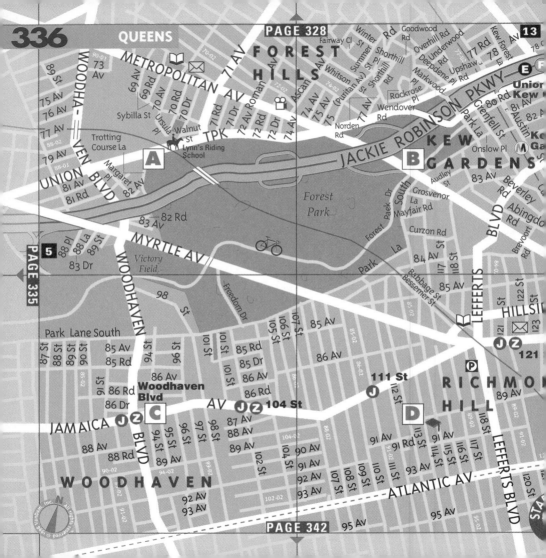

PAGE 328
13

FOREST HILLS

METROPOLITAN AV

73 AV

89 St
75 AV
76 AV
77 AV
79 AV
81 Rd
81 Pl

WOODHAVEN BLVD

69 AV
69 Rd
70 Rd
70 Dr
70 St
Ursula

Sybilla St
Trotting Course La
Walnut St
Margaret Pl
82 St

71 Rd
TPK
71 St
71 Dr
72 Av
72 Rd
72 Dr
74 St
Roman Av
Ascan Av
Whitson St
(Puritan Av)
Shorthill St Pl

Winter Rd
Fairway Cl
Summer Rd
Goodwood Rd
Overhill Rd
Underwood
Deadpene Pl
Markwood Pl
Shorthill Rd
Rockrose Pl
Wendover Rd
Norden Rd

Kew forest La
77 Rd
78 Rd
Upshaw Av
80 Rd
81 Pl
Austin
Grenfell St
Park La

JACKIE ROBINSON PKWY

E F
Union Kew G
82 Av
Kew Ga

A
Lynn's Riding School

UNION BLVD

B
KEW GARDENS

Onslow Pl Ⓜ
Kew Ga

83 Av
Beverley Rd
Abingdo
Rd

Forest Park

Grosvenor La
Mayfair Rd
South
Forest Park Dr
Curzon Rd
Audley St
84 AV
117 St
118 St
85 Av
Babbage St
Bessemer St
85-92
Brevoort Rd

83 Av
82 Rd
82 Rd

MYRTLE AV

PAGE 335
5

88 Pl
88 La
89 St
83 Dr

Victory Field

98 St

Freedom Dr
107 St
106 St
105 St

Park La

LEFFERTS BLVD

121 St
122 St
123 St

HILLSI

J Z
121

Park Lane South
85 AV
85 Rd
85 Rd
85 Dr
86 AV
86 AV

87 St
88 St
89 St
90 St
94 St
96 St
101 St
101 St

85 Av
85 Rd
86 Av
86 Rd

86 AV
86 Dr

Woodhaven Blvd

C

AV Ⓙ Ⓩ 104 St

111 St
J
112 St
113 St

P

RICHMO

HILL

89 Av

D

91 Av

JAMAICA Ⓙ Ⓩ
88 AV
88 Rd

BLVD

94 St
95 St
96 St
97 St
98 St
102 St

87 AV
88 AV
89 AV
89 AV
90 AV
91 AV
92 AV
93 AV

104-02
104 St
107 St
108 St
109 St
110 St
111 St

91 Av
91 Rd
93 Av
113 St
114 St
115 St
116 St
117 St
118 St

LEFFERTS BLVD

WOODHAVEN

92 AV
93 AV

102-02

ATLANTIC AV

95 Av

120 St
ST

PAGE 342

N

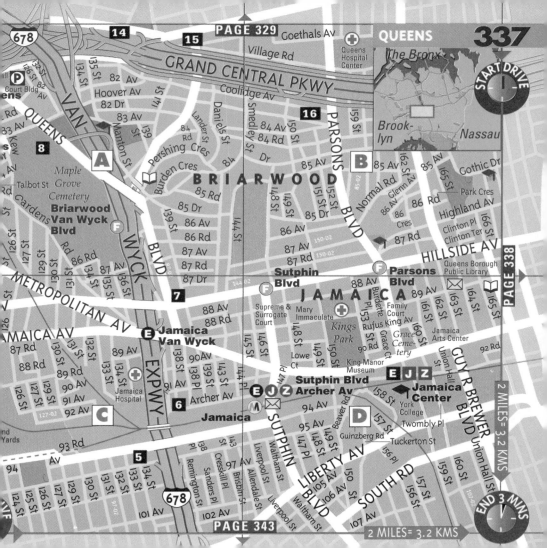

678
14
15
Goethals Av
Village Rd
GRAND CENTRAL PKWY
Queens Hospital Center

The Bronx

Brooklyn
Nassau

START DRIVE

P
Court Bldg
ens
82 St
82 Av
135 St
134 St
Hoover Av
82 Av
82 Dr
83 Av
Coolidge Av
Daniels St
141 St
139 St
Manton St
Lander St
84 Rd
84 St
84 Av
84 Rd
150 St
16
159 St
162 St
165 St
Gothic Dr
33 Av
Kew
AV
s
Rd
QUEENS
VAN
A
Pershing Cres
Burden Cres
85 Av
B
85 Av
Normal Rd
Glenn Av
Park Cres
Highland Av
8
Maple Grove Cemetery
BRIARWOOD
144 St
148 St
149 St
151 St
152 St
85 Dr
86 Av
86 Rd
Clinton Pl
Clinton Ter
166 St
Talbot St
85 Rd
85 Dr
86 Cres
86 Rd
Rd Gardens
Briarwood Van Wyck Blvd
F
139 St
86 Av
86 Rd
87 Av
87 Rd
87 Dr
87 Rd
HILLSIDE AV
126 St
127 St
129 St
130 St
134 St
135 St
86 Rd
87 Av
136 St
WYCK
BLVD
Sutphin Blvd
88 Av
Parsons Blvd
F
Queens Borough Public Library
PAGE 338
METROPOLITAN AV
7
F
JAMAICA
Burdette
89 Av
161 St
162 St
163 St
164 St
165 St
88 Av
88 Rd
Supreme & Surrogate Court
Mary Immaculate
Family Court
Rufus King Av
160 St
Jamaica Arts Center
MAICA AV
E
Jamaica Van Wyck
89 Av
148 St
146 St
145 St
Kings Park
153 St
90 St
Grace Ct
Grace Cemetery
92 Rd
87 Rd
130 St
131 St
132 St
88 Rd
89 Rd
90 Av
91 Av
133 St
134 St
138 St
90 Av
138 St
139 St
143 St
91 Av
144 St
149 St
150 St
Lowe Ct
King Manor Museum
E J Z
126 St
127 St
129 St
92 Av
EXPWY
Jamaica Hospital
C
6
Archer Av
E J Z
Sutphin Blvd Archer Av
M
Jamaica Center
York College
Twombly Pl
GUY R BREWER BLVD
Union Hall St
2 MILES = 3.2 KMS
nd Yards
93 Rd
5
Jamaica
94 Av
95 Av
147 Pl
148 St
149 St
Beaver Rd
158 St
D
157 St
Guinzberg Rd
Tuckerton St
156 St
157 St
159 St
160 St
Union Hall St
94 Av
678
134 St
133 St
132 St
131 St
130 St
129 St
126 St
125 St
124 St
138 St
143 St
Cresskill Pl
Sanders Pl
Brisbin St
Allendale St
Liverpool St
Waltham St
97 Av
101 Av
102 Av
Liverpool St
Waltham St
SUTPHIN
LIBERTY BLVD
105 Av
106 Av
107 Av
150 St
SOUTH RD
156 St
157 St

QUEENS

The Bronx

Brook-lyn

Nassau

START DRIVE 1

Doncaster Pl
Midland Pkwy
Radnor Rd
Avon Rd
GRAND CENTRAL PKWY
McLaughlin Av
85 Rd
Sutro St
Palo Alto
Palermo Ken
Santiago
Nero Av
Como Av
Marengo
Pinto St
St
Keno Av
Romeo Ct
Av
Wicklow Pl
Chevy Chase Rd
Hovenden Rd
Cambridge Rd
Soho Dr
HOLLISWOOD
Clio Av
Henley
Somerset St
Barrington St
Chelsea Rd
Rio Dr
St
Salerno Av
Pompeii
Radnor
Avon St
Wareham Pl
Kruger Rd
Eton Rd
188 St
Palo Alto Av
Dunton Av
Cloverhill Rd
Clover Pl
Dunton Av
Foothill
Edgerton Blvd
Dalny
Rd
A
Haywood Rd
Foothill Av
Holliswood Hospital
B
197 St
89 Av
198 St
201 St
202 St
204 St
205 St
FRANCIS LEWIS BLVD
207 St
jord
JAMAICA
Wexford Ter
87 Dr
Ter
25
196 St
195 St
89 Rd
195
HOLLIS
93 Av
ESTATES
191 St
192 St
193 St
196 St
91 Av
94 St
DE AV
F
Jamaica 179 St
89 Av
187 Pl
188 St
189 St
190 St
195 St
91 Av
JAMAICA AV
178 St
179 St
90 Av
181 St
182 St
183 St
184 St
90 Av
186 St
185 St
184 Pl
193 St
Pl
Hiawatha Av
Carpenter Av
199 St
201 St
99 Av
202 St
203 St
204 St
205 St
PAGE 340
180 St
179 Pl
91 Rd
Woodhull
Sagamore Av
Sagamore Rd
193 St
194 St
195 St
196 St
197 St
198 St
199 St
200 St
201 St
100 Av
104 Av
176 St
178 Pl
180 Pl
181 Pl
182 Pl
JAMAICA AV
HOLLIS AV
191 St
102 Av
103 Av
109 Av
176 St
177 St
183 St
Henderson Av
184 St
185 St
186 St
187 St
188 St
189 St
104 Av
191 St
105 Av
192 St
193 St
110 Av
HOLLIS AV
103 Rd
104 Av
Liberty Av
C
Arcade Av
Babylon Av
Camden Av
Ludlum
FARMERS
109 Rd
190 Pl
194 St
111 Av
D
110 Rd
105 Av
106 Av
106 Rd
107 Av
Ruscoe St
Watson Pl
108 Av
Dunlop Av
Elmira Av
Brinkerhoff Av
Einwood Pl
Rye Pl Av
Jordan Av
111 Rd
112 Av
111 Av
END 3 MINS
Fern Pl
Wren Pl
Rex Pl
177 St
176 St
175 St
179 Pl
Fonda Av
Galway Av
Hilburn Av
Ilion St
Hannibal St
BLVD
PAGE 345
112 Rd
113 Av
2 MILES= 3.2 KMS

2 MILES= 3.2 KMS

PAGE 332

QUEENS VILLAGE

HOLLIS

ST ALBANS

HEMPSTE

SPRINGFIELD BLVD

FRANCIS LEWIS BLVD

Dunton Av
Pompeii Rd
Foothill Av
202 Av
204 St
25

HILLSIDE AV
88 Rd
Hollis 89 Av
243 St
212 St
211 St
210 Pl
209 St
208 St
207 St
205 St
204 St
202 St
201 St
199 St
198 St
197 St
196 St
89 Av
89 Rd

214 St
213 St
90 Av
90 Ct
89 Rd Court
91 Av
92 Av
93 Av
93 Rd
Blvd
211 Pl

214 St
215 St
216 St
217 St
218 St
219 St
91 Rd
92 Av
92 Rd
92 Rd
Dav
Edm
Fairb
93 Av
93 Rd
94 Av
94 Rd
94 D

Vandeveer St

Winchester Blvd
Springfield
221 Rd
219

92 Rd
93 Rd
94 Av
94 Dr
94 St

214 Pl

B

Amboy La

A

91 Av

94 Av
94 Rd
93 Rd

JAMAICA AV

Queens Village
M
96
97Av

Hiawatha Av
Carpenter Av
199 St
201 St
99 Av

Soca Paradise

98 Av
99
Sigourney Av
100 Av
101 Av

219 St
218 St

100 Av
196 St
197 St
198 St
199 St
200 St
201 St
202 St
203 St
204 St
205 St
205 Pl
207 St
208 St
209 St
210 St
211 St
99 Av
104 Av
109 Av

Bellaire Pl

211 Pl
212 St
213 St

99 Av
102 Av
103 Av
104 Av
106 Av

215 St
216 St
217 St
217 La

217 St
103 Av
218 Pl
104 Av
105 Av

220 St
221 St
220 Av
101
100

HOLLIS AV

Roland La
217 Pl
Monterey

103 A
104 Av
105 Av
106 Av
107 Av
108 Av
109 Av
110 Av

195 St

C

110 Av
110 Rd
111 Av
194 St
111 Rd
111 Av
112 Av
113 Av
112 Rd

Bardwell Av
Colfax
209 Pl

212 St
213 St
214 St
215 St
216 St
217 St

110 Av
110 Rd
111 Av
111 Rd
111 Av
112 Rd
112
113

Witthoff St
Delevan Av
Nashville Blvd

111 Av
112
Av

D

Convent

222 St
223 St
110 Av
111 Av
112 Av
112 Rd
113 Av
Murdock Av
113 Dr

209 St
210 St
211 St

SPRINGFIELD BLVD

219-02
221-02
219-02
225-02
114 Av

Murdock Av
ST ALBANS

PAGE 339

BRADDOCK AV

240 St
241 St
242 St

Gettysburg St
224 St
225 St
239 St
240 St
241 St
242 St

88 Dr
89 Av
90 Av
91 Av

247 St
Common-
wealth Blvd

87 Dr
87 Rd

88 Rd

250 St
251 St

The Bronx

START DRIVE

Av

Av

JAMAICA AV

5 Av
6 Av

7 Av

22-02

9 Av

244 St
245 St
246 St
247 St

JERICHO TPK

Queens County
Nassau County

Brook-
lyn

Nassau

27

A

26D

Bellerose

Ⓜ

B

FLORAL
PARK

TULIP AV

PLAINFIELD AV

CROSS ISLAND PKWY

Belmont Race
Track

D

02

26B,C

C

24

HEMPSTEAD TPK

2 MILES = 3.2 KMS

26A

ELMONT

ELMONT RD

END 3 MINS

2 MILES = 3.2 KMS

The Bronx

Brook-lyn

Nassau

START DRIVE

95 Av
114 St
113 St
112 St
111 St
95-02 St
116 St
117 St
118 St

101 Av

ZONE PARK

103 Av

41 St
(Greenwood Av)

120 St
121 St
123 St
124 St
125 St
126 St
127 St

101 Av

102 Av
102 Rd

97-02

130 St
131 St
132 St
133 St

101 Av

4

103 Rd

105 Av
134 St

LEFFERTS BLVD

A
A LIBERTY AV
Lefferts Blvd
A

107 Av

Van Sicklen St

135 St

B

107 Av

107-02

109 Av

Hawtree Creek Rd

109-02

109-02

678

107 Rd
Lakewood Av
109 Rd
Glassboro Av
139-02

3

111 Av

111-02

111-02

111-02

141 St
140 St
139 St
142 St
111-02

111 St

LINDEN   BLVD

115 Av

115-02

116 Av

VAN WYCK EXPWY

Dr Charles Andrews Memorial Park

Sutter Av

Aqueduct Race Track

C

133 Av

131 St

135 Av
117 St
118 St

114 St
114 Pl
115 St
116 St
149 Av

150 Av

149-02

150-02

Hawtree Creek Rd

LEFFERTS   BLVD

133-02

120 St
121 St
122 St
122 Pl

123 St
124 St
125 St
126 St
127 St
128 St

ROCKAWAY BLVD

Foch   Blvd

Lincoln St

115-02

116-02

116 Av

SOUTH OZONE PARK

Gotham Rd
Cedric Rd

D

117 Rd

120 Av

123 Av

131 Av

129 St
130 St

131-02

110-02

132 St
133 St
134 St

Alwick Rd

2

135 Av
135 Pl

140 St

2 MILES = 3.2 KMS

2 MILES = 3.2 KMS

END 3 MINS

PAGE 343

PAGE 339

PAGE 345

QUEENS

ST ALBANS

112 AV
178 St
177 St
111 Rd
173 St
176 St
175 Pl
Adelaide Rd
Murdock Av
113 AV
178
179
178 St
114 Rd
Pl St
Dunkirk St
Ovid St
Rome Dr
Dormans Rd
Quencer Rd
Sullivan Rd
Mexico
Dr
Suffolk Dr
Tioga St
Newburg St
Turin Dr
Dunkirk St

114
Rd
Dr
194-02

115 Av

Sayres Av
St Albans
Memorial
Park
113 AV

115 Rd
115 Dr
194-02
116 Rd

116 Av

LINDEN

BLVD

St Albans
(M)
St. Albans
Veterans Adm.
Exit Care Center

LINDEN BLVD

115 AV
174 St
175 St
173 St
172 St
A

117 Rd
118 AV
118 Rd
119 AV
Montauk
Everitt
Lovingham Pl
Foch Blvd
118 Rd
B

200 St
201 St
199 St
198 St
197 St
196 St
195 St
194 St
193 St

167 St
170 St
168 St
169 St
116 AV
166 St
171 St

FARMERS BLVD

192 St
191 St
190 St
189 St

120 AV
194 St
195 St
196 St
197 St
199 St

Foch Blvd
170-02

Roy Wilkins
So.uthern Queens
Park

Baisley Blvd
177 Pl
178 St
178 Pl
119 Rd
179 St
180 St
119 Dr
119 Rd

Riverton St
118 Rd
119 Rd

120 Rd

120 AV
193 St
194 St
195 St
196 St

118 AV
118 Rd
119 Rd
Marsden St
Bedell St
Ring Pl
Victoria
Rd
Victoria Dr
Amelia St
Brocher
Rd
Merrill St
Roe Rd
120 AV
Sunbury Rd
Troutville Rd
Ursina Rd
Inwin
Leslie Rd
121 AV
Grayson St
Benton St
Lucas St
Milburn St
122 AV
192 St

165 St
166 St
120 AV
Smith St
168 St
170 St
171 St
172 St
125
124 AV
126 AV
127 AV
174 Pl
172 St
176 St
Selover Rd
Anderson Rd
Zoller Rd
Sidway Pl
Eveleth Pl
177 St
Veterans
Square
Nellis St
Montauk St
193 St
Nashville
Williamson Av
191 St
SPRING

217 St
218 St
219

128 AV

BAISLEY BLVD
127 AV
Bedell St
129 AV
172 St
173 St
Garrett St
176 St
177 St
179 St
Adair
St
Pineville La
Nepton St
Defoe St
132 AV
132 Rd
133 Rd
133

GUY BREWERS BLVD
130 AV
C
Rochdale
Village
130 AV
103
Eveleth Pl
130 Rd
131 AV
176 Pl
132 AV
133 AV
133 Rd
134
178 St
178 St
130 Rd
Mathewson
Ct
Bennet Ct
Denis St
Crandall St
134 Av
135 AV
135 AV
136
Cheney Av
Belknap
St
E Gate Plaza
Sloan St
D
Ridgedale St
217 St
218 St
219
220 St
220 Pl
221 St
222 St
MERRICK
134 Rd
136 Rd
136 AV
137 St
137 AV
137 Rd

132
AV
134 AV
166 Pl

133 AV
133 Rd
174 St
175 St
173 St
134 Rd

Locust
Manor

Southgate St
Bennet St
137 St
138 Rd
138 AV

PAGE 352

N

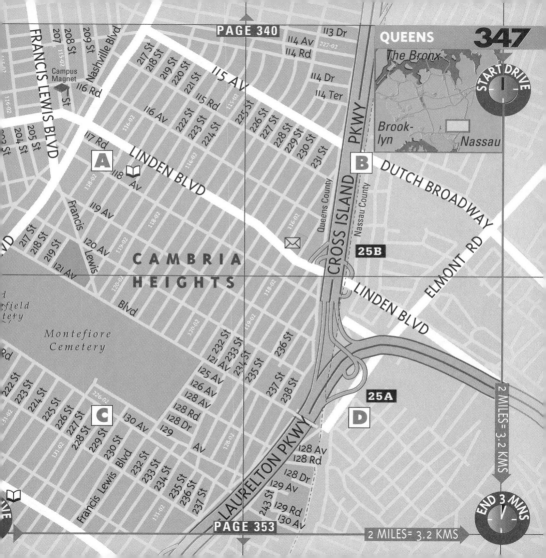

The Bronx

START DRIVE

Brooklyn

Nassau

FRANCIS LEWIS BLVD

207 St 208 St 209 St
Nashville Blvd
116 Rd
Campus Magnet
116-02
204 St 205 St
117 Rd
118 Av

113 Dr
114 Av
114 Rd
227-02
114 Dr
114 Ter

115 AV

217 St 218 St 219 St 220 St 221 St 115 Rd
116 Av 222 St 223 St 224 St
225 St 226 St 227 St 228 St 229 St 230 St 231 St

114 Dr
114 Ter

CROSS ISLAND PKWY

DUTCH BROADWAY

A

LINDEN BLVD

118 Av

119 Av

120 Av

121 Av

217 St 218 St 219 St

Francis Lewis

C A M B R I A
H E I G H T S

Queens County
Nassau County

B

25B

ELMONT RD

LINDEN BLVD

field
tery

Montefiore Cemetery

Blvd

232 St 233 St
121 Av
125 Av
126 Av
128 Av
128 Rd
128 Dr
129
Av

234 St
235 St

236 St
237 St
238 St

25A

D

222 St 223 St 224 St 225 St 226 St 227 St 228 St 229 St 230 St
Francis Lewis Blvd
232 St 233 St 234 St 235 St 236 St 237 St

C

128 Av
128 Rd
128 Dr
129 Av
129 Rd
130 Av
243 St

LAURELTON PKWY

2 MILES= 3.2 KMS

END 3 MINS

2 MILES= 3.2 KMS

QUEENS

PAGE 342

17S

153 Av
79 St
80 St
81 St
82 St
83 St
82-02
84-02
84 St
86 St
88 St
155 Av
89 St
St
155 Av
156 Av
81-02
81-13 Av
159-02
90-01
156-02

A

B

17

77 St
157 Av

BELT PKWY

94 St

Killarney St
Lahn St
Huron St
Bridgeton St
Cohancy St
98 St

Tahoe St
Raleigh Av
Huron St
Hawtree St
166 Pl

Aqueduct
North
Conduit Av

Race Track Rd

82 St
83 St
84 St
85 St
86 St
87 St
88 St
89 St
90 St
91 St
92 St

158 Av
79 St
80 St
81 St
159 Av
159-02

96 St
97 St
98 St
99 St
100 St
101 St
102 St

157 Av
158 Av
158-02
159 Av

Coleman
Square
159 Rd
159-02
103 Rd

A Howard B
JFK Airpo

78 St

H O W A R D

B E A C H

160 Av

160-02
161 Av
81-02

159-02
160 Av

161 Av

103 St

C

PAGE 419

162 Av

163 Av

164 Av

165 Av

Queens County
Kings County

*Spring Creek
Park*

162-01
162-02
163-02
164-02

162-01
162-02
163-02
164-02

CROSS BAY BLVD

161-02

Shellbank Basin

161 Av

162 Av

163 Av

164 Av

165 Av

162-02
163-02
164-02

Ped
Bridge

Russel St

1 St
Rau Ct
Davenport Ct
163 Dr

164 Rd
164 Dr

Hawtree Basin

D

*F M Charles
Memorial
Park*

*Hamilton
Beach
Park*

Grassy Bay

Congressman Joseph
Addabo Bridge

PAGE 433

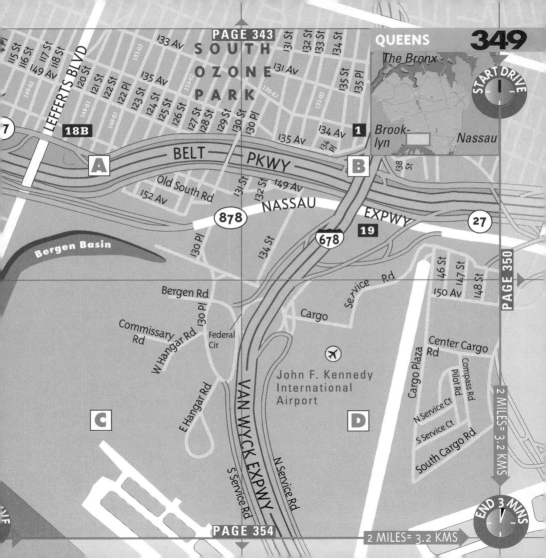

SOUTH OZONE PARK

PAGE 343

A Aqueduct North Conduit Av

18B

114 St
114 Pl
115 St
116 St
149 Av
118 St
LEFFERTS BLVD
120 St
121 St
122 St
122 Pl
123 St
124 St
125 St
126 St
127 St
128 St
129 St
130 St
130 Pl
131 Av
131 St
132 St
133 St

133 Av
135 Av
150 AV
135 Av

134

A

157 AV
98 St
99 St
100 St
101 St
158 AV
158-02
159 AV
Coleman Square
102 St
Race Track Rd

19

BELT PKWY

B

Old South Rd
152 Av
149 Av
131 St
132 St
184

878

678

A Howard Beach JFK Airport
103 Rd

Bergen Basin

130 Pl

134 St

PAGE 349

160 AV
03 St
Russel St
Ped Bridge 1 St
Rau Ct
Davenport St
163 Dr
164 Rd
164 Dr

C

Hamilton Beach Park

Hawtree Basin

Grassy Bay

Bergen Rd
Commissary Rd
W Hangar Rd
Federal Cir
Cargo

E Hangar Rd

D

VAN WYCK EXPWY

S Service Rd
N Service Rd

General Aviation Building

PAGE 355

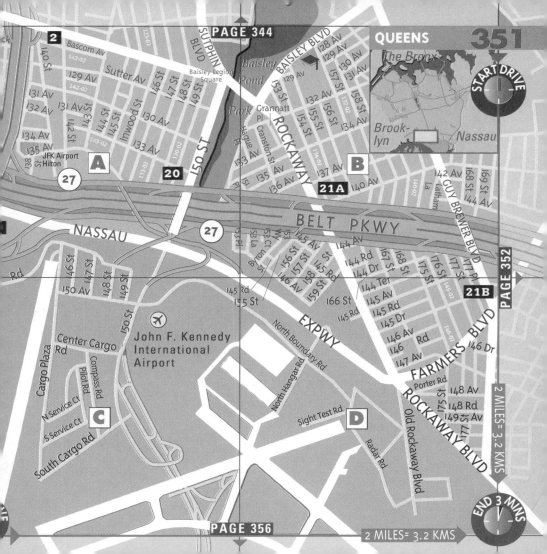

2
Bascom Av
142-02
Sutter Av
129 Av
141 St
131 Av
132 Av
131 Av
142 St
142 St
144 St
141 St
130 Av
146 St
147 St
148 St
149 St
1-13-02
134 Av
135 Av
138 St
JFK Airport Hilton
133 Av
A
27
20

SUTPHIN BLVD
Baisley Legion Square
Baisley Pond
Park
Grannatt Pl
Hague St
Cranston St
153 St
135 St
136 St

BAISLEY BLVD
128 Av
129 Av
130 Av
129 Av
132 Av
155 St
156 St
154 St
157 St
158 St
134 Av
137-02
ROCKAWAY
B
21A

The Bronx
START DRIVE
Brooklyn
Nassau

142 Av
144 Av
168 St
169 St
140-02
GUY BREWER BLVD

NASSAU
27
BELT PKWY
Latham La
177 PL

146 St
147 St
148 St
149 St
150 Av
155 St
53 Pl
53 St
53 Ct
53 La
W St
Byron St
145 Av
156 St
157 St
145 St
146 Av
158
159
144 Av
144 Rd
144 Dr
167 St
168 St
175 St
176 St
177 St
149-02
21B

Rd
Center Cargo Rd
Cargo Plaza
Compass Rd
Pilot Rd
N Service Ct
S Service Ct
C
South Cargo Rd

John F. Kennedy International Airport
North Hangar Rd
North Boundary Rd
145 Rd
155 St
166 St
144 Ter
145 Av
145 Rd
145 Dr
146 Av
146 Rd
147 Av
EXPWY
Sight Test Rd
D
Radar Rd

145 Av
145 Rd
146 Dr
FARMERS BLVD
Porter Rd
175 St
177
ROCKAWAY BLVD
148 Av
148 Rd
149 Av
149 St

2 MILES= 3.2 KMS
2 MILES = 3.2 KMS

PAGE 352
END 3 MINS

QUEENS

PAGE 349

VAN WYCK

S Service Rd

A

B

Grassy

Bay

PAGE 433

CROSS BAY BLVD

East Pond

C

Broad

Creek

D

Marsh

East
High
Meadow

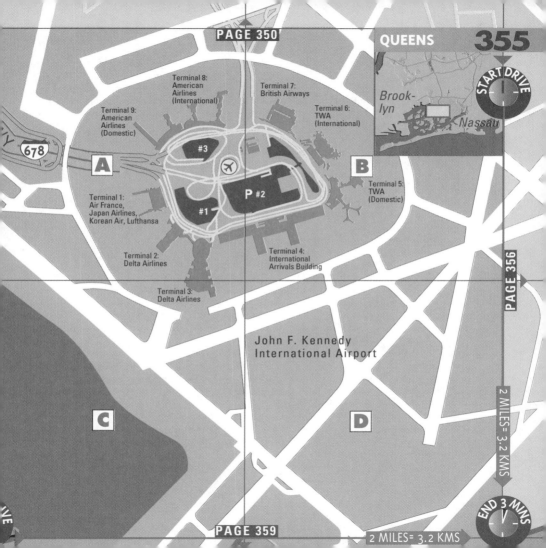

Brook-lyn

Nassau

START DRIVE

678

Terminal 9:
American
Airlines
(Domestic)

Terminal 8:
American
Airlines
(International)

Terminal 7:
British Airways

Terminal 6:
TWA
(International)

A

#3

B

Terminal 5:
TWA
(Domestic)

Terminal 1:
Air France,
Japan Airlines,
Korean Air, Lufthansa

P #2

#1

Terminal 2:
Delta Airlines

Terminal 4:
International
Arrivals Building

Terminal 3:
Delta Airlines

John F. Kennedy
International Airport

C

D

PAGE 356

2 MILES= 3.2 KMS

END 3 MINS

2 MILES= 3.2 KMS

QUEENS

PAGE 351

*Brookville
Park*

Bog Creek

Terminal 6:
TWA
(International)

Terminal 5:
TWA
(Domestic)

A

B

ROCKAWAY BLVD

Thurston Basin

PAGE 355

John F. Kennedy
International Airport

C

D

Broa
Ba

Head of Bay

STA

N
Thomas Bros. Maps Inc. © 1998 all rights reserved

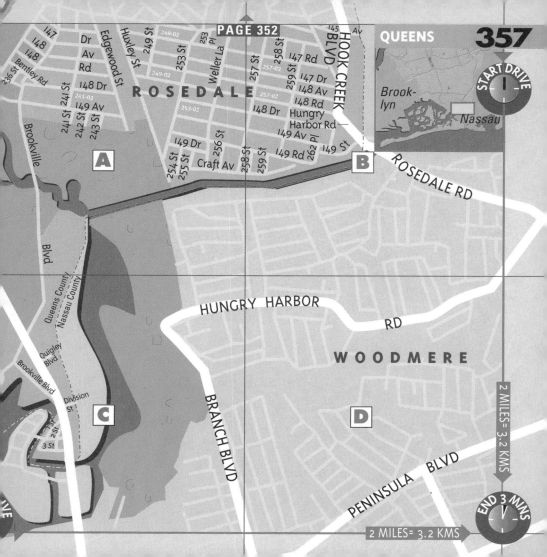

147
148
148
236 St
Bentley Rd
Dr
Av
Rd
Edgewood St
Huxley St
249 St
249-02
253 St
253 St
253
Pl
Weller La
257 St
258 St
249-02
257-02
HOOK CREEK BLVD
145 Av
147 Rd
147 Dr
148 Av
148 Rd

R O S E D A L E

241 St
241 St
242 St
243 St
241-02
149 Av
253-02
148 Dr
Hungry
Harbor Rd
149 Av 262 Pl
149 Rd
149 St
149 Dr
256 St
Craft Av
254 St
255 St
257-02
258 St
259 St
259 St

Brookville

A

B

ROSEDALE RD

Brook-
lyn
Nassau

START DRIVE

Blvd

Queens County
Nassau County

HUNGRY HARBOR

RD

Quigley
Blvd
Brookville Blvd

Division
St

2 St
3 St

C

W O O D M E R E

D

BRANCH BLVD

PENINSULA BLVD

2 MILES= 3.2 KMS

END 3 MINS

2 MILES= 3.2 KMS

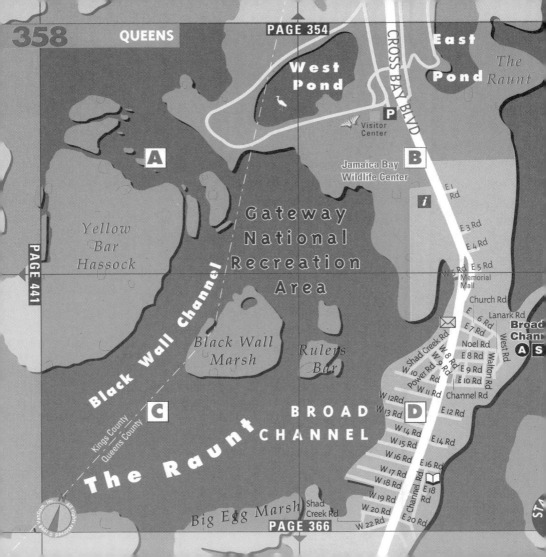

PAGE 354

CROSS BAY BLVD

West Pond

East Pond

The Raunt

P

Visitor Center

B

Jamaica Bay Wildlife Center

i

E 1 Rd

E 3 Rd

E 4 Rd

W 5 Rd   E 5 Rd

Memorial Mall

Church Rd

E 6 Rd   Lanark Rd

Broad Chan

A S

E 7 Rd

West Rd

Shad Creek Rd

Noel Rd

Power Rd   W 8 Rd   E 8 Rd

W 9 Rd   E 9 Rd

Walton Rd

W 10 Rd   E 10 Rd

W 11 Rd   Channel Rd

W 12 Rd

W 13 Rd   **D**   E 12 Rd

W 14 Rd   E 14 Rd

W 15 Rd

W 16 Rd   E 16 Rd

W 17 Rd

W 18 Rd

W 19 Rd

Channel Rd

E 18 Rd

W 20 Rd   E 20 Rd

W 22 Rd

A

Yellow Bar Hassock

Black Wall Channel

Gateway National Recreation Area

Black Wall Marsh

Rulers Bar

C

Kings County
Queens County

The Raunt

BROAD CHANNEL

D

Big Egg Marsh   Shad Creek Rd

PAGE 366

PAGE 441

© 1998 Thomas Bros. Maps, Inc. ALL RIGHTS RESERVED

STA

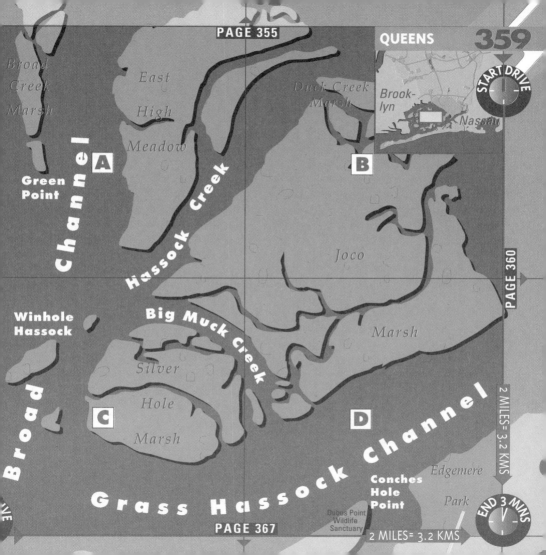

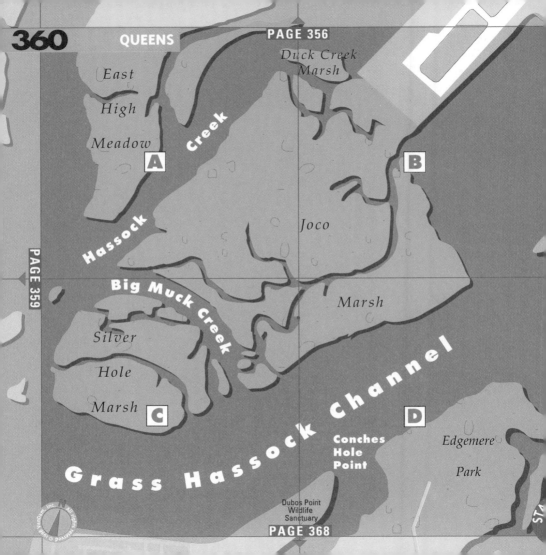

QUEENS

PAGE 356

Duck Creek
Marsh

East

High

Meadow

A

Hassock Creek

B

PAGE 359

Joco

Big Muck Creek

Marsh

Silver

Hole

Marsh **C**

Grass Hassock Channel

D

Conches
Hole
Point

Edgemere
Park

Dubos Point
Wildlife
Sanctuary

PAGE 368

ST.

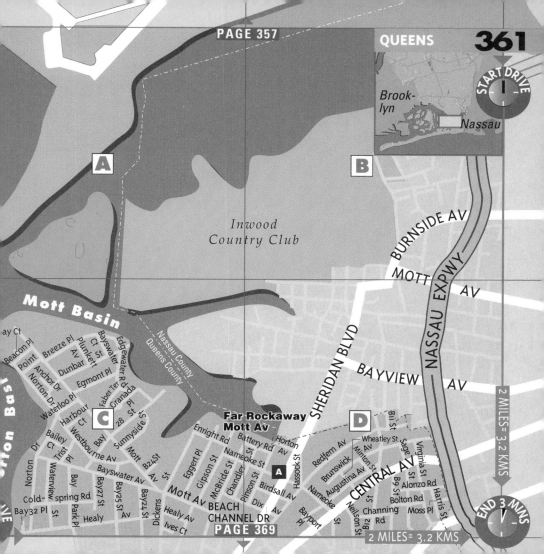

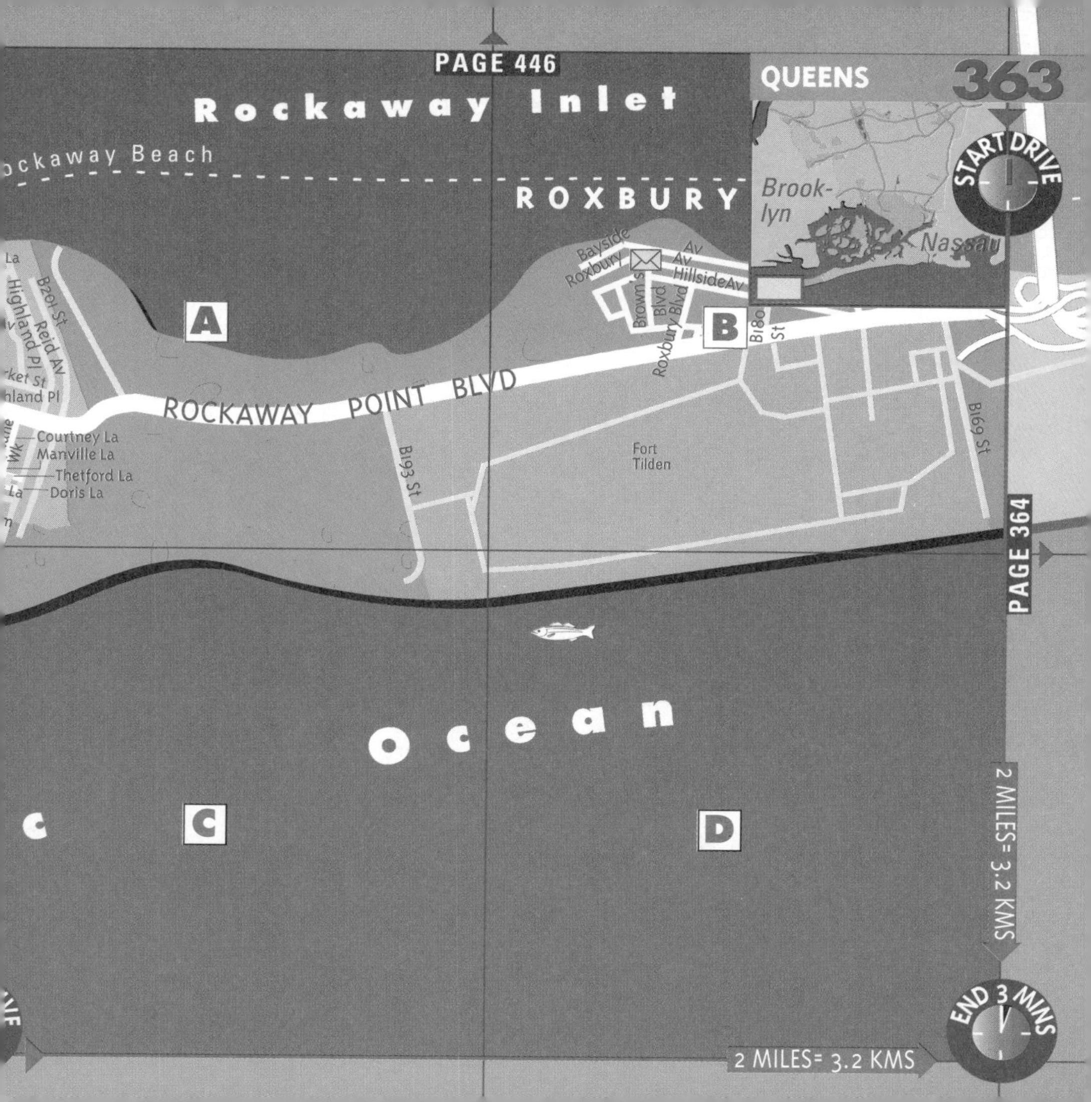

Rockaway Inlet

Rockaway Beach

ROXBURY

QUEENS

Brook-
lyn

Nassau

START DRIVE

La

B201 St

Reid Av

Highland Pl

hland Pl

ker St

A

Bayside
Roxbury St

Brown St

Roxbury Blvd

Av
Hillside Av

B

B180 St

ROCKAWAY   POINT   BLVD

Courtney La

Manville La

Thetford La

Doris La

La

B193 St

Fort
Tilden

B169 St

PAGE 364

O c e a n

C

c

D

2 MILES= 3.2 KMS

AV

END 3 MINS

2 MILES= 3.2 KMS

START DRIVE

Brook-lyn

Nassau

Beach Channel

A BEACH CHANNEL DR
Marine Park
126
120-01
502
502

B Beach 105 St
Wainwright Ct
Bl10 St
A **S**
Seaside Av

R O C K A W A Y   P A R K

Bl33 St
Bl32 St
Bl31 St
Bl30 St
Bl29 St
Bl28 St
Bl27 St
Bl26 St
Bl25 St
407
502

Rockaway Park
Beach 116 St
A **S**
113-01

Rockaway Water
Pollution Control Plant
Bl8 St
Bl7 St
Bl6 St
Bl5 St

Seaside
Rockaway
Houses
Bl02 La

Bl24 St

Bl34 St

B E L L

H A R B O R

202

Memorial Cir

Bl22 St
Bl23 St
Bl21 St
Bl20 St
Bl19 St
Bl18 St
Bl17 St
Bl16 St
Bl15 St
Bl14 St
Bl13 St
Bl12 St
Bl11 St
Bl10 St
Bl09 St

Bl06 La

Shore Front Pkwy
105-01
BOARDWALK

Ocean
Promenade
Rockaway Park

C

D

A t l a n t i c   O c e a n

way Beach

AVE

END 3 MINS

2 MILES = 3.2 KMS

2 MILES = 3.2 KMS

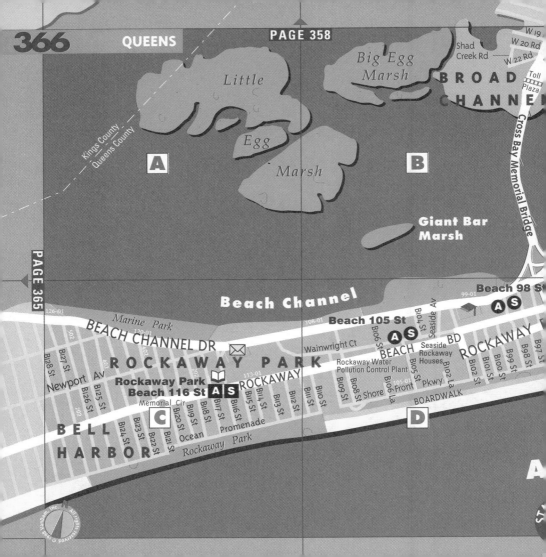

W 19
W 20 Rd
Shad
Creek Rd
W 22 Rd

*Big Egg
Marsh*

B R O A D

C H A N N E L

Toll
Plaza

Little

Egg

A

Marsh

B

Kings County
Queens County

Cross Bay Memorial Bridge

*Giant Bar
Marsh*

Beach Channel

126-01

99-01

Beach 98 St

A S

Marine Park

105-01

Beach 105 St

B104 St

Seaside Av

A S

BEACH CHANNEL DR

120-01

Wainwright Ct

BEACH

BD

A S

B105 St

B106 St

B97 St

R O C K A W A Y   P A R K

Rockaway Water
Pollution Control Plant

Seaside
Rockaway
Houses

ROCKAWAY

B98 St
B99 St
B100 St
B101 St
B102 St

Newport Av

B27 St
B28 St

B25 St
B26 St

102

ROCKAWAY

113-01

B108 St
B109 St

B107 St

B101 St
B102 St

B99 St

**Rockaway Park
Beach 116 St** A S

B11 St
B12 St

Shore
Front
Pkwy

B106 La

102

Memorial Cir

B17 St
B16 St
B15 St

C

D

BOARDWALK

B E L L

B24 St
B23 St

B20 St
B19 St
B18 St

Ocean
Promenade

H A R B O R

B22 St

B21 St

Rockaway Park

A

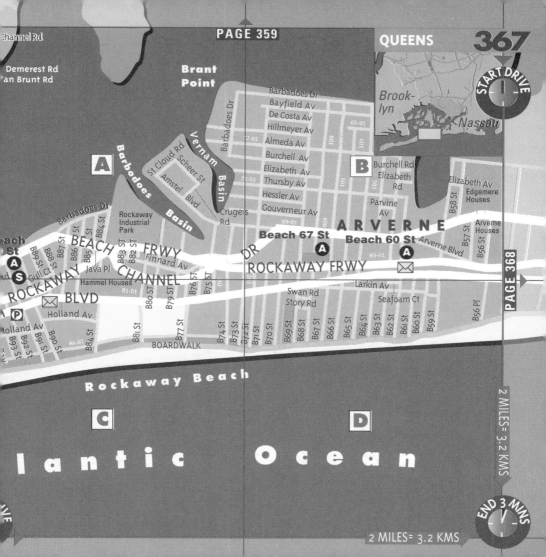

368

PAGE 360

Edgemere

Park

Dubos Point
Wildlife
Sanctuary

Basin

Conch Basin

Basin

Norton

Dr

Trist
Pl

Norton

Waterview

St

Bay
Park Pl

Cold-
spring Rd

Bay 32 Pl

Hea

B A Y S W A

Bessemund Av

DeCosta Av

65-01

601

Almeda Av

Sommerville

Basin

Bayswater

Bay31 St

Bay30 St

Cor

Burchell Rd
Elizabeth
Rd

101

Elizabeth
Av

Edgemere Houses

Elizabeth
Av

Almeda Av

Norton

Conch
Rd
Av

B

Norton

Dwight

Av

Falcon

Bay
32 St

Ocean

Beach C

Parvine
Av

B58 St

54-01

Hantz Rd

202

Norton Av

Far Rockaway

A R V E R N E

B57 St

B56 St

BEACH CHANNEL DR

B48 St

B47 St

B46 St

E D G E M E R E

38-01

BEACH C

Arverne
Houses

Peninsula
Hospital Central

Reinhart Rd

312

A

Beach 36 St

30-01

Bro

Arverne Blvd

B53 St

A

63-01

A Beach 60 St

ROCKAWAY BEACH

ROCKAWAY FRWY

A Beach 44 St

B44 Pl

B41 St

BLVD

B35 St

B31

Edgemere Rd

Seagir

Larkin Av

Seafoam Ct

B56 Pl

B54 St

B52 St

B51 St

B50 St

B49 St

B46 St

B45 St

B44 St

B43 St

B42 St

B41 St

B40 St

B39 St

B38 St

B37 St

B36 St

Lewmay

B34 St

Surf
Rd

B33 St

B32 St

B30 St

ST

B64 St

B63 St

B62 St

B61 St

B60 St

B59 St

B48 St
B48 Way
B47 St

B46 Way
B46 Pl
B47 Way

BOARDWALK

Rockaway Beach

C

D

A t l a n t i c   O c e a n

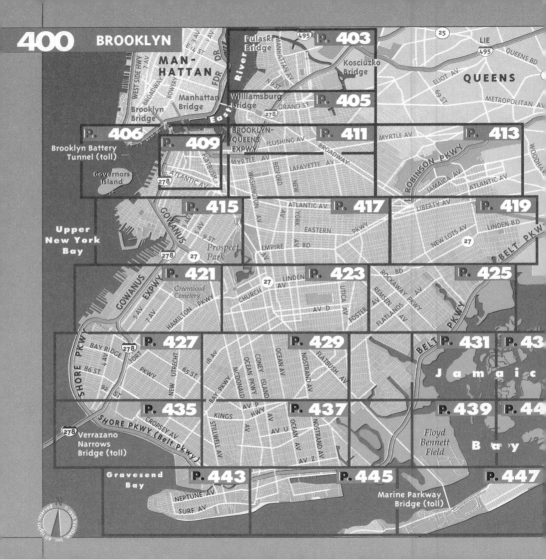

MAN-
HATTAN

QUEENS

LIE
495

25

495

ELIOT AV

METROPOLITAN AV

69 ST

WOODHA

East River

WEST SIDE HWY

7 AV

E 14 ST

E 3 AV

BROADWAY

BOWERY

FDR DR

Manhattan
Bridge

Brooklyn
Bridge

Pulaski
Bridge

Kosciuzko
Bridge

Williamsburg
Bridge

N ST

MANHATTAN AV

GRAND ST

278

MYRTLE AV

P. 406

Brooklyn Battery
Tunnel (toll)

Governors
Island

278

BROOKLYN-
QUEENS
EXPWY

FLUSHING AV

MYRTLE AV

ATLANTIC AV

FLATBUSH

BEDFORD

NEW

LAFAYETTE AV

WASHINGTON

BROADWAY

JACKIE ROBINSON PKWY

JAMAICA AV

ATLANTIC AV

Upper
New York
Bay

GOWANUS

4 AV

5 AV

9 ST

278

27

Prospect
Park

ATLANTIC AV

YORK

AV

EASTERN PKWY

EMPIRE BD

AV

LIBERTY AV

NEW LOTS AV

27

LINDEN BD

BELT PKW

GOWANUS EXPWY

5 AV

7 AV

278

Greenwood
Cemetery

HAMILTON PKWY

27

LINDEN AV

CHURCH

UTICA AV

AV D

FOSTER

ROCKAWAY PKWY

BD

REMSEN AV

FLATLANDS AV

BELT PKWY

SHORE PKWY

BAY RIDGE

4 AV

FORT

86 ST

92 ST

PKWY

NEW UTRECHT

65 ST

278

18 AV

BAY PKWY

MCDONALD

CONEY ISLAND

OCEAN PKWY

OCEAN AV

NOSTRAND AV

FLATBUSH AV

BELT

Jamaic

Verrazano
Narrows
Bridge (toll)

278

SHORE PKWY (Belt Pkwy)

CROPSEY AV

STILLWELL AV

KINGS HWY

AV P

AV U

OCEAN AV

NOSTRAND AV

AV Z

Floyd
Bennett
Field

B a y

Gravesend
Bay

NEPTUNE AV

SURF AV

Marine Parkway
Bridge (toll)

Brooklyn's Best

Brooklyn, NYC's most populous borough, is a metropolis in its own right, and home to 2.3 million people. It has been a cultural Mecca, shipping capital, ocean front resort, and the gateway to America. One could fit four Manhattans into its 81.8 sq miles of land. One out of every six Americans hails from what would still be the country's fourth largest city if it wasn't for "the mistake": the annexation by New York City in 1898.

River Café

This haute dining barge boasts the most fabulous views of Manhattan and competes with the best food palaces anywhere. Reserve. 1 Water St, 718-522-5200. **407A**

Botanic Garden

50 acres of flora plus the largest public rose and bonsai collections in the country. 1000 Washington Av, 718-622-4433. **416C**

Brooklyn Museum of Art

The museum's permanent collection includes paintings and sculpture by Rodin, Modigliani, Degas, Monet, Chagall, Gauguin, Sargent, Bierstadt, plus one of the foremost collections of Egyptian art. 200 Eastern Pkwy, 718-638-5000. **416A**

The Brooklyn Museum by McKim, Mead & White

BAM

The loadstar of the avant-garde performing arts scene is an annual rite and de rigueur for New Yorkers in the mix. The careers of composer Philip Glass, multimedia artist Laurie Anderson and choreographers Mark Morris and Bill T. Jones were launched here under the auspices of BAM's Next Wave Festival and visionary impressario, Harvey Lichtenstein. Brooklyn Academy of Music 30 Lafayette St, 718-636-4100. **407D**

mpressariocing

Peter Luger

Candle-lit antebellum atmosphere, and the best steaks around. Cash only. Reservations are essential. 178 Broadway at Driggs Av, 718-387-7400. **404A**

Prospect Park

America's leading landscape architects, Olmsted & Vaux, designed this urban oasis. The arch, by John Duncan, was built in honor of the Union Army in 1870. Flatbush Av & Plaza Street. **416B**

Grand Army Arch

PAGE 308

PAGE 119

HUNTE

LONG ISLAND EX

Pulaski Bridge

Newtown Cre

East River

River

Queens County
Kings County

New York County
Kings County

Circle Line

Greenpoint Piers

A

Ash St

Commercial St
Clay
Box
St
St

Dupont St

Eagle St

Freeman St

West St

FRANKLIN ST

MANHATTAN

Paidge Av

MCGUINESS BD

B

Green St

Huron St

India St

Java St

Kent St

Provost St

Kingsland

GREENPOINT

St

Russell St

Greenpoint Av

A

Milton St

Noble St

Oak St

B

Calyer St

Quay St

G **Greenpoint Av**

AV

Calyer

GREENPOINT

Jewel St

Moultrie St

Av

Diamond

McGuiness Blvd S

Norman St

Newel St

Eckford St

Nassau

HUMBOLDT ST

Mo
Me

Leonard

Lorimer St

Guernsey St

Clifford Pl

Bushwick Inlet

P Meserole Av

Banker St

Gem N

Dobbin St

N 14 St

N 13 St

N 12 St

N 11 St

N 10 St

C

KENT AV

Wythe Av

N 9 St

N 8 St

N 7 St

N 6 St

N 5 St

N 4 St

N 3 St

N 1 St

River St

Metropolitan

Grand St

BERRY ST

N 9 ST

NORTH SIDE

L **Bedford Av**

Oznots

D

McCarren Park

G **Nassau Av**

Driggs Av

Broome St

Engert Av

Newton St

T Raymond
Nutley Square

Bayard St

Mt Carmel Square

Roebling

BROOKLYN-QUEEN

33

R

PAGE 404

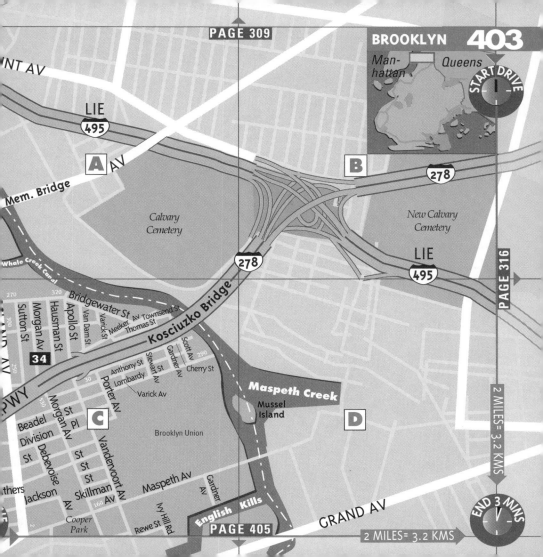

NT AV

LIE
495

Man-
hattan   Queens

START DRIVE
I

A AV

B

278

Mem. Bridge

Whale Creek Canal

Calvary
Cemetery

New Calvary
Cemetery

LIE
495

278

PAGE 316

270   320
Bridgewater St

Van Dam St

Varick St

Meeker AV Townsend St

Thomas St

300

Morgan Av

Sutton St

Hausman St

Apollo St

Kosciuzko Bridge

Scott Av

290

Gardner Av

Stewart Av

Cherry St

2 MILES = 3.2 KMS

34

PWY

250

Anthony St

Porter Av

Lombardy

Varick Av

30

C

Beadel

Division

St

Debevoise

thers

Jackson

Morgan Av

St

St

St

St

Pl

Vanderwoort Av

Av

160

Skillman Av

Maspeth Av

Maspeth Creek

Mussel
Island

D

Brooklyn Union

Gardner
Av

Cooper
Park

Rewe St

Ivy Hill Rd

English Kills

PAGE 405

GRAND AV

END 3 MINS

2 MILES= 3.2 KMS

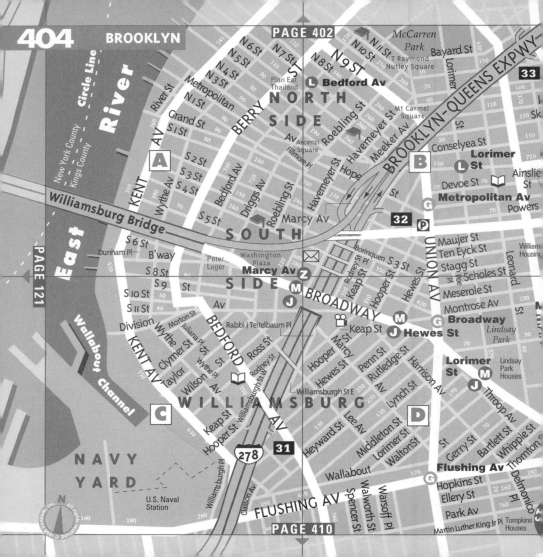

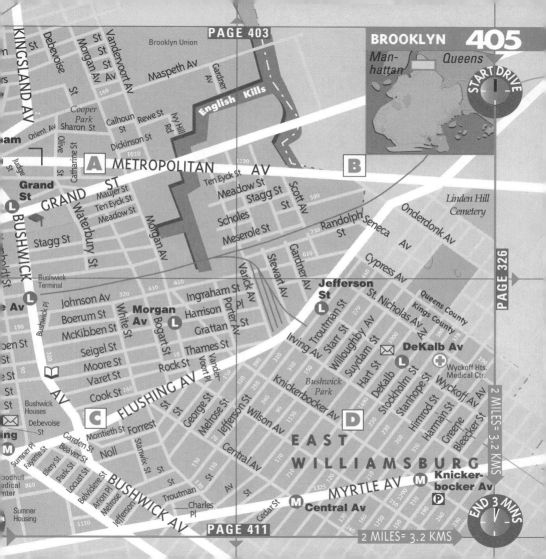

PAGE 104

River
Bargemus
Old F

Liberty & Ellis
Island Ferries

*Battery
Park*

A

Governors
Island
Ferry

B

FULTON
FERRY

East River

Brooklyn
Heights
Promenade

Brooklyn

2

3

4

5

Staten
Island
Ferry

Carder Rd

Castle
Williams

Hay
Rd

**Governors
Island**

Wheeler Av

Gresham Rd

Craig Rd N

Early Bird Rd

C

Division Rd

Enright Rd

Craig Rd S

Tango
Pier

Lima
Pier

Yankee
Pier

Fort Jay

**BROOKLYN
HEIGHTS**

New York County
Kings County

6

7

8

9A

9B

27   🛡 **278**

Long Island
College Hospital

Furman St

Columbia Pl

Willow Pl

D

Warren St

Baltic St

Kane St

Irving St

Sedgwick St

Degraw St

Sackett St

Union St

President St

Carroll St

Columbia St

Tiffany Pl

Van Brunt St

Hicks St

Cheever Pl

Warren St

HENRY

Strong P

BOE

Brooklyn
Battery
Tunnel
(Toll)

Ferry Pl

Hamilton Av

Summit St

10

Buttermilk Channel

PAGE 414

220

150

220

PAGE 407

East River

Brooklyn Heights Promenade

Brooklyn Heights Promenade

Brooklyn Heights Promenade

BROOKLYN BRIDGE

28

Old Fulton St

Poplar St

Prospect

St → Pedestrian Walkway Access

Pearl St

Middagh St

Cranberry St

Ⓐ Ⓒ **High St**

Brooklyn Bridge

Ⓐ Ⓒ **High St**

Orange St

Red Cross Pl

2

Pineapple St

Brooklyn War Memorial

A

3

Heights

90

Pineapple Wk

B

Bridge Plaza

Eastern Athletic Club

BACA

Clark St

2 **3**

Clark St

Parkes Cadman Plaza

Pedestrian Walkway

4

B R O O K L Y N

Sterling Pl

Columbia Park

Willow

College Pl

Love La

P

Monroe Pl

H E I G H T S

Cadman Plaza E

Walt Whitman Park

PLAZA WEST

U.S. District Court

5

Brooklyn Business Library

TILLARY ST

NY

Pierrepont St

410

NYS Appellate Court

Johnson St

M

Pierrepont St

Montague Ter

Montague St

150

Brooklyn Historical Society

Surrogates & Family Court

NY Marriott Brooklyn

Remsen St

Ⓝ Ⓡ

St. Ann's Center

Grace Ct

Court St

Grace Ct Alley

Hunts La

Ⓜ Ⓝ Ⓡ

Social Security

NYS Supreme Court

ADAMS ST

Pearl St

278

JORALEMON ST

Columbia Pl

Willow Pl

HICKS ST

Garden Pl

280

HENRY ST

Aitken Pl

Sidney Pl

CLINTON ST

St Francis College

Borough Hall

D

Civic Center

Br Ur

Furman St

BQE

Borough Hall

2 **3**
4 **5**

Brooklyn Law School

Red Hook La

Gage & Tollner

27

Columbia St

P

La Bouillabaisse

COURT ST

Schermerhorn St

Livingston St

120

Civil & Small Claims Court

Smith St

C

ATLANTIC AV

State

St

BOERUM PL

NY Transit Museum

220

170

Long Island College Hospital

130

Police Central Booking Criminal Court

N

Congress St

Pacific St

PAGE 406

© 1998 Vandam Inc. All rights reserved

BROOKLYN **409**
Manhattan   Queens

START WALK
1

York St

Bridge St

Gold St

York St

Farragut

Navy St

DOT Towaway Lot

Brooklyn Navy Yard Industrial Park

Sands St

29

Housing

29A

BROOKLYN-QUEENS EXPWY

A

Nassau St   Flushing Av

B

ncord St

Duffield St

Gold St

Prince St

Commodore J Barry Park

N Elliot Pl

N Portland Av

N Oxford St

Cumberland St

el St

ral Pl

lin Park

St

RIDGE

190

40

140

Park Av

29B

Navy St

FORT

Cumberland Hospital

GREENE

I College

RO

H

Tech Pl

Raymond Ingersoll Houses

Auburn Pl

Walt Whitman Houses

70

90

110

380

PAGE 410

Polytechnic University

Fire Dept HQ

Brooklyn Chamber

F

lawrence

Duffield St

Bridge St

MYRTLE AV

Fair Pl

Fleet

University Towers Housing

Kings View Housing

St Edwards St

Fort Greene Park

D

Washington Park

Carlton Av

Adelphi St

Clermont Av

160

380

1 MILE = 1.6 KMS

FLATBUSH AV EXT

Metro-Tech BID

LLOUGHBY ST

N **R** Lawrence St

C

University Plaza

Long Island University (Brooklyn Campus)

Ashland Pl

Brooklyn Downtown

S Portland Av

S Oxford St

150

190

210

230

2 **3** Hoyt St

MALL

Albee Sq W

Albee Sq

Junior's

D **M** **N**

Thelma Hill Performing Arts Center

Hudson Av

Rockwell Pl

P

Brooklyn Tech

Ft Greene Pl

S Elliott Av

De Kalb Av

Hoyt St

Elm Pl

Bond St

Q **R** De Kalb Av

City Tax Offices

IRS DMV

St Felix St

2 **3** Nevins

4 **5** St

END 20 MINS

1 MILE = 1.6 KMS

Moore St 📖 Moore St PAGE 405

Varet St   Varet St

Cook St   Cook St

Bushwick Houses

Throop Av

Bartlett St

Whipple St

Thornton St

ing Av

s St

Delmonico Pl

Flushing Av Ⓙ

FLUSHING AV

Wilson Av

George St

Melrose St

Jefferson St

Central Av

Montieth St   Forrest

Garden St   Noll

Beaver St

Starwix St

St

Debevoise St

✉

Sumner Pl

Fayette St

Ellery St

Park St

Locust St

Belvidere St

Arion Pl

Melrose

Jefferson

BUSHWICK

Av

Troutman

St

St

Charles Pl

MYRTLE Ⓜ Central Av

B Av

Woodhull Medical Center ➕

A

Sumner   Housing

King Jr Pl

Tompkins Houses

kton St

Myrtle Av Ⓙ Ⓜ Ⓩ

Ditmas St

Willoughby St

Suydam St

Hart St

Lawton St

Dodworth St

Cedar St

Evergreen Av

Kosciusko St

B U S H W I C K

Menahan St

Grove St

PAGE 412

Vernon Av

Willoughby Av

Hart St

Eleanor Roosevelt Housing

Kosciusko St Ⓙ

Kosuth Pl

Lafayette Av

Van Buren St

Greene

Goodwin Pl

BROADWAY

Myrtle Av Willoughby Av

Pulaski St

DE KALB AV

Kosciusko St

✉

LAFAYETTE AV

Brevoort Housing

Van Buren St

Stuyvesant

MALCOLM X BLVD

Patchen Av

P 🅿

Gates St Ⓩ Ⓙ

ON

Tompkins Park

P 🅿 Greene Av

Throop Av

Tompkins Av

Marcus Garvey Blvd

Lewis Av

Av

Av

Av

Lexington

Quincy St

Gates Av

Monroe St

C

Madison St

Putnam Av

Jefferson Av

Hancock St

Halsey St

Macon St

B E D F O R D

S T U Y V E S A N T

D

Ralph Av

Howard Av

MacDonough St

Decatur St

2 MILES = 3.2 KMS

END 3 MINS

2 MILES = 3.2 KMS

📖 PAGE 417

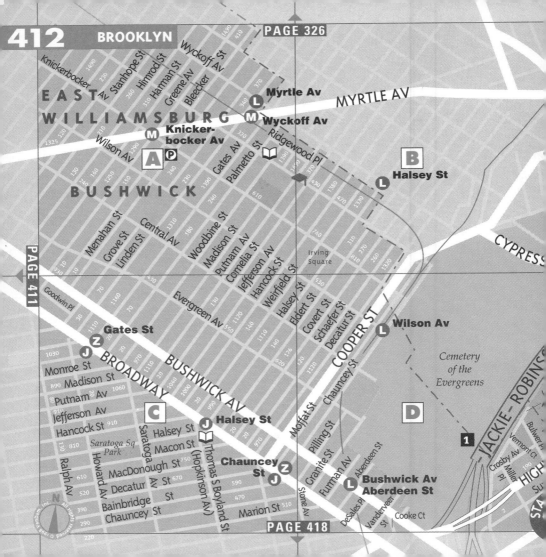

PAGE 326

Knickerbocker Av

Wyckoff Av

Wyckoff St

Stanhope St

Himrod St

Harman St

Greene Av

Bleecker

Myrtle Av

MYRTLE AV

E A S T

W I L L I A M S B U R G

Wyckoff Av

Wilson Av

Ridgewood Pl

Knicker-bocker Av

A P

Gates Av

Palmetto St

B

Halsey St

B U S H W I C K

Menahan St

Central Av

Grove St

Linden St

Woodbine St

Madison St

Putnam Av

Cornelia St

Jefferson Av

Hancock St

Weirfield St

Halsey St

Eldert St

Covert St

Schaefer St

Decatur St

Chauncey St

Irving Square

CYPRESS

Evergreen Av

Goodwin Pl

Gates St

J Z

Monroe St

Madison St

Putnam Av

Jefferson Av

Hancock St

BROADWAY

BUSHWICK AV

COOPER ST

Wilson Av
L

Cemetery
of the
Evergreens

D

JACKIE - ROBINSO

1

Moffat St

Granite St

Pilling St

Furman Av

Aberdeen St

Vermont Ct

Crosby Av

Bulwer

C

Saratoga Sq
Park

Ralph Av

Howard Av

Saratoga

Halsey St

Macon St

MacDonough St

Decatur

St

Bainbridge

Chauncey St

Thomas S Boyland St
(Hopkinson Av)

Halsey St
J

Chauncey St
Z
J

Marion St

Stone Av

DeSales Pl

Vanderveer St

**Bushwick Av
Aberdeen St**
L

Cooke Ct

HIGH

STA

PAGE 411

PAGE 418

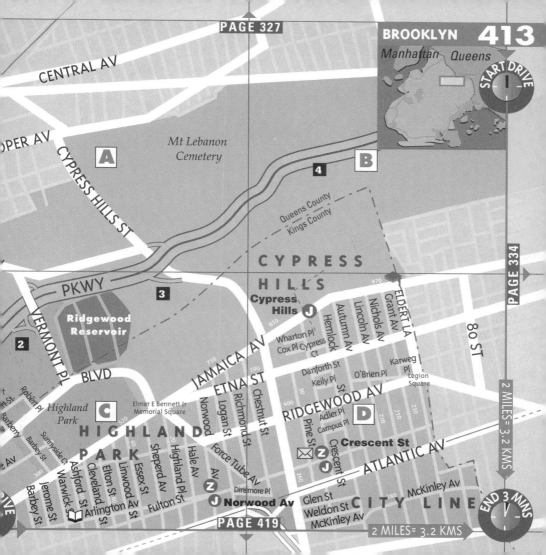

BROOKLYN **413**

Manhattan Queens

START DRIVE

CENTRAL AV

PER AV

Mt Lebanon Cemetery

A

CYPRESS HILLS ST

4

B

Queens County
Kings County

PKWY

3

PAGE 334

C Y P R E S S

H I L L S

Cypress Hills

J

Ridgewood Reservoir

VERMONT PL

2

970

ELDERT LA

80 ST

Grant Av
Nichols Av
Lincoln Av
Autumn Av
Hemlock

Wharton Pl
Cox Pl Cypress
Ct

JAMAICA AV

ETNA ST

BLVD

Robert Pl

Highland Park

C

Elmer E Bennett Jr Memorial Square

Norwood

Logan St

Richmond St

Chestnut St

710

190

Danforth St
Keily Pl

St

O'Brien Pl

Karweg
Pl
Legion
Square

RIDGEWOOD AV

D

Adler Pl
Campus Pl

210 210 210

400

30

H I G H L A N D

P A R K

Sunnyside Ct
Barbey St

320

Ashford St

Elton St
Linwood St

Shepherd Av

Essex St

Highland Pl

Hale Av

Force Tube Av

Av

Pine St

Crescent St

Crescent St

✉ **Z**

Z
J

ATLANTIC AV

240

Jerome St
Warwick St
Barbey St

Cleveland St
Arlington St

Fulton St

Z

Dinsmore Pl

J Norwood Av

Glen St
Weldon St
McKinley Av

180

McKinley Av

C I T Y   L I N E

END 3 MINS

2 MILES = 3.2 KMS

2 MILES = 3.2 KMS

Buttermilk Channel

10
12

Atlantic Basin

PAGE 406

Summit St

Carroll St

26

278

HENRY ST

CLINTON St

Douglass St

Smith St

Degraw

Sackett St

Union St

President St

Baisley House

Pioneer St

King St

Imlay St

Bowne St

Seabring St

Commerce St

Coles St

Toll Plaza

150
220

Court St

240

210

Carroll St

F G

C A R R O L L

Sullivan St

Ferris St

39

Coffey St

41

VAN BRUNT ST

Delavan St

Verona St

Woodhull St

2 Pl

3 Pl

Rapelye St

4 Pl

70

G A R D E N S

3 St

Richards St

Wolcott St

Dikeman St

A

Visitation Pl

Red Hook Park

Huntington

Luquer

B

St

Smith St

Nelson St

5 St

Demer Pl

4 St

R E D
H O O K

Dwight

Conover St

Reed St

Columbia St

W 9 St

60

Mill St

St

Smith St
9 St

Canal

6 St Basin

7 St Basin

44

46

20

Van Dyke St

Beard St

Sigourney

Creamer

Lorraine St

Hicks

Centre

Bush St

F G

Garnet St

St

9 ST

Otsego St

Halleck St

Halleck St

Henry

Clinton

Bay St

St

Hamilton Pl

9

Breakwater Terminal

Columbia St

Port Auth Grain Terminal

Bryant St

Court St

Court St

Percival St

Gowanus

Hamilton Av

1

GOWANUS EXPWY

2A

M

Erie Basin

C

20 St

21 St

23 St

2

D

23

N

R

2B

18 St

Gowanus Bay

29 St

30 St

31 St

33 St

35 St

200

210

19 St

20 St

21 St

22 St

210

23 St

278

STA

PAGE 420

Manhattan   Queens

MALCOM X BLVD

Lewis Av

Lewis Av

Bainbridge St

Fulton Chauncey St
Park

Marion St

Hattie Jones Ct

Ⓐ Ⓒ FULTON ST

Utica Av

faith
pital and
lical Center

Jewell McKoy La

ATLANTIC   AV

A

Brevoort
Housing

Ralph Av

Chauncey St

Marion St

Sumpter St

Ralph Av

MacDougal

Saratoga Av

Ⓐ Ⓒ ✉

O C E A N   H I L L

Hunterfly Pl

Suydam Pl

Kane Pl

Columbus Pl

Prescott Pl

Bancroft Pl

Dewey Pl
Louis Pl

🅿

Roosevelt Pl

B

Rockaway Av

W E E K S V I L L E

Weeksville
Society

Kingsborough
Housing

🅿

*St Johns
Park*

Troy Av

Schenectady Av

Utica Av

St Mary's
Hospital ✚

Rochester Av

Buffalo Av

Ralph Av

Howard Av

Saratoga Av

Hopkinson Av

PKWY

YORK AV

🅿

Howard
Housing

B R O W N S V I L L E

PAGE 418

ERN PKWY
TE

3 **4**

Utica Av

Ford St

*Lincoln
Terrace
Park*

Portal St

Union St

EASTERN

EAST   NEW

Pitkin Av

Amboy St

Strauss St

Herzl St

KINGS

Grafton Av

Legion St

Saratoga Av

Bristol ✉ St

Chester St

Thatford St
Rockaway Av

Sutter Av

Tapscott St

Union St

E A S T

C

RE BLVD

S E N

L A G E

Kingsbrook
Jewish
Medical
Center ✚

E 49 St

E 48 St

UTICA AV

REMSEN AV

ROCK-

Rutland

Winthrop St

105 Av

Clarkson

Rutland Rd

F L A T B U S H

Sutter Av
Rutland Rd **3**

3

**Saratoga
Av**

Blake
Square

Blake Av

Howard Av

Howard
Gardens

D

Dumont Av

Livonia Av

Hopkinson Av

Riverdale Av

Newport St

END 3 MINS

AWAY PKWY

Lenox
Rd

2 MILES= 3.2 KMS

2 MILES= 3.2 KMS

PAGE 423

Z J Norwood Av

PAGE 413

C I T Y   L I N E

BROOKLYN 419

Manhattan *Queens*

START DRIVE

Weldon St
McKinley Av
Hill St

Wells St

A Grant Av

A C Euclid Av

C Shepherd Av

N Conduit Av

S Conduit Av

EUCLID AV

A

Berriman St
Sheperd Av
Atkins Av
Milford St
Logan St
Fountain Av
Crystal St
Chestnut St
Doscher St

Linwood St
Belmont Av
Essex St

P

Pine St
Crescent St
Hemlock St
Autumn Av
Lincoln Av
Sheridan Av
Grant Av
Eldert La
Forbell St
Drew St
Ruby St

Emerald St

Amber St

B

Sutter Av

Blake Av

Dumont Av

Pitkin Av
Subway
Yards

Cypress
Hills
Housing

N E W   Y O R K

LINDEN BLVD

New Lots
Av

Logan St
Milford St
Montauk Av
Atkins Av
Berriman St
Sheperd Av
Essex St
Linwood St
Elton Av
Cleveland St
Hartford St
Bremen St

Fountain Av

(27)

C

Louis H Pink

Loring Av

Euclid Av
Holly St

Stanley Av

Hemlock St

Lincoln Av

Sheridan Av

Housing

D Wortman Av

Queens County
Kings County

Boulevard

Stanley Av

Old Mill Rd

Wortman Av

Cozine Av

Cozine Av

Flatlands Av

Flatlands Av

157 Av

Housing

PAGE 425

PAGE 342

2 MILES = 3.2 KMS

END 3 MINS

2 MILES= 3.2 KMS

Gowanus

Bay

35 St

39 St   36 St

7

6

5

Bush Terminal Docks

Marginal St

34

37 St

39 St

40 St

44 St

250

250

Ferry

57 St

4

3

2

I

1A

Lutheran
Medical
Center

52 St

250

250

1 AV

54 St

76

2 AV

58 St

250

250

3 AV

GOWANUS EXPWY

250

440

46 St

47 St

48 St

49 St

50 St

51 St

N R 53 St

53 St

440

54 St

55 St

56 St

57 St

4 AV

5 AV

6 AV

540

540

540

N R

C

M Bay Ridge

1

745

253

D

N R 59 St

59 St

60 St

61 St

440

62 St

63 St

64 St

440

540

540

540

540

650

65 St

Owls
Head
Park

Sedgwick Pl

Bergen Pl

Wakeman Pl

Shore Rd

67 St

68 St

N

P

278

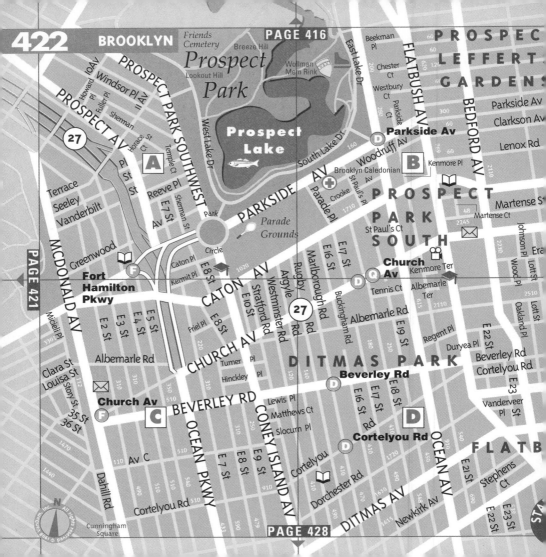

Manhattan   Queens

START DRIVE
1

Fenimore St
Hawthorne St
Winthrop St

Winthrop St
690

Kings County Hospital

Kingsbrook Jewish Medical Center

Kingsboro Psychiatric Center

Health Science Center SUNY

A

(27)

Fairview Pl
Raleigh Pl

LINDEN BLVD

B

Ralph Av

ch Av

CHURCH AV

CHURCH AV

E 31 St
E 32 St

E 34 St
E 35 St
Brooklyn Av
E 37 St
E 38 St
E 39 St
Snyder Av
E 40 St
Albany Av
E 42 St
E 43 St
Troy Av
E 45 St
E 46 St
Schenectady Av
E 48 St
E 49 St

E 51 St
E 52 St
E 53 St
E 54 St
E 55 St

E 58 St
E 59 St

UTICA AV

Tilden Av

Beverly Rd

E 56 St

E 57 St

Av

P

Holy Cross Cemetery

NEW YORK AV

Beverley Rd

CLARENDON RD

KINGS HWY

PAGE 424

F A R R A G U T

Newkirk Av

E 28 St
E 29 St

C

AV D

Newkirk Av
Victor Rd

Brooklyn Av

E 37 St

E 38 St
E 39 St

E 40 St
Albany Av
E 42 St
E 43 St

Foster Av

Troy Av
E 45 St
E 46 St

D

Jodie Ct

Whitty La

2 MILES = 3.2 KMS

H

TER AV

E 27 St

Farragut Pl

Brooklyn Rd

Paerdegat Park

Farragut Rd

Harwood Pl

FOSTER AV

END 3 MINS

2 MILES= 3.2 KMS

PAGE 418

PAGE 423

PAGE 431

Willmohr St
Hopkinson Av
Lott Av
Chester St
Rockaway Av
Thatford Av
Watkins St
Osborn St
Sackman St
Herzl St
Amboy St
Bristol St
Hegeman St
Hegeman Av
LINDEN BLVD
Georgia
Malta St
Anna Ct
Will Pl
De Witt Av
Church Av
Abraham Miller Square
LINDEN
Brookdale Hospital
Brookdale Plaza
BLVD
27
E 105 Wk
Bank St
Stanley Av
Williams Av
Louisie
Breukelen Housing
A
ROCKAWAY PKWY
Av A
E 92 St
E 91 St
Av B
E 95 St
E 96 St
E 94 St
E 93 St
Av
Ditmas
E 89 St
E 88 St
E 87 St
E 86 St
Coventry Rd
Av D
Ames La
Kyler Pl
Nolans La
Rockaway
E 101 St
E 100 St
E 101 Av
B
E 105 St
E 105 St
E 108 St
Turnbull
E 107 St
E 106 St
Flatla
E 104 St
Dorset St
Branton St
Ralph Av
Pieter Claesen Wyckoff House Museum
Chase Ct
Preston Ct
Brooklyn Terminal Market
Av D
Bedell La
Bayview Pl
School La
Farragut Rd
Smiths La
Glenwood Rd
Conklin Av
Rockaway Pkwy Canarsie
L
FLATLANDS AV
Trucklemans La
E 103 St
E 102 St
E 101 St
E 100 St
E 99 St
Tiemans La St
E 98 St
FOSTER AV
C
E 59 St
E 82 St
E 80 St
E 79 St
E 78 St
E 71 St
E 76 St
Varkens Hook Rd
E 89 St
E 88 St
E 87 St
E 86 St
E 85 St
E 84 St
E 83 St
Durland Pl
Skidmore
Hoyt La
La
Av J
E 95 St
E 94 St
E 93 St
Av K
D
Holmes La
E 96 St
E 92 St
E 91 St
Church La
REMSEN AV
Canarsie Cemetery
Stillwells Pl
Av L
CANARS
Av M
Rost Pl
Kaufman Pl
Av N

Manhattan   Queens

START DRIVE

Wortman Houses

Wortman AV

Schenck Av

Cozine Av

Flatlands Av

Linden Houses

Vermont St

Vandalia Av

S P R I N G   C R E E K

NYS Office
of Mental Retardation and
Developmental Disabilities

Erskine St

Dale Pl

Ardsley Loop

AV

Van Siclen Av

Bethel Loop

A

Vandalia

Schenck Av

Walker St

Elton St

Seaview Av

Seaview Loop

St

B

Croton Loop

Delmar Loop

Elmira Loop

Schroeders Av

S T A R R E T T
C I T Y

Twin Pines Dr

Freeport Loop

Geneva Loop

Seaview Av

Spring Creek
Park
(no access)

PAGE 348

F4 St

F5 St

F6 St

Homell Loop

F7 St

F8 St

Border Av

F r e s h   C r e e k

14

D

2 MILES= 3.2 KMS

F9 St

F10 St

C

Seaview Av

B E L T   P K W Y

Basin

N o r t h   C h a n n e l

Bayview
Houses

E l d e r s
P o i n t
M a r s h

END 3 MINS

2 MILES= 3.2 KMS

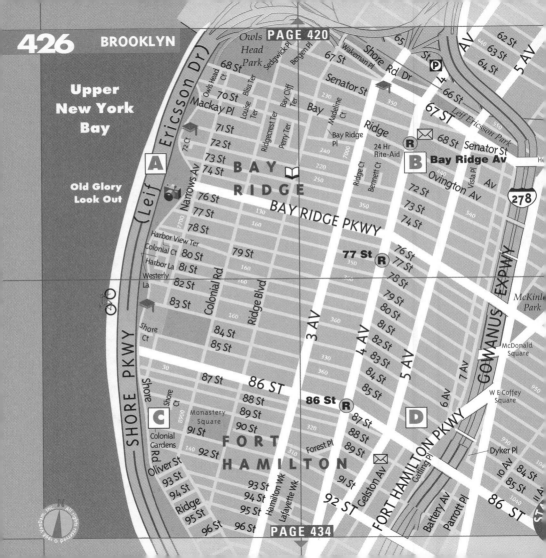

Upper
New York
Bay

Old Glory
Look Out

Owls
Head
Park

PAGE 420

Leif Ericsson Dr

68 St
70 St
Mackay Pl
71 St
72 St
73 St
74 St

Owls Head Ct
Bliss Ter
Louise Ter
Ridgecrest Ter
Perry Ter
Bay Cliff Ter

72 Ct

A

B A Y

R I D G E

Narrows Av

76 St
77 St
78 St

Harbor View Ter
Colonial Ct
Harbor La
Westerly La

80 St
81 St

79 St

Colonial Rd

82 St
83 St

Shore Ct

84 St
85 St

Ridge Blvd

87 St
88 St
89 St
90 St
91 St
92 St

86 ST

C

Monastery
Square

Colonial
Gardens

Oliver St

93 St
94 St
Ridge
95 St
96 St

F O R T
H A M I L T O N

Hamilton Wk
Lafayette Wk

93 St
94 St
95 St
96 St

Shore Ct

Shore

Shore Rd

SHORE PKWY

130
160
160
160
160
30
8900
140

BAY RIDGE PKWY

Bay Ridge Pl

Bay
Ridge

Madeline Ct
Bay Cliff Ter

24 Hr
Rite-Aid

Ridge Ct
Bennett Ct

Sedgwick Pl
Bergen Pl

67 St

Wakeman Pl
Senator St

65 St
4 St
66 St

62 St
63 St
64 St

5 AV

Shore Rd Dr

P

67 ST

Leif Ericsson Park

230
350
1700
7000
240
220
250

R

68 St
Senator St

B **Bay Ridge Av**

Ovington Av

Vista Pl
Av

72 St
73 St
74 St

350

540

77 St R

76 St
77 St
78 St
79 St
80 St
81 St
82 St
83 St
84 St
85 St

3 AV

4 AV

5 AV

6 AV

7 AV

350
360
130
360
230

He

278

GOWANUS EXPWY

McKinley
Park

McDonald
Square

W E Coffey
Square

86 St R

87 St
88 St
89 St

91 St

Forest Pl

Gatling Pl

Celston Av

92 ST

D

FORT HAMILTON PKWY

Dyker Pl

Battery Av
Parrott Pl

9 AV
10 AV

84 St
85 St

86 ST

950
1040
320
310

PAGE 434

PAGE 428

8 Av

8 Av

A

Fort
Hamilton Pkwy

FORT HAMILTON PKWY

Leif
Ericsson
Square

Bocchino D
Memorial Plaza

49 St

50 St

52 St
53 St
54 St
55 St

50 St
51 St

55 St

B

56 St
57 St
58 St
59 St
60 St
61 St

11 AV
12 AV
13 AV
14 AV
15 AV
16 AV
17 AV

62 St

63 St

Tabor Ct

New
Utrecht Av

62 St

64 St

Regina
Opera

65 ST

66 St

67 St

Ovington Av

Bay Ridge Av

70 St

71 St

72 St

73 St

74 St

RIDGE PKWY

YKER

EIGHTS

C

76 St

77 St

78 St

79 St

80 St

81 St

82 St

83 St

NEW UTRECHT AV

Dunyea Ct

Ovington Ct

71 St

D

Wallaston Ct
Cameron Ct

18 Av

NEW UTRECHT

68 St

END 3 MINS

2 MILES = 3.2 KMS

Manhattan   Queens

START DRIVE

FOSTER AV

Stephens Ct

690

E 27 St

554

561

Farragut Pl   Brooklyn Rd

3310

Farragut Rd

Av

OCEAN AV

Farragut Rd

539

2690

2610

Kenilworth Pl

Amersfort Pl

Brooklyn Rd

Flatbush Av Brooklyn College

572

793

742

650

520

Glenwood Rd

Av H

820

2 **5**

Glenwood Rd

1639

940

940

870

Glenwood Rd

A

Rd

Campus Rd

Hillel Pl

740

750

1650

FLATBUSH AV

B

E 45 St

Troy Av

980

590

1710

980

Brooklyn Center for Performing Arts

Campus

Brooklyn College

Aurelia Ct

Av I

3610

E 35 St

E 36 St

E 37 St

E 38 St

E 39 St

E 40 St

E 42 St

Albany Av

E 43 St

E 46 St

990

990

Amersfort Park

1150

E 19 St

E 18 St

E 17 St

E 21 St

E 22 St

E 23 St

E 24 St

Bedford Av

E 26 St

E 27 St

E 28 St

E 29 St

E 31 St

E 32 St

New York Av

E 34 St

1727

1050

1090

3180

1040

P

Av J

FLATLANDS

PAGE 430

1920

E 39 St

1170

120

1821

1179

1160

1270

1070

1140

Av K

Hubbard Pl

Alton Pl

E 40 St

E 41 St

M I D W O O D

1640

1190

1250

1260

1340

1130

1180

1210

1050

NOSTRAND AV

1130

1120

Av L

Overbaugh Pl

HWY

Lott Pl

Harden St

E 43 St

2110

1530

2 MILES = 3.2 KMS

KINGS

Ryder St

E 38 St

Father Kehoe Sq

Baughman Pl

1510

C

Beth Israel Kings Highway Hospital

Fraser Sq

Av M

D

AV

Coleman

Hendrickson St

nut Av

Av M

Elm Av

Dorman Square

Bay

Mansfield Pl

Delamere Pl

1250

1260

1350

1440

1380

1460

1510

Kimball St

Ryder St

1510

Av

Cedar Av

1380

AV

Olean St

1410

1510

1530

Av N

1450

FLATLANDS

E 38 St

E 37 St

E 34 St

E 33 St

E 32 St

E 31 St

E 36 St

E 35 St

Av P

Quentin Rd

1510

1600

1510

Av R

END 3 MINS

Av N

1490

1670

PAGE 437

2 MILES= 3.2 KMS

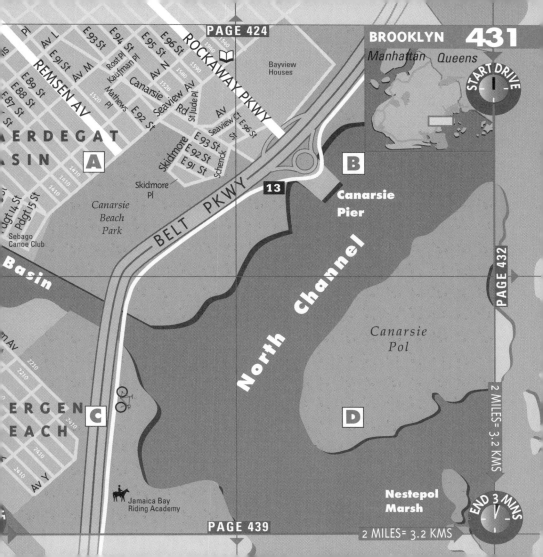

Pl
Av L
E 93 St
E 94 St
E 95 St
E 96 St

REMSEN AV
E 91 St
Av M
Rost Pl
Kaufman
Av N
Canarsie
Seaview Av
Rd
St Jude Pl
Seaview Ct
Av

ROCKAWAY PKWY

Bayview
Houses

Manhattan   Queens

START DRIVE

E 89 St
E 88 St
E 87 St
St

Mathews
E 92 St
Pl
Skidmore
E 93 St
E 92 St
E 91 St
Schenck
St

Av
E 96 St

A

ERDEGAT
ASIN

Canarsie
Beach
Park

Skidmore
Pl

13

BELT PKWY

B

**Canarsie
Pier**

Sebago
Canoe Club

Pdgt 14 St
Pdgt 15 St

Basin

North Channel

**Canarsie
Pol**

nAv

ERGEN
EACH

C

D

2 MILES= 3.2 KMS

Jamaica Bay
Riding Academy

Av Y

**Nestepol
Marsh**

END 3 MINS

2 MILES= 3.2 KMS

PAGE 425

Av L

E 93 St

E 104 St

E 103 St

E 102 St

E 101 St

E 100 St

E 99 St

E 98 St

F 9 St
F 10 St

ROCKAWAY

Av M

E 96 St

E 95 St

E 94 St

Av N

Rost Pl

Kaufman Pl

Canarsie

Seaview Av

Mathews Pl

E 92 St

Rd

St Jude Pl

Skidmore

E 91 St

Skidmore Pl

E 93 St

E 92 St

Av
Seaview Ct

Schenck St

Schenck St

E 96 St

PKWY

1540

1580

1520

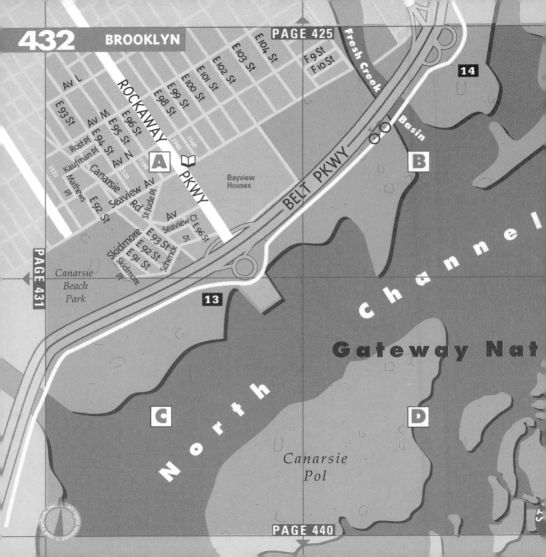

A

B

C

D

Bayview
Houses

*Canarsie
Beach
Park*

Fresh Creek

Basin

BELT PKWY

Channel

Gateway Nat

North

*Canarsie
Pol*

14

13

PAGE 431

PAGE 440

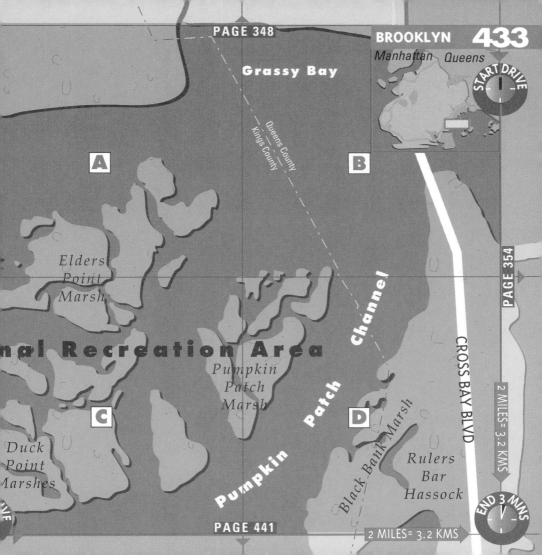

PAGE 348

Manhattan   Queens

START DRIVE

Grassy Bay

Queens County
Kings County

A

B

*Elders
Point
Marsh*

PAGE 354

al Recreation Area

*Pumpkin
Patch
Marsh*

P
u
m
p
k
i
n

P
a
t
c
h

C
h
a
n
n
e
l

CROSS BAY BLVD

2 MILES= 3.2 KMS

C

D

*Duck
Point
Marshes*

Black Bank Marsh

*Rulers
Bar
Hassock*

END 3 MINS

PAGE 441

2 MILES= 3.2 KMS

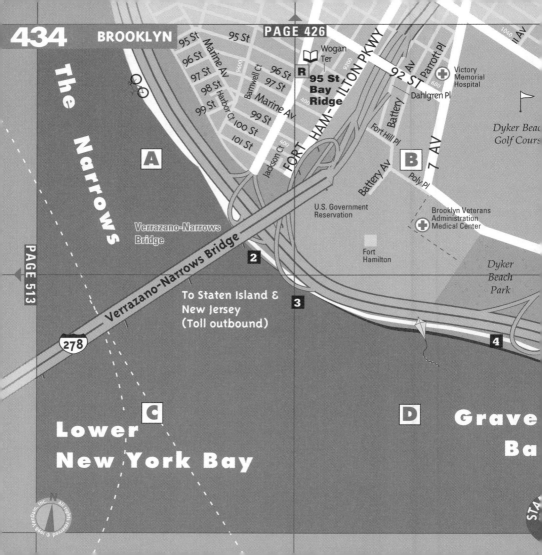

PAGE 426

95 St

95 St

96 St

97 St

98 St

99 St

Marine Av

Marine Av

Barnwell Ct

Harbor Ct

100 St

101 St

Jackson Ct

96 St

97 St

99 St

Wogan Ter

R **95 St Bay Ridge**

FORT HAMILTON PKWY

92 ST

Parrott Pl

Victory Memorial Hospital

Dahlgren Pl

Battery Av

Fort Hill Pl

7 AV

1040 = AV

Dyker Beach Golf Course

B

Battery Av

Poly Pl

A

U.S. Government Reservation

Brooklyn Veterans Administration Medical Center

The

Narrows

Verrazano-Narrows Bridge

2

Fort Hamilton

Dyker Beach Park

Verrazano-Narrows Bridge

To Staten Island & New Jersey (Toll outbound)

3

4

278

PAGE 513

C

Lower New York Bay

D

Grave

Ba

STA

N

Manhattan Queens

START DRIVE

83 St
81 St
82 St
84 St
85 St
13 Av
15 Av

B E N S O N H U R S T

86 ST

16 Av

17 Av

BAY RIDGE PKWY

72 St
73 St
74 St
76 St
77 St
78 St
79 St
80 St

NEW UTRECHT AV

79 St

Ⓑ Ⓜ

18 AV

A

B

Bay 7 St
Bay 8 St
Benson Av
Bay 10 St
Bay 11 St
Bay 13 St
Bay 14 St

16 St
Rutherford Pl
17 St

Bath Av

Ⓑ Ⓜ 18 Av

19 Av

20 AV

CROPSEY AV

Independence
Av

Bay

Bay

17 Ct

Ⓑ Ⓜ 20 Av

21 Av

BAY PKWY

23 Av

24 AV

Bay 19 St
20 St
22 St
23 St

Benson Av

Bay
Bay
Bay 25 St
Bay 26 St
Bay 28 St
Bay 29 St

Ⓟ

B A T H
B E A C H

Ⓑ Ⓜ
Bay Pkwy

Benson Av
Bath Av
Bay 35
Bay 34
Bay 37 St
Bay 38 St

25 Av

SHORE

Ⓒ

SHORE PKWY (Belt Pkwy)

20 Dr

19 La

20 La

21 Dr 21 La

Rd

Bensonhurst
Park

Bay 31 St
Bay 32 St

D

Bay 40 St

n d

Shore Rd

24 Av

END 3 MINS

5

2 MILES= 3.2 KMS

2 MILES= 3.2 KMS

PAGE 428

PAGE 435

PAGE 443

BAY RIDGE PKWY

BAY PKWY

67 St
68 St
69 St
70 St
71 St
72 St
73 St
74 St
76 St
77 St
78 St
79 St
80 St

19 AV
20 AV
21 AV

63 St
64 St
23 AV
65 ST

Bay Pkwy

Av N

Av N

Av O

Roder Av

Ryder Av

CONEY ISLAND

OCEAN
PARKWAY

Marboro
Square

Av O

Av P

Av P

W 4 St
W 3 St
W 2 St
W 1 St

Dahill Rd

Estate Rd

Quentin Rd

Av R

KINGS

24 Hr
Rite-Aid

Archie C Ketchum
Square

Kings Hwy

Quentin Rd

Kings Hwy

HWY

Woodside
Av

Kings Hwy

Billings Pl

OCEAN PKWY

Highlawn Av

Kings Pl

LLoyd Ct

Colin Pl

Av S

Applegate
Ct

Van Sicklen St
Lake St

MCDONALD

Sloan Pl

Hut
Ho

Av

81 St
82 St
83 St
84 St
85 St

23 AV
24 AV

Bay Pkwy

86 ST

STILLWELL

AV

Bay 32 St
Bay 34 St
Benson Av
Bay 35
Bay 37 St
Bay 38 St
Bath Av
Bay 40 St
25 AV
Bay 41 St
26 AV
Bay 43 St

W 13 St
W 12 St
W 11 St
W 10 St
W 9 St
W 8 St
W 7 St
W 6 St
W 5 St

Av T

Av U

25 Av

Meucci Sq

86 St

Lake Pl

Garibaldi Sq

Av V

Wolf Pl

Av W

Av U

Whitney
Pl

West St

Lady
Moody Sq

Village Rd N

Cemetery
Village Rd S

Village Ct
Village Rd E

GRAVESEND NECK

GRAVESEND

Stryker St
Stryker
Ct
Southgate Ct

E 5 St
E 4 St
E 3 St
E 1 St
E 2 St
E 7 St

Blvd
Ct

STA

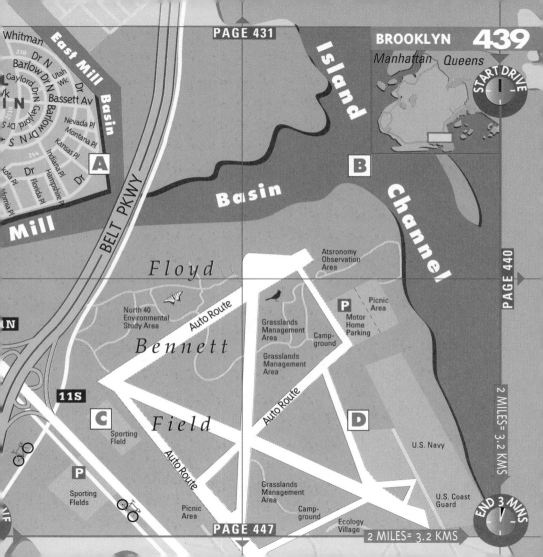

Manhattan   Queens

START DRIVE

Whitman
Dr N
Barlow Dr N
Gaylord Dr N
Bassett Av
Utah
Wk
210
Gaylord Dr N S
Barlow Dr N S
Nevada Pl
Montana Pl
Kansas Pl
Indiana Pl
Florida Pl
Hampshire Pl
Dr
254
Dr
Wk
California Pl

A

B

Island

Basin

Channel

Mill

East Mill Basin

BELT PKWY

Floyd

Atsronomy
Observation
Area

North 40
Environmental
Study Area

Auto Route

Grasslands
Management
Area

P   Picnic
Area

Motor
Home
Parking

Bennett

Grasslands
Management
Area

Camp-
ground

Auto Route

C

D

Field

11S

Sporting
Field

2 MILES = 3.2 KMS

Auto Route

U.S. Navy

P
Sporting
Fields

Picnic
Area

Grasslands
Management
Area

Camp-
ground

U.S. Coast
Guard

END 3 MINS

Ecology
Village

2 MILES= 3.2 KMS

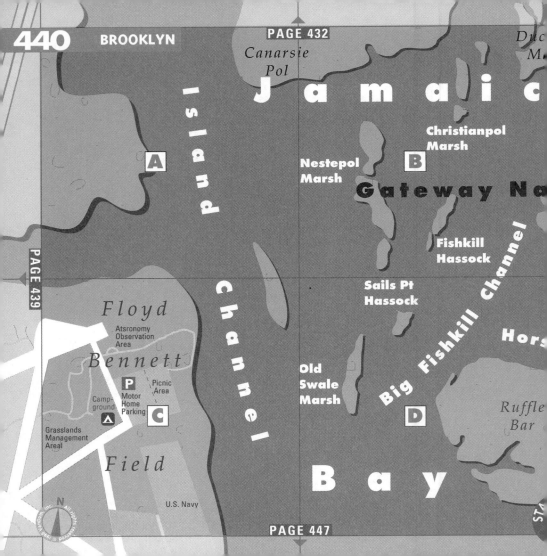

PAGE 432

Canarsie Pol

Duc M.

J a m a i c

Island

A

Christianpol Marsh

Nestepol Marsh

B

Gateway Na

Fishkill Hassock

Channel

Sails Pt Hassock

PAGE 439

Floyd

Atsronomy Observation Area

Bennett

P Picnic Area

Camp- Motor ground Home Parking

△

Grasslands Management Areal

C

Field

U.S. Navy

Old Swale Marsh

D

Big Fishkill Channel

Hors

Ruffle Bar

B a y

N

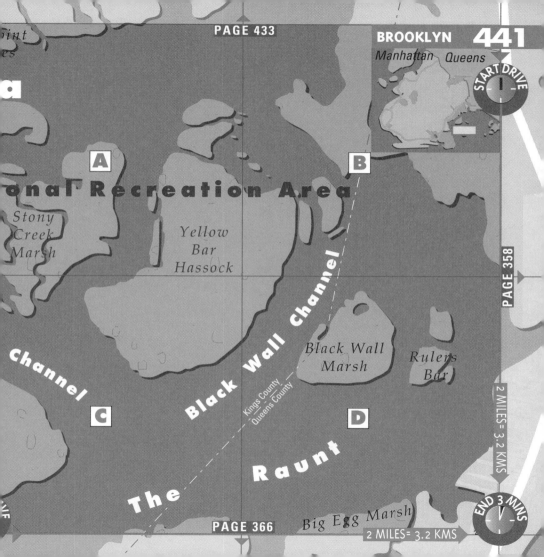

Manhattan *Queens*

START DRIVE

int
es

A

onal Recreation Area

Stony
Creek
Marsh

Yellow
Bar
Hassock

B

Black Wall Channel

Black Wall
Marsh

Rulers
Bar

Channel

C

Kings County
Queens County

D

2 MILES= 3.2 KMS

The Raunt

Big Egg Marsh

2 MILES= 3.2 KMS

END 3 MINS

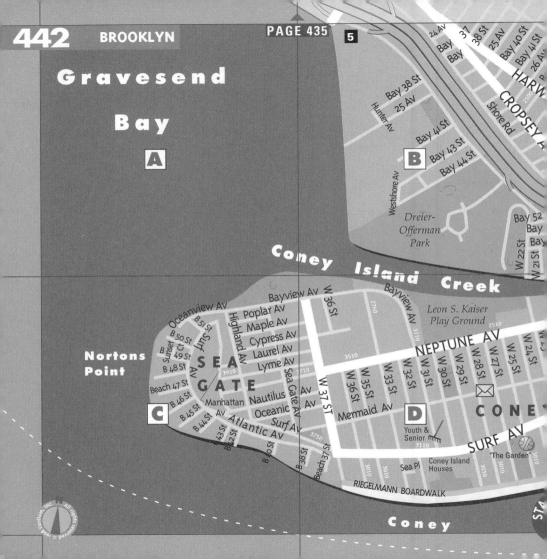

Gravesend

Bay

A

24 AV
37
38 St
25 AV
Bay 40 St
Bay 41 St
Bay
Bay
26 AV
HARW
CROPSEY A

Bay 38 St
25 AV
Hunter Av

Shore Rd

Bay 4 St
Bay 43 St
B
Bay 44 St

Westshore Av

Bay 52
Bay
Bay

Dreier-
Offerman
Park

W 22 St
W 21 St

Coney Island Creek

Bayview Av
W 36 St
Bayview Av

Leon S. Kaiser
Play Ground

2740

3110

2510

Oceanview Av
B 51 St
Poplar Av
Bayview Av
NEPTUNE AV
W 24 St
W 25 St

B 50 St
Surf St
Highland Av
Maple Av
Cypress Av
W 28 St
W 27 St

Sunset Ct
B 49 St
Laurel Av
Lyme Av
W 35 St
W 33 St
W 32 St
W 31 St
W 30 St
W 29 St

B 48 St
S E A
3910

**Nortons
Point**

Beach 47 St
G A T E

Sea Gate Av
3710
W 37 St
W 36 St

3510

C
B 46 St
Manhattan
Nautilus
CONE

B 45 St
Av
Oceanic
Mermaid Av
D

B 44 St
Surf Av
3750

B 43 St
Atlantic Av
Youth &
Senior

B 42 St
W 50 St
Beach 37 St
W 38 St
3110

SURF AV

"The Garden"

Sea Pl
Coney Island
Houses
3010

3010

3010

0310

RIEGELMANN BOARDWALK

ST 4

Coney

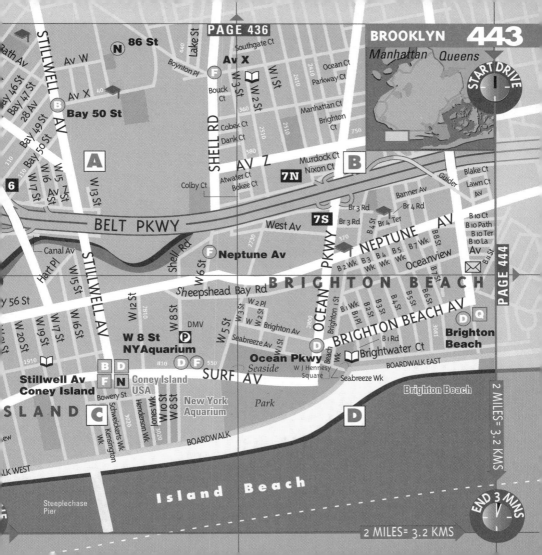

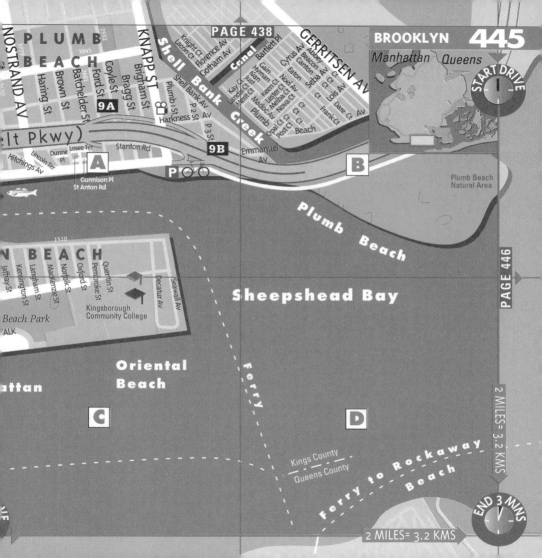

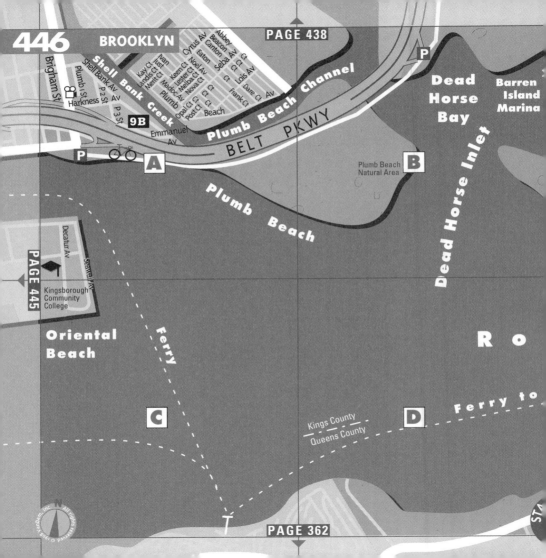

BROOKLYN

PAGE 438

Brigham St

Shell Bank Creek

Shell Bank Av

Plumb St

P 2 St

Av

P 3 St

Harkness

Cyrus Av

Abbey Ct

Beacon Av

Canton Ct

Eaton Ct

Seba Av

Kay Ct

Ivan Ct

Landis Ct

Merit Ct

Neal Av

Lester Av

Keen Ct

Madoc Av

Melba Ct

Nova Ct

Lois Av

Dare Ct

Frank Ct

Oral Ct

Post Ct

Plumb

Beach

9B

Emmanuel Av

Plumb Beach Channel

BELT PKWY

Dead Horse Bay

Barren Island Marina

P

A

B

Plumb Beach Natural Area

Plumb Beach

Dead Horse Inlet

P

PAGE 445

Decatur Av

Seawall Av

Kingsborough Community College

Oriental Beach

Ferry

C

Kings County

Queens County

D

Ferry to

R o

St

PAGE 362

N

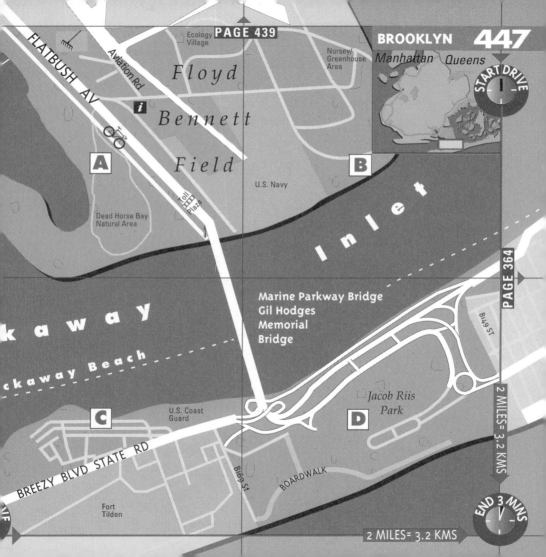

Manhattan Queens

FLATBUSH AV

Aviation Rd

Floyd

Bennett

Field

Ecology
Village

Nursey/
Greenhouse
Area

i

A

Toll
Plaza

Dead Horse Bay
Natural Area

U.S. Navy

B

Inlet

START DRIVE

PAGE 364

B149 ST

Marine Parkway Bridge
Gil Hodges
Memorial
Bridge

kaway

ckaway Beach

U.S. Coast
Guard

*Jacob Riis
Park*

C

D

BREEZY BLVD STATE RD

B169 St

BOARDWALK

2 MILES = 3.2 KMS

Fort
Tilden

END 3 MINS

2 MILES = 3.2 KMS

Staten Island's Best

Often praised as the most tranquil and verdant of New York City's five boroughs, Staten Island is rich in its physical beauty. While spiritually more connected to NJ, its residents have the best of both worlds, not the least of which is the Wu-Wear Store, home to Wu-Tan Clan, one of the grittiest and mega-selling hip-hop groups in the world—a place of pilgrimage for suburban youth around the world.

Snug Harbor

The cultural heart of the island is composed of 28 historic buildings in Victorian, Beaux Arts and Greek Revival styles. The jazz, classical and pop concerts are legendary as is the historical tour on weekends. 1000 Richmond Terrace @ Tysen St, 718-448-2500. **506B**

Wu-Wear Store

As parents can attest, this is Mecca for their teenage offspring who rank this experience above a visit to the Statue of Liberty. 61 Victory Blvd @ Bay Street, 718-720-9043 (daily 11-7, closed Sunday). **507A**

The Greenbelt

At 2,500 acres easily the city's largest park, with landscapes so varied one can forsake the Hamptons for these shaded woodlands, wetlands and hiking trails. Nearby Prall's Island sports the largest egret and heron rookery on the East Coast. 200 Nevada Av, 718-667-2165. **517C**

Staten Island Ferry

Spectacular views of the Downtown Manhattan skyline make this a must-do for visitors. **507B**

Verrazano-Narrows Bridge

The world's largest suspension bridge has become virtually synonymous with the NY Marathon when 30,000 runners funnel through. **513D**

SI Institute of Arts & Sciences

Designed by Peter Eisenman Architects and slated for a 2002 opening, this is bound to be the most dramatic new structure in NY Harbor. **507B**

SI Stats:
Population:
378,977

Area:
60.2 sq miles

SI Institute of Arts & Sciences
by Eisenman Architects

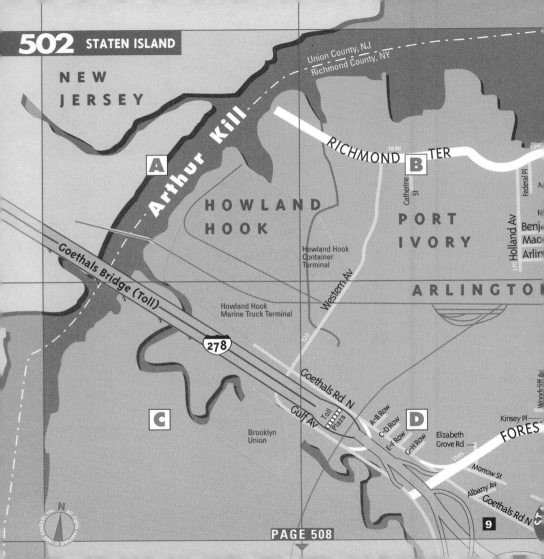

NEW
JERSEY

Union County, NJ
Richmond County, NY

A

Arthur Kill

RICHMOND B TER

3630

**HOWLAND
HOOK**

Catherine St

PORT
IVORY

Federal Pl

Holland Av

Fa
Benj
Mac
Arlin

170

Howland Hook
Container
Terminal

Western Av

Goethals Bridge (Toll)

ARLINGTO

Howland Hook
Marine Truck Terminal

522

278

Goethals Rd N

Wood-liff Av

C

Toll
Plaza

A-B Row

C-D Row

E-F Row

D

Kinsey Pl

FORES

Gulf Av

Brooklyn
Union

G-H Row

Elizabeth
Grove Rd

Morrow St

3542

Albany Av

Goethals Rd N

N

9

NJ

START DRIVE

Shooter's Island

Hudson County, NJ
Richmond County, NY

Van Kull

A

B

Toll

Richmond Ct
Grandview Av
Cowen Pl
Post La
Christopher St
Andros St
Mersereau
Davidson Ct
Davidson St
Lockman Av
Arlington Ct
Anderson Pl

Coonley Ct

Sylvan Pl

Orinoco Pl
Erastina Pl
Giordan Ct
DMV

RICHMOND TER

Mariners
Harbor La

Emeric Ct
Wright Av
Housman Av
Winant

Newark Av
LaSalle St

Nicholas Av
Slaight St
Harrison Av
Castleton Av
Grove Pl
Charles Av
Crittenden
Treadwell
Shape

De Hart Av
Forest Ct
Linden Av
Heusden St
Gigi St

John St
St Josephs St
Eaton Pl
Innis St
Charles
Hatfield Pl
Clinton Pl

SOUTH AV
Roxbury St
Mariner's Harbor
Brabant Av
Harbor Loop Houses
Continental
Downey Pl
Netherland

Lockman Loop
Leyden Av
Walloon St
Journeay St
Union St

Bush St
Union Av
Maple Pkwy

M A R I N E R ' S
H A R B O R

Charles Pl
De Ruyter Pl
Princess La
Princess St
Michelle Ct

Walker St
Walker Dr

Hooker Pl
Kalver Pl

David Av

Bayonne
Bridge
Plaza
LaForge Pl
LaForge Av
Burden Av
Blackford Av
Hooker Pl
Trantor Pl

Tate St

MARTIN LUTHER KING JR EXPWY

MORNINGSTAR RD

Richmond Av

Catherine St
LaGrange
Montell St
Beekman St
Riley Pl
Tabb Pl
Orange Av
Seymour Av
Hagaman Pl
Smith Pl

Lockman Av
Harbor Rd
Gridley Av
Bruckner Av
Confederation Av
Dublin Pl

C

Van Pelt Av
Van Name Av
Simonson Av

Conklin Av
Granite Av
Pulaski Av

Dixon
Ronald Av
Wenlock St
Westbrook Av

St Adalbert Pl

D

Bowles Av
Murdock Av
Gordon Pl

Villa Av
Van Riper St

PORT RICHMOND AV

Albert Ct
Wemple St
Spartan Av
Cedar Wood Ct
Andrea
Briarwood Rd
Yale
Birch
St Lisk Av
Wolcoff La

Samuel Pl
Amity Pl
Francesca La
Summerfield Pl
Carol Pl
Doreen Dr
Eleanor Pl
Adrianne Pl
Wilcox St
Heaney Av
Coonley Av

Roselolli Rd
Woodcrest Rd
Knollwood
Ludwig La
Jupiter La

Van Name Av
Eunice Pl
Overlook Av

Heafy St
Sanders St

Melyn Pl
Hudson Pl
Monsey Pl
N Tremont

Richmond Av

Egbert Sq
Amprior St

Vedder Av
James Ct
Lynn Ct

Rieglemann St
Pontiac Pl

Houston St
Houston La

FOREST AV
Galloway Av

Baron Hirsch Cemetery

440

END 3 MINS

2 MILES = 3.2 KMS

2 MILES = 3.2 KMS

NEW JERSEY

NJ

START DRIVE

K u l l

Ferry

Hudson County, NJ
Richmond County, NY

A

B

North St

RICHMOND TER

Fraser Park

Gales La — Ferry St
2060

North St

Howard Ct
Harrison Pl
Davis Ct

Larkin St

Church St

N Burgher Av

Elm St
Bement Ct

Av

Ann St

Grove Av

Bennett St

Vreeland St
St
Av B

Van St
Barrett La
Tompkins Ct

Edwin Markham Gardens

Wayne St

Henderson Av

Slaight St

St

Maple

Cottage Pl
St

New Bond St
Wygant Pl

Fountain Cemetery

Staten Island Cemetery

Trinity Pl
Woodruff La
Wayne St
Chappell St

WEST

Campbell Av

Nicholas Av

Harrison Av

Faber
Park Av

Rector St

Bodine St
Dorigan St
Taylor St
Barker St
Alaska St

BRIGHTON

Castleton Av
1610

Anderson Av

De Groot Pl
Taylor Ct

Market St — Doe Pl

Shappe
Treadwell

Albion Pl
Post Av
Simonson

Hurst St

CASTLETON AV

Roe St
Elizabeth St
Caroline St

Britton St
South St

Hatfield
Clinton

Palmer
Pl
Washington
Catherine Ct

White Pl
Cary Av

State St
West St
Noble Pl

Broadway

Seneca St

Bement Av
Sheffield St
Oakland Av

Blackford Av
Burden Av

Homestead Av
Heberton Av

PORT

Olive St

Greenleaf Av

Cornell Av
Raymond Pl
Disosway Pl

Delafield Av

D

Rainbow Av

Post Av

Dubois Av

Catherine St
Montell St
Beekman St

RICHMOND

Holbemt Ct
Kramer Pl

Marion St
Brooks St

Derby Ct

Arcadia Pl

Myrtle Av

FOREST

AV

Morrison Av

Decker Av
Lexington Av
Cortlandt St
Dryden Ct

Floyd St

Allen Ct
Ludwig St
Clove Lake Pl
Purcell St

Loret Ct
Freeman Pl
Lynnhaven Pl
Ford Pl

E Raleigh Av
Harvest Av

Sharrett Pl
Newkirk Pl

Haughwout Av

Delafield Av

Colonial
Lloyd Ct
Benwin La
Hardin Av

Bosworth St
Blaine Av

Tabb Pl
Cornell St

Hamlin Pl

Green Ct
Arthur Ct

Dore Ct

W Raleigh Av

Law Pl

Orange Av

Ordell Av
Veltman Av

Zachary Ct

Mundy Pl

Brooks Lake

Brooks Pond Pl

END 3 MINS

C

JEWETT

PAGE 511

Brooks Lake

2 MILES= 3.2 KMS

2 MILES = 3.2 KMS

PAGE 506

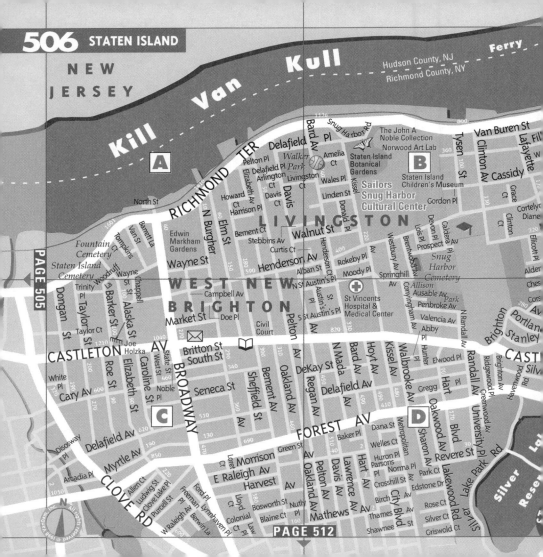

PAGE 502

A

B

B L O O M F I E L D

NJ

Lamberts La

Gulf Av

440

Union County, NJ
Richmond County, NY

Bloomfield Av

River Rd

Staten
Island
Corpora
Park

Prall's
Island

Chelsea

Edward Curry Av

Hughes Av

Saw Mill Creek

Prall's River

Arthur Kill

C

D

WEST SHORE EXPWY

The Tele

Teleport Dr

SOUTH

Industry Rd

Bloomfield Rd

Glen St

Spencer St

South Av

PAGE 514

NJ

START DRIVE

Spartan Av
Cedar Wood St
Rosecliff Rd
Woodcrest Av
Amador
Andrea Pl
Yale
Wilcox St
Van Name Pl
Overlook Av
Heafy St
Sanders St
Eunice
Garick St
Briarwood Rd
Birch Rd
Francesca La
Carol Pl
Doreen Dr
Eleanor Pl
Adriane Pl
Baron Hirsch Cemetery
ethals
Leon St
Belknap St
Lisk Av
Knollwood
Ga Rd N
Wolcoff La
Regal Wk
Selvin Loop
Ludwig La
Benjamin Dr
Rodman St
Peter St
Anita St
Regal Wk
Ada Dr
Marc St
Cypress Crest
Farragut St
Regis Dr
Melissa St
Leo St
Armand St
Aye Ct
A
278
STATEN ISLAND EXPWY
Elson Ct
Jules Dr
Essex St
Lambert St
Arlene Ct
Lenore Ct
Comstock Av
Deppe Pl
B
Home
Watchogue
Leonard Av
Waters Rd
Bee St
Gauldy Av
Faby Av
Cooke St
Domain St
North Av
Madison
Farraday St
Sumner Av
Canterbury Av
Echo Pl
Levitt St
Lyon St
Willow Rd E
WILLOWBROOK RD
Felton St
Caswell La
Leigh Av
Kingsbridge Rd
Longdale St
May Av
Seldin Av
Astor Av
Globe Av
Willow Rd
Tremont Av
Caswell Av
Stewart Av
Bryson Av
Colfield Av
Crystal Av
Lamberts
Elson St
Roman Av
Willow Rd
440
Francine La
Thurston St
Kirshon Av
Lander Av
Holgate St
Fieldstone Rd
Saybrook St
Loring Ct
Croton Pl
Cambridge Av
Woodbine St
Hawthorne St
Aubum Av
Nadal Pl
Oliver Pl
Hillman Av
Morgan La
Renee Pl
Leggett Pl
Yona Pl
Crocheron Av
Akron St
Nina Av
Denton Pl
Montauk Pl
Commerce St
Arlene St
Hillman Av
Jardine Av
Merrill Av
Jennifer St
Debbie St
Parkview Loop
Wyona Av
Neptune Pl
Decatur Av
Bellhaven Pl
Berglund Av
Plank Rd
Firth Rd
Morani
Leona St
Gary
Richard La
RICHMOND CHRISTOPHER LA
Graham Av
Paulding Av
Greentree La
B U L L ' S   H E A D
VICTORY BLVD
Darcy Av
D
278
Stewart Av
Colfield
Sommer Av
Nostrand Av
Speedwell Av
C
Dreyer Av
Hall Av
Bascom Pl
Westwood Av
Av
Sideview Av
Lisa Rd
Jones St
Clifton St
Saybrook St
Goller Pl
Dinsmore St
Dawson Cir
Dawson Ct
Camegie Av
Croft Pl
Eton Pl
Willow Brook Park
The College of Staten Island (CUNY)
Spark Pl
Amsterdam Av
Dawson Cir
Signs Rd

W I L L O W B R O O K

END 3 MINS

2 MILES = 3.2 KMS

2 MILES = 3.2 KMS

PAGE 510

STATEN ISLAND **511**

NJ

START DRIVE

Zachary

Egbert Av

Curtis Av

Brooks Pond

Pl

Brooks Pond Cemetery

Staten Island Zoological Society

Coughlan Av

Dallas St

Hartford Av

Karen Ct

Ravenhurst Av

Alpine Ct

Douglas Av

Elias

Pl

Greenleaf Av

Brookside Av

Brooks Lake

Tyler Av

Benedict Av

Colorado Av

Glenwood Pl

St Peters

Cemetery

Starr Av

Kingsley Av

New York Pl

Alabama Av

MANOR

Carolina

Martling Av

Richmond Pond

Clove Way

College

Virginia St

Delaware Pl

190

Slosson

Av

Fairview Av

Av

Ohio Pl

Elmira Av

Maryland Pl

Merriman Pl

New York State Armory

100

Clove Lakes Park

Clove

Fox Hunt Ct

Constant

Av

Miller St

Av

Drake Av

60

Waldron Av

edge Pl

Av

A

Ct

Smith

Utter Av

Keiber

180

260

Rice Av

B

Lake

Glenwood Av

Margaretta Ct

Joan Pl

260

Potter Av

140

Dudley Av

Royal Oak Rd

Sawyer

70

Av

Goodell Av

Sturges St

Lakeland Rd

Niagara St

CLOVE RD

Goodwin

110

S Greenleaf Av

Governor Rd

Av

Knox Pl

Genesee St

Schoharie Av

Seneca St

Crowell

Av

Westcott Blvd

Sanford Pl

Renwick Av

Cypress Av

Ontario

Cayuga Av

kham Pl

Kemball

70

Dongan Av

Hodges Pl

Ellsworth Pl

Brenton

Albert St

Walters St

Aymar

Bristol Av

Northern

Logan Av

Dobbs Pl

Oswego

I Loop

Av

Chandler Av

Av

Beechwood Pl

Winthrop

1610

Marx St

Cattaraugus St

Vogel La

St

Treetz Pl

Coale Av

Raymond

Henning Av

Windsor Rd

Little

Otsego Av

Tioga St

TLETON

Josephine St

Sommers Av

Todt Hill Rd

Windsor Ct

Clove Rd

PAGE 512

NERS

Lester St

Mountain View

Gansevoort

Clermont

Garden St

Elvin St

Penn St

Reon Av

Wheeler

Perry

Quinlan

Cemetery

278

Milford Dr

Ocean Ter

Witte Pl

Alexandra Pl

Gower St

Schmidts

Lortel Av

La

Melhorn Rd

College of Staten Island (Sunnyside Campus)

Milford Av

STATEN ISLAND EXPWY

MANOR

150

Todt Hill Rd

Lightner Av

Motley Av

Staten Island Blvd

2 MILES = 3.2 KMS

C

Waldo Pl

Athena Av

Deere Park

Buttonwood Av

Deer Park

Mohn Pl

Beebe

Julie Ct

Poland Pl

De Noble La

Portsmouth Av

Roosevelt Ct

Livingston Av

P

Franklin Av

Area Pl

Fine Blvd

Andes Pl

Valleyview Pl

D

Louise La

Coverly Av

Suffolk

Graves St

Holden Blvd

Blvd

Norwalk Av

Townley Av

Portsmouth

TER

Wellbrook Av

Duke Pl

Tillman St

LaGuardia Av

OCEAN

END 3 MINS

Queen St

Fanning

Lincoln St

Dresden La

Tilber Av

Oceanview La

Vermont Ct

Gower St

Melba

Croak Av

Elmhurst Av

Wooddale Av

Woodhaven Av

Merrick Av

Basket Willow Swamp

Shady Pl

Harold St

Bolivar Av

2 MILES = 3.2 KMS

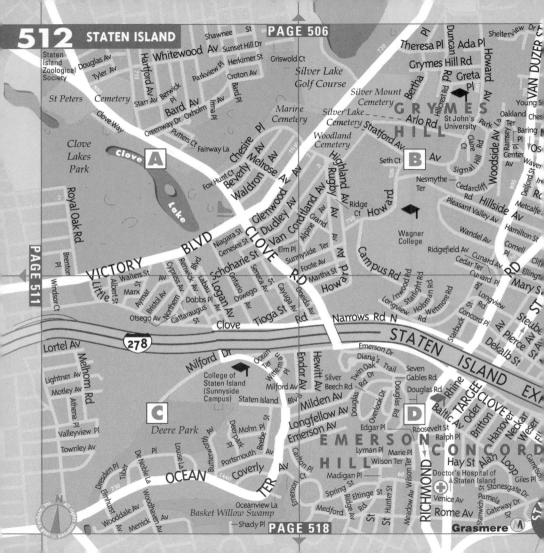

514 STATEN ISLAND

Spencer St

SOUTH AV

Crane Av

Meredith Av

CHELSEA

VICTORY BLVD

TRAV

NJ

Glen St

8

Union County, NJ
Richmond County, NY

Ridgeway Av

Bates Av

Shenandoah Av

A

Kennebeck Av

Wakefield

Latimer Av

Baron Blvd

B

William T D
Wildlife Re

Cannon Av

440

Cannon   Av

Leroy St

Riche

Gaspar

Parish Av

Prices La

Simmons La

Ridgeway Av

Wild

Melvin Av

Church Av

Towers La

Burke Av

Shelley Av

Hamilton Pl

Melvin
Av

Mildred Av

Temple Ct

Sylvan
Cemetery

Roswell Av

Watson Av

Pearson St

7

Alberta Av

Melvin Av

Rawson Pl

TRAVIS

Main

Beresford Av

Fieldmeyers La

Wild

Beresford Av

Cartledge Av

Schmul
Park

Springvile

Crabbs La

Wild

Walton Av

Dean

Arthur Kill

Av

486

Veterans Rd W

Veterans Rd E

C

WEST SHORE EXPWY

Victory Blvd Ext

D

Creek

Fresh
Kills
Park

Park Drive East

N

Little Fresh Kill

Park Drive West

STA

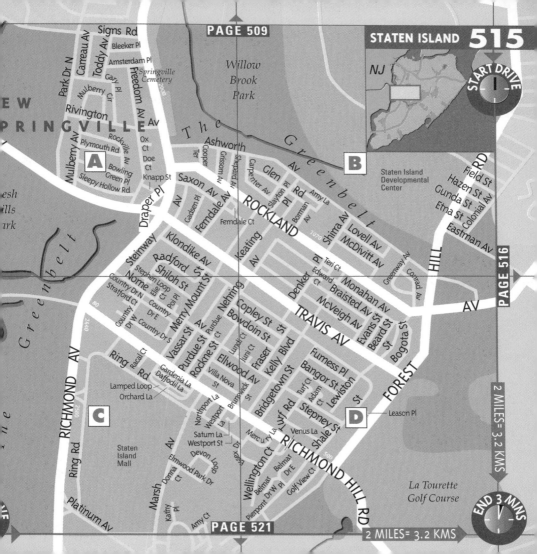

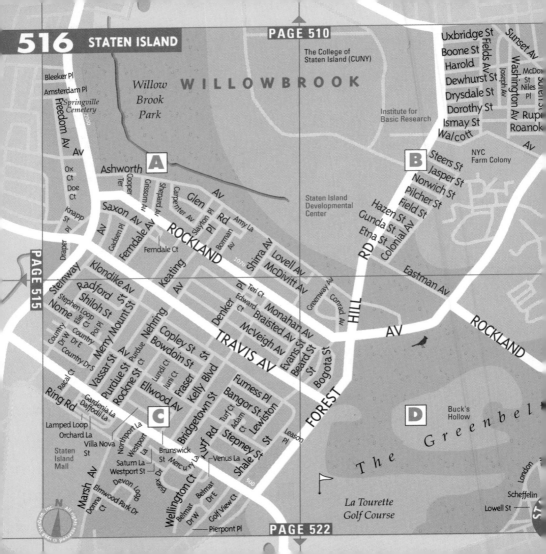

The College of
Staten Island (CUNY)

Uxbridge St
Boone St
Harold
Dewhurst St
Drysdale St
Dorothy St
Ismay St
Walcott

Fields Av
Sunset Av
Washington Av

McDo
Joseph Av
Niles St
Rupe
Roanok

WILLOWBROOK

Willow
Brook
Park

Institute for
Basic Research

Bleeker Pl
Amsterdam Pl
Springville
Cemetery

Freedom Av

AV

Ox
Ct
Doe
Ct
Knapp
St

Ashworth

A

Cooper
Ter

Grissom Av
Shepard Av
Carpenter Av
Clayton Pl

Glen
Rd

Av

Amy La

Shinia Av
Lovell Av
McDivitt Av

B

NYC
Farm Colony

Staten Island
Developmental
Center

Steers St
Jasper St
Norwich St
Pilcher St
Field St
Hazen St
Gunda St
Etna St
Colonial Av

Saxon Av

Gadsen Pl
Femdale Av

ROCKLAND

Femdale Ct

Bonham Av

HILL

RD

Eastman Av

ROCKLAND

Steinway
Klondike Av
Radford St
Shiloh St
Stephen Loop
Norne
Country
Dr W

Keating
Av

1070

McDivitt Av

Teri Ct
Edward
Ct
Braisted Av

Monahan Av

Greenway Av
Conrad Av

AV

Country
Dr E
Country Dr S
Racal Ct

Merry Mount St
Vassar St
Purdue St
Rockne St

Nehring
Av

Copley St
Bowdoin St

Lundi Ct
Juni Ct

Denker
St

Fraser
St

TRAVIS AV

McVeigh Av
Beard St
Evans St

Bogota St

D

Buck's
Hollow

Ring Rd

Gardenia La
Daffodil La

Ellwood Av

Kelly Blvd

Furness Pl

Bangor St

Greenbel

Lamped Loop
Orchard La
Staten Island
Mall

Villa Nova
St

Northport La
Westport La

Bridgetown St

Turf Rd

Turf Ct
Adam

Lewiston
St

Stepney St

Leason
Pl

The

Marsh Av
Doma
Ct

Brunswick
St

Satum La
Westport St
Devon Loop
Elmwood Park Dr

Essex
Dr

Mercury La

Venus La

Shale
St

C

Wellington Ct

Belmar
Dr W

Belmar
Dr E

Golf View Ct

Pierpont Pl

500

FOREST

La Tourette
Golf Course

London
Scheffelin
Lowell St

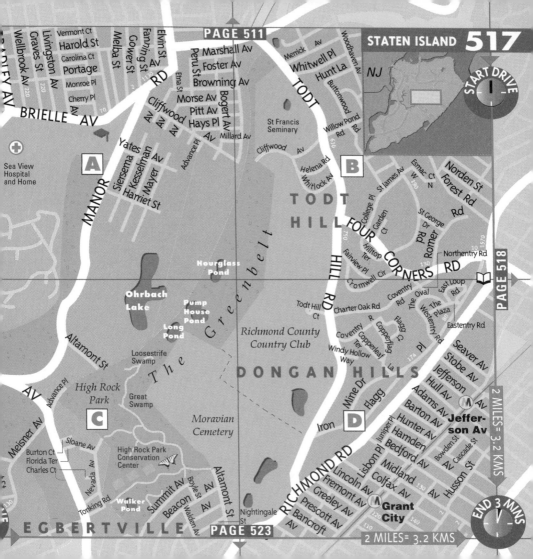

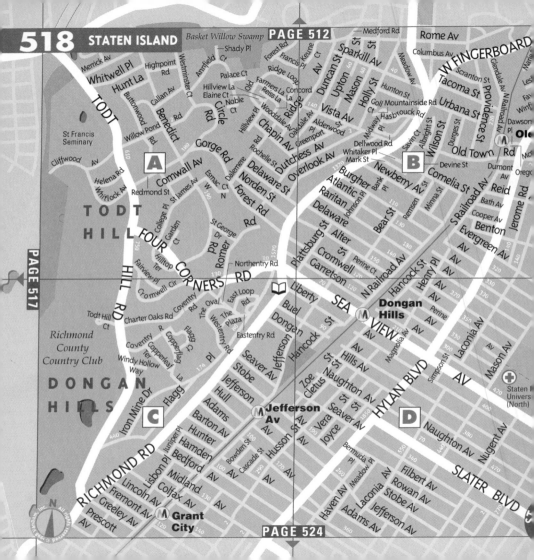

START DRIVE

NJ

A S M E R E

Vista Pl
Piedmont Av
Pouch Ter
Columbia Al
chicago Al
Columbia Av
Chicago Av
Knauth Pl
Landis Av
Tompkins Av
Duer Av

Cameron Pond
Allendale Rd
Normalee Rd.
Beverly Rd
Briarcliff Rd
Radcliff Rd
Hastings St
Florida Av

STEUBEN ST
RD
A R R O C H A R
Pickersgill Av
Major St
MacFarland Av
Wallace Av
Waterford Ct
Galesville St
Palisade St
Guilford St

BLVD
970
200

Mallory
Norway
Kramer St
Linwood Av
McClean Av
Railroad Av
Jackson Av
Conger St
Windom Av
Ocean Av

St Marys
130

A
Jerome Av
Hickory Av
Pershing Av
Cedar Av
Mills Av
Austin Av
Retner Av
Jackson
Linda Av

Bionia Av
Humbert St
Diaz St
SAND LA
Arthur Av
Drury La

Reid Av
550
Kensington Av
Lamport
Cambria St
Robin Rd
Doty Av
B

Cameron Av
Oberlin St
Foch Av
Olympia
Blvd
Lorne St
Balfour St
Agby
Orlando St
Wills Pl
South Beach Park

Scott Av
Appleby Av
Andrews
Pearsall
South Beach Av
Tuscany Ct
Lansing St

Nugent Av
Vulcan Av
Lava St
Wentworth Av
240

Winfield St
Patterson St
McLaughlin
South Beach

Quintard St
Quincy St
Agnes Pl
Reynaud Av
Oceanside Av

S O U T H
B E A C H

C
FATHER CAPODANNO BLVD
BOARDWALK
FRANKLIN D. ROOSEVELT

South Beach Psychiatric Center
780
Oceanside Av
Quincy Av

Lower

New

York

Bay

D

PAGE 432

2 MILES= 3.2 KMS

Hoffman Island

END 3 MINS

2 MILES= 3.2 KMS

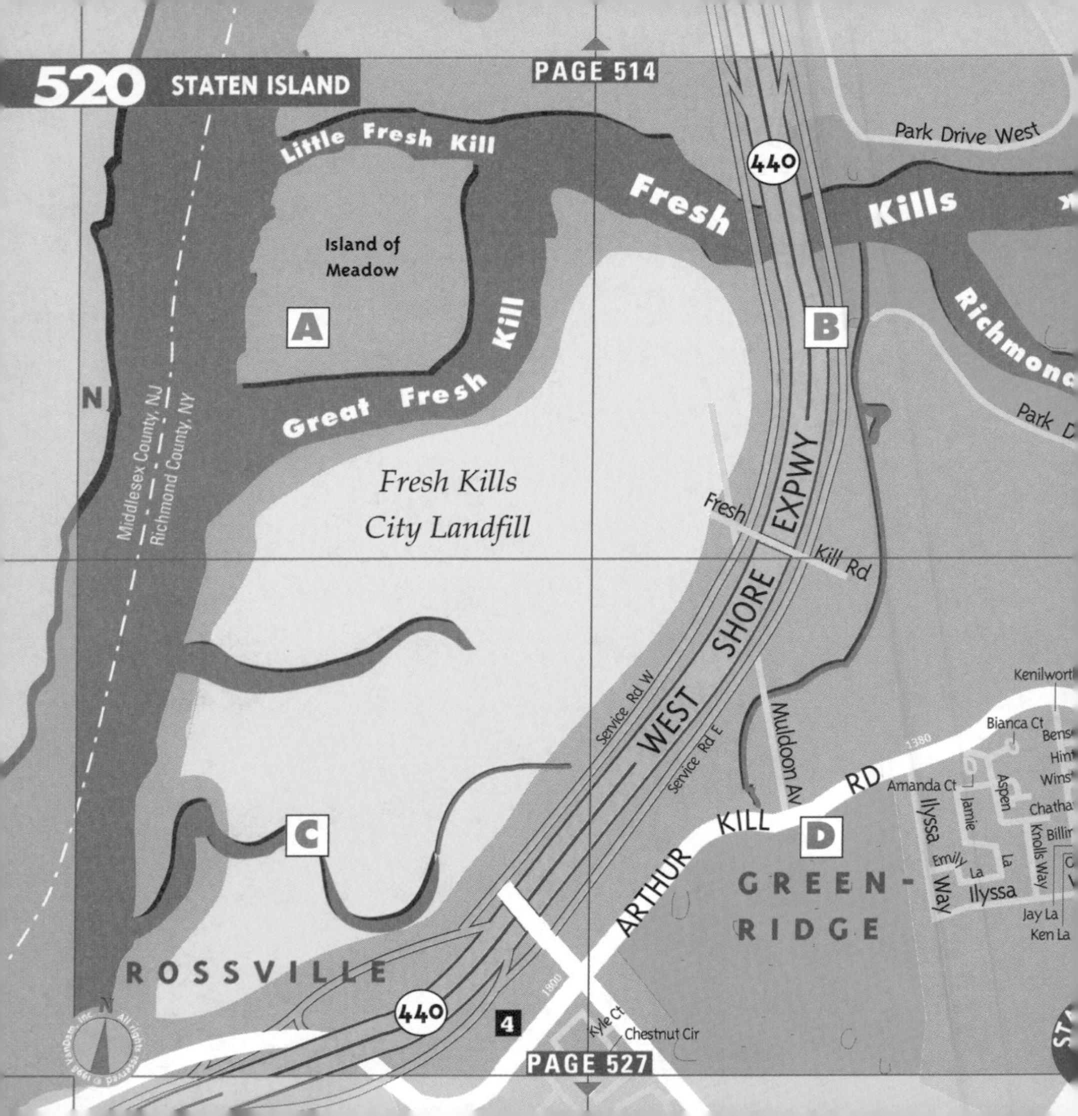

PAGE 514

Little Fresh Kill

Fresh

Kills

Park Drive West

440

Richmond

Island of
Meadow

Park D

A

Great Fresh Kill

B

Middlesex County, NJ
Richmond County, NY

N.

*Fresh Kills
City Landfill*

Fresh

Kill Rd

WEST SHORE EXPWY

Service Rd. W

Service Rd E

Kenilworth

Bianca Ct

Bense

Hin

Winst

Amanda Ct

Aspen

Chatha

C

Muldoon Av

Ilyssa Way

Jamie

La

Knolls Way

Billin

Emily La

Ilyssa

ARTHUR KILL RD

D

Jay La

1380

Ken La

**GREEN-
RIDGE**

ROSSVILLE

440

4

1900

Kyle Ct

Chestnut Cir

N

NJ

START DRIVE

Park Drive East

Ring Rd

Staten Island Mall

Marsh Av

Platinum Av

Windham Pl Kathy Pl

Loop Amy Ct

Gregory Pl

Pierpont Pl

Arielle La

Stone La

Gregory Rd

Canon Dr

Yukon Av

Rumson Rd

Fresh Kills Park

A

Independence Av

Independence Hill

Alaska Pl

Forest Hill Rd

B

Old Mill Rd

Historic Richmond Town

Forest Hill

La Tourette Park

Revere La

Newvale Av

Franklin La

Tanglewood Dr

Lacon St

Otho St

Mena St

Cromer St

Troy St

Corbin Av

Vinton St

Pemberton Av

Daleham St

Greaves

Teakwood Ct

Cicero Av

Glencoe St

Elkhart

Miles St

St

Gurley

Fairfield

Eric La

Hereford St

Islington St

Abbey Rd

KILL RD

Arkansas

Barlow Av

Lennon Ct

AV

Lexington La

Jumel St

C

Alexandra Ct

E Gurley

Doane Av

Elverton Av

Shieg Av

Kennington St

Abingdon Ct

Colon Av

Brookfield Av

AV

Annadale Rd

Futurity Pl

Token St

Ladd Av

E Brandis Av

Abingdon Av

GIFFORDS LA

Linton Pl

End Pl

ynan St

Berry Av

Watkins Av

ARTHUR

E Macon Av

Armstrong

D

Leverett Av

rauf St

enmore St

Berry Av W

Dorval Av

Gurley Av

Opp Ct

Getz Av

Cortelyou Av

Cheryl Av

Sunfield Av

Gold

Brandis Av

Ridgewood Blvd

Fenway Cir

E Reading Av

val Pl

Alexander Av

Wainwright Av

Bartlett Av

restdale

AV

RICHMOND PKWY

Macon Av

Eltingville Blvd

Crossfield

Barlow Av

END 3 MINS

2 MILES = 3.2 KMS

2 MILES = 3.2 KMS

RICHMOND AV

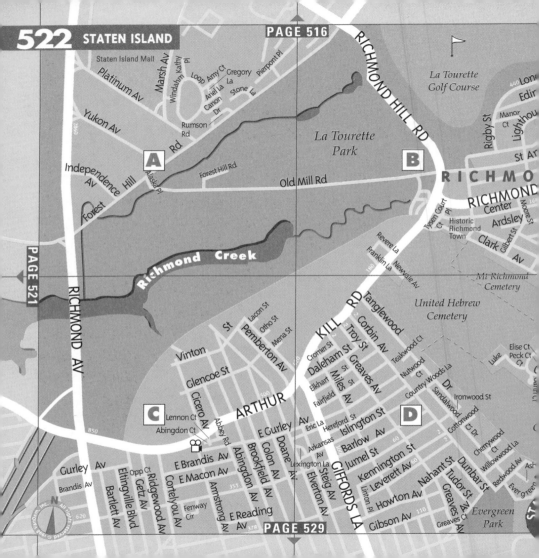

PAGE 518
PAGE 523
PAGE 531

Grant City

Colfax Av
Bedford Av
Midland Av
Greeley Av
Bancroft Av
Otis Allison Pl
Locust
Kruser St
N Railroad
S Railroad
Prescott Av
St Av
Bryant Av
Grant Pl
Zeni Pl
Zwicky Av
Burbank
Steele Av
Edison Av
Av
Maplewood Pl
MIDLAND AV
Beachview Av
Haven Av
Laconia Av
Stobe Av
Jefferson Av
Rowan Av
Adams Av
Filbert Av
SLATER
Bache Av
Jacques Av
New
Idlease Pl
Nugent Av
Graham Blvd
St
Grimsby
Freeborn St
Wahler St
Mapleton
Jay St Quin

G R A N T
C I T Y

New Dorp

N E W

HYLAN

BLVD

Boundary Av
Sanilac St
Rudyard St
Poultney St
Lincoln Av
Oldfield St
Mason St
Moreland St
Kiswick St
Greeley Av
Elm Tree Av
Olympia Blvd
Colony Av
Baden Pl
Patterson
Hempstead Av

D O R P

Coddington Av
Rose Av
Ross Av
Sterling Av
Beach Av
Allison Av
Lindbergh Av
Cannon Blvd
Thomas Pl
Reno Av
9 St
Colgate Pl

NEW DORP LA

N E W
D O R P
B E A C H

Beacon
Celtic Pl
Ima St
Mill Rd
Winham Av
Marine Way
Ebbitts St
Clapboard St
Manila Av

Miller Field
(Gateway National
Recreation Area)

M I D L A N D
B E A C H

FATHER CAPODANNO BLVD

O A K W O O D

Primrose Pl
Tysens La
Malden Pl
Penn Av
Falcon
Peter Av
Titus Av
Cuba Av
Ebbitts St
Weed Av
Diaz Pl
Isernia Av
Manila Av
Milton Av
Finley
Hett
Roma
Navesink Pl
Michelle La
Jennifer La

Gerard P
Dugan Park
Eva Av

Isabella Av
Amherst St
Riga St
Lynn Av
Guyon Av
Roberts Dr
Agda Av
Foss Av
Old Mill Rd
Mill
1st

Neptune St
Waterside St
Seafoam St
Wavecrest St
Maple Ter
Center St
Topping St
Dustan St
Garibaldi Av
Cedar Grove Ct
Millbank Rd
Neutral Av
Cedar Grove Av

C
D

New Dorp
Beach

Great Kills
Park

Great Kills Park

O A K W O O D
B E A C H

Cedar Grove
Beach

A **B**

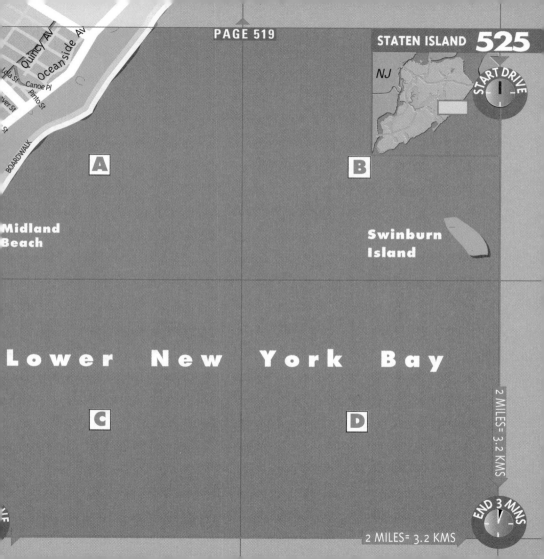

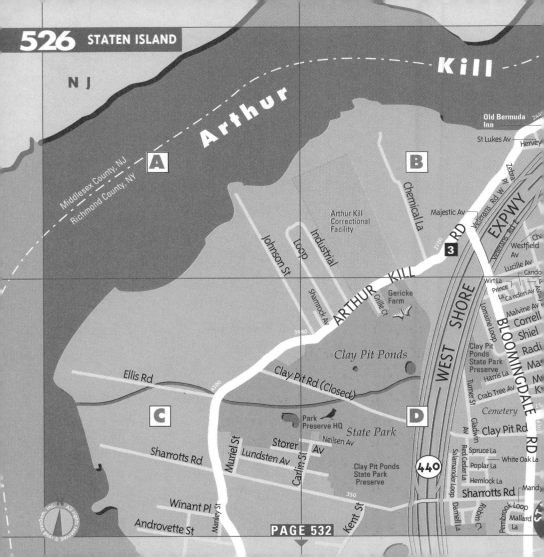

Arthur **Kill**

NJ

Old Bermuda Inn

244

St Lukes Av — Hervey

A

Middlesex County, NJ
Richmond County, NY

Arthur Kill Correctional Facility

Chemical La

Majestic Av

B

Zebra Pl

Veterans Rd W

Veterans Rd E

EXPWY

Westfield Av

Lucille Av

Cando

Chi

Johnson St

Loop

Industrial

3

2700

WEST SHORE RD

Wirt La

Prince La

Candon La

Ashley

Pl

BLOOMINGDALE RD

Malvine Av

Correll

Shamrock Av

ARTHUR KILL

Grille Ct

Gericke Farm

Lorraine Loop

Shiel

Radi

3990

Clay Pit Ponds

Clay Pit Ponds State Park Preserve

Harris La

Mae

N

Ellis Rd

4100

Clay Pit Rd (Closed)

Turner St

Crab Tree Av

Cemetery

K

C

D

Clay Pit Rd

Park Preserve HQ

State Park

Neilsen Av

Av

Gladwin

Sharrotts Rd

Muriel St

Storer Av

Lundsten Av

Carlin St

Spruce La

Red Cedar La

White Oak La

440

Poplar La

Salamander Loop

Clay Pit Ponds State Park Preserve

Hemlock La

Mandy

Sharrotts Rd

Winant Pl

Manley St

350

Kent St

Darnell La

Robin Ct

Pembrook Loop

Mallard La

Androvette St

© 1998 VanDam, Inc. All rights reserved

WEST SHORE EXPWY
440

ARDEN HEIGHTS

WOODROW RD

4

Crocker Ct

Chestnut Cir

Kyle Ct

Carlyle Green

Carlyle Green

Green

ARDEN AV

Macon Av

Isb

Barlow Av

Waring Av

Shotwell Av

Tyron Av

Sm

W

HUEGUENOT

Cody Ct
Pratt Ct
Poets Cir
Lombard Ct
Raily Ct
Alcott
Bunnell Ct
Mimosa La
Ashton Dr
Russek
Yucca Dr
Princeton Green
Country La
Harford
La
Regent Cir
Maple Ct
Daffodil

Forest Green
Birch La

Princeton Green

Bunell St

Barclay Cir
Beekman Cir
Nedra La

Cornell Av

Legate Av

Regina La

Suzama La
Evan Pl
Row

Carlton Blvd

Grantwoo

A

South Shore
Golf Course

Sussex
Green

Dogwood

Geyser Dr

Sutton Pl

Hickory
Cir

Hill Green

Almond St

Halpin AV

B

Carlton Blvd

Totten
Gunton Pl
Selkirk St
Pl

Avon Green

Rumba Pl

Lisa La
Wyma La

Hammock La

Stack Dr

Valley

Rolling
Rd

Manchester Dr

Tulip

Ebey
La

Victoria Rd

Everton Pl

Ruxton Av

Vespa Av

Jefferson

Canton Av

Holcomb Av

Belfield Av

AV

Stafford Av

Vineland

Sinclair

Sheldon

Rensselaer Av

Rathbun Av

A

ROSSVILLE

Barrow Pl

Rossville Av

Mallow St

Hemlock St

Alverson Av

ARDEN AV

Rosedale

Powell La
Shift Pl
W Castor Pl
Castor Pl
Coventry
Loop

Cardiff St

Boulder La

Anaconda St

Ballard Av

Delmar Av

Everton Av

Sperry Pl

Crown

Crown
Pl

Vineland AV

Heenan

Stafford Av

Sinclair

Sheldon

Sheldon Av

AV

Berne

Gilroy St

Alverson

Cemetery

Dahlia St

Powell St

Walker Pl

Deserte Av
Ellsworth Av
Powell St

Vineland
Nippon Av
Stafford Av
Sinclair

Rensselaer Av

Rathbun

Ramona

Delmar Av

Drumgoole Rd E

RICHMOND PKWY

Drumgoole Rd

Ionia

Belfield A

Edgegrove Av

Detroit Av

Carlto

A

Spar Av

1270

Helios Pl
Latham Pl
Wieland Av
Elks
Pl

Lenevar Av

Ramapo

Stafford
Sinclair

Sheldon

Rensselaer

Rathbun

Ramona

Lamont

Ionia

Edgegrove Av

FOSTER RD

AV

AV

AV

AV

Vernon Av

Marcy AV

Ellsworth Av

C

Lamont AV

Ionia Av

Edgegrove Av

Darlington Av

D

Drumgoole Rd E

Rathbun Av

N. Railroad St

S Railroad

Buffington Av

Downes Av

Archwood Av

Bennett

Collyer Av

Leva Pl

Albee Av

Tenafly

Alvine Av

Hod

Carlton Ct

NJ

START DRIVE 1

Brandis Av

Macon Av

Barlow Av

Monterey Perkiomen Av

Marne Av

Gothic Pl

Reading Av

Leverett Av

Stroud Av

Scranton Av

Lovelace

Pompey

Genesee

Augusta Av

Av

Figurea Av

Katan Av

Wainwright Av

RICHMOND AV

Getz Av

Eltingville Blvd

Bartlett Av

Ridgewood Av

Cortelyou Av

Sweet Brook Rd

Fenway Cir

Armstrong Av

E Reading Av

Middle Loop Rd

E Stroud Av

E Scranton Av

Stanley Cir

E Augusta Av

E Figurea Av

Patty Ct

Ovas Ct

Star Ct

Katan Av

Demopolis Av

Fern Av

Escanaba Av

Notre Dame Av

Doane Av

Colon Av

Brookfield Av

Abingdon Av

ELTINGVILLE

Wolcott Av

Laredo Av

Filer St

Orchard St

Memphis Av

Lamoka Av

Serrell Av

Petrus Av

Rochelle Pl

Bartlett Av

Lamoka Av

Maria Gil Ct La

Cortelyou Av

Annadale Rd

Rye

Mott

Moffett St

Adair Cir

Bent St

Van Brunt St

Whalley Av

Stuyvesant Av

Wilson Av

Sylvia St

Village La

Chesebrough St

Bayard St

Eltingville Blvd

White Plains

Putnam St

St Albans Pl

Eltingville

Great Kills

Baltimore Hardy St

Property St

Lindenwood St

Giffords Glen

Brown

Adrienne Pl

Clovis Rd

Hillside Ter

Dent Rd

Nolan

Locust Pl

Pleasant St

Seeley

Scarsdale St

Fontaine St

Belden Pl

Rustic Ct

Cleveland Av

Beth Pl

School St

Park Ter

Sherwood

La

Hillcrest

NELSON AV

LINDENWOOD AV

AMBOY RD

Amboy Rd

Plo

Montyvale Pl

Highmount Rd

Holly Av

Acacia Av

Ramblewood Av

Cloverdale Av

Elmwood Av

Armstrong St

Robinson Av

Beach

Pacific Av

Sycamore St

Eleanor La

Edgewood Rd

Hilltop Pl

Ocean View Pl

Monticello Ter

DALE

Ray St

Barb

Arthur Pl

St

Ralph Av

Jeannette Av

Lomain Av

Endview St

Posen St

Sneden

Mosley Av

Seguine Pl

Bamberger La

Bovanizer St

Gillard Av

Ross St

Ogden St

Walmer Pl

Lyndale La

Oakdale St

Thornycroft

Winchester

Ridgecrest

Crest

Loop

Pacific St

Bennington St

Oceanview Pl

David

Osbom

Driggs

King St

Presley St

Lillian Pl

William Av

Russell St

Annadale

Sheridan St

Mosley AV

Eagan Av

Fabian St

May Pl

Blue Heron Dr

Hillis St

Summit Pl

Rogers St

Fomes Pl

Rae Av

Edwin

Fingal

Winslow Pl

Sycamore

Tallman

Eylandt

Lipsett Av

Booth Av

Kraft Av

Berkley St

Eastman St

Seldman St

Rankin St

Osborne St

Liss St

ARDEN AV

RICHMOND AV

Lyndale

Retford

Park Rd

Preston

Hales

King St

Hillcrest

Hilltop Rd

Heinz Av

Walnut Av

Groton St

Littlefield Av

END 3 MINS

PAGE 530

2 MILES= 3.2 KMS

2 MILES= 3.2 KMS

PAGE 523

PAGE 529

PAGE 535

GIFFORDS

Howton Av

Tudor St
Dunbar St
Evergreen Ct

Woodcutters La
Nancy Ct
Dr

Benton Av
S Railroad Av
Twombley Av
Spratt Av
Hopkins Av
Buffalo St
Currie Av

AMBOY RD

Linton Pl
Steig Av
Elverton Av
Gibson Av
Exeter St
Greaves St
Greaves Ct
Greaves Pl
Dewey Pl
Evergreen Ridge

Bay
Terrace

O'Gorman Av
Hooper Av
Durant Av
Thollen Av
Justin Av
Kelvin Av
Block St

Doane Av
Colon Av
Woodland Av
Miles Av
Shafter St
Schley Av
Sampson Av
Katan Av

Taunton St
Redgrave Av
Bartow St
Bay Ter
Maybury Ct
Baldwin Av
Ovis Pl
Thayer Pl

Brookfield Av
Dewey
Kaan Loop
N Rhett Av
Rhett Av
Stem Ct
Greaves La
Lamoka Av

G R E A T

K I L L S

Ainsworth Av
Cranford St
Keegans La
Trent Av

Grattan Av

Abingdon Av
Margaret St
Hardy St
Property St

Great
Kills

Oak Ct
Clinton Rd
Stonecrest Ct

Keats St
Fieldway Av
Highland Rd

Grea
(Gatew
Recre

Baltimore Av
Lindenwood Av
Giffords Glen
Adrienne St
Clovis St
Ramble Rd
Great Kills Rd

HYLAN BLVD

Mansion Av

Sherwood Pl
Beth Pl
Pleasant St
Scarsdale St
Fontaine Pl
Hillside Av
Dent St
Locust Pl
Midland Rd
Ocean Rd
Maybury
Greencroft Av

Rustic Pl

Montyvale Pl
Highmount Rd
Sealey Av
School St
Park Ter
Belden Pl
Cleveland Pl
Rustic Pl
Grandview

Fairlawn
Loop
Fairlawn Av
Waterside
Pkwy
N Ct
S Ct

Oakdale St
Ramblewood Av
Holly Av
Acacia Av
Hilcrest Av
Edgewood Rd
Eleanor La
Monticello Ter
Durant Ter
Nash Ct
Av Whitman
Cottage Av
Ter
Mckee Av

Elmwood Av
Cloverdale Av
Ocean View Pl
Hilltop Pl
Florence St
Melrose Pl
Mercer Av

Armstrong Av
Robinson Av
Ocean View Pl
David St
Driggs
Tarlee Pl
Hartford St
Cornish St
Morris Av

Beach St
Bennington St
Osbom
King
Lillian Pl
Presley St
Sweetwater
Ackerman Av
Ponta Av
Hartford St

Thornycroft Rd
Hillcrest St
William Av
Russell St
Witman Av
Goodall St
Fitzgerald Av
Cinda Av
Beach La
Harbour Ct

Winchester Av
King St
Heinz Av
Glover St
Walnut Av
Byrd Pl
Highland La

**Great
Kills
Harbor**

Groton St
Littlefield Av
Tennyson Dr
Filipe La
Point St

**Crookes
Point**

Great Ki

HYLAN BLVD

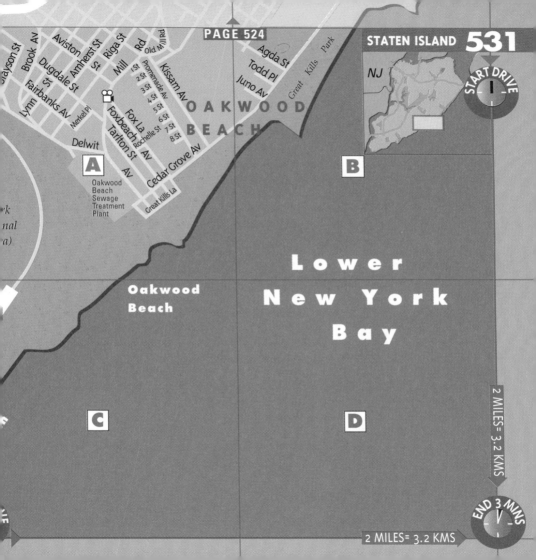

NJ

START DRIVE

Graysom St
Brook Av
Aviston St
Amherst St
Riga St
Mill Rd
Old Mill Rd
Dugdale St
Fairbanks Av
Lynn Av
Merkel Pl
Delwit

Kissam Av
Promenade Av
1 St
2 St
3 St
4 St
5 St
6 St
7 St
8 St
Fox La
Foxbeach Av
Rochelle St
Tariton St
Cedar Grove Av
Great Kills La

Agda St
Todd Pl
Juno Av
Great Kills Park

O A K W O O D
B E A C H

A

Oakwood
Beach
Sewage
Treatment
Plant

rk
nal
(a)

B

**L o w e r
N e w Y o r k
B a y**

Oakwood
Beach

C

D

2 MILES = 3.2 KMS

2 MILES= 3.2 KMS

END 3 MINS

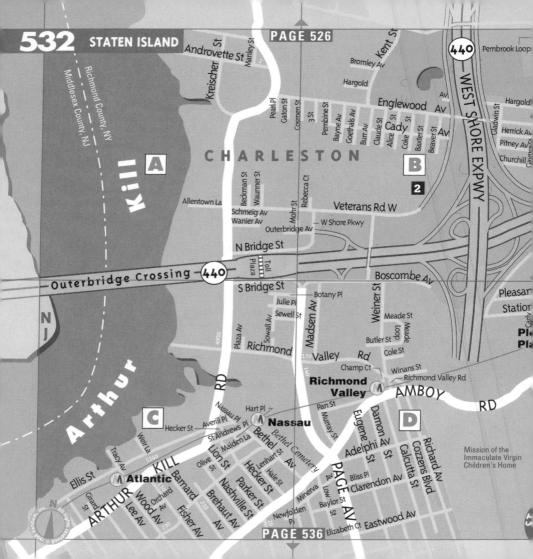

532 STATEN ISLAND

440

Pembrook Loop

CHARLESTON

A

Richmond County, NY
Middlesex County, NJ

Androvette St

Kreischer St

Manley St

Pearl Pl

Gaton St

Cosmen St

3 St

Pembine St

Bayne St

Goethals Av

Burr Av

Claude St

Alice St

Coke St

Baxter St

Beaver St

Bromley Av

Hargold

Kent St

Englewood Av

Cady

Av

Gladwin St

Hargold

Herrick Av

Pitney Av

Churchill

B

2

WEST SHORE EXPWY

440

Allentown La

Beckman St

Waumer St

Rebecca Ct

Schmeig Av

Wanier Av

Mohr St

Outerbridge Av

W Shore Pkwy

Veterans Rd W

N Bridge St

Plaza

Toll

Outerbridge Crossing 440

Boscombe Av

Pleasan
Station

S Bridge St

Julie Pl

Botany Pl

Sewell St

Weiner St

Meade St

Meade
loop

Pl
Pla

Arthur

Plaza Av

Sowall Av

Madsen Av

Richmond

Valley

Rd

Butler St

Cole St

Champ Ct

Winans St

Richmond Valley Rd

Richmond Valley Ⓜ

AMBOY

RD

NJ

Hart Pl

Nassau Pl

St Andrews Pl

Averill Pl

Hecker St

Pan St

Ⓜ **Nassau**

Bethel

Bethel Cemetery

Eugene St

Damon St

Adelphi Av

Richard Av

Cozzens Blvd

Calcutta St

Mission of the
Immaculate Virgin
Children's Home

D

C

ARTHUR KILL

Weir La

Tracy Av

52nd

Ellis St

Ⓜ **Atlantic**

Girard St

Lee Av

Wood Av

Orchard St

Barnard

Fisher Av

Brehaut Av

Nashville St

Parker St

Lion St

Olive St

Maiden La

Lenhart Av

Hale St

Hecker St

Murray St

PAGE AV

Minerva

Newfolden Pl

Bliss Pl

Clarendon Av

Baylor St

Low St

Elizabeth Ct

Eastwood Av

NJ

START DRIVE

Alysia Ct
Sharon La
Helene Ct
nona Av

Lamont Av
Ionia Av
Edgegrove Av
Darlington Av
Carlton Av

MaGuire Av

FOSTER RD

Vernon Av

Marcy Av

Carlton Ct

470
1720

Ashland Av E
Albourne Av E

Bloomingdale Park

Drumgoole Rd E

RICHMOND PKWY

Woodhull Av

Addison Av
Vernon Av
Richmond Pkwy Rd

A

MaGuire Ct
Fonda Pl
Depew Pl
Minturn Av

Rd W
Ashland Av
Lenevar Av
Bradford Av

Parkwood Av

Queensdale St
Valdemar Av
Wheeling Av
Haynes Av
Princewood Av
Wrenn St

B

Deisuis St
Prall Av
Luten Av
Androvette Av

HUEGUENOT AV

Tuckahoe Av

Drumgoole

Albourne Ct

Albourne Av
Uncas Av
Cleamont Av

Nathan Ct

618th

Chisholm St
Eylandt Av

Victor St
Maretzek Ct
Goff Av
Vogel Av
Petersons La
MaGuire Av
Terrace Av

Vogel Av

Boynton St

Scudder Av

Madera St

Idaho Av

S Drum St
erbridge Av
Durham St

Maree Av

Utica St

Waterbury Av
Florence Pl

Oswald Pl

SEGUINE AV

Herbert St

Prince's Bay

MacGregor Av

Wolfe's Pond Park

Jansen St
Short Pl

PAGE 534

Georges La

Ficarelle Dr

Percival Pl
Elizabeth Pl

Knox St
Singleton St

Johanna Loop

Hathaway Av

Atkins Av

Holten Av

HYLAN BLVD

Maxwell Av
Cornelia Av

Penton St
Bedell St
Gilbert Pl
LaTourette St

Bayview

Di Renzo Ct
Hanover Av

Wolf St

Harriet Av
Belle Dr

Sharrott Av
Cordelia Av
S Goff Av
Woodvale Av
Elder Av
Excelsior Av
Finlay Av
Shadyside Av

Everett Av

Trenton Ct
Inez St

Staten Island
University
Hospital
(South)
Keating

Armour Pl
Ormsby Av
St Case Av
Cooper Pl

Resurrection Cemetery

C

Kenneth Pl
Stevenson Pl

Vail Av

Vail

Creston Av

Burton Av

Woodvale Loop

Carol Ct

Kingsland St

D

Norman Pl

Melville St
Walch St

Wilbur St

Memo St

Wolfe's Pond

Sherwood Av

Resurrection Cemetery

HYLAN BLVD

Admiralty
Commodore
Flagship
Loop Cir
Indale
Marine Dr

Lemon Creek Park

Hank Pl

Marscher Pl

Van Wyck Av

Trenton Ct

Purdy Pl

Johnston

2 MILES= 3.2 KMS

END 3 MINS

Johnston Ter

2 MILES= 3.2 KMS

PAGE 529

PAGE 533

HUGUENOT

Ⓜ **Huguenot**

AMBOY

HUEGUENOT AV

Lexa Pl
Collyer AV
Bland Pl
Alvine Av
Billiou St
Philip Av
Deisius St
Community La
Edwin St
RD
Kraft Pl
Edwin St
Lipsett Av
Sycamore St
Tallman St
Eylandt St
Sanbom St
Barclay
ARDEN AV
Seldman St
Liss St
Oban St
Woo

Ruggles St

Rose La
Eugene Pl
Sala Ct

Rockport St
Stecher St
Algonkin St
Christine Ct
Comely St
Arbutus
Kingdom Av
Tudahoe Av
St

Poillon AV

Koch Blvd
Jansen St
Harold Av
Weaver St
Holdridge
Shirley Av
St
Noel
Lenzie
Luna Cir
Lenzie St
Ravenna St
Elman
Bathgat

A

*Blue Heron
Pond Park*

B

Deisius St
Prall Av
Androvette Av
Luten Av

St
Colon
St
Denise Ct
Walsh St
Eadie Av
Bertram AV
Louise St
Arbutus Way
AV
Jansen Ct
Jansen St
Wendy Dr
Allegro St
Newton St
Dole St
Tyndale St
Kinghom St
Allen Pl
Lipsett
Peare Pl
Ryan Pl
Bennet
Pl
Sandgap

Capellan St

Lotus AV
Rockport St
Pierre Pl
Leonard St

BLVD
Lynch St
Philip
AV
Kenwood Av
Leola Pl
Petersburg Av
Poughkeepsie Av
Orangeburg Av
Zephyr Av

HYLAN
Oceanview Av
1 Ct
2 Ct
3 Ct
4 Ct
Bayview Ter
Boardwalk Av
4895

*Wolfe's
Pond
Park*

Jansen St
Short Pl
5400

Swaim Av
Stecher Av
Jarvis Av
Arbutus
AV

Arbutus Lake

Nicolosi Loop
Dr

HYLAN
Maxwell Av
Dixwell Av
Cornelia Av
Edith Av
Irvington St
Chester Av
Shore Av
Veith Pl
Yeomalt Av
Trout Pl
Az
Nicolosi

**Huguenot
Beach**

Harriet Av
Belle Dr

C

Wolfe's Pond

D

Atla

STA

N

Lyndale
Retford
King St
Av
Av
Av
BLVD
Seacrest Av
Groton S
Littlefield Av
Oceanic Av
Prol Pl
rchard
len
berry
Wakefield Rd
Rd
Promenade

**Crookes
Point**

NJ

START DRIVE

adale
ch

A

B

O c e a n

t i c

C

D

2 MILES= 3.2 KMS

END 3 MINS

VE

2 MILES= 3.2 KMS

PAGE 532
Richmond Valley Ⓜ AMBOY

Arthur Kill

Middlesex County, NJ
Richmond County, NY

ARTHUR KILL

Nassau Pl
Hart Pl
Pan St
Murray Av
Hecker St
Averill Pl
St Andrews Pl
Nassau
Bethel Av
Olive St
Lori St
Maiden La
Bethel Av
Bethel Cemetery

Ⓜ Atlantic

Weir La
Tracy Av
5240
Bamard
Orchard
Wood Av
Lee Av
Yetman
Fisher Av
KILL RD
Brehaut Av
Nashville St
Parker St
Hecker St
Lenhart St
Hale St
Low St
Minerva
Baylor St
Bliss Pl
Clarendon Av

Richard Av
Cozzens Blvd
Calcutta St
Damon St
Eugene St
Adelphi Av

Ellis St

Utah St
Girard St
A
Johnson St
Tynell St
Craig Av
Main St
Earley Pl
Lafayette St
230
240
250
260
210
220
Joyce La
Sanford St
Newfolden Pl
Poe St
Geigerich Av
Joline Ct
Bedell Av
Haywood St
Elizabeth Ct
Jeffrey Pl
Eastwood Av
Estelle Pl
Academy
Beecher Pl
Bartow
Camden Av

B

PAGE AV

Ⓜ Tottenville
P

BENTLEY ST

Asp Pl
Patten St
7740
800
900
Hopping Av

AMBOY

📖
✉

Summit Rd
Academy
Paradise Pl
Keppel Av
Jacob St
Truman St
Jacob St
La
Kalioh
Sylvan
Blossom La
Kathleen Ct
Kerry La
Celina La
Adlers La
Amaron La
Roman
Geigerich Pl

Sprague Av
Nancy La
Jacob St

TOTTENVILLE

7780

Wards Point Av
Tottenville Pl
Perth Amboy Pl
Summit Rd
Bryan St
Shore Rd
Pittsville Av

CARTERET ST
Pittsville Av
Main St
Brighton St
Chelsea St
Swinnerton St
Manhattan Av
Yetman Av
Sleight Av
George St
Fayann La

HYLAN BLVD

CRAIG AV
Satterlee St
Pittsville Av
Finlay St
Aspinwall St
Connecticut St
Massachusetts St

C

Clemont Av
550
540
560
7800
260 St
250 St

Loretto St
Rockaway St
Sunset La
Seacrest La
Wildwood La
Sandy La
Forest La
Woods Loop
Sunrise Pl
Sea Breeze
670
350

Joline La
Tricia Way

D

The Conference House

Surf Av

Billop Av

Surf Av

Tottenville Beach

Wards Point

Conference House Park

© 1998 THOMAS BROS. MAPS INC. ALL RIGHTS RESERVED.

Everett Pl

Kenneth Pl

Elder Av

S Goff Av

Creston St

Vail

Everett Av

Inez St

Resurrection Cemetery

Stevenson Pl

Vail Av

Carol Ct

Burton Av

Bayview

HYLAN BLVD

Lemon Creek Park

NJ

START DRIVE

Sherwood Av

Woodvale

Admiralty

Commodore

Woodvale Av

Indale Av

Marine Dr

Flagship Loop Cir

Av

Dr

Sharrott Av

Resurrection Cemetery

6220

Johnston Ter

A

B

Purdy Pl

Johnston Ter

on of the culate Virgin en's Home

80

MOUNT LORETTO

Seguine Point

Prince's Bay

B a y

C

D

2 MILES = 3.2 KMS

Raritan

END 3 MINS

2 MILES= 3.2 KMS

Locating a street is easy. All streets in NYC are indexed alphabetically by borough. Each borough has a unique color bar for easy reference to its maps and indices as shown at right.

Each street is followed by a page number and a grid coordinate. In order to find West Broadway in Manhattan simply go to the Manhattan index starting on page 608. West Broadway....104 B. 104 represents the page number and "B" the grid coordinate.

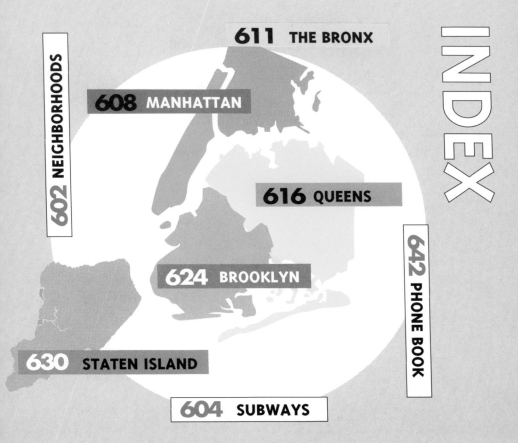

Page
Grid

AIRPORTS & HELIPORTS

BUS & TRAIN TERMINALS

FERRY TERMINALS

TO FIND A BASIC

Simply turn to page and locate the basic in grids **A,B,C or D.**

MA = Manhattan
BX = The Bronx
BK = Brooklyn
QS = Queens
SI = Staten Island

TUNNELS & BRIDGES

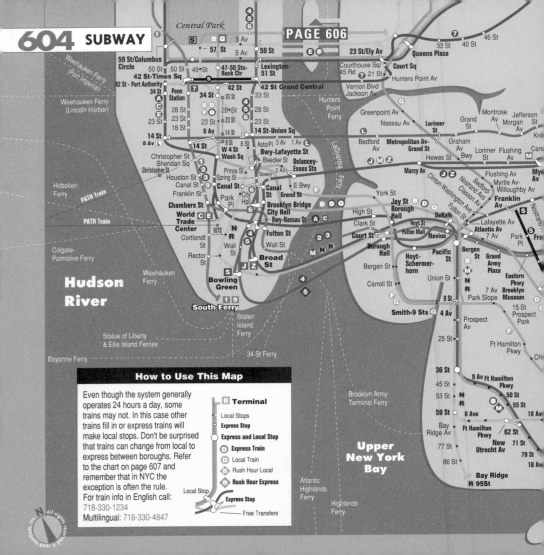

PAGE 606

How to Use This Map

Even though the system generally operates 24 hours a day, some trains may not. In this case other trains will fill in or express trains will make local stops. Don't be surprised that trains can change from local to express between boroughs. Refer to the chart on page 607 and remember that in NYC the exception is often the rule.
For train info in English call:
718-330-1234
Multilingual: 718-330-4847

B Terminal
Local Stops
Express Stop
Express and Local Stop
D Express Train
D Local Train
B Rush Hour Local
D Rush Hour Express
Local Stop
Express Stop
Free Transfers

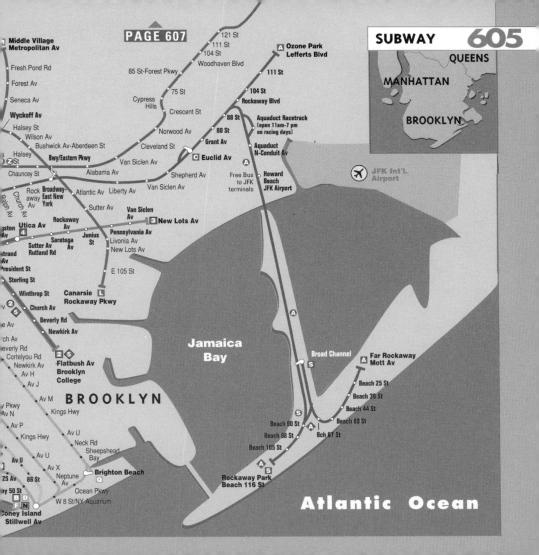

QUEENS

MANHATTAN

BROOKLYN

Middle Village
Metropolitan Av

Fresh Pond Rd

Forest Av

Seneca Av

Wyckoff Av

Halsey St
Wilson Av
Bushwick Av-Aberdeen St

Halsey St

Bwy/Eastern Pkwy

Chauncey St

Broadway-
East New
York

Utica Av

Sutter Av
Rutland Rd

Saratoga
Av

Junius
St

Rockaway
Av

Pennsylvania Av

Livonia Av

New Lots Av

Van Siclen
Av

New Lots Av

E 105 St

Canarsie
Rockaway Pkwy

121 St
111 St
104 St
Woodhaven Blvd

85 St-Forest Pkwy

75 St

Cypress
Hills

Crescent St

Norwood Av

Cleveland St

Van Siclen Av

Alabama Av

Atlantic Av   Liberty Av

Sutter Av

Shepherd Av

Van Siclen Av

Euclid Av

Ozone Park
Lefferts Blvd

111 St

104 St
Rockaway Blvd

88 St

80 St

Grant Av

Aquaduct Racetrack
(open 11am-7 pm
on racing days)

Aquaduct
N-Conduit Av

Free Bus
to JFK
terminals

Howard
Beach
JFK Airport

JFK Int'l.
Airport

New Lots Av

Winthrop St

Church Av

Beverly Rd

Newkirk Av

Cortelyou Rd

Newkirk Av

Av H

Av J

Av M

Kings Hwy

Av P

Kings Hwy

Av U

Neck Rd

Av U

Av X

Neptune
Av

Flatbush Av
Brooklyn
College

Sterling St

President St

Strand
Av

Kingston
Av

Rockaway
Av

Sutter Av

Rock
away
Av

Ralph Av

Church
Av

Beverly Rd

Sheepshead
Bay

Av U

86 St

Ocean Pkwy

W 8 St/NY Aquarium

Brighton Beach

Coney Island
Stillwell Av

BROOKLYN

**Jamaica
Bay**

Broad Channel

Far Rockaway
Mott Av

Beach 25 St

Beach 36 St

Beach 44 St

Beach 60 St

Bch 67 St

Beach 90 St

Beach 98 St

Beach 105 St

Rockaway Park
Beach 116 St

Atlantic Ocean

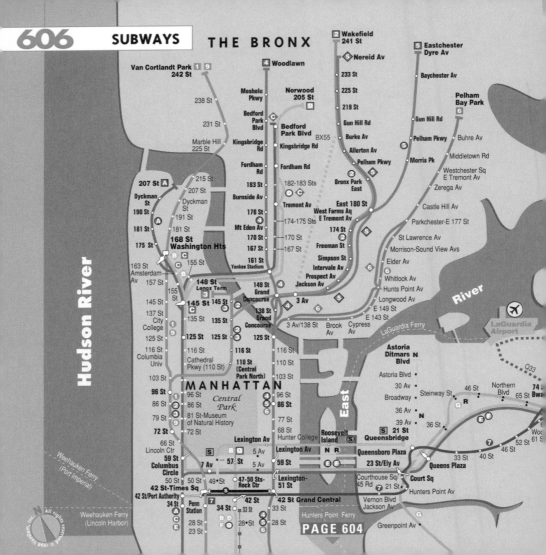

THE BRONX

Van Cortlandt Park 1 9
242 St

238 St

231 St

Marble Hill
225 St

Mosholu
Pkwy

Norwood
205 St

Bedford
Park
Blvd

Bedford
Park Blvd

BX55

Kingsbridge
Rd

Kingsbridge Rd

Fordham
Rd

Fordham Rd

183 St

182-183 Sts

Burnside Av

176 St

174-175 Sts

Mt Eden Av

170 St

170 St

167 St

167 St

161 St
Yankee Stadium

148 St
Lenox Term

149 St
Grand
Concourse

138 St
Grand
Concourse

125 St 125 St 125 St

116 St 116 St 116 St

110 St
(Central
Park North)

103 St 103 St

Wakefield 2
241 St

Nereid Av

233 St

225 St

219 St

Gun Hill Rd

Burke Av

Allerton Av

Pelham Pkwy

Bronx Park
East

East 180 St

West Farms Aq
E Tremont Av

Tremont Av

174 St

Freeman St

Simpson St

Intervale Av

Prospect Av

Jackson Av

3 Av

3 Av/138 St

Brook
Av

Cypress
Av

E 149 St

E 143 St

Eastchester 5
Dyre Av

Baychester Av

Pelham
Bay Park

Gun Hill Rd

Pelham Pkwy Buhre Av

Morris Pk Middletown Rd

Westchester Sq
E Tremont Av

Zerega Av

Castle Hill Av

Parkchester-E 177 St

St Lawrence Av

Morrison-Sound View Avs

Elder Av

Whitlock Av

Hunts Point Av

Longwood Av

6

Woodlawn 4

Wowoodlawn 4

LaGuardia Ferry

River

LaGuardia
Airport

207 St A

Dyckman
St

190 St

181 St

175 St

168 St
Washington Hts

163 St
Amsterdam
Av

157 St

155
St

145 St 145 St 145 St

137 St
City
College

135 St 135 St

125 St

116 St
Columbia
Univ

103 St

215 St

207 St

Dyckman
St

191 St

181 St

155 St

MANHATTAN

Central
Park

96 St 96 St 96 St

86 St 86 St 86 St

79 St

81 St-Museum
of Natural History

72 St 72 St

66 St
Lincoln Ctr

59 St
Columbus
Circle

7 Av 57 St

50 St 50 St 49 St

42 St/Port Authority

42 St-Times Sq

34 St

Penn
Station

28 St

23 St

34 St

33 St

28 St

96 St

86 St

77 St

68 St
Hunter College

Lexington Av

Lexington Av

5 Av

5 Av

59 St

47-50 Sts-
Rock Ctr

42 St

33 St

28 St

Roosevelt
Island

Lexington
-51 St

Lexington-
Grand Central

Hunters Point Ferry

PAGE 604

Astoria
Ditmars
Blvd

Astoria Blvd

30 Av

Broadway Steinway St

36 Av

39 Av

36 St

21 St

Queensbridge

Queensboro Plaza

23 St/Ely Av

Courthouse Sq
45 Rd 21 St

Court Sq

Hunters Point Av

Vernon Blvd
Jackson Av

Greenpoint Av

Northern
Blvd

46 St

65 St

74

Woo
61 St

52 St 61 St

33 St
40 St

46 St

Queens Plaza

Queens Plaza

Q33

East

Hudson River

Weehauken Ferry
(Port Imperial)

Weehauken Ferry
(Lincoln Harbor)

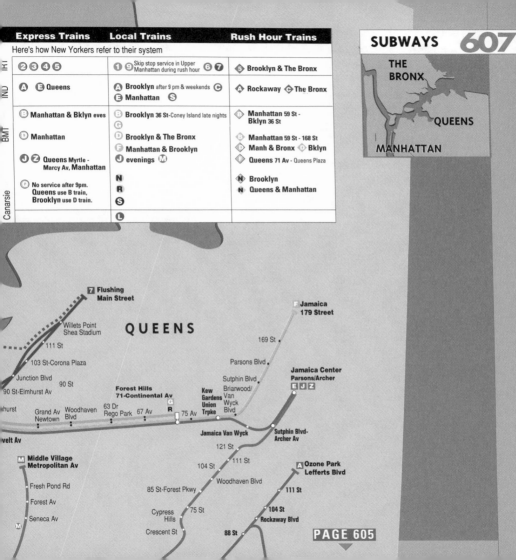

THE BRONX

QUEENS

MANHATTAN

Express Trains **Local Trains** **Rush Hour Trains**

Here's how New Yorkers refer to their system

IRT

②③④⑤ | ①⑨ Skip stop service in Upper Manhattan during rush hour ⑥⑦ | ⑤ Brooklyn & The Bronx

IND

Ⓐ Ⓔ Queens | Ⓐ Brooklyn after 9 pm & weekends Ⓒ Ⓔ Manhattan Ⓢ | Ⓐ Rockaway Ⓒ The Bronx

BMT

Ⓑ Manhattan & Bklyn eves | Ⓑ Brooklyn 36 St-Coney Island late nights Ⓖ | Ⓑ Manhattan 59 St - Bklyn 36 St

Ⓓ Manhattan | Ⓓ Brooklyn & The Bronx | Ⓓ Manhattan 59 St - 168 St

Ⓙ Ⓩ Queens Myrtle - Marcy Av, Manhattan | Ⓕ Manhattan & Brooklyn | Ⓕ Manh & Bronx Ⓖ Bklyn

Ⓙ evenings Ⓜ | Ⓖ Queens 71 Av - Queens Plaza

Canarsie

Ⓩ No service after 9pm. Queens use B train, Brooklyn use D train. | Ⓝ | Ⓝ Brooklyn

Ⓡ | Ⓝ Queens & Manhattan

Ⓢ

Ⓛ

QUEENS

⑦ Flushing Main Street

Willets Point Shea Stadium

111 St

103 St-Corona Plaza

Junction Blvd

90 St-Elmhurst Av

90 St

Ⓕ Jamaica 179 Street

169 St

Parsons Blvd

Sutphin Blvd

Briarwood/ Van Wyck Blvd

Jamaica Center Parsons/Archer Ⓔ Ⓙ Ⓩ

Forest Hills 71-Continental Av Ⓖ

63 Dr Rego Park 67 Av Ⓡ 75 Av

Kew Gardens Union Trpke

Grand Av Newtown Woodhaven Blvd

hurst

velt Av

Ⓜ Middle Village Metropolitan Av

Fresh Pond Rd

Forest Av

Seneca Av

Ⓜ

Jamaica Van Wyck

121 St

104 St

111 St

Sutphin Blvd-Archer Av

Ⓐ Ozone Park Lefferts Blvd

85 St-Forest Pkwy

Woodhaven Blvd

111 St

Cypress Hills

75 St

104 St Rockaway Blvd

Crescent St

88 St

PAGE 605

Washington St	102B -112B
Washington Ter	157A
Water St	103A
Watts St	106A
Waverly Pl	112B
Weehawken St	108B
W Broadway ..	104B
West End Av	
.... 128C	-140A
W Houston St	108B
West Side Hwy	
.... 102C	-124A
West Dr. 129C	-141A
West Rd	
(Roosevelt Is).	308A
West St	102B
W Thames St..	102A
W Washington Pl...	
....	113C
Wheeler Rd	
(Governors Is)	406C
White St	106D
Whitehall St.....	103C
Willett St.........	111C
William St........	103A
Wooster St......	106B
Worth Sq	117B
Worth St..........	104B
York Av .. 131D	-139D
York St............	106B

NUMBERED
AV • PI • ST

1 Av 110B	-147A
1 Pl..............	102D
2 Av 110A	-151C
2 Pl..............	102B
3 Av 114C	-150D
3 Pl..............	102B
4 Av	113B
5 Av 113B	-150B
6 Av 106B	-129D
7 Av 117C	-130C
..............145C	-153A
7 Av S	109A
8 Av 112B	-125A

9 Av 116D -124B	,161C
10 Av	
........116D -124B	,161C
11 Av 116B	-124B
12 Av	
......116A -124B	,148C
65 St Transverse ...	
....	130A
79 St Transverse	
....	133A
85 St Transverse	
....	137C
97 St Transverse	
....	137A

E 1-2 St	110A
E 3 St	114C
E 4 St............	113D
E 5-6 St	114C
E 7 St	114A
E 8 St............	113B
E 9-14 St........	113B
E 15-20 St	117D
E 21 St...........	118C
E 22-29 St	118A
E 30-36 St	121D
E 37-40 St	121B
E 41-43 St	122A
E 44-49 St	125D
E 50 St...........	125B
E 51 St...........	126B
E 52-57 St	126A
E 58-64 St	130D
E 65-72 St	130B
E 73-79 St	133D
E 80-82 St	133B
E 83-86 St	134B
E 87-91 St	137D
E 92-95 St	137B
E 96-99 St	138B
E 100 St	143C
E 101-03 St	141D
E 104-07 St......	141B
E 108-10 St	142B
E 111-12 St	146D
E 113-14 St	147C
E 115-17 St	146D

E 118-25 St	146B
E 126-32 St	150D
E 135 St...........	150B
E 138 St	150B
W 3 St..............	113C
W 4 St..............	112B
W 8-9 St	113A
W 10-11 St	112D
W 12-14 St	112A
W 15-21 St	116D
W 22-25 St	116B
W 26-29 St	116A
W 30-36 St	120D
W 37-38 St	120B
W 39-44 St	120A
W 45-49 St	124D
W 50-57 St	124B
W 58-64 St	128D
W 65-72 St	128B
W 73-79 St	132C
W 80-86 St	132A
W 87-91 St	136C
W 92-99 St	136A
W 100-03 St	140C
W 104-09 St	140A
W 111-17 St	145C
W 118-25 St	145A
W 126-29 St	148D
W 130-32 St	148C
W 133 St	148A
W 134 St	148B
W 135-40 St	148A
W 141-49 St	152D
W 150-59 St	152B
W 160-64 St	154D
W 165-68 St	154B
W 169-73 St	154A
W 174-80 St	157C
W 181-90 St	157A
W 191-93 St	159C
W 196 St	158D
W 201-07 St	159A
W 208 St	159A
W 211-18 St	161C
W 219-20 St	161A
W 225 St	161A
W 227 St	161A

Arithmetic of The Avenues

To locate an address on an avenue in Manhattan without knowing the cross street is quite simple. Just drop the last figure, divide by 2 and add or subtract as listed below. The resulting number is the nearest cross street. This does not apply to Broadway below 8 St.

Avs A, B, C, D add 3	**Broadway**
1 & 2 Av add 3	754–858 subtract 29
3 Av add 10	858–958 subtract 25
4 Av add 8	> 100 St subtract 30
5 Av to 200 add 13	**Columbus Av** add 60
to 400 add 16	**Convent Av** add 127
to 600 add 18	**Central Park W** divide St
to 775 add 20	number by 10 & add 60
to 775 - 1286 drop last	**Edgecombe Av** add 134
figure & subtract 18	**Lenox Av** add 110
to 1500 add 45	**Lexington Av** add 22
to 2000 add 24	**Madison Av** add 26
Av of the Americas subtract 12	**Manhattan Av** add 100
7 Av add 12, > 110 St add 20	**Park Av** add 35
8 Av add 10	**Pleasant Av** add 101
9 Av add 13	**Riverside Dr** divide house
10 Av add 14	number by 10 & add 72
Amsterdam Av add 60	up to 165 St
Audubon Av add 165	**West End Av** add 60

East	**Cross Streets**	**West**

To find a crosstown street address and
the avenues it is in between, follow the key.

Manhattanwide	Below 59th St	Above 59th Street
1–49 5–Madison Avs	**1–99** 5–6 Avs	**1–99** Central Park W–Columbus Avs
50–99 Madison–Park Avs	**100–199** 6–7 Avs	**100–199** Columbus–Amsterdam Avs
100–149 Park–Lexington Avs	**200–299** 7–8 Avs	**200–299** Amsterdam–West End Avs (WEA)
149–199 Lex–3 Avs	**300–399** 8–9 Avs	**300–399** West End Av–Riverside Dr
200–299 3–2 Avs	**400–499** 9–10 Avs	
300–399 2–1 Avs	**500–599** 10–11 Avs	
400–499 1–York Avs (Av A below 14 St)		
500–599 Avs A–B		

ang Av 204D
atford Av ...216D
ong St.........209D
burban Pl....222B
llivan Pl 218B
mmit Av 221C
mmit Pl 209C
nset Bd.......225C
nset Ter 219C
therland St..207C
vinton Av 218D
camore Av ..208A
camore Dr .217A
van Av 203C
n Pl 217B
ylor Av 216D
ler Av 221B
nbroeck Av..211A
nny Pl 221A
rrace Pl......205B
rrace St.....207C
ieriot Av 217C
rogmorton Av.....
.....................218B
rogs Neck Bd.....
.....................218B
rogs Neck
pwy 218B
roop Av 211A
waites Pl 210D
bett Av........208D
bout Av 215A
emann Av ...205C
er St............213A
erney Pl 219A
fany St 222D
den St........210B
lotson Av...205C
n Hendrick Pl .....
.....................209C
mpson Pl 228A
ton Av.........222D
mlinson Av ..211C
pping Av 215C

Torry Av 225A
Townsend Av...221A
Trafalgar Pl....216C
Tratman Av.....217B
Trinity Av........221D
Truxton St......223C
Tryon Av 209B
Tudor Pl.........221C
Tulfan Ter 208D
Turnbull Av 217D
Turneur Av 225A
Tyndall Av......202D
Undercliff Av ..220B
Underhill Av ...217C
Union Av 222D
Union Pl 221C
Unionport Rd ..216B
University Av ..209C
University Av ..215A
Unknown Soldier
Plz 215C
Valentine Av...209D
Valhalla Av 212D
Valles Av........203C
Van Buren St..216D
Van Cortlandt Av E
.....................209D
Van Cortlandt Av W
.....................209C
Van Cortlandt Park
E 203D
Van Cortlandt Park
S 209A
Van Cortlandt
Village Sq 209C
Van Hoessen Av.....
.....................211C
Van Nest Av....216D
Vance St.........211B
Varian Av 205A
Verveelen Pl...209C
Victor St 216B
Viele Av..........223D
Villa Av 209D

Vincent Av 218B
Vineyard Pl.....216C
Vireo Av 204A
Virgil Av 217D
Virginia Av 217C
Vreeland Av ...218A
Vyes Av..........222B
Waldo Av 208B
Wales Av 227B
Wallace Av......210B
Walnut Av 227D
Walton Av 215A
Ward Av 223A
Waring Av 210D
Washington Av.....
.....................215B
Washington Park
Av.....................221B
Waterbury Av..212D
Waterloo Pl 216C
Waters Av 211D
Waters Pl 211D
Watson Av 217C
Watt Av............212D
Wayne Av 209B
Webb Av 209C
Webster Av.....
...................204C-221D
Weeks Av 215C
Weiher Ct 221D
Wellman Av 212C
Wenner Pl........218C
West Av 217C
W Burnside Av.....
.....................214D
W Clarke Pl 221A
W Farms Rd ...216D
W Farms Sq 216D
W Fordham Rd215A
W Gun Hill Rd 209B
W Kingsbridge Rd ..
.....................215A
W Mosholu Pkwy
N 209B

W Mosholu Pkwy S
.....................209A
W Mt Eden Av 221A
W Tremont Av 215C
Westchester Av .....
...................212C-227B
Westchester Sq.....
.....................217B
Westervelt Av 211B
Whalen St........203C
Wheeler Av 223A
White Plains Rd .....
...................210D-224B
Whitehall Pl 204A
Whitlock Av 223A
Whittier St 223C
Whittmore Av 218A
Wickham Av ...204B
Wilcox Av 218B
Wilder Av 204B
Wilkinson Av ..211D
Willett Av 210B
William Av 213A
William Pl.......218A
Williamsbridge Rd..
.....................210D
Willis Av 227A
Willow Av 227D
Willow La 212C
Wilson Av........211A
Windward Ln..213B
Winters St 213B
Wissman Av....219A
Wood Av 217C
Wood Rd..........217C
Woodhull Av ...211B
Woodmansten Pl....
.....................211C
Woodycrest Av .....
.....................221C
Worthen St......223C
Wright Av 205C
Wyatt St 216D
Wythe Pl..........221A

Yates Av 211A
Young Av.........211A
Yznaga Pl.......218D
Zerega Av........217B
Zulette Av 212C

**NUMBERED
AV • Pl • ST**

1-2 Av 219A
3 Av 215D-227A
4-5 Av 219A
7 Av 219A
9 Av 219A
11 Av 219A

E 132 St 227C
E 133 St 227D
E 134-38 St 227C
E 139 St 227D
E 140-48 St 227A
E 149 St 227B
E 150-51 St 226B
E 152 St 227A
E 153 St 226B
E 154-55 St 227A
E 156 St 221D
E 157-59 St 221C
E 160-61 St 221D
E 162-65 St 221C
E 166 St 221D
E 167 St 221C
E 168-71 St 221A
E 172 St 216D
E 173 St 216C
E 174-75 St 215D
E 177 St 215C, 218B
E 178-83 St 215C
E 184-89 St 215B
E 190-93 St 215A
E 194-96 St 211D
E 197-207 St ...209D
E 208-13 St 209B
E 214-17 St 210B

E 218-19 St 204D
E 220-21 St 204C
E 222 St..........204D
E 223-26 St 204C
E 227-29 St 204D
E 229 Dr N & S 204D
E 230-36 St 204C
E 233 St..........203D
E 236-38 St 203D
E 239-43 St 204A

W 161-68 St 221C
W 169-76 St 221A
W 177-83 St 215C
W 184 St..........215A
W 188 St...........215A
W 190 St...........215A
W 192 St...........215A
W 193 St...........214B
W 195 St...........215A
W 197 St...........209C
W 205 St...........209C
W 227-28 St 208D
W 229 St...........209C
W 230-32 St 208D
W 233 St...........209C
W 234-40 St 208D
W 242 St...........208B
W 244-45 St 208B
W 246-49 St 208A
W 250-53 St 208B
W 254-55 St 203C
W 256-63 St 202D

FIND A BASIC

Simply turn to page
and locate the
basic in grids
A,B,C or D.

MA = Manhattan
BX = The Bronx
BK = Brooklyn
QS = Queens
SI = Staten Island

FIND A BASIC

Simply turn to page
and locate the
basic in grids
A,B,C or D.

MA = Manhattan
BX = The Bronx
BK = Brooklyn
QS = Queens
SI = Staten Island

QUEENS

Abbot Rd..........307D
Aberdeen Rd .330D
Abigail Adams Av ..
................................338B
Abingdon Rd ..336B
Adair St............345D
Adelaide Rd ...345A
Admiral Av 326D
Aguilar Av.......329D
Alameda Av 324D
Albert Rd 342D
Albert Short Sq316B
Albion Av 319C
Alderton St.....327B
Alexander Gray
Triangle............306B
Allendale St 337D
Almeda Av 367C
Almont Rd.......369B
Alonzo Rd 361D
Alstyne Av 319C
Alwick Rd 343D
Amber St.........342C
Amboy La 340B
Amelia Rd 345C
Amory Ct.........326C
Amstel Bd........367A
Anchor Dr........361C
Anderson Rd ..345D
Andrews Av 326C
Ankener Av......319C
Annandale La 325A
Annapolis St ..369B
Apex Pl............328A
Arcade Av........339C
Arch St............316B
Archer Av 337C
Archway Pl 328D
Ardsley Rd 315D
Arion Rd 342C
Arleigh Rd 315D
Arlington Ter ..344B
Arnold Av 326C
Arthur St..........352D
Arverne Bd......367B
Ascan Av 336B

Ash Av..............321B
Ashby Av..........322C
Ashford St 332D
Aske St 319B
Aspen Pl 338B
Asquith Cres ...327D
Astoria Bd 309A
Astoria Park S 302C
Atlantic Av 336D
Atlantic Wk 362B
Aubrey Av........335B
Auburndale La322D
Audley St 336B
Augusta Ct 344B
Augustina Av ..361D
Austell Pl 316B
Austin St327B-336B
Ava Pl 338B
Avery Av 321A
Avon Rd 330D
Avon St 339A
Aztec Pl 369A
Babbage St 336D
Babylon Av 339C
Bagley Av.........322D
Bailey Ct 361C
Baisley Bd 345C
Baisley Legion Sq ..
...............................344D
Baldwin Av 328C
Barbadoes Dr 367A
Barclay Av 321D
Bardwell Av 340C
Barnett Av 317A
Barnwell Av 319C
Barrington St ..339A
Barron St 344D
Barrows Ct.......324B
Barton Av 322A
Bascom Av.......344D
Bath Wk 362B
Battery Rd 361D
Baxter Av 319A
Bay Ct 361C
Bay Dr 315C
Bay Ter 362B
Bay Park Pl......361C
Bay 24-25 St ..361C

Bay 27-28 St ..361C
Bay 30-32 St ..368B
Bay 32 Pl 361C
Bay Park Dr 304B
Bayfield Av......367B
Bayport Pl 361C
Bayside Av 312C
Bayside Dr ....
..................362B, 363B
Bayside La 313D
Bayside St 307C
Bayside Wk 362B
Bayview Av........
...............315D, 356C
Bayview Wk....362B
Bayshore Rd ..315C
Bayswater Ct ..361C
Bayswater La ..361C
Bayway Wk 362B
Beach Channel Dr ..
..............365A-368A
Beach 3-7 St ..369D
Beach 8-9 St ..369B
Beach 11-12 St ..
...............................361D
Beach 13-17 St ..
...............................369C
Beach 18-22 St ..
...............................369A
Beach 24 St ...361C
Beach 25-28 St......
...............................369C
Beach 29-41 St......
...............................368D
Beach 41 Pl ...368B
Beach 42-46 St......
...............................368D
Beach 46 Pl ...368D
Beach 46 Wy ..368D
Beach 47 St ...368B
Beach 47 Wy ..368D
Beach 48 St ...368A
Beach 48 Wy ..368C
Beach 48-52 St......
...............................368C
Beach 53 St ...368A
Beach 54 St ...368C
Beach 56 Pl ...367D

Beach 56-58 St......
...............................367B
Beach 59-72 St......
...............................367D
Beach 73-77 St......
...............................367C
Beach 79-81 St......
...............................367C
Beach 82-89 St......
...............................367A
Beach 90-93 St......
...............................367C
Beach 96-99 St......
...............................366D
Beach 100-02 St......
...............................366D
Beach 102 La 365B
Beach 104-05 St......
...............................365B
Beach 106 La 365B
Beach 106 St ..365B
Beach 108-17 St......
...............................365B
Beach 118-35 St......
...............................365A
Beach 136-46 St......
...............................364B
Beach 145-49 St......
...............................364D
Beach 169 St ..363B
Beach 180 St ..363B
Beach 193 St ..363A
Beach 201 St ..363A
Beach 204 St ..362B
Beach 207-09 St......
...............................362B
Beach 214-21 St......
...............................362B
Beach 222 St ..362A
Beacon Pl.......361C
Beatrice Ct......369A
Beaver Rd 337C
Beck Rd 369B
Bedell St..........344B
Bedford Av 362B
Beech Av 321B
Beech Ct 305C
Beechknoll Av 325A

Beechknoll Pl 328D
Belknap St 345D
Bell Bd 314B
Bellaire Pl........340A
Belmont Av 342C
Belt Pkwy ....
..............348A-352A
Benham St 319B
Bennet Ct 345D
Bennet St 346D
Bentley Rd 357C
Benton St 345D
Bergen Rd 349C
Berkley Av 325A
Berrian Bd 303C
Bessemer Ct ..336D
Bessemund Av ......
...............................368B
Beverly Rd 315C
Billings St 332D
Birdsall Av 365D
Birmington Pkwy ...
...............................323D
Blake Av 342C
Bleecker St 326C
Blossom Av 321A
Boardwalk ....
...............365B-368B
Boelsen Cres ..327D
Bohack Sq 326C
Boker Ct 304D
Bolton Rd 361D
Bonnie La 307C
Boody St 310C
Booth Mem Av ......
...............................321C
Booth St 328A
Borage Pl 328D
Borden Av 316A
Borkel Pl 332D
Borough Pl 309D
Boss St 342D
Boulevard 305D
Bourton St 327B
Bow St 328D
Bowden Av......323A
Bowne St 321B
Boyce Av 323A

Braddock Av ..332
Bradley Av 31
Brant Wk 362
Brattle Av 325
Breezy Point Bd ......
...................................36.
Brevoort Rd ...330
Brian Cres 30
Briar Pl 36
Bridgeton St...34
Bridgewater Av ......
...................................32
Brinkerhoff Av 33
Brisbin St 33
Bristol Av 342
Britton Av 31
Broad St 35
Broadway........30
Brocher Rd 34
Brookhaven Av......
...................................36
Brooklyn Queens
Expwy (BQE) .31
Brookside St .31
Brookville Bd .353
Brown's Bd 36
Brown Pl..........32
Browvale La....325
Brunswick Av 36
Bud Pl 32
Buell St 31
Burchell Av 36
Burchell Rd 36
Burden Cres...33
Burdette Pl......33
Burling St 32
Burns St 32
Burrough Pl ...31
Burton St 32
Butler Av..........32
Butler St 31
Bye Rd 32
Byrd St 32
Byron St 35
C.R. Sohncke Sq......
...................................31
Cabot Rd 33
Caffrey Av........36

Street	Grid
W Hangar Rd ..349C	
W Market St ..362B	
Westgate St....352B	
Westbourne Av 361C	
Westmoreland Pl	
...............315D	
Westmoreland St	
...............325A	
Westside Av....320C	
Westaway Rd 307D	
Wetherole St .328A	
Wexford Ter ..339A	
Wheatley St 361D	
Whistler Av 307D	
Whitehall Ter .331B	
Whitelaw St 342D	
Whitestone Expwy	
...............305D	
Whitney Av.....319B	
Whitston St ...336B	
Wicklow Pl 339A	
Willets Point Bd......	
...............320B	
Villets St 307D	
William Ct.......369C	
Williamson Av 345D	
Willoughby Av 326C	
Willow St 324B	
Vinchester Bd 332D	
Vinter St 328D	
Vitthoff St 340D	
Wood St 345A	
Woodbine St .326D	
Woodhaven Bd	
...............327D	
Woodhaven Ct	
...............342D	
Woodhull Av ..339D	
Woodside Av ..318B	
Woodward Av 326C	
Vren Pl 339C	
Wyckoff Av.....334A	
Xenia St 320C	
Yates Rd 344D	
Yellowstone Bd	
...............328B	
Yion St............324C	
Zoller Rd 345D	

NUMBERED
AV • PI • ST

Street	Grid
1 St 302C, 348D	
1 St...............357C	
2 Av 305B-306A	
2 St 302D, 316A	
2 St...............357C	
3 Av 305B-306A	
3 St 302C, 357C	
4 Av 305B-306A	
4 Av 362B	
4 St...............302C	
5 Av 305A-306A	
5 Av 362B	
5 St 316A	
6 Av 305A-306B	
6 Rd 306B	
7 Av 305A-306A	
7 Av 362B	
8 Av 304D-306C	
8 Av 362B	
8 St 302C-309A	
8 Rd 305D-306D	
9 Av 305C-306D	
9 Av 362B	
9 Rd 305C	
9 St.........302C-308C	
10 Av 305C-307C	
10 Av 362B	
10 St 308B	
11 Av 305C-307C	
11 Pl..............316A	
11 St 308BC	
12 Av 305C-306D	
12 Av 362B	
12 Rd 305D-314B	
12 St 302C-309A	
13 Av 305C-306D	
13 Rd 305D, 313A	
13 St 308BD	
14 Av 304D-306D	
14 Pl..............302C	
14 Rd......304D, 313A	
14 St..............302C	
15 Av 304D-314B	
15 Dr 305D-314B	
15 Rd 305D-314B	

Street	Grid
16 Av 306D-314B	
16 Dr 306D-313A	
16 Rd 305D-314A	
17 Av 305D-314B	
17 Rd 305D-314A	
18 Av 305D-314B	
18 St 302C-309A	
19 Av 303C-314B	
19 Dr 310B	
19 Rd 310B	
19 St 302D	
20 Av 302D	
20 Rd 302D	
20 St 302D	
21 Av 302D-314C	
21 Dr 302D	
21 Rd 302D-312B	
21 St 302D-316B	
22 Av 312A	
22 Dr 302D-311A	
22 Rd 302D-312B	
22 St 308D	
23 Av 302D-314D	
23 Dr 302D	
23 Rd	
.......309B, 311C, 314B	
23 St 302D-316B	
24 Av 302D-314D	
24 Dr 302C	
24 Rd	
.......302C, 313C, 314C	
24 St 302D-308D	
25 Av 311C-314C	
25 Dr 313C	
25 Rd......302C, 312B	
25 St 316B	
26 Av 302C-314C	
26 Rd 309A	
26 St 302D	
27 Av 309A-314D	
27 Rd 309A	
27 St 302D-316B	
28 Av 309A-314D	
28 Rd 312D-315C	
28 St 302D-316B	
29 Av 309A-314D	
29 Rd 312D	

Street	Grid
29 St 302D-316B	
30 Av 309A-314D	
30 Dr 309A	
30 Pl 316B	
30 Rd 309A-309D	
30 St 308D	
31 Av 309A	
31 Dr 309A-312D	
31 Pl 316B	
31 Rd	
......309A, 312C, 315C	
31 St 302D-316B	
32 Av 310D-313D	
32 Av (Vista Av)	
...............314C	
32 Pl 317A	
32 Rd 313D	
32 St 302D-309C	
33 Av 309A-314D	
33 Rd 308B-314A	
33 St 302D-317A	
34 Av 309A-320B	
34 Rd 312D-314D	
34 St 309C-317A	
35 Av 308D-323A	
35 Rd 319A	
35 St 309C	
36 Av 308D-321A	
36 Rd 321A	
36 St 310A-317A	
37 Av 308D-324A	
37 Dr 320A	
37 Rd 318B	
37 St 310A-317A	
38 Av 308D-324A	
38 Dr 324B	
38 Rd 315D	
38 St 310A-314C	
39 Av 308D-324B	
39 Dr 317B	
39 Pl 317A	
39 Rd 315D	
39 St 317A	
40 Av 308D-324B	
40 Dr 319B	
40 Rd......308D, 319B	
40 St 317A	
41 Av 308D-324A	

Street	Grid
41 Dr 317B	
41 Rd......319B, 321A	
41 St 310A-317A	
42 Av 319B-324B	
42 Pl 309C	
42 Rd 308D-322B	
42 St 310A-317A	
43 Av 308C-325A	
43 Rd 308C-322B	
43 St 310A-317C	
44 Av 308C-325A	
44 Dr 308C	
44 Rd 308C	
44 St 310A-317C	
45 Av 308C-322B	
45 Dr 322D	
45 Rd 308C-322D	
45 St 310A-317A	
46 Av 308C-324A	
46 Rd 308C-322D	
46 St 310A-317C	
47 Av 316A-324C	
47 Rd 316A	
47 St 310A-318A	
48 Av 316A-324C	
48 St 310A-326A	
49 Av 316A-324C	
49 La 326A	
49 Pl 326A	
49 Rd 323D	
49 St 310A-326A	
50 Av 316A-324C	
50 St 309D-326A	
51 Av 316A-325A	
51 Dr 319C	
51 Rd 317D-319C	
51 St 309D	
52 Av 317D-325A	
52 Ct 319C	
52 Dr 317D-327A	
52 Rd 317D-325A	
52 St 317B-318A	
53 Av 318D-324D	
53 Dr 318D-326B	
53 Pl 309D	
53 Rd 325A	
53 St 326C	
54 Av 316A-324D	

Street	Grid
54 Dr 317C	
54 Pl 326C	
54 Rd 317C	
54 St 309D-326C	
55 Av 316A-326A	
55 Dr 326B	
55 Rd 326B-327A	
55 St 309D-326C	
56 Av 318C-324C	
56 Dr 317C-326B	
56 Pl 309D	
56 Rd 317C-326B	
56 St 309D-326C	
56 Ter 326A	
57 Av 319D-325C	
57 Dr 324D-326B	
57 Pl 326A	
57 Rd 321C-326A	
57 St 309D-326C	
57 St...............334C	
58 Av 319D-325C	
58 Dr 326A	
58 La 317D	
58 Pl 317D-326A	
58 Rd 321C-326B	
58 St 309D-318C	
59 Av 319D-325C	
59 Dr 326D	
59 Pl 317D-326B	
59 Rd 326B	
59 St 318Dt-326B	
59 St...............334C	
60 Av 319D-325C	
60 Ct 326D	
60 Dr 326D	
60 La 326B	
60 Pl 326B	
60 Rd 325C-327B	
60 St 309D-326D	
60 St...............334A	
61 Av 325C	
61 Dr 327B	
61 Rd 321C-327C	
61 St 309D-326D	
61 St...............334C	
62 Av 321C-325C	
62 Dr 320D-327C	
62 Rd 317B-328A	

Street	Grid
62 St	309D-334B
63 Av	321C-325C
63 Dr	327B-328A
63 Pl	326B
63 Rd	321C-329A
63 St	318D-326D
64 Av	321C-325C
64 Cir	330B
64 La	334B
64 Pl	334B
64 Rd	327B-329A
64 St	318B-334B
65 Av	328A-324D
65 Cres	331A
65 Dr	327C-328C
65 La	326D
65 Pl	317D-334B
65 Rd	327B
65 St	318B-334B
66 Av	324D-328A
66 Dr	327C
66 Pl	334B
66 Rd	327C
66 St	318D-334B
67 Av	324D-334A
67 Dr	327C
67 Pl	334B
67 Rd	327C
67 St	318B-334B
68 Av	324D-334A
68 Dr	328B
68 Pl	334B
68 Rd	327C-334A
68 St	309D-334B
69 Av	335A-325C
69 Dr	335A
69 La	326B
69 Pl	318D-334B
69 Rd	328D-336A
69 St	310C-334B
70 Av	324D-334A
70 Dr	336A
70 Rd	328D-336A
70 St	310C-334B
71 Av	325C-334A
71 Cres	330B
71 Dr	336A
71 Pl	335A
71 Rd	325C-336A
71 St	310C334B
72 Av	325C-328D
72 Pl	319C-335A
72 Cres	329C
72 Dr	328C-336A
72 Rd	325C-336A
72 St	310C-335A
73 Av	325C-335B
73 Pl	319C-335A
73 Rd	331B
73 St	310C-335A
73 Ter	329C
74 Av	325D-335B
74 Pl	335C
74 St	310C-335A
75 Av	333B-334A
75 Pl	327C
75 Rd	329C
75 St	310C-335C
76 Av	332A-335B
76 Dr	328C
76 Rd	328D
76 St	310C-342A
77 Av	325C-335A
77 Cres	333A
77 Pl	327A
77 Rd	336B
77 St	310C-348A
78 Av	329C-334A
78 Cres	336B
78 Dr	329C
78 Rd	329C-335A
78 St	310C-348A
79 Av	333B-334A
79 La	335A
79 Pl	335A
79 St	310C-348A
80 Av	333B-334A
80 Dr	330D
80 Rd	330D-336B
80 St	310D-348A
81 Av	333B-335B
81 Rd	335B
81 St	310D-348A
82 Av	333C-335B
82 Dr	333C
82 Pl	327B
82 Rd	333C-337A
82 St	310D-348A
83 Av	333C-335B
83 Dr	335B, 337A
83 Pl	327B
83 Rd	337A
83 St	310D-348A
84 Av	337D
84 Dr	333C-338A
84 Pl	327B
84 Rd	333C-338A
84 St	310D-348A
85 Av	333D-335D
85 Dr	335C
85 Rd	331C-339B
85 St	310D-348A
86 Av	333C-335C
86 Cres	337B
86 Dr	335D-336C
86 Rd	331C-338B
86 St	310D-348A
87 Av	333C-335C
87 Dr	333C, 339A
87 Rd	333C-338B
87 St	310D-348A
87 Ter	333D
88 Av	333C-335C
88 Dr	333C
88 La	335B
88 Pl	335B
88 Rd	333C, 335C
88 St	310D-348A
89 Av	335D-341A
89 Rd	337C, 340A
89 St	310D-348A
90 Av	335C-341A
90 Ct	340A
90 Pl	310D
90 Rd	335C
90 St	310D-348A
91 Av	335D-341A
91 Pl	319D
91 Rd	332D-340B
91 St	310D-348B
92 Av	332D-335D
92 Rd	332D-340B
92 St	310D-348B
93 Rd	335D-340B
93 Rd	337C, 340B
93 St	319B-328A
94 Av	340D-342B
94 Dr	340B
94 Pl	342D
94 Rd	340A
94 St	311A-348B
95 Av	341A-342A
95 Pl	342D
95 St	342D-348B
96 Av	341A
96 Pl	342D
96 Rd	340D
96 St	311C-348B
97 Av	341A-342A
97 Pl	319D
97 St	311C-348B
98 Av	340B
98 Pl	319D
98 St	311C-350A
99 Av	339D
99 Pl	342D, 350A
99 St	311C-350A
100 Av	339D-340B
100 Dr	340D
100 Rd	341C
100 St	311C-350A
101 Av	340D-342A
101 Rd	342B
101 St	311C-350A
102 Av	340D-342A
102 Rd	342A-343B
102 St	311C-350A
103 Av	340D-342A
103 Dr	342B
103 Rd	339C
103 St	311C-350A
104 Av	339C-340D
104 Rd	338D
104 St	311C-342B
105 Av	340D-343B
105 Pl	342B
105 St	311C-342D
106 Av	340D-342A
106 Rd	339C
106 St	311C-342D
107 Av	340D-342A
107 Rd	343B
107 St	311C-342D
108 Av	340D-342A
108 Dr	344B
108 Pl	344B
108 Rd	338D, 339C
108 St	311C-342D
109 Av	340D-342A
109 Dr	344B
109 Rd	339D, 344A
109 St	320D-342B
110 Av	340D-344B
110 Rd	339D-345A
110 St	304D-343A
111 Av	340D-343C
111 Rd	339D-346A
111 St	304D-343A
112 Av	340D, 344B
112 Pl	320D
112 Rd	339D-340D
112 St	304D-343A
113 Av	340C-344B
113 Dr	340D
113 Rd	345B
113 St	304D-343A
114 Av	340D
114 Dr	345B-347B
114 Pl	343C-350A
114 Rd	344B, 347B
114 St	304D-350A
114 Ter	347B
115 Av	343D-347A
115 Dr	344B, 346B
115 Rd	344B-347C
115 St	304D-350A
116 Av	343D-347A
116 Dr	344D
116 Rd	344D-347A
116 St	304D-350A
117 Rd	343D-347A
117 St	304D-349A
118 Av	344D-347A
118 Rd	344D-346B
118 St	304D-350A
119 Av	344D-347A
119 Dr	344D
119 Rd	344D-346B
119 St	304B
120 Av	343D-347A
120 Rd	345D-346B
120 St	304D-350A
121 Av	344D-347C
121 St	304D-350B
122 Av	344D-346D
122 Pl	343C
122 St	311D-350B
123 Av	344C
123 St	305C-350E
124 Av	344D-346C
124 Pl	336E
124 St	305C-350B
125 Av	344D-347C
125 St	305C-350B
126 Av	345C-347C
126 Pl	311D, 312C
126 St	305C-350B
127 Av	345C
127 Pl	312C
127 St	305C-350B
128 Av	344D-347B
128 Dr	347C
128 Rd	347C
128 St	305C-350B
129 Av	344C-347C
129 Rd	347D-353B
129 St	305C-350B
130 Av	344C-353B
130 Dr	346C
130 Pl	344C-349A
130 Rd	345D-353B
130 St	305C-350B
131 Av	343D-353B
131 Rd	353B
131 St	305C-350B
132 Av	351D-353B
132 Rd	345D-353B
132 St	305C-350B
133 Av	342C-353B
133 Dr	353B
133 Pl	305C
133 Rd	345D-353B
133 St	312C, 350B
134 Av	342D-353B
134 Pl	350B
134 Rd	342D-346C
134 St	321C-350B
135 Av	343C-353B

BROOKLYN

Abbey Ct...........445B
Aberdeen St....412D
Abraham Miller Sq
.................424A
Adams St........407C
Adelphi St........407D
Adler Pl............413D
Agate Ct 416B
Ainslie St 404B
Aitken Pl..........407C
Alabama Av 418B
Albany Av
.............416B-429B
Albee Sq..........407C
Albee Sq W 407C
Albemarle Rd..421D
Albemarle Ter 422D
Alben Mem Sq421D
Alice Ct............416B
Allen Av 437D
Alton Pl............429D
Amber St 419B
Amboy St 417D
Amersfort Pl....429A
Ames La 424A
Amherst St.......444D
Amity St 407C
Anchorage Pl..407A
Anna Ct............424B
Anthony St 403C
Apollo St..........403C
Applegate Ct ...436D
Archie C Ketchum
Sq 436A
Ardsley Loop ...425A
Argyle Rd 422C
Arion Pl............405C
Arkansas Dr.....438B
Arlington Av 413C
Arlington Pl 416B
Ascenzi Sq 404B
Ash St 402B
Ashford St 418B
Ashland Pl 407D

Aster Ct............438C
Atkins Av 419A
Atlantic Av
................407C-418B
Atlantic Av 442C
Atwater Ct 443A
Auburn Pl.........407D
Aurelia Ct 429A
Autumn Av 413D
Av A-B..............424A
Av C 422D
Av D 424A
Av F 428B
Av H 428B
Av I 428B
Av J-M 424D
Av N 424D-436B
Av O 430C-436B
Av P 429D
Av R 429D
Av S 430C-436B
Av T-W ..430D-436D
Av X-Y 431C
Av Z 443A
Aviation Rd.......447A
Bainbridge St..417A
Balfour Pl 416D
Baltic St 406D
Bancroft Pl......417B
Bank St 424B
Banker St 402D
Banner Av 443B
Barberry Ct.....413D
Barbey St.........413C
Barlow Dr NS 439A
Barnwell Ct 434A
Bartel Pritchard Sq
........................415C
Bartlett Pl 445B
Bartlett St........404D
Baruch St.........407D
Bassett Av 439A
Bassett Wk 407D
Batchelder St 437B
Bath Av............435A

Battery Av 426D
Baughman Pl...429D
Bay Av..............429C
Bay St 414D
Bay Pkwy 428D
Bay 7-8 St........435A
Bay 10-11 St....435A
Bay 13-14 St....435A
Bay 16-17 St....435A
Bay 19-20 St....435C
Bay 22-23 St....435D
Bay 25-26 St....435D
Bay 28-29 St....435D
Bay 31-32 St....435D
Bay 34-35 St....435D
Bay 37-38 St....435D
Bay 40 St 435D
Bay 41 St..........436C
Bay 43 St..........436C
Bay 44 St 443A
Bay 46-47 St....443A
Bay 49-50 St....443A
Bay 52-54 St....442B
Bay 56 St..........443C
Bay Cliff Ter 426A
Bay Ridge Av ..426B
Bay Ridge Pkwy
........................426B
Bay Ridge Pl ..426B
Bayard St.........402C
Bayview Av 442D
Bayview Pl.......424C
Beach Wk 443B
Beach 37 St 442D
Beach 38 St 442D
Beach 40 St 442D
Beach 42-51 St 442D
Beacon Ct 445B
Beadel St 403C
Beard St 414A
Beaumont St ..444D
Beaver St 405C
Bedell La..........424C
Bedford Av
.............404A-437C

Bedford Pl 416A
Beekman Pl 416C
Belmont Av 419A
Belt Pkwy
.............425C-446A
Belvidere St 405C
Bennett Ct 426B
Benson Av 435A
Bergen Av 430B
Bergen Ct........430B
Bergen Pl 420C
Bergen St 407C
Berkeley Pl......415A
Berriman St 419A
Berry St 402D
Bethel Loop 425A
Beverley Rd 422C
Bevy Ct 438C
Bijou Av 438C
Billings Pl 436B
Bills Pl.............421D
Blake Av 417D
Blake Ct 443B
Blake Sq..........417D
Bleecker St 405D
Bliss Ter 426A
Boardwalk 443C
Boardwalk E .443D
Boardwalk W..443C
Bocchino D Mem
Plz 427A
Boerum Pl.......407C
Boerum St 405C
Bogart St 405C
Bokee Ct 443B
Bond St............407C
Border Av 425C
Borinquen Pl .404B
Bouck Ct 443A
Boulevard St ...436D
Bowery St 443C
Bowne St 414A
Box St 402B
Boynton Pl 443A
Bradford St 418B

Bragg St 437D
Branton St 424C
Brevoort Pl.....416A
Brevoort Pl......416A
Bridge St 407A
Bridge Plz Ct ..407A
Bridgewater St.......
........................403C
Brigham St.......437D
Brighton Ct......443B
Brighton 1 Pl ..443D
Brighton 1 Rd..443D
Brighton 1 St ..443D
Brighton 1 Wk 443D
Brighton 2 St ..443D
Brighton 2 Wk 443B
Brighton 3 Rd..443B
Brighton 3 St ..443D
Brighton 3 Wk 443D
Brighton 4 Rd..443B
Brighton 4 St ..443B
Brighton 4 Ter 443B
Brighton 4 Wk 443B
Brighton 5 St ..443D
Brighton 5 Wk 443B
Brighton 6 St ..443D
Brighton 7 St ..443B
Brighton 7 Wk 443B
Brighton 8 St ..443B
Brighton 10 Ct 443B
Brighton 10 La 443B
Brighton 10 Path
........................443B
Brighton 10 St 444B
Brighton 10 Ter......
........................443B
Brighton 11 St 443B
Brighton 12-14 St......
........................444B
Brighton 15 St 444D
Brighton Beach Av
........................443D
Brightwater Av.......
........................444D
Brightwater Ct 443D

Bristol St..........417D
Broadway.......404D
Brookdale Plz 424A
Brooklyn Av ...423A
Brooklyn Rd ...423B
Brooklyn-Queens
Expwy (BQE)
.............402D-407B
Broome St 402B
Brown St 437B
Bryant St 414D
Buckingham Rd ......
........................422D
Buffalo Av.......417C
Bulwer Pl 412D
Burnett St........437B
Bush St 414D
Bushwick Av ..405A
Bushwick Pl....405D
Butler Pl 415B
Butler St 407C
Cadman Plz EW ......
........................407A
Calder Pl.........415D
Calhoun St 405A
California Pl 439A
Calyer St..........402D
Cambridge Pl..410D
Cameron Ct 427B
Campus Pl 413D
Campus Rd......429D
Canal Av 443A
Canarsie Rd ...431A
Canton Ct 445B
Carlton Av 407C
Carroll St 406D
Cary Ct 428D
Cass Pl 444D
Catharine St....405A
Cathedral Pl....407A
Caton Av 422D
Caton Pl 422D
Cedar Pl..........405B
Cedar St 429C
Celeste Ct........443B

Bentley St.......536A
Benton Av 518B
Benton Ct 523C
Benziger Av ...507A
Beresford Av .514C
Berglund Av ...509C
Berkley St........517A
Bermuda Pl 518D
Berne Pl 527C
Berry Av 521C
Berry Ct 527A
Bertha Pl 512B
Bertram Av 534A
Berwick Pl 512A
Berwin La 505D
Beth Pl 529B
Bethel Av 532C
Beverly Av 512A
Beverly Rd ....
..............315D, 336B
Bianca Ct 520D
Bidwell Av 510B
Billings St 520D
Billiou St 528D
Billop Av 536C
Bionia Av 519A
Birch Av 506D
Birch La 527B
Birch Rd 503C
Birchard Av 510D
Bishop St 523A
Bismarck Av ...507A
Bismarck Ct ...507A
Blackford Av ..503D
Blaine Ct 505D
Bland Pl 534A
Bleeker Pl......515A
Bliss Pl 532D
Block St 523C
Bloomfield Av 508D
Bloomingdale Rd ....
.....................526D
Blossom La ...536B
Blueberry La .535A

Blue Heron Dr 529C
Blythe Pl 522D
Boardwalk Av 534B
Bodine St 505D
Bogert Av 517A
Bogota St 515D
Bolivar St 511C
Bombay St 527C
Bond St..........505C
Boone St........510D
Booth Av 529C
Borman Av 515B
Borough Pl 507B
Boscombe Av 532B
Bosworth St ...505D
Botany Pl 532D
Boulder St 527D
Boundary Av .524A
Bovanizer St...529C
Bowden St 517D
Bowdoin St ...515D
Bowen St 513A
Bower Ct 527A
Bowles Av 503D
Bowling Green Pl....
.....................515A
Boyce Av 523C
Boyd St 507C
Boylan St 521C
Boyle Pl 523A
Boyle St 517C
Boynton St 533A
Brabant St 503C
Bradford Av ...533A
Bradley Av 511C
Bradley Ct 517A
Braisted Av ...515D
Brandis Av 521C
Brehaut Av 532C
Brenton Pl 511B
Brentwood Av 506B
Brewster St ...507C
Briarcliff Rd ...519A
Briarwood Rd .503C

Bridgetown St 515D
Brielle Av 517A
Brighton Av ...506D
Brighton St 536C
Bristol Av 511D
Britton Av 512D
Britton St 505D
Broad St 507D
Broadway......505D
Bromley Av 532B
Brook Av 523D
Brook St 507A
Brookfield Av .521D
Brooks Pl 505C
Brooks Pond Pl .....
.....................505D
Brookside Av .511A
Brown Av 529B
Brown Pl.........513D
Brownell St 513A
Browning Av ..517A
Bruckner Av ...503C
Brunswick St .515D
Bryan St 536C
Bryant Av 524A
Bryson Av......509B
Buchanan Av ..510D
Buel Av 518C
Buffalo St 523C
Buffington Av 528D
Bunnell Ct......527B
Bunnell St......527B
Burbank Av ...524A
Burchard Ct ...528D
Burden Av 503D
Burgher Av 518B
Burke Av 514B
Burnside Av ...510B
Burr Av 532B
Burton Av 533C
Burton Ct 517C
Bush Av 503C
Butler Av 536A
Butler Bd 536D

Butler Pl 513A
Butler St 532D
Butler Ter 507C
Butterworth Av ......
.....................511D
Buttonwood Rd .....
.....................517B
Byrd Pl 530C
Byrne Av 510D
C-D Row 502D
Cable Wy 503C
Cabot Pl 513D
Cady Av 532B
Calcutta St 532D
Caldera Pl......506B
Call St 523A
Callan Av 518A
Calvin Av 507C
Cambria St 519A
Cambridge Av 509D
Camden Av 536B
Camden St 513A
Cameron Av ...519A
Campbell Av ..505B
Campus Rd 512B
Canal St 507C
Candon Av 526D
Candon Ct......526B
Cannon Av 514A
Cannon Bd 523B
Canoe Pl 525A
Canon Dr 521B
Canton Av 527B
Capellan St....534A
Cardiff St 527D
Carlin St 526C
Carlton Av 527D
Carlton Bd 527B
Carlton Ct 527D
Carlton Pl 512C
Carly Ct 532C
Carlyle Green .527B
Carmel Av.......510D
Carneaux Av ..527B

Carnegie Av ...509C
Caro St 510D
Carol Ct 533C
Carol Pl 503C
Carolina Av 517A
Carolina Pl 511A
Caroline St 505D
Carpenter Av ..515B
Carreau Av 515A
Carroll Pl........507A
Carteret St 536C
Cartledge Av ..514D
Cary Av 505D
Cascade St.....517D
Case Av 533D
Cassidy Pl......506B
Castleton Av ..503B
Castleton Ct ..507C
Castor Pl........527D
Caswell Av 509B
Caswell La 509A
Catherine Ct ..505C
Catherine St...502B
Catlin Av 507C
Cattaraugus St .....
.....................511D
Cayuga Av 511D
Cebra Av 507C
Cedar Av 519A
Cedar Grove Av .....
.....................524D
Cedar St 507C
Cedar Ter 512B
Cedar Wood Ct......
.....................503C
Cedarcliff Rd .512B
Cedarview Av 523C
Celina La........536D
Celtic Pl.........524C
Center Av 512B
Center Pl 524D
Center St 522B
Central Av 507B
Champ Ct 532D

Champlain Av..523C
Chandler Av ...511A
Channel View Ct ....
.....................523C
Chapin Av 518A
Chappell St.....505B
Charles Av 503B
Charles Ct......517C
Charles Pl 503C
Charleston Av 526B
Charter Oak Rd......
.....................517D
Chatham St 520D
Chelsea Rd 508D
Chelsea St 536C
Chemical La ..526B
Cherokee St ...525A
Cherry Pl........517A
Cherrywood Ct ......
.....................522D
Cheryl Av 521C
Chesebrough St .....
.....................529C
Chesire Pl......512A
Chester Av 534C
Chester Pl......507C
Chesterton Av 523C
Chestnut Av ...513A
Chestnut Cir ..520D
Chestnut Pl....506D
Chestnut St ...512B
Chicago Al 513C
Chicago Av 519A
Chisholm St ...533B
Christine Ct ...534A
Christopher La 509D
Christopher St 503A
Church Av 514B
Church La 513B
Church St 505A
Churchill Av ...532B
Cicero Av 521D
Cindra Av 530C
Circle Loop 513A

Forrestal Av – Heusden St

Street	Ref	Street	Ref	Street	Ref
Latham Pl	527C	Lily Pond Av	519B	Loring Av	528B
Lathrop Av	510B	Lincoln Av	517D	Loring Ct	509D
Latimer Av	514B	Lincoln Pl	513D	Lorrain Av	529C
LaTourette St	533C	Lincoln St	511C	Lorraine Loop	526D
Laurel Av	512B	Linda Av	519B	Lortel Av	511C
Lava St	519A	Lindbergh Av	523B	Lotus Av	534A
Law Pl	505D	Linden Av	503C	Louis St	507C
Lawn Av	523A	Linden St	506B	Louise La	511D
Lawrence Av	506D	Lindenwood Av	529B	Louise St	534A
Layton Av	507A	Lindenwood Pl	529B	Lovelace Av	529A
Leason Pl	515D	Linton Pl	521D	Lovell Av	515B
Ledyard Pl	519A	Linwood Av	519A	Low St	532D
Lee Av	532C	Lion St	532C	Lowell St	516D
Leeds St	523D	Lipsett Av	529C	Lucille Av	526B
Legate Av	528C	Lisa La	527B	Ludlow St	528B
Leggett Pl	509C	Lisa Pl	509C	Ludwig La	503C
Legion Pl	513C	Lisbon Pl	517D	Ludwig St	505D
Leigh Av	509A	Lisk Av	503C	Luigi Ct	523A
Lenevar Av	527C	Liss St	529D	Luigi Pl	523B
Lenhart St	532C	Little Clove Rd	511C	Luke Ct	522D
Lennon Ct	521D	Littlefield Av	529D	Luna Cir	534B
Lenore Ct	509B	Livermoore Av	510B	Lundi Ct	515C
Lenzie St	534B	Livingston Av	511C	Lundsten Av	526C
Leo St	509B	Livingston Ct	506A	Luten Av	533B
Leola Pl	534B	Llewelyn Pl	505C	Lyle Ct	523C
Leon St	509A	Lloyd Ct	505D	Lyman Av	513D
Leona St	509C	Lockman Av	503A	Lyman Pl	512D
Leonard Av	509B	Lockman Loop	503C	Lynch St	534B
Leonard St	534A	Lockwood Pl	510B	Lyndale Av	529C
Leroy St	514B	Logan Av	511D	Lyndale La	529C
Leslie Av	518B	Lois Pl	506B	Lynhurst Av	513A
Lester St	511C	Lola St	525A	Lynn Ct	503D
Leverett Av	521D	Lombard Ct	527A	Lynn St	523D
Levit Av	509B	London Ct	523A	Lynnhaven Pl	505D
Lewiston St	515D	London Rd	516D	Lyon Pl	509B
Lexa Pl	527C	Long Pond La	513A	MacArthur Av	529A
Lexington Av	505C	Longdale St	509A	Mace St	522B
Lexington La	521D	Longfellow Av	512D	MacFarland Av	519A
Leyden Av	503C	Longview Rd	512B	MacGregor St	533D
Liberty Av	518D	Loret Ct	505D	Macon Av	521C
Lighthouse Av	522B	Loretto St	536D	Macormac Pl	502D
Lightner Av	511D			Madera St	533B
Lilac Ct	503C			Madigan Pl	512D
Lillian Pl	529D				

Street	Ref	Street	Ref	Street	Ref
Madison Av	509B	Marianne St	510B	McCully Av	523
Madsen Av	532D	Marie Pl	512D	McDermott Av	518
Magnolia Av	518D	Marie St	518B	McDivitt Av	515
MaGuire Av	527C	Marine Dr	533C	McDonald St	516
MaGuire Ct	533A	Marine Way	524C	McKee Av	530
Maiden La	532C	Mariners La	503A	McKinley Av	522
Main St	536A	Marion Av	507C	McLaughlin St	519
Maine Av	510B	Marion St	505C	McVeigh Av	515
Majestic Av	526B	Marisa Cir	526D	Meade Loop	532
Major Av	519A	Mark St	518B	Meade St	532
Malden Pl	523D	Markham Pl	511A	Meadow Av	512
Mallard La	526D	Marne Av	529A	Meadow Ct	527
Mallory Av	519A	Marscher Pl	533D	Meadow Pl	518
Mallow St	527C	Marsh Av	515C	Medford Rd	512
Malone Av	523C	Marshall Av	517A	Medina St	523
Malvine Av	526D	Martha St	512D	Meeker St	516
Manchester Dr	527B	Martin Av	510D	Meisner Av	517
Mandy Ct	526D	Martin Luther King Jr Expwy	503D	Melba St	511
Manee Av	533A	Martineau St	502B	Melhorn Rd	511
Manhattan St	536C	Martling Av	511A	Melissa St	509
Manila Av	523D	Marvin Rd	533A	Melrose Av	512
Manila Pl	524C	Marx St	511D	Melrose Pl	530
Manley St	526C	Mary St	512D	Melville St	533
Mann Av	510D	Maryland Av	513D	Melvin Av	514
Manor Ct	522B	Maryland Pl	511A	Melyn Pl	503
Manor Rd	511A	Mason Av	518D	Memo St	533
Manorville Ct	513C	Mason Bd	526D	Memphis Av	529
Mansion Av	530B	Mason St	518B	Mena St	521
Manton Pl	513C	Massachusetts St	513	Mendelsohn St	513
Maple Av	505A		536	Mercer Pl	530
Maple Ct	527B	Mathews Av	506D	Mercury La	515
Maple Pkwy	503C	Maxwell Av	533D	Meredith Av	514
Maple Ter	524D	May Av	509A	Merkel Pl	531
Mapleton Av	524B	May Pl	529C	Merle Pl	513
Maplewood Av	523A	Mayberry Promenade	535A	Merrick Av	50
Maplewood Pl	524A	Maybury Av	530A	Merrill Av	50
Marble St	510B	Maybury Ct	530B	Merriman Av	51
Marc St	509B	Mayer Av	517A	Merry Mount St	51
Marcy Av	527D	McBaine Av	526D	Mersereau Av	50
Maretzek Ct	533A	McClean Av	519A	Metcalfe St	51
Margaret St	530A	McCormick Pl	518B	Metropolitan Av	50
Margaretta Ct	511A				
Maria La	529A				

Street	Page	Street	Page	Street	Page	Street	Page	Street	Page
ers St	511B	Weser Av	512D	Wieland Av	527C	Windom Av	519B	Woodvale Loop	533C
on Av	514C	West St	505D	Wilbur Pl	510D	Windsor Av	523A	Woodward Av	510D
del Av	512B	W Buchanan St	506B	Wilbur St	533D	Windsor Ct	511D	Wooley Av	510B
ier Av	532A	W Castor Pl	527C	Wilcox St	503C	Windsor Rd	511C	Wrenn St	533D
d Av	507C	W Cedarview Av	522B	Wild Av	514A	Windy Hollow Way	517D	Wright Av	503B
ds Point Av	536C	W Fingerboard Rd	518B	Wilder Av	523A	Winfield Av	518B	Wright St	507C
dwell Av	510B	W Raleigh Av	505D	Wildwood La	536D	Winfield St	519C	Wygant Pl	505C
ing Av	528B	West Shore Expwy	508D-526B	Wiley Pl	523A	Wingham St	513D	Wyona Av	509D
ner Av	527C	W Willow Rd	509B	Willard Av	510B	Winham Av	524C	Xenia St	519A
ren Hill St	513A	Westbrook Av	503D	Willard Pl	510B	Winslow Pl	529C	Yale St	503C
wick Av	510D	Westbury Av	506B	William Av	529D	Winston St	520D	Yates Av	517A
shington Av	516B	Westcott Bd	511A	William St	507C	Winter Av	507A	Yeomalt Av	534C
shington Pl	505D	Westentry Rd	517D	Willis Av	507C	Winthrop Pl	511A	Yetman Av	536A
chogue Rd	509B	Western Av	502D	Willow Av	513A	Wirt Av	526B	Yona Av	509D
er St	507D	Westervelt Av	507A	Willow Rd E & W	509B	Wirt La	526D	York Av	507A
erbury Av	533A	Westfield Av	526B	Willow St	507C	Witteman Pl	511D	York Ter	507A
terford Ct	519B	Westminster Ct	518A	Willow Pond Rd	517B	Wolcoff La	503C	Young St	512B
ters Av	509B	Westport La	515C	Willowbrook Ct	510B	Wolcott Av	529A	Yucca Dr	527B
terside Pkwy	530D	Westport St	515C	Willowbrook Rd	509B	Wolf St	533D	Yukon Av	521A
terside St	524D	Westwood Av	509D	Willowood La	522D	Wolverine St	523C	Zachary Ct	505C
kins Av	521C	Wetmore Rd	512D	Wills Pl	519A	Wood Av	532C	Zebra Pl	526B
tson Av	514B	WhalleyAv	529C	Wilson Av	529C	Wood Ct	527A	Zeck Ct	509B
unner St	532A	Wheeler Av	511C	Wilson St	518B	Woodbine Av	509B	Zeni Pl	524A
ve St	507D	Wheeling Av	533B	Wilson Ter	512D	Woodbridge Pl	510B	Zephyr Av	534D
vecrest St	524D	Whitaker Pl	518B	Wiman Av	530C	Woodcliff Av	502D	Zev Pl	513C
verly Pl	512B	White Ct	529C	Wiman Pl	513B	Woodcrest Rd	503C	Zoe St	518D
yne St	505B	White Pl	505D	Winans St	532D	Woodcutters La	530B	Zwicky Av	524A
Boylan St	521C	White St	513D	Winant Av	527C	Wooddale Av	511D		
aver St	534B	White Hall St	523D	Winant Pl	526C	Woodhaven Av	517B		
bster Av	507C	White Oak La	526D	Winant St	503B	Woodhull Av	533B		
ed Av	523D	White Plains Av	513A	Winchester Av	529C	Woodland Av	530A		
einer St	532D	Whitewood Av	512A	Windemere Av	523C	Woodlawn Av	519A		
eir Av	533C	Whitlock Av	517B	Windemere Rd	513C	Woodrow Rd	527B		
eir La	532C	Whitman Av	530C	Windham Loop	521B	Woodruff La	505B		
ellbrook Av	511C	Whitney Av	518B	Winding Woods Loop	536D	Woods of Arden Rd	534B		
elles Ct	506D	Whitwell Pl	517B			Woodside Av	512B		
ellington Ct	515D	Wiederer Pl	512B			Woodstock Av	507C		
emple St	503C					Woodvale Av	533C		
endy Dr	534A								
enlock St	503D								
entworth Av	519C								

NUMBERED CT • ST

1 Ct	534B
1 St	523B
2 Ct	534B
2 St	523B
3 Ct	534B
3 St	523B
4 Ct	534B
4 St	523B
6 St	531A
7 St	523B
8 St	523D
9 St	523B
10 St	523D

NUMBERED HIGHWAYS

Highway names appear alphabetically in each borough street list.

1	157C-205C
9A	128A-202A
25	308D-340A
25A	309C-324B
27	422A-353B
87	203D-226B
95	157C-205C
278	224B-502C
295	218B-314B
440	503D-532B
495	316B-325B
678	218C-349B
695	218B
895	223A

ABBREVIATIONS

Al	Alley
Av	Avenue
Bd, Blvd	Boulevard
Cir	Circle
Cl	Close
Cres	Crescent
Ct	Court
Dr	Drive
Expwy	Expressway
Ft	Fort
Hts	Heights
Hwy	Highway
La	Lane
Pkwy	Parkway
Pl	Place
Plz	Plaza
Pt	Point
Rd	Road
Sq	Square
St	Street
Ter	Terrace
Tri	Triangle
Wk	Walk

EMERGENCIES

AAA Road Service
800-222-4357

Ambulance, Fire, Police 911

Animal Bites
212-566-2068

Animal Med. Ctr
212-838-8100

Arson Hotline
718-722-3600

Battered Women
800-621-4673

Coast Guard
800-735-3415

Child Abuse
800-342-3720

Deaf Emergency
718-899-8800

Dental Emergency
212-677-2510

Domestic Violence
800-621-4673

Drug Abuse
800-395-3400

**Emergency Medical
Technician Info**
718-416-7000

**Hazardous
Materials**
718-699-9811

Locksmith (24hr)
212-247-6747

Missing Persons
212-719-9000

**Park Emergencies
(24hr)** 800-201-7275

Pharmacy (24hr)
212-755-2266

**Poison Control
Center (24hr)**
212-764-7667

Rape Hotline
212-577-7777

Runaway Hotline
212-966-8000

**Sex Crimes
Reports**
212-267-7273

Suicide Prevention
212-532-2400

**Victim Services
Hotline**
212-577-7777

ESSENTIALS

AAA
212-757-2000

B & B Reservations
212-737-7049

Big Apple Greeters
212-669-2896

Bridge & Tunnels
212-221-9903

ChequePoint USA
212-869-6281

**Convention &
Visitor's Bureau**
212-397-8222

Customs (24hr)
800-697-3662

**Directory
Assistance** 411

**Foreign Exchange
Rates** 212-883-0400

**Foreign
Newspapers**
212-840-1868

Immigration
212-206-6500

Hotel Reservations
800-444-7666

**Jacob Javits
Convention Center**
212-216-2000

**Lost Travelers
Checks**
• AMEX
800-221-7282
• Citicorp
800-645-6556
• VISA
800-227-6811

Movies
212-777-FILM

NYC On Stage
212-768-1818

Passport Info
212-399-5290

Post Office
212-967-8585

Telegrams
800-325-6000

Time
212-976-1616

Traffic Information
212-442-7080

Traveler's Aid
212-944-0013

UN Information
212-963-1234

Weather
212-976-1212

TOURS & EXCURSIONS

**Adventure on a
Shoestring**
212-265-2633

**All American
Stage Tours**
800-735-8530

Art Tours
212-239-4160

**Backstage at
Broadway**
212-575-8065

Big Apple Greeters
212-669-2896

Big Onion Tours
212-439-1090

**Bronx Heritage
Trail** 718-881-8900

**Brooklyn
Historical Society**
718-624-0890

City Walks
212-989-2456

Circle Line
212-563-3200

**Doorways to
Design**
718-339-1542

Ellis Island Ferry
212-269-5755

Express Navigation
800-262-8743

Gray line/Shortline
212-397-2600

**Harlem
Renaissance**
212-722-9534

**Harlem Visitors &
Convention Assoc.**
212-427-3317

Heritage Trails NY,
1-888-4TRAILS

Hoboken Ferry (NJ)
201-420-4422

Liberty Helicopters
212-967-6464

**Manhattan
Sightseeing**
212-354-5122

**NY Big Apple
Tours Double
Decker Tours**
212-967-6008
212-691-7866

NY Helicopter
800-645-3494

NY Walks
212-797-2388

NY Waterway
800-53-FERRY

**Parents League of
NY** 212-737-7385

The Petrel (1938)
212-825-1976

The Pioneer (1885)
212-669-9417

**Radical Walking
Tours** 718-462-0069

**Seaport Liberty
Cruises**
212-630-8888

Seaport Line
212-608-9840

Spirit of NY
212-727-2789

Urban Explorat
718-721-5254

**Walking Tours
of Chinatown**
212-619-4785

Wild Foods Tou
718-291-6825

**World Yacht
Cruises**
212-630-8100

**92nd St.
YM–YWHA**
212-996-1100

TRANSPORT

Airlines–Domes
• American
800-433-7300
• Continental
800-523-3273
• Delta
800-221-1212
• Northwest
800-441-1818
• TWA
800-221-2000
• United
800-241-6522
• USAir
800-428-4322

Airlines–Foreign
• Aeromexico
800-237-6639
• Air Canada
800-776-3000
• Air France
800-321-4538
• ANA–ALL Nippo
800-235-9262
• British Airways
800-247-9297
• Lufthansa
800-645-3880

Bus & Subway
Main
718-330-1234
Access -Disabled
718-596-8585
Greyhound
212-971-6300
Hampton Jitney
800-936-0440

Ferries
Ellis Island
212-269-5755
Express Navigation
800-262-8743
Harbor Shuttle
888-254-RIDE
NY Waterway–
800-53-FERRY
Staten Island
718-815-BOAT
Statue of Liberty
212-269-5755

George Washington Bridge Bus Station
212-564-1114

Helicopter
Helicopter Flight Services
212-355-0801
Liberty
212-487-4777
National
800-645-3494
Port Authority
212-348-7240

JFK Airport
Main
718-244-4444
Parking
718-656-5699
Train to Plane
718-858-7272

LaGuardia Airport
• Main
718-476-5000
• Airport Bus
718-476-5353
• Ferry
800-54-FERRY
• Parking
718-476-5000

Limousine Service
212-777-7171

Newark Airport
• Main
201-961-6000
• Airport Bus
201-762-5100
• Parking
201-623-6334

NY Passenger Ship Terminal
212-246-5451

Port Authority Bus Terminal
212-564-8484

Roosevelt Island
Tram 212-832-4543

Trains
• Amtrak
800-523-8720
212-582-6875
• Long Island Railroad (LIRR)
718-217-5477
• Metro North
800-532-4900
• NJ Transit
800-626-7433
• PATH
800-234-7284

Teterboro Airport
201-288-1775

BUSINESS & CONSUMER
Better Bus .Bureau
212-533-6200

Chamber of Commerce
BK 718-875-1000
BN 718-829-4111
MA 212-493-7400
QS 718-898-8500
SI 718-727-1900

Consumer Affairs
212-487-4444

Gas,Electric,Water Complaints
800-342-3377

Small Business Administration (SBA) 212-264-4354

Taxi Complaints
212-221-8294

GOVERNMENT
Borough President
BK 718-802-3700
BX 718-590-3500
MA 212-669-8300
QS 718-286-3000
SI 718-816-2236

City Council
212-788-7100

Mayor's Office
212-788-7585

Tax Info
• City Tax (24hr)
718-935-6736
• Federal (IRS)
800-829-1040
• State Tax
800-225-5829

HEALTH & HUMAN
AIDS Hotline
800-462-6787

Alcoholics Anonymous
212-870-3400

All Night Pharmacy
212-755-2266

Bail 212-669-2879

Crisis Center
800-621-4673

Department of Aging 212-442-1000

Disabled Info
212-229-3000

Gay and Lesbian Switchboard
212-777-1800

Health Department
212-442-1999

Health Info (24hr)
212-434-2000

Legal Aid Society
212-577-3300

Medicaid
718-291-1900

Medicare
800-638-6833

Salvation Army
212-337-7200

Senior Citizens
212-442-1000

Salvation Army
212-337-7200

Social Security
800-772-1213

LIBRARIES
Bronx
718-579-4200

Brooklyn
718-230-2100

Brooklyn Business
718-722-3333

NY Public
212-340-0849

NY Science, Industry & Business (SIBL)
212-592-7001

Queens
718-990-0700

Staten Island
St George Center
718-442-8560

PARKING & TRAFFIC
Potholes
212-442-7942

Sidewalks
212-442-7942

Towed-Away ?
212-869-2929

Registration Plates
212-645-5550

Parking Violations
212-477-4430

UTILITIES
Brooklyn Union
718-643-4050

ConEdison
718-802-6000

Bell Atlantic
890-1550

WEBSITES NY
All internet addresses listed are assumed to begin with "www."

Café los Negroes
losnegroes.com

Central Park
centralpark.org

Citysearch NY
citysearch.com

Metrobeat
metrobeat.com

Official City of New York Web Site
ci.nyc.ny.us/home.html

NYC Reference a.k.a.Clay Irving's Home Page
panix.com/~clay/

New York Sidewalk
sidewalk.com

The New York Times
nytimes.com

The New York Web
nyw.com

NYC Beer Guide
nycbeer.org

Total New York
totalny.com

VanDam, Inc.
vandam.com

Village Voice
villagevoice.com

ATTRACTIONS

Abyssinian Baptist Church
132 W 138 St, MA
212-862-7474 **149C**

American Craft Museum
40 W 53 St, MA
212-956-6047 **125C**

American Museum of Natural History
CPW @ 79 St, MA
212-769-5000 **133C**

The Apollo Theater
253 W 125 St, MA
212-749-5838 **149C**

Battery Park City Esplanade **102A**

Bloomingdale's
1000 Third Av, MA
212-705-2000 **130D**

Brighton Beach
Btwn Ocean & West End Avs, Coney Island, BK **443D**

The Bronx Museum of the Arts
1040 The Grand Concourse, BX
718-681-6000 **221C**

Bronx Zoo – Int'l Wildlife Conservation Park
Bronx River Pkwy @ E Fordham Rd, BX, 718-367-1010 **216A**

Brooklyn Academy of Music (BAM)
30 Lafayette Av, BK
718-636-4100 **407D**

Brooklyn Botanic Gardens
1000 Washington Av BK, 718-622-4433 **415D**

Brooklyn Bridge
Enter @ City Hall Park, MA or Adams St, BK **105A-408B**

Brooklyn Heights Promenade **406B**

Brooklyn Museum of Art (BMA)
200 Eastern Pkwy BK, 718-638-5000 **415D**

Carnegie Hall
881 Seventh Av, MA
212-247-7800 **125A**

Cathedral Church of St. John the Divine
Amsterdam Av @ 112 St, MA
212-662-2133 **144C**

Central Park **129A**

Children's Museum of Manhattan
212 W 83 St, MA
212-721-1223 **132B**

Chinatown, Manhattan **107C**

Chrysler Bldg
E 42 St @ Lexington Av MA **126D**

Circle Line
W 42 St @ 12 Av, MA
212-563-3200 **120A**

The Cloisters
Fort Tryon Pk, MA
212-923-3700 **158B**

Columbia University
W 116 St @ Broadway, MA
212-854-1754 **144B**

Coney Island USA
1208 Surf Av, BK
718-372-5159 **443C**

Cooper-Hewitt Museum
2 E 91 St, MA
212-849-8300 **137D**

El Museo del Barrio
1230 Fifth Av, MA
212-831-7272 **141B**

Ellis Island Nat'l Monument
Take ferry from Battery Park, MA
212-363-3200 **102C**

Empire State Bldg
350 Fifth Av, MA
212-736-3100 **121D**

F.A.O. Schwarz
767 Fifth Av, MA
212-644-9400 **129D**

Federal Hall Nat'l Memorial
26 Wall St, MA
212-264-8711 **103A**

Flatiron Bldg
Fifth Av @ 23 St, MA **117B**

Fraunces Tavern Museum
54 Pearl St, MA
212-425-1778 **103A**

Frick Collection
1 E 70 St, MA
212-288-0700 **130B**

Grant Nat'l Mem
Riverside Dr
@ W 122 St, MA
212-666-1640 **144A**

Guggenheim (SoHo)
575 Broadway @ Prince St, MA
212-423-3500 **109B**

Hayden Planetarium
CPW @ W 81 St, MA
212-769-5900 **133A**

Heritage Trails NY
26 Wall St, MA
888-4-TRAILS **103A**

Int'l Center of Photography (ICP)
1135 Fifth Av, MA
212-860-1777 **137B**

ICP Midtown
6 Av @ W 43 St, MA
212-768-4680 **125D**

Intrepid Sea-Air-Space Museum
W 46 St @ 12 Av, MA
212-245-0072 **124C**

Isamu Noguchi Garden Museum
32-37 Vernon Bd, QS
718-204-7088 **308B**

Jamaica Bay Nat'l Wildlife Refuge
Broad Channel & First St, QS
718-318-4300 **358B**

Jewish Museum
1109 Fifth Av
@ E 92 St, MA
212-423-3200 **137B**

Lincoln Center for the Performing Arts
Broadway
@ 65 St, MA
212-875-5000 **128B**

Little Italy **107A**

Lower East Side Tenement Museum
90 Orchard St, MA
212-431-0233 **110B**

Macy's Herald Sq
151 W 34 St, MA
212-695-4400 **121B**

Madison Sq Garden
4 Penn Plz, MA
212-465-6741 **121A**

The Metropolitan Museum of Art
5 Av @ E 82 St, MA
212-535-7710 **133D**

Museum for African Art
593 Broadway, MA
212-966-1313 **109B**

Museum of American Folk Art
2 Lincoln Sq, MA
212-977-7298 **128B**

Museum of the City of New York
1220 Fifth Av, MA
212-534-1672 **141B**

Museum of Chinese in the Americas
70 Mulberry St, MA
212-619-4785 **107C**

The Museum of Jewish Heritage
18 First Pl, MA
212-968-1800 **102A**

**useum of Modern
rt (MoMA)**
W 53 St, MA
2-708-9480   **125**B

**he Museum of
elevision & Radio**
W 52 St, MA
2-621-6600   **125**B

**at'l Museum of the
merican Indian**
ustoms House @
owling Green, MA
2-825-6700   **102**D

**at'l Academy
Design**
83 Fifth Av
E 89 St, MA
2-369-4880   **137**D

BC Studio Tour
Rockefeller Plz,
A, 212-664-4000
125D

**ew Museum of
ontemporary Art**
3 Broadway, MA
2-219-1222   **109**B

Y Aquarium
8 St
Surf Av, BK
8-265-3400   **443**C

Y Botanical Garden
0 St @ Southern
d, BX
8-817-8700   **210**C

W Hall of Science
-01 111 St, QS
8-699-0005   **320**B

W Public Library
St @ 5 Av, MA
2-661-7220   **122**A

**NY Stock Exchange
(NYSE)**
20 Broad St, MA
212-656-5165   **102**B

**The Pierpont
Morgan Library**
29 E 36 St, MA
212-685-0610   **122**B

The Plaza Hotel
768 Fifth Av @
Central Park S, MA
212-759-3000   **129**D

**Queens Museum
of Art (QMA)**
Flushing Meadows–
Corona Park, QS
718-760-0064   **320**D

**Queens Theatre
in the Park**
Flushing Meadows
Corona Park, QS
718-760-0064   **320**D

**Radio City
Music Hall**
Sixth Av @ W 50 St,
Rockefeller Ctr, MA
212-247-4777   **125**B

Riverside Church
490 Riverside Dr
@ W 120 St, MA
212-222-5900   **144**A

Rockefeller Center
Bet. Fifth–Sixth Avs
& 48–51 Sts, MA
212-698-2950   **125**D

**St Patrick's
Cathedral**
Fifth Av @ E 50 St,
MA, 212-753-2261
125B

St Paul's Chapel
B'way @ Fulton St,
MA, 212-602-0872
104D

Seagram Bldg
375 Park Av, MA
212-572-7000   **126**B

Shea Stadium
Flushing Meadows
Corona Pk, QS
718-507-8499   **320**B

**Snug Harbor
Cultural Center**
1000 Richmond Ter,
SI, 718-448-2500
506B

**Socrates
Sculpture Park**
B'way @ Vernon Bd,
Long Island City, QS
718-956-1819   **308**B

**Solomon R
Guggenheim
Museum (Uptown)**
1071 Fifth Av, MA
212-423-3500   **138**C

**Sony Wonder
Technology Lab**
550 Madison Av
@ 56 St, MA
212-833-8100   **126**B

SoHo
Houston–Canal Sts
& SixthAv– Lafayette
St, MA   **109**D

**South Street
Seaport Museum**
Seaport Plz
207 Front St, MA
212-748-8600   **105**C

Staten Island Ferry
Take ferry from
Battery Park, MA
212-363-3200   **103**C

**Statue of Liberty
Liberty Island**
212-363-3200 Ferry,
212-269-5755   **102**C

**Studio Museum in
Harlem**
144 W 125 St, MA
212-864-4500   **145**B

Tiffany & Co.
727 Fifth Av, MA
212-755-8000   **126**A

Times Square 125C

Trinity Church
89 B'way @ Wall St,
MA, 212-602-0872
102B

Trump Tower
725 Fifth Av
@ E 56 St, MA
212-832-2000   **126**A

United Nations
First Av @ E 45 St,
MA, 212-963-1234
127C

**Van Cortlandt
Mansion Museum**
B'way @ 246 St, BX
718-543-3344   **209**A

**Verrazano Narrows
Bridge   434**A

**Waldorf–Astoria
Hotel**
301 Park Av, MA
212-355-3000   **126**B

**Warner Bros.
Studio Store**
Fifth Av @ 57 St, MA
718-754-0300   **129**D

**Washington Square
Park, MA   113**C

Wave Hill
675 W 252 St, BX
718-549-3200   **208**A

**Whitney Museum
of American Art**
945 Madison Av, MA
212-570-3600   **134**D

Woolworth Bldg
233 Broadway, MA
104D

**World Financial
Center (WFC)**
Liberty St @ the
Hudson River, MA
212-945-0505   **104**C

**World Trade Center
Observation deck**
WTC 2 @ Liberty St,
MA, 212-435-7000
104A

Yankee Stadium
161 St & River Av, BX
718-760-6200   **221**C

TO FIND A TOP 100

Simply turn to page
and locate the
attraction in grids
A, B, **C** or D.

MA = Manhattan
BX = The Bronx
BK = Brooklyn
QS = Queens
SI = Staten Island

BUSINESS

ADVERTISING

WPP Group USA
309 W 49 St, MA
212-632-2200 **125C**

Ogilvy & Mather
309 W 49 St, MA
212-237-4000 **125C**

Saatchi & Saatchi
375 Hudson St, MA
212-463-2000 **108B**

OmniCom Group
437 Madison Av, MA
212-415-3600 **130D**

**Interpublic Group
of Companies**
1271 Sixth Av, MA
212-399-8000 **126A**

CONSUMER GOODS

Avon
1345 Sixth Av, MA
212-282-5000 **126A**

**Bristol-Meyers
Squibb Company**
345 Park Av, MA
212-546-4000 **126B**

Colgate Palmolive
300 Park Av, MA
212-310-2000 **126D**

Estée Lauder
767 Fifth Av, MA
212-572-4200 **129D**

Kinney Shoe Corp
233 Broadway, MA
212-720-3700 **104D**

Pfizer
235 E 42 St, MA
212-573-2323 **123A**

MAFCO
36 E 63 St, MA
212-688-9000 **130D**

Philip Morris
120 Park Av, MA
212-880-5000 **122B**

RJR Nabisco
1301 Sixth Av, MA
212-258-5600 **126A**

Seagram
375 Park Av, MA
212-572-7000 **126B**

Unilever
390 Park Av, MA
212-888-1260 **126B**

Woolworth Corp
233 Broadway, MA
212-553-2000 **104D**

FINANCIAL SERVICES

American Express
200 Vesey St, MA
212-640-2000 **104C**

Bank of NY
48 Wall St, MA
212-495-1784 **103A**

Bankers Trust NY
280 Park Av, MA
212-250-2500 **126D**

Bear Stearns
245 Park Av, MA
212-272-2000 **126D**

**Chase
Manhattan Bank**
270 Park Av, MA
212-270-6000 **126D**

Citibank
399 Park Av, MA
212-559-1000 **126B**

Transammonia
350 Park Av, MA
212-223-3200 **126B**

**Donaldson, Lufkin
& Jenrette**
277 Park Av, MA
212-892-3000 **126D**

Ernst & Young
787 Seventh Av, MA
212-773-3000 **125A**

**Federal Reserve
Bank of NY**
33 Liberty St, MA
212-720-5000 **105C**

Fortis
1 Chase Manhattan
Plz, MA
212-859-7000 **103A**

Goldman Sachs
85 Broad St, MA
212-902-1000 **103A**

**KPMG Peat
Marwick**
345 Park Av, MA
212-758-9700 **126B**

JP Morgan
60 Wall St, MA
212-483-2323 **103A**

Lehman Brothers
3 WFC
@ 200 Vesey St, MA
212-526-7000 **104D**

Merrill Lynch
N & S Tower, WFC,
MA, 212-449-1000
104C

**Morgan Stanley,
Dean Witter,
Discover & Co**
1585 Broadway, MA
212-761-3000 **125C**

Paine Webber Group
1285 Sixth Av, MA
212-713-3000 **125B**

**Prudential
Securities**
199 Water St, MA
212-214-1000 **105C**

**Republic
National Bank**
452 Fifth Av, MA
212525-5000 **122A**

**Salomon Bros
Smith Barney**
388 Greenwich St,
MA, 212-816-6000
106C

INSURANCE

**Empire Blue Cross
& Blue Shield**
622 Third Av, MA
212-476-1000 **122B**

The Equitable
1290 Sixth Av, MA
212-554-1234 **125A**

Guardian Life
201 Park Av S, MA
212-598-8000 **118D**

Marsh & McLennan
1166 Sixth Av, MA
212-345-5000 **126C**

Met Life
1 Madison Av, MA
212-578-2211 **118A**

Mutual Life of NY
1740 Broadway, MA
212-708-2000 **125A**

**NYLCare Health
Plans**
1 Liberty Plz, MA
212-437-1000 **104D**

NY Life
51 Madison Av, MA
212-576-7000 **118**

**Teachers Insuranc
and Annuity Assoc
of America**
730 Third Av, MA
212-490-9000 **126**

**Reliance Group
Holdings**
55 E 52 St, MA
212-909-1100 **126**

Travelers Group
388 Greenwich St, M
212-816-8000 **106**

MEDIA

ABC
77 W 66 St, MA
212-456-7777 **129**

Bertelsmann
1540 Broadway, M
212-782-1000 **125**

CBS
51 W 52 St, MA
212-975-4321 **125**

FOX
205 E 67 St, MA
212-452-5555 **131**

Hearst
959 Eighth Av, MA
212-649-2000 **125**

NBC
30 Rockefeller Plz, M
212-664-4000 **125**

**News America
Holdings**
1211 Sixth Av, MA
212-852-7000 **125**

BUSINESS

ony Corp
50 Madison Av, MA
12-833-6800 **126B**

ime Warner
5 Rockefeller Plz,
1A, 212-484-8000
125B

urner Corporation
75 Hudson St, MA
12-229-6000 **108B**

iacom
515 Broadway, MA
12-258-6000 **125C**

UBLISHING

arnes & Noble
22 Fifth Av, MA
12-633-3300 **118C**

antam Doubleday
ell Group
540 Broadway, MA
12-354-6500 **125C**

rain's NY Business
20 E 42 St, MA
12-210-0100 **122A**

ow Jones
00 Liberty St, MA
12-416-2000 **102B**

runer & Jahr
75 Lexington Av, MA
12-499-2000 **122B**

arperCollins
1 E 53 St, MA
12-207-7000 **126C**

achette Filipacchi
833 Broadway, MA
2-767-6000 **125A**

earst Books
50 Sixth Av, MA
2-261-6500 **126A**

McGraw Hill
1221 Sixth Av, MA
212-512-2000 **125A**

New York Times
229 W 43 St. MA
212-556-1234 **125A**

Penguin Putnam
375 Hudson St, MA
212-366-2000 **109A**

Random House
201 E 50 St, MA
212-751-2600 **127A**

St Martin's Press
175 Fifth Av, MA
212-674-5151 **118A**

Simon & Schuster
1230 Sixth Av, MA
212-698-7000 **125D**

Warner Books
1271 Sixth Av, MA
212-522-7200 **125A**

REAL ESTATE

Forest City Ratner
1 MetroTech Center,
BK, 718-722-3500
408D

Helmsley–Spear
60 E 42 St, MA
212-687-6400 **122A**

Loew's
667 Madison Av, MA
212-545-2000 **130D**

Mitsui & Co USA
200 Park Av, MA
212-878-4000 **126D**

Trump Organization
725 Fifth Av, MA
212-832-2000 **126B**

TECHNOLOGY

AT&T
32 Sixth Av, MA
212-387-5400 **106B**

Bell Atlantic
1095 Sixth Av, MA
212-395-2121 **126C**

Dover Corp.
280 Park Av, MA
212-922-1640 **126D**

ITT Corp
1330 Sixth Av, MA
212-258-1000 **126A**

Mitsubishi Int'l
520 Madison Av, MA
212-605-2000 **126B**

Nissho Iwai
1211 Sixth Av, MA
212-704-6500 **125A**

Philips Electronics
100 E 42 St, MA
212-850-5000 **122B**

Siemens
1301 Sixth Av, MA
212-258-4000 **126A**

Toshiba America
1251 Sixth Av, MA
212-596-0600 **125A**

UTILITIES & TRANSPORT

Con Edison
4 Irving Pl, MA
212-460-4600 **118D**

MTA
347 Madison Av, MA
212-878-7000 **126D**

Brooklyn Union
1 MetroTech Ctr, BK
718-403-2000 **408D**

BUSINESS IMPROVEMENT DISTRICTS (BIDS)

Alliance for Downtown, NY
120 Broadway, MA
212-566-6700 **102B**

Fashion Center
249 W 39 St, MA
212-764-9600 **121A**

Fifth Av
600 Fifth Av, MA
212-265-1310 **126C**

Fulton Mall Assoc.
356 Fulton St, BK
718-852-5118 **407C**

Grand Central Partnership
6 E 43 St, MA
212-818-1777 **122A**

Lincoln Square
10 Columbus Cir, MA
212-974-9100 **129C**

Madison Av
903 Madison Av, MA
212-249-4095 **130B**

MetroTech
4 MetroTech, BK
718-488-8200 **409C**

Times Square
1560 Broadway, MA
212-768-1560 **125C**

14 St
223 E 14 St, MA
212-674-1164 **118D**

34 St Partnership
6 E 43 St, MA
212-818-1913 **122A**

CHAMBERS OF COMMERCE

The Bronx
226 E Fordham Rd,
BX, 718-829-4111
215C

Brooklyn
7 MetroTech Center,
BK, 718-875-1000
409C

NYC Partnership 1
Battery Park Plz, MA
212-493-7400 **121C**

Queens
75-20 Astoria Bd, QS
718-898-8500 **310D**

Staten Island
130 Bay St, SI
718-727-1900 **507B**

CONVENTIONS

Jacob Javits
11 Av @ 36 St, MA
212-216-2000 **120A**

NY Coliseum
10 Columbus Cir, MA
212-757-3440 **129C**

NY Convention Pier
Pier 92, MA **124A**

TO FIND A TOP 100

Simply turn to page and locate the company in grids A,B,C or D.

MA = Manhattan
BX = The Bronx
BK = Brooklyn
QS = Queens
SI = Staten Island

DINING

AMERICAN

Arcadia $$$$
21 E 62 St, MA
212-223-2900   **130D**

Aureole $$$$
34 E 61 St, MA
212-319-1660   **130D**

Gramercy Tavern $$$$ 42 E 20 St, MA
212-477-0777   **118D**

March $$$$
405 E 58 St, MA
212-754-6272   **131D**

New Prospect Cafe $$ 393 Flatbush Av, BK, 718-638-2148   **415B**

Union Sq Cafe $$$
21 E 16 St, MA
212-243-4020   **118C**

CHINESE

Canton $$$
45 Division St, MA
212-226-4441   **107C**

Chin Chin $$$
216 E 49 St, MA
212-888-4555   **127C**

PRICE KEY

Price ranges include the average cost of a dinner and an alcoholic drink without tax and tip. Tip 15%.

$ = $5–$20
$$ = $21–$35
$$$ = $36–$55
$$$$ = Over $55

Joe's Shanghai $$
136-21 37 Av, QS
718-539-3838   **321A**

Shun Lee Palace $$$ 155 E 55 St, MA
212-371-8844   **126B**

Tse Yang $$$
34 E 51 St, MA
212-688-5447   **126B**

CONTINENTAL

Four Seasons $$$$
99 E 52 St, MA
212-754-9494   **126B**

Marylou's $$$
21 W 9 St, MA
212-533-0012   **113A**

One if by Land, TIBS $$$$ 17 Barrow St, MA, 212-228-0822   **113C**

Petrossian $$$$
182 W 58 St, MA
212-245-2214   **130C**

Peacock Alley $$$
Waldorf-Astoria
301 Park Av, MA
212-872-4895   **126B**

21 Club $$$
21 W 52 St, MA
212-582-7200   **125B**

DELI/KOSHER

Barney Greengrass $
541 Amsterdam Av, MA, 212-724-4707   **136D**

Carnegie Deli $
854 Seventh Av, MA
212-757-2245   **125A**

Katz's $
205 E Houston St, MA
212-254-2246   **110B**

Ratners $$
138 Delancy St, MA
212-677-5588   **110B**

2nd Av Deli $
156 Second Av, MA
212-677-0606   **114A**

DINER

Coffee Shop $$
29 Union Sq W, MA
212-243-7969   **118C**

Empire Diner $$
210 Tenth Av, MA
212-243-2736   **116B**

Juniors $
386 Flatbush Ext. Av
BK, 718-852-5257   **409C**

Market Diner $$
572 Eleventh Av, MA
212-695-0415   **120B**

Vynl Diner $
824 Ninth Av, MA
212-974-2003   **124B**

FRENCH

Daniel $$$$
20 E 76 St, MA
212-982-6930   **134D**

Chanterelle $$$$
2 Harrison St, MA
212-966-6960   **104B**

La Bouillabaisse $$
145 Atlantic Av, BK
718-522-8275   **408C**

La Côte Basque $$$$ 60 W 55 St, MA
212-688-6525   **126A**

Le Cirque 2000 $$$$
455 Madison Av, MA
212-303-7788   **126B**

Les Célébrités $$$$
155 W 58 St, MA
212-484-5113   **129C**

FUN FOOD

Brooklyn Diner USA $$ 212 W 57 St, MA
212-581-8900   **125A**

Fashion Cafe $$
51 Rockefeller Plz,
MA, 212-765-3131   **125B**

Hard Rock Cafe $$
221 W 57 St, MA
212-489-6565   **125A**

Official All Star Cafe $$ 1540 B'way, MA
212-840-TEAM   **125C**

Planet Hollywood $$ 140 W 57 St, MA
212-333-7827   **126B**

Tavern on the Green $$$ CPW & 67 St, MA
212-873-3200   **129A**

FUSION

Cendrillon $$
45 Mercer St, MA
212-343-9012   **109D**

Jo Jo $$$
160 E 64 St, MA
212-223-5656   **130D**

Verbena $$$
54 Irving Pl, MA
212-260-5454   **118D**

Le Colonial $$$
149 E 57 St, MA
212-752-0808   **130D**

Mesa Grill $$$
102 Fifth Av, MA
212-807-7400   **117D**

GREEK & MIDDLE EASTERN

Agrotikon $$
322 E 14 St, MA
212-473-2602   **114**

Karyatis $$
35-03 Broadway, Q
718-204-0666   **30**

Moustache Pitza $
405 Atlantic Av, BK
718-852-5555   **40**

Oznots Dish $$
79 Berry St, BK
718-599-6596   **40**

Periyali $$$
35 W 20 St, MA
212-463-7890   **117**

Telly's Taverna $$
28-13 23 Av, QS
718-728-9194   **30**

INDIAN

Baluchi's $$
193 Spring St, MA
212-226-2828   **10**

Bay Leaf $$
49 W 56 St, MA
212-957-1818   **12**

Dawat $$$
210 E 58 St, MA
212-355-7555   **13**

Jackson Diner $
37-03 74 St, QS
718-672-1232   **31**

Shaan $$$
57 W 48 St, MA
212-977-8400   **12**

DINING

ITALIAN

Caffé Bondi $$$
W 20 St, MA
212-691-8136 **117**D

Felidia $$$$
43 E 58 St, MA
212-758-1479 **131**C

Il Giglio $$$
1 Warren St, MA
212-571-5555 **104**B

Il Mulino $$$$
6 W 3 St, MA
212-673-3783 **113**C

Il Nido $$$
51 E 53 St, MA
212-753-8450 **127**A

JAPANESE

Masaki $$
10 E 9 St, MA
212-473-3327 **114**A

Iso $$
75 Second Av, MA
212-777-0361 **115**C

Nobu $$$$
105 Hudson St, MA
212-219-0500 **106**C

**MEXICAN/
NEW MEXICAN**

Santa Fe $$
2 W 69 St, MA
212-724-0822 **129**A

Zarela $$$
953 Second Av, MA
212-644-6740 **127**A

**Rocking Horse Cafe
Mexicano** $$
182 Eighth Av, MA
212-463-9511 **117**C

**OLDE
NEW YORK**

Café des Artistes
$$$ 1 W 67 St, MA
212-877-3500 **129**A

Fanelli $
94 Prince St, MA
212-226-9412 **109**B

Fraunces Tavern
$$$ 54 Pearl St, MA
212-269-0144 **103**A

Gage & Tollner $$$
372 Fulton St, BK
718-875-5181 **408**D

Old Bermuda Inn
$$$ 2512 Arthurkill
Rd, SI, 718-948-7600 **526**B

Old Homestead $$$
56 Ninth Av, MA
212-242-9040 **117**C

PIZZA

Joe's Pizza $
233 Bleecker St, MA
212-366-1182 **113**C

John's Pizzeria $
278 Bleecker St, MA
212-243-1680 **113**C

Lombardi's $$
32 Spring St, MA
212-941-7994 **110**C

Mario's $$
2342 Arthur Av, BX
718-584-1188 **215**B

Patsy Grimaldi's $
19 Old Fulton St, BK
718-858-4300 **407**A

SEAFOOD

Le Bernardin $$$$
155 W 51 St, MA
212-489-1515 **125**A

Le Pescadou $$$
18 King St, MA
212-924-3434 **108**A

Oceana $$$$
55 E 54 St, MA
212-759-5941 **126**B

River Café $$$$
1 Water St, BK
718-522-5200 **406**A

Ocean Palace $$
5423 Eighth Av, BK
718-871-8080 **421**C

**SOUTHERN &
SOULFOOD**

Cafe Beulah $$$
39 E 19 St, MA
212-777-9700 **118**D

Jezebel $$$
630 Ninth Av, MA
212-582-1045 **124**D

Mekka $$
14 Av A, MA
212-475-8500 **114**D

Miss Ann's $
86 S Portland St, BK
718-858-6997 **407**A

Shark Bar $$
307 Amsterdam Av,
MA, 212-874-8500 **132**D

Sylvia's $$
328 Lenox Av, MA
212-996-0660 **149**D

SPANISH/TAPAS

Bolo $$$
23 E 22 St, MA
212-228-2200 **118**A

El Cid $$
322 W 15 St, MA
212-929-9332 **117**C

Marichu $$$
342 E 46 St, MA
212-370-1866 **127**C

STEAK

**Palm &
Palm Too** $$$
837 Second Av, MA
212-687-2953
212-697-5198 **127**C

Peter Luger $$$$
178 Broadway, BK
718-387-7400 **404**C

Post House $$$$
28 E 23 St, MA
212-935-2888 **130**D

Smith & Wollensky
$$$ 797 Third Av, MA
212-753-1530 **126**D

Sparks $$$$
210 E 46 St, MA
212-687-4855 **127**C

THAI

Jai-Ya Thai $$
396 Third Av, MA
212-889-1330 **118**B

Plan-Eat-Thailand $
184 Bedford Av, BK
718-599-5758 **404**D

Vong $$$
200 E 54 St, MA
212-486-9592 **127**A

TROPICAL

Asia de Cuba $$$
Morgans Hotel
237 Madison Av, MA
212-726-7755 **122**B

Bambou $$$
243 E 14 St, MA
212-505-1180 **118**D

Brawta $
347 Atlantic Av, BK
718-855-5515- **406**C

Circus $$$
808 Lexington Av,
MA, 212-223-2965 **130**D

**Tropica Bar &
Seafood House** $$$
200 Park Av, MA
212-867-6767 **126**D

Casa Brasil $$
316 E 53 St, MA
212-355-5360 **127**A

VEGETARIAN

Angelica Kitchen $
300 E 12 St, MA
212-228-2909 **114**A

Hangawi $$$
12 E 32 St, MA
212-213-0077 **122**C

Mavalli Palace $$
46 E 29 St, MA
212-679-5535 **118**B

Quantum Leap $
88 W 3 St, MA
212-677-8050 **113**C

Souen $$
28 E 13 St, MA
212-627-7150 **113**B

**TO FIND A
TOP 100**

Simply turn to
page and locate
the restaurant
in grids
A,B,C or D.

MA = Manhattan
BX = The Bronx
BK = Brooklyn
QS = Queens
SI = Staten Island

EDUCATION

ARTS

Culinary

French Culinary Institute
462 Broadway, MA
212-219-8890 **109D**

NY Restaurant School
75 Varick St, MA
212-226-5500 **109C**

Performing

Alvin Ailey American Dance Center
211 W 61 St, MA
212-767-0940 **128D**

American Academy of Dramatic Arts
120 Madison Av, MA
212-686-9244 **122D**

Harlem School of the Arts (HSA)
645 St Nicholas Av, MA, 212-926-4100 **153C**

Joffrey Ballet School
434 Sixth Av, MA
212-254-8520 **113A**

The Juilliard School of Music
60 Lincoln Center, MA
212-799-5000 **128B**

Manhattan School of Music
120 Claremont Av, MA
212-749-2802 **144A**

Mannes College of Music
150 W 85 St, MA
212-580-0210 **132B**

Martha Graham School
316 E 63 St, MA
212-838-5886 **131C**

School of American Ballet
165 W 65 St, MA
212-877-0600 **128B**

Steller Adler Conservatory
419 Lafayette St, MA
212-260-0525 **113D**

Visual & Design

Arts at University Settlement
184 Eldridge St, MA
212-674-9120 **110B**

Nat'l Academy of Design School of Fine Art
5 E 89 St, MA
212-996-1908 **137D**

Fashion Institute of Technology (FIT)
227 W 27 St, MA
212-217-7999 **117A**

Parsons School of Design
2 W 13 St, MA
212-229-8900 **113A**

Pratt Institute
• Manhattan
259 Lafayette St, MA
212-925-8481 **110A**
• Brooklyn
200 Willoughby St, BK
718-636-3669 **410D**

School of Visual Arts
209 E 23 St, MA
212-679-7350 **118B**

COLLEGES & UNIVERSITIES

Audrey Cohen College
75 Varick St, MA
800-338-4465 **106A**

Bank Street College
610 W 112 St, MA
212-875-4467 **144C**

Barnard College
3009 Broadway, MA
212-854-5262 **144A**

Baruch College (CUNY)
17 Lexington Av, MA
212-802-2000 **118B**

Benjamin N Cardozo School of Law
55 Fifth Av, MA
212-790-0200 **113B**

Berkeley College
3 E 43 St, MA
212-996-4343 **126D**

Boricua College
186 North 6 St, BK
718-782-2200 **404B**

Boro of Manhattan Community College (CUNY)
199 Chambers St, MA
212-346-8000 **104A**

Bronx Community College (CUNY)
181st St & University Av, BX
718-289-5100 **215C**

Brooklyn Law School
250 Joralemon St, BK, 718-625-2200 **408D**

Brooklyn College (CUNY)
2900 Bedford Av, BK
718-951-5000 **429A**

City College (CUNY)
Convent Av @ 138 St, MA, 212-650-7000 **148B**

College of Insurance
101 Murray St, MA
212-962-4111 **104C**

College of Mount Saint Vincent
6301 Riverdale, BX
718-405-3200 **202D**

College of Staten Island (CUNY)
2800 Victory Bd, SI
718-982-2000 **509D**

Columbia University
W. 116 St , MA
212 854-1754 **144B**

Cornell University Medical College
1300 York Av, MA
212-746-5454 **131B**

Cooper Union
30 Cooper Sq, MA
212-254-6300 **114A**

CUNY Law
65-21 Main St QS
718-575-4200 **329A**

CUNY Graduate Center opens fall '98
365 Fifth Av, MA
212-642-1600 **122C**

Fordham University
Rose Hill
441 E Fordham Rd, BX
718-817-1000 **215B**

Fordham University
Lincoln Center
113 W 60 St, MA
212-636-6000 **128B**

Health Science Center (SUNY)
450 Clarkson Av, BK
718-270-1000 **423A**

Hebrew Union College
1 W 4 St, MA
212-674-5300 **113B**

Hostos Community College (CUNY)
475 Grand Concourse, BX
718-518-4444 **226A**

Hunter College (CUNY)
695 Park Av, MA
212-772-4000 **130A**

John Jay College of Criminal Justice
899 Tenth Av, MA
212-237-8000 **128A**

Kingsborough Community College
2001 Oriental Bd, BK
718-368-5000 **445A**

La Guardia Community College
31-10 Thomson Av, QS
718-482-7200 **316A**

Lehman College (CUNY) Bedford Park Bd W, BX
718-960-8000 **209A**

Long Island University (LIU)
1 University Plz, BK
718-488-1000 **409A**

Manhattan College
4513 Manhattan
College Pkwy, BX
718-862-8000 **208B**

Marymount College
221 E 71 St, MA
212-517-0400 **131A**

**Medgar Evers
(CUNY)**
1650 Bedford Av, BK
718-270-4900 **416C**

Monroe College
2501 Jerome Av, BX
800-556-6676 **215A**

**New School for
Social Research**
66 W 12 St, MA
212-229-5600 **113A**

**New York City
Technical College**
300 Jay St, BK
718-260-5000 **408D**

**The NY College of
Podiatric Medicine**
53 E 124 St, MA
212-410-8000 **146B**

New York Law
57 Worth St, MA
212-431-2100 **104B**

**New York
University (NYU)**
Washington Sq, MA
212-998-4636 **113D**

Pace University
Pace Plz, MA
212-346-1200 **105C**

**Polytechnic
University**
MetroTech Ctr, BK
18-260-3100 **409C**

**Queens College
(CUNY)**
65-30 Kissena Bd, QS
718-997-5411 **329A**

**Queensborough
Community College
(CUNY)**
222-05 56 Av, QS
718-631-6262 **323D**

**Rockefeller
University**
1230 York Av MA
212-327-8000 **131B**

St Francis College
180 Remsen St, BK
718-522-2300 **408B**

**St John's
University**
800 Utopia Pkwy, QS
718-990-6132 **330C**

St Joseph's College
245 Clinton Av, BK
718-636-6800 **410C**

**Schuyler Maritime
College (SUNY)**
Fort Schulyer, BX
718-409-7200 **219D**

Teacher's College
525 W 120 St, MA
212-678-3000 **144B**

**University of
the Streets**
130 E 7 St, MA
212-254-9300 **114D**

Wagner College
631 Howard Av, SI
718-390-3100 **512B**

Yeshiva University
500 W 185 St, MA
212-960-5400 **157A**

York College (CUNY)
94-20 Guy R Brewer
Bd, Jamaica, QS
718-262-2000 **337D**

LIBRARIES

Bronx
Fordham Library Ctr
2556 Bainbridge Av,
BX, 718-579-4200
215A

Brooklyn
Grand Army Plz, BK
718-780-7700 **415D**

Brooklyn Business
280 Cadman Plz W
BK, 718-722-3333
408B

**Donnell
Library Center**
20 W 53 St, MA
212-621-0618 **126B**

**The Kurdish
Library Museum**
144 Underhill Av, BK
718-783-7930 **415B**

**The Langston
Hughes Community**
102-09, Northern
Bd, Corona ,QS
718-651-1100 **320A**

Pierpont Morgan
29 E 36 St, MA
212-685-0610 **122D**

NY Public
455 Fifth Av, MA
212-661-7220 **122A**

**NY Public Library
for the Performing
Arts** 40 Lincoln
Center Plz, MA
212-870-1630 **128D**

**NY Science, Industry
& Business (SIBL)**
188 Madison Av, MA
212-592-7000 **122D**

Queens
89-11 Merrick Bd,
Jamaica, QS
718-990-0781 **338D**

Staten Island
St George Center, SI
718-442-8560 **507B**

**SPECIAL
HIGH SCHOOLS**

Bronx HS of Science
75 W 205, BX
718-295-0200 **209C**

Brooklyn Technical
Brooklyn Tech Pl, BK
718-858-5150 **409D**

Campus Magnet
207-01 116 Av
Cambria Heights, QS
718-978-6432 **347A**

**HS of Fashion
Industries**
225 W 24 St, MA
212-255-1235 **117A**

**HS of Graphic
Communication Arts**
439 W 49 St, MA
212-245-5925 **124D**

**Manhattan Center
for Science & Math**
E 116 & FDR Dr, MA
212-876-4639 **147D**

**Murry Bergtraum
HS for Business
Careers**
411 Pearl St, MA
212-964-9610 **105A**

St George School
450 St Marks Pl, SI
718-273-3225 **507A**

Aviation
45-30 36 St, LIC, QS
718-361-2032 **317A**

Samuel Gompers
455 Southern Bd, BX
718-665-0950 **227B**

Stuyvesant
345 Chambers St, MA
212-312-4800 **104A**

TECHNICAL

**College of
Aeronautics**
La Guardia Airport,
QS, 718-429-6600
310D

**College of
Technology**
320 W 31 St, MA
800-225-8246 **121C**

**College of
Optometry (SUNY)**
33 W 42 St, MA
212-780-4900 **122B**

**NY Institute of
Technology**
1855 Broadway, MA
212-261-1500 **129C**

TO FIND A TOP 100

Simply turn to page
and locate the
college or school in
grids **A,B,C** or **D.**

MA = Manhattan
BX = The Bronx
BK = Brooklyn
QS = Queens
SI = Staten Island

GOVERNMENT

BOROUGH & CITY HALLS

The Bronx
851 Grand Concourse
718-590-3500 **221**C

Brooklyn
209 Joralemon St
718-802-3700 **408**D

Manhattan
Municipal Bldg
212-669-8300 **105**A

Queens
120-55 Queens Bd,
Kew Gardens
718-286-3000 **337**A

Staten Island
10 Richmond Ter
718-816-2236 **507**B

City Hall, MA
• City Council
212-788-7100 **105**A
• Mayor's Office
212-788-3000 **105**A

BUSINESS SERVICES

NYC Department of Business Services
110 Williams St, MA
212-513-6300 **105**C

Small Business Administration (SBA)
26 Federal Plz, MA
212-264-4354 **105**A

US Customs
6 WTC, MA
800-697-3662 **104**D

COURTS

The State & City court system is undergoing a major overhaul in the year 2000. Here is a short key to the jurisdictions of the current system.

• Civil–for disputes under $25,000
• Criminal–for misdemeaners
• Family–for child custody issues
• Surrogate–for probation of wills
• Supreme–civil cases over $25,000, divorce and felony cases.

Municipal– Bronx County
Civil
851 Grand Concourse
212-791-6000 **221**C

Criminal
215 E 161 St
718-374-5880 **221**C

Family
900 Sheridan Av
718-590-3321 **221**C

Supreme–Bronx Co
851 Grand Concourse
718-590-3723 **221**C

Surrogate's
851 Grand Concourse
718-590-3618 **221**C

Small Claims
851 Grand Concourse
212-791-6000 **221**C

Kings County
Civil
141 Livingston St
718-643-5069 **408**D

Criminal
120 Schermerhorn St
718-643-4044 **408**D

Family
283 Adams St
718-643-2652 **408**D

Supreme–Kings Co
360 Adams St
718-643-8076 **408**D

Surrogate's
2 Johnson St
718-643-5262 **408**D

Small Claims
141 Livingston St
408D

New York County
Civil
111 Centre St
212-791-6000 **106**D

Criminal
100 Centre St
212-374-5880 **105**A

Family–NYS & Co
60 Lafayette St
212-374-8743 **105**A

Supreme– New York Co
60 Centre St **107**C

Surrogate's
31 Chamber St
212-374-8233 **105**A

Small Claims
111 Centre St
212-374-5776 **106**D

Queens County
Civil
120-55 Queens Bd
718-643-5069 **337**A

Criminal
125-01 Queens Bd
212-374-5880 **337**A

Family
89-14 Parsons Bd
718-520-3991 **337**D

Supreme– Queens Co
88-11 Sutphin Bd
718-520-3713 **337**D

Surrogate's
88-11 Sutphin Bd
718-520-3132 **337**D

Small Claims
120-55 Queens Bd
212-791-6000 **336**B

Richmond County
Civil
927 Castleton Av
212-791-6000 **506**C

Criminal
67 Targee St
212-374-5880 **507**C

Family
100 Richmond Ter
718-390-5462 **507**A

Supreme– Richmond Co
18 Richmond Ter
718-390-5352 **507**B

Surrogate's
18 Richmond Ter
718-390-5400 **507**B

Small Claims
927 Castleton Av
718-390-5421 **506**C

State– Supreme Civil
60 Centre St, MA
212-374-8359 **107**C

Criminal
100 Centre St, MA
212-374-5880s **105**A

Family
60 Lafayette St, MA
212-374-8743 **105**A

Supreme Appellate
• First Division
27 Madison Av, MA
212-340-0400 **118**B
• Second Division
45 Monroe Pl, BK
718-875-1300 **408**B

Surrogate's
31 Chamber St, MA
105A

Small Claims
111 Centre St, MA
106D

Federal– US Bankruptcy
1 Bowling Green,
MA, 212-688-2870
102B

US Court of Appeals
40 Foley Sq, MA
212-857-8500 **105**A

US District–
• Southern
500 Pearl St, MA
212-805-0136 **105**A
• Eastern
225 Cadman Plz E, BK
718-260-2600 **408**

US Int'l Trade
1 Federal Plz, MA
212-264-2800 **105**A

GOVERNMENT

EMERGENCY & ENFORCEMENT

Coast Guard
212 Coast Guard Dr
SI, 718-354-4037
513D

Drug Enforcement Administration (DEA)
99 Tenth Av, MA
212-337-3900 **116**D

Federal Bureau of Investigation (FBI)
26 Federal Plz, MA
212-384-1000 **105**A

Fire Dept Hdqrs
9 MetroTech Center
BK **409**C

Police Dept Hdqrs & Central Booking
The Bronx
2 E 169 St
718-590-2804 **221**A

Brooklyn
120 Schermerhorn St
718-875-6586 **409**C

Manhattan
1 Police Plz
212-374-3838 **105**A

Queens
125-01 Queens Bd,
Kew Gardens
718-268-4523 **337**A

Staten Island
78 Richmond Ter
718-876-8490 **507**A

IMMIGRATION & NATURALIZATION
26 Federal Plz, MA
212-206-6500 **105**A

MOTOR VEHICLE

DMV
The Bronx
2265 E Tremont Av
212-645-5550 **217**A

Brooklyn
• 481 Hudson Av
718-966-6155 **409**C
• 2875 W 8 St,
Coney Island
718-966-6155 **443**C

Manhattan
• 155 Worth St
212-645-5550 **105**A
• 2110 Adam
Clayton Powell Bd
212-645-5550 **149**C

Queens
• 92-35 165 St,
Jamaica, QS
718-966-6155 **338**D
• 168-35 Rockaway
Bd Springfield Grdns
718-966-6155 **352**C
• 30-56 Whitestone
Expwy, Flushing
718-966-6155 **312**D

Staten Island
2795 Richmond Ter
800-368-1186 **503**A

Parking Violations
770 Broadway, MA
212-477-4430 **113**B

Read the signs for street cleaning and alternate side parking times carefully.

Errors can cost $200.00 or more!

Tow-Away Lots (DOT)

The Bronx
745 E 145 St **227**B

Brooklyn
Navy Yard **409**A

Manhattan
• 203 Ninth Av. **116**B
• 38 St & 12 Av **120**A

Queens
129-05 31 Av **312**C

Staten Island
350 St Marks Pl
718-876-5307 **507**A

Traffic Violations

The Bronx
2455 Sedgwick Av
718-488-5710 **214**B

Brooklyn
• 30 Rockwell Pl
718-488-5710 **409**C
• 2875 W 8 St
718-488-5710 **443**C

Manhattan
• 19 Rector St
718-488-5710 **102**B
• 2110 Adam Clayton
Powell Jr. Bd
718-488-5710 **149**C

Queens
• 168-35 Rockaway
Bd, Springfield Grdns
718-488-5710 **352**C
• 30-56 Whitestone
Expwy, Flushing
718-488-5710 **312**D

Staten Island
2795 Richmond Ter
718-488-5710 **503**A

PASSPORT

NY Passport Office
376 Hudson St, MA
212-206-3500 **108**B

SOCIAL SERVICES

Alcoholism & Substance Abuse
55 W 125 St, MA
212-961-8471 **149**D

Aging
2 Lafayette St, MA
212-442-1322 **106**D

Family & Children
80 Maiden La, MA
212-383-1825 **104**D

Medicaid
330 W 34 St, MA
718-291-1900 **121**C

Human Rights
40 Rector St, MA
212-306-7500 **102**C

Victim Services
2 Lafayette St, MA
212-577-7700 **106**D

Youth & Community
156 William St, MA
212-442-5900 **105**C

Social Security
• 26 Federal Plz, MA
212-264-8819 **105**A
• 226 161 St, BX
718-537-4637 **204**C
• 59-07 175 Pl, Fresh
Meadows, QS
718-357-8805 **330**D
• 200 Montague St,
BK, 718-330-7861
408D

TAXES

Internal Revenue Service (IRS)
The Bronx
3000 White Plains Rd
800-829-1040 **210**D

Brooklyn
10 MetroTech Center
800-829-1040 **409**C

Manhattan
• 110 W 44 St
800-829-1040 **125**D
• 55 W 125 St
800-829-1040 **149**D

Queens
1 Lefrak City Plz
800-829-1040 **319**D

Staten Island
45 Bay St
718-488-8432 **507**B

City Tax Offices
25 Elm Pl, BK
718-935-6739 **409**C

State Tax Info
Albany, NY
800-225-5829

TO FIND A TOP 100

simply turn to page
and locate the
agency in grids
A,B,C or D.

MA = Manhattan
BX = The Bronx
BK = Brooklyn
QS = Queens
SI = Staten Island

AIRPORTS

The Crowne Plaza LaGuardia $$$
104-04 Ditmars Bd, QS 800-692-5429
311C

JFK Airport Hilton $$$ 138-10 135 Av,QS
800 HILTONS **351**A

LaGuardia Marriott $$ 102-05 Ditmars Bd, QS
718-565-8900 **311**B

Sheraton LaGuardia East $$ 135-20 39 Av, QS
718-460-6666 **321**A

BED & BREAKFAST
All B & B's require reservations prior to arrival.

Baisley House $ 294 Hoyt St, BK
718-935-1959 **414**B

The Gracie Inn $$ 502 E 81, MA
212-628-1700 **135**B

Le Refuge Inn $$ 620 City Island, BX
718-885-2478 **207**C

SoHo $$ 167 Crosby St, MA
212-925-1034 **114**C

Upper West Side $$ W 77 St, MA
212-472-2000 **132**D

MANHATTAN
Downtown

Best Western Seaport Inn $$ 33 Peck Slip, MA
212-766-6600 **105**C

Holiday Inn Downtown $$ 138 Lafayette St, MA
212-966-8898 **106**B

Marriott Financial Center $$$ 85 West St, MA
212-385-4900 **102**B

Marriott WTC, New York $$$ 3 WTC, MA
212-938-9100 **104**D

The Millenium Hilton $$$ 55 Church St, MA
800-835-2220 **104**D

SoHo & The Village

The Larchmont $ 27 W 11 St, MA
212-989-9333 **113**A

The Mercer $$$ 99 Prince St, MA
212-966-6060 **109**C

Off-SoHo Suites $ 11 Rivington St, MA
212-979-9808 **110**A

SoHo Grand $$$ 310 W Broadway, MA
212-965-3000 **106**B

Washington Sq $ 103 Waverly Pl, MA
212-777-9515 **113**A

Chelsea & Gramercy Park

Chelsea $$ 222 W 23 St, MA
212-243-3700 **117**A

Gramercy Park $$ 2 Lexington Av, MA
800-221-4083 **118**B

Inn at Irving Place $$ 56 Irving Pl, MA
212-533-4600 **118**D

Southgate Tower $$ 371 Seventh Av, MA
212-563-1800 **121**C

Midtown East

Beekman Tower $$ 3 Mitchell Pl, MA
212-355-7300 **127**C

Crowne Plaza at the United Nations $$ 304 E 42 St, MA
212-986-8800 **123**A

The Doral Court $$ 130 E 39 St, MA
800-685-1100 **122**B

Doral Tuscany $$$ 120 E 39 St, MA
800-686-1600 **122**B

The Doral Inn $$ 541 Lexington Av, MA, 212-755-1200
126D

The Doral Park Av $$ 70 Park Av, MA
212-687-7050 **122**B

The Drake $$$ 440 Park Av, MA
800-63SWISS **126**B

Dumont Plaza Suite $$$ 150 E 34 MA
800-ME-SUITE **122**D

Eastgate Tower Suite $$ 222 E 39 St, MA
800-ME-SUITE **123**A

The Fitzpatrick $$$ 687 Lexington Av, MA
212-355-0100 **126**B

The Four Seasons $$$$$ 57 E 57 St, MA
212-758-5700 **130**D

Grand Hyatt NY $$$ Park Av @ 42 St, MA
800-228-9000 **122**B

Helmsley Middletowne $$ 148 E 48 St, MA
800-221-4982 **126**C

Hotel Élysée $$ 60 E 54 St, MA
212-753-1066 **126**B

Hotel Inter-Continental NY $$$ 111 E 48 St, MA
800-327-0200 **126**D

Loews NY $$ 569 Lexington Av, MA
212-752-7000 **126**B

Morgans $$$ 237 Madison Av, MA
800-686-0300 **122**D

NY Helmsley $$$ 212 E 42 St, MA
800-221-4982 **122**B

The NY Palace $$$$ 445 Madison Av, MA
212-888-7000 **126**B

The Omni Berkshire Place $$$ 21 E 52 St, MA
800-THEOMNI **125**B

Pickwick Arms $$ 230 51 St, MA
212-355-0300 **127**A

Regal UN Plaza $$$$ 1 UN Plz, MA
800-222-8888 **127**C

The Roger Williams $$$ 131 Madison Av, MA, 212-488-7000
122D

Roger Smith $$ 501 Lexington Av, MA
212-755-1400 **126**D

St Regis $$$$$ 2 E 55 St, MA
800-759-7550 **126**A

San Carlos $$ 150 E 50 St, MA
800-722-2012 **126**B

Shelburne $$ 303 Lexington Av, MA
800-689-5200 **122**B

Swissôtel NY $$$ 440 Park Av, MA
800-63SWISS **126**B

Vanderbilt YMCA $ 224 E 47 St, MA
212-756-9600 **126**C

The Waldorf–Astoria $$$ 301 Park Av, MA
800-WALDORF **126**B

The Waldorf Towers $$$$ 100 E 50 St. MA
800-WALDORF **126**E

Midtown West

The Algonquin *$$$*
59 W 44 St, MA
800-548-0345 **125D**

Best Western President *$*
234 W 48 St, MA
800-826-4667 **125C**

The Essex House– Nikko Hotel *$$$*
160 CPS, MA
800-NIKKO-US **129C**

Hampshire Ambassador
132 W 45 St, MA
212-961-7600 **125C**

Hotel Edison *$*
228 W 47 St, MA
212-840-5000 **125C**

Quality Hotel & Suites *$*
59 W 46 St, MA
212-719-2300 **125D**

Holiday Inn Crowne Plaza *$$$*
605 Broadway, MA
800-227-6963 **125A**

The Mansfield *$$*
12 W 44 St, MA
212-944-6050 **125D**

The Manhattan *$$*
17 W 32 St, MA
212-736-1600 **121C**

Marriott Marquis *$$$* 1535 B'way, MA
800-228-9290 **125C**

Michelangelo *$$$*
152 W 51 St, MA
800-237-0990 **125A**

The Millenium Broadway *$$$*
145 W 44 St, MA
800-622-5569 **125C**

The NY Hilton *$$$*
1335 Sixth Av, MA
800-HILTONS **125B**

Paramount *$$*
235 W 46 St, MA
800-225-7474 **124C**

Le Parker Meridien *$$$* 118 W 57 St, MA
800-543-4300 **125B**

The Peninsula NY *$$$$* 700 Fifth Av, MA
800-262-9467 **126A**

The Plaza *$$$*
768 Fifth Av, MA
800-759-3000 **129D**

Quality Inn Midtown *$* 157 W 47 St, MA
800-826-4667 **125C**

RHIGA Royal *$$$*
151 W 54 St, MA
800-937-5454 **125A**

The Royalton *$$$*
44 W 44 St, MA
800-635-9013 **125D**

St Moritz on-the-Park *$$*
50 CPS, MA
800-221-4774 **129D**

Sheraton NY Hotel & Towers *$$*
811 Seventh Av, MA
800-325-3535 **125A**

The Shoreham *$$$*
33 W 54 St, MA
212-247-6700 **125B**

The Warwick *$$$*
65 W 54 St, MA
212-247-2700 **125B**

Westin Central Park
$$$$ 112 CPS, MA
212-757-1900 **129D**

The Wyndham *$$*
42 W 58 St, MA
212-753-3500 **129D**

Upper Eastside

The Carlyle *$$$$*
35 E 76 St, MA
212-744-1600 **134D**

The Franklin *$$*
164 E 87 St, MA
212-369-1000 **139C**

Hotel Plaza Athénée *$$$$*
37 E 64 St, MA
800-734-9100 **130B**

The Lowell *$$$$*
28 E 63 St, MA
800-221-4444 **130D**

The Mark *$$$$*
25 E 77 St, MA
800-THE MARK **133D**

The Regency *$$$$*
540 Park Av, MA
212-759-4100 **130D**

The Pierre *$$$$*
5 Av @ E 61 St, MA
800-332-3442 **129D**

Sherry–Netherland *$$$$$* 781 Fifth Av,
MA, 800-247-4377 **129D**

The Stanhope *$$$$*
995 Fifth Av, MA
800-828-1123 **133B**

Surrey *$$*
20 E 76 St, MA
212-288-3700 **133D**

The Westbury *$$$*
69 St @ Madison Av
MA, 212-535-2000 **130D**

92nd St YMCA *$*
de Hirsch Residence
1395 Lexington Av,
MA, 800-858-4692 **139A**

Upper Westside

Beacon Hotel *$$*
2130 Broadway, MA
800-572-4969 **132D**

Inn New York City *$$* 266 W 71 St, MA
212-580-1900 **128B**

Mayflower Hotel on the Park *$$*
15 Central Park W,
MA, 800-223-4164 **129C**

NY Int'l American Youth Hostel *$*
891 Amsterdam Av,
@ W 103, MA
212-932-2300 **140D**

Radisson Empire *$$*
44 W 63 St, MA
212-265-7400 **128C**

Trump International Hotel & Tower *$$$$*
1 Central Park W,
MA, 800-44TRUMP **129C**

63rd St YMCA *$*
5 W 63 St, MA
212-787-4400 **129C**

OUTER BOROS

New York Marriott Brooklyn *$$$*
333 Adams St, BK
718-246-7000 **408D**

The Staten Island Hotel *$$*
1415 Richmond Av, SI
800-532-3532 **510C**

RESERVATIONS

At Home in NY
800-692-4262

City Lights B & B
212-737-7049

NY by Phone
888-NYC-APPLE

New World
800-443-3800

Urban Ventures
212-594-5650

PRICE KEY

$ = less than $100
$$ = $100-$200
$$$ = $200-$300
$$$$ = $300-$400
$$$$$ = $400-$500

Price ranges given
are for single occu-
pancy midweek.
It's smart to call for
weekend specials
and promotional
rates.

MA = Manhattan
BX = The Bronx
BK = Brooklyn
QS = Queens
SI = Staten Island

MUSEUMS

Abigail Adams Smith House Museum
421 E 61 St, MA
212-838-6878 **131**C

African–American Wax Museum
316 W 115 St, MA
212-678-7818 **145**C

Alice Austen House
2 Hylan Bd, SI
718-816-4506 **513**B

Alternative Museum
594 Broadway
Suite #402, MA
212-966-4444 **109**B

American Academy of Arts & Letters
633 W 155 St, MA
212-368-5900 **152**B

American Craft Museum
40 W 53 St, MA
212-956-6047 **125**B

American Museum of the Moving Image (AMM)
35 Av @ 36 St, QS
718-784-4520 **309**C

American Museum of Natural History
21 Central Park
West @ 79 St, MA
212-769-5000 **133**C

American Numismatic Society
Audubon Ter, MA
212-234-3130 **152**B

The Americas Society
680 Park Av, MA
212-249-8950 **130**B

The Asia Society
725 Park Av, MA
212-249-6400 **130**B

Asian American Art Centre
26 Bowery, MA
212-233-2154 **107**C

Bartow–Pell Mansion Museum
Shore Rd N, BX
718-885-1461 **206**D

The Black Fashion Museum
155 W 126 St, MA
212-666-1320 **149**D

The Bronx Museum of the Arts
1040 Grand Concourse, BX
718-681-6000 **221**C

Brooklyn Children's Museum
145 Brooklyn Av, BK
718-735-4432 **416**B

Brooklyn Historical Society
128 Pierrepont St, BK
718-624-0890 **408**D

Brooklyn Museum of Art (BMA)
200 Eastern Pkwy, BK
718-638-5000 **415**D

Children's Museum of the Arts
182 Lafayette St, MA
212-941-9198 **109**B

Children's Museum of Manhattan
212 W 83 St, MA
212-721-1223 **132**B

China Institute in America
125 E 65 St, MA
212-744-8181 **130**B

The Cloisters
Fort Tryon Pk, MA
212-923-3700 **158**D

Cooper–Hewitt National Design Museum
2 E 91 St, MA
212-849-8300 **137**D

Dahesh Museum
601 Fifth Av, MA
212-759-0606 **125**D

Dia Center for the Arts
548 W 22 St, MA
212-989-5912 **116**B

The Drawing Center
35 Wooster St, MA
212-219-2166 **109**D

Dyckman Farmhouse Museum
4881 Broadway, MA
212-304-9422 **159**A

Edgar Allan Poe Cottage
Grand Concourse & E Kingsbridge Rd, BX
718-881-8900 **215**A

El Museo del Barrio
1230 Fifth Av
@ E 104 St, MA
212-831-7272 **141**D

Ellis Island Immigration Museum
Ellis Island, MA
212-363-7620 **102**C

Exit Art / The First World
548 Broadway, MA
212-966-7745 **109**D

Federal Hall
26 Wall St, MA
212-825-6888 **103**C

Federal Reserve Bank of NY
33 Liberty St, MA
212720-6130 **105**C

Fraunces Tavern
54 Pearl St, MA
212-425-1778 **103**C

Forbes Magazine Galleries
62 Fifth Av, MA
212-206-5548 **113**A

Frick Collection
1 E 70 St, MA
212-288-0700 **130**B

Garibaldi Meucci Museum
420 Tompkins Av, SI
718-442-1608 **513**A

Guggenheim Museum–SoHo
575 Broadway
@ Prince St, MA
212-423-3500 **109**D

Hayden Planetarium
Central Park W
@ W 81 St, MA
212-769-5900 **133**A

The Hispanic Society of America
613 W 155 St, MA
212-690-0743 **152**B

Historic Richmond Town
441 Clarke Av, SI
718-351-1611 **522**B

Int'l Center of Photography, (ICP) Uptown
1130 Fifth Av, MA
212-860-1777 **137**D

ICP Midtown
6 Av @ W 43 St, MA
212-768-4680 **125**D

Intrepid Sea–Air– Space Museum
W 46 St @ 12 Av, MA
212-245-0072 **124**C

Isamu Noguchi Garden Museum
32-37 Vernon Bd, QS
718-204-7088 **308**D

Jacques Marchais Museum of Tibetan Art
338 Lighthouse Av, SI
718-987-3500 **523**A

Jamaica Arts Center
161-04 Jamaica Av, QS, 718-658-7400 **337**D

Japan Society
333 E 47 St, MA
212-832-1155 **126**D

Jewish Museum
1109 Fifth Av, MA
212-339-3430 **137**D

The John A Noble Collection
1000 Richmond Ter, SI
718-447-6490 **506**B

The Judaica Museum
4961 Palisades Av, BX
718-548-1006 **202**D

King Manor Museum
King Park, QS
718-523-0029 **337**D

Kingsland Homestead
143-35 37 Av, QS
718-939-0467 **313**B

The Kurdish Library Museum
144 Underhill Av, BK
718-783-7930 **415**B

The Liberty Science Center
Liberty State Pk, NJ
201-200-1000 **104**C

Lower East Side Tenement Museum
90 Orchard St, MA
212-431-0233 **110**D

The Metropolitan Museum of Art
1000 Fifth Av, MA
212-535-7710 **133**A

Morris-Jumel Mansion
65 Jumel Ter, MA
212-923-8008 **154**D

Museum for African Art
593 Broadway, MA
212-966-1313 **109**B

Museum of Amer. Financial History
28 Broadway, MA
212-908-4110 **102**B

Museum of American Folk Art
2 Lincoln Sq, MA
212-977-7298 **128**B

Museum of Amer. Illustration
128 E 63 St, MA
212-838-2560 **130**D

Museum of Bronx History
3309 Bainbridge Av,
BX, 718-881-8900
  209D

Museum of the City of NY
1220 Fifth Av, MA
212-534-1672 **141**B

Museum of Jewish Heritage
18 First Pl, MA
212-968-1800 **102**D

Museum of Modern Art (MoMA)
11 W 53 St, MA
212-708-9480 **125**B

Museum of Chinese in the Americas
70 Mulberry St, MA
212-619-4785 **107**C

Museum of TV & Radio
25 W 52 St, MA
212-621-6600 **125**B

National Academy Museum
1083 Fifth Av, MA
212-369-4880 **137**D.

National Museum of the American Indian
1 Bowling Green, MA
212-825-6700 **102**C

New Museum of Contemporary Art
583 Broadway, MA
212-219-1222 **109**B

NYC Fire Museum
278 Spring St, MA
212-691-1303 **109**C

NY Hall of Science
47-01 111 St, QS
718-699-0005 **320**B

New–York Historical Society
170 CPW, MA
212-873-3400 **133**C

NY Public Library
42 St @ Fifth Av, MA
212-661-7220 **122**A

NY Transit Museum
Boerum Pl, BK
718-243-3060 **408**D

Nicholas Roerich Museum
319 W 107 St, MA
212-864-7752 **140**A

North Wind Undersea Institute
610 City Island Av, BX
718-855-0701 **207**C

Old Merchant's House
29 E 4 St, MA
212-777-1089 **114**C

Pierpont Morgan Library
29 E 36 St, MA
212-685-0610 **122**B

Pieter Claeson Wyckoff House Museum
5816 Clarendon Rd, BK
718-629-5400 **424**C

Police Museum
235 E 20 St, MA
212-477-9753 **118**D

Queens County Farm Museum
73-50 Little Neck Pkwy, QS
718-347-3276 **333**A

Queens Museum of Art (QMA)
Flushing Meadows–
Corona Park, QS
718-760-0064 **320**D

PS 1
22-25 Jackson Av, QS
718-784-2084 **316**A

Rose Museum
154 W 57 St, MA
212-247-7800 **125**A

Skyscraper Museum
44 Wall St, MA
212-968-1961 **103**A

Snug Harbor Cultural Center
1000 Richmond Ter,
SI, 718-448-2500 **506**B

Socrates Sculpture Park
B'way @ Vernon Bd
Long Island City, QS
718-956-1819 **308**B

Solomon R Guggenheim Museum (Uptown)
1071 Fifth Av, MA
212-423-3500 **138**C

Sony Wonder Technology Lab
550 Madison Av, MA
212-833-8100 **126**B

South Street Seaport Museum
207 Front St
Seaport Plz, MA
212-748-8600 **105**C

Staten Island Children's Museum
1000 Richmond Ter, SI
718-273-2060 **506**B

Staten Island Institute of Arts and Sciences
75 Stuyvesant Pl, SI
718-727-1135 **507**B

Studio Museum in Harlem
144 W 125 St, MA
212-864-4500 **145**B

Theodore Roosevelt Birthplace
28 E 20 St, MA
212-260-1616 **118**C

Ukranian Museum
203 Second Av, MA
212-228-0110 **114**A

Van Cortlandt Mansion Museum
B'way @ 246 St, BX
718-543-3344 **209**A

Whitney Museum of American Art
945 Madison Av, MA
212-570-3600 **134**D

Whitney Museum at Philip Morris
120 Park Av, MA
212-878-2550 **122**B

TO FIND A TOP 100

Simply turn to page to locate museums in grids A,B,C or D.

MA = Manhattan
BX = The Bronx
BK = Brooklyn
QS = Queens
SI = Staten Island

NATURE 3

AQUARIA & ZOOS

Bronx Zoo–Int'l Wildlife Conservation Park
Bronx River Pkwy @ E Fordham Rd, BX, 718-367-1010 **216AB**

Central Park Zoo Wildlife Conservation Ctr
830 Fifth Av, MA
212-439-6500 **129D**

Prospect Park Wildlife Conservation Ctr
450 Flatbush Av, BK
718-339-7339 **415D**

NY Aquarium
W 8 St & Surf Av, BK
718-265-3400 **443D**

Queens Wildlife Conservation Ctr
53-51 111 St, QS
718-271-7761 **320D**

Staten Island Zoo
614 Broadway, SI
718-442-3100 **512A**

BEACHES

Brighton BK **443D**
Coney Island BK **443C**
Great Kills SI **530D**
Jacob Riis QS **364C**
Manhattan BK **444D**
Ferry Point BX **218D**
Orchard BX **206D**
Rockaway QS **365C**

CEMETERIES

The Bronx
St Raymonds **218D**
Woodlawn **203D**

Brooklyn
Canarsie **424C**
Friends **422A**
Greenwood **421A**
Holy Cross **423C**
Washington **428D**

Manhattan
African Burial Grounds **104A**
St Paul's **104D**
Trinity **152B**

Queens
Calvary **317C**
Cemetery of the Evergreens **334C**
Cypress Hills **334B**
Flushing **322C**
Lutheran **326D**
Montefiore **347C**
Mt Carmel **334B**
Mt Hebron **329A**
Mt Lebanon **335A**
Mt Judah **334D**
Mt Olivet **326B**
Mt Zion **317D**
New Calvary **317D**
St John's **327D**
St Michael's **310C**

Staten Island
Baron Hirsch **510A**
Moravian **517C**
Ocean View **522D**
Snug Harbor **506B**
Resurrection **533C**
United Hebrew **522D**

GARDENS

Botanical
Brooklyn Botanic
1000 Washington Av
BK, 718-622-4433 **416C**

New York Botanical
200 St & Southern Bd BX
718-817-8700 **210C**

Queens Botanical
4350 Main St, QS
718-939-0647 **321C**

Staten Island Botanical
1000 Richmond Ter, SI
718-273-8200 **506B**

Wave Hill
675 W 252 St, BX
718-549-3200 **208A**

Community
Through fortitude and grit, New Yorkers have taken over 700 vacant lots and transformed them into beautiful and productive gardens that help strengthen their communities.

Aided by Green Thumb, city gardeners get access to city land and horticultural training. Here are a few of the finest in the five boroughs.

Brisas La Caribe
237 E 3 St, MA **114D**

Howard
750 Howard Av, BK **417B**

Joe Holzka
1171 Castleton Av, SI **506C**

The One Love
Inwood St, QS **344A**

Taqwa
90 W 164 St, BX **221C**

Youth & Senior
Surf Av @ 32 St, BK **442D**

6th & B
624 E 6 St, MA **115A**

Special
Biblical Garden
St John the Divine, MA **144D**

Cloisters
Ft Tryon Pk, MA **158B**

Peace
UN Plz, MA **127C**

Conservatory
Central Pk, MA **141B**

St Luke's-in-the-Field
487 Hudson St, MA **112D**

Sterling Park
Brooklyn Heights, BK **408A**

Shakespeare
Central Park, MA **133A**

Strawberry Fields
Central Park, MA **129A**

INTERPRETIVE CENTERS

Alley Pond Park Environmental
228-06 Northern Bd, Douglaston, QS
718-229-4000 **324A**

Brooklyn Center for the Urban Environment
Tennis House, Prospect Park, BK
718-788-8549 **415C**

Charles A Dana Discovery
Lenox Av & 110 St, MA
212-860-1370 **141B**

Clay Pits Ponds State Preserve
83 Nielsen Av, SI
718-967-1976 **526C**

Henry Luce Nature Observatory
Belvedere Castle
Central Park, MA
212-772-0210 **133A**

High Rock Conservation
200 Nevada Av, SI
718-667-6042 **517C**

Jamaica Bay Nat'l Wildlife Refuge
Cross Bay Bd, QS
718-318-4340 **358B**

Urban Ecology
Inwood Pk, MA
212-304-2365 **160B**

Urban Forest Ecology
Van Cortlandt Pk, BX
718-548-0912 **209A**

PARKS

TO FIND A TOP 100

simply turn to page
and locate a park or
garden in grids
A, B, C or D.

MA = Manhattan
BX = The Bronx
BK = Brooklyn
QS = Queens
SI = Staten Island

NIGHTLIFE

BLUES, FOLK, ROCK & SOUL

Venues may offer many styles of music. Call for more details.

Arlene Grocery
95 Stanton St, MA
212-358-1633 **110**B

Arthur's Tavern
57 Grove St, MA
212-675-6879 **112**D

Bitter End
147 Bleecker St, MA
212-673-7030 **113**D

The Blue Lounge
625 Broadway, MA
212-473-8787 **113**D

Bottom Line
15 W 4 St, MA
212-228-7880 **113**D

Brownies
169 Av A, MA
212-420-8392 **114**B

CBGB
315 Bowery, MA
212-982-4052 **114**C

Chicago B.L.U.E.S.
73 Eighth Av, MA
212-924-9755 **112**B

Coney Island High
15 St Mark's Pl, MA
212-674-7959 **114**A

The Cooler
416 W 14 St, MA
212-645-5189 **112**B

Fez
380 Lafayette St, MA
212-533-2680 **114**C

Gonzalez y Gonzalez
625 Broadway, MA
212-473-8787 **113**D

Irving Plaza
17 Irving Pl, MA
212-777-6800 **119**D

Knitting Factory
74 Leonard St, MA
212-219-3055 **106**D

Le Bar Bat
311 W 57 St, MA
212-307-7228 **129**C

Louisiana Grill
622 Broadway, MA
212-460-9633 **113**D

Manny's Car Wash
1558 Third Av, MA
212-369-BLUES, **139**C

Mercury Lounge
217 E Houston St,
MA, 212-260-4700
114D

Rock'n Roll Cafe
149 Bleecker St, MA
212-677-7630 **113**D

Terra Blues
149 Bleecker St, MA
212-777-7776 **113**C

Tramps
51 W 21 St, MA
212-727-7788 **117**B

West End Gate
2911 Broadway, MA
212-662-8830 **144**D

Wetlands Preserve
161 Hudson St, MA
212-966-4225 **106**A

CABARET

Bemelmans Bar
35 E 76 St, MA
212-744-1600 **134**D

Café Carlyle
35 E 76 St, MA
212-570-7189 **134**D

Chez Josephine
414 W 42 St, MA
212-594-1925 **120**D

The Chestnut Room
Tavern on the Green
CPW @ 67 St, MA
212-873-3200 **129**A

Danny's Skylight Room
346 W 46 St, MA
212-265-8133 **125**C

Don't Tell Mama
343 W 46 St, MA
212-757-0788 **125**C

Eighty Eight's
228 W 10 St, MA
212-924-0088 **112**D

Judy's
49 W 44 St, MA
212-764-8930 **125**D

The Oak Room
59 W 44 St, MA
212-840-6800 **125**D

Rainbow & Stars
30 Rockefeller
Center Plz, MA
212-632-5000 **125**D

Tatou
151 E 50 St, MA
212-753-1144 **126**D

Triad
58 W 72 St, MA
212-799-4599 **128**B

COMEDY CLUBS

Boston Comedy
82 W 3 St, MA
212-477-1000 **113**C

Caroline's
1626 Broadway, MA
212-757-4100 **125**A

Catch a Rising Star
253 W 28 St, MA
212-244-3005 **117**A

Comedy Cellar
117 MacDougal St,
MA, 212-254-3480
113C

Chicago City Limits
1105 First Av, MA
212-888-5233 **131**C

Dangerfield's
1118 First Av, MA
212-593-1650 **131**C

Gotham
34 W 22 St, MA
212-367-9000 **117**B

New York Comedy Club
241 E 24 St, MA
212-696-LAFF **118**B

The Original Improv
433 W 34 St, MA
212-279-3446 **120**D

Rebar
127 Eighth Av, MA
212-627-1680 **117**C

Soho Arts Group
36 W 17 St, MA
212-463-8732 **117**D

Stand-Up NY
236 W 78 St, MA
212-595-0850 **132**D

DANCE CLUBS

The Apollo
253 W 125 St, MA
212-749-5838, **149**C

Au Bar
41 E 58 St, MA
212-308-9455 **130**D

The Bank
225 E Houston St,
MA, 212-505-5033
114D

Club Broadway
2700 Queens Plz S, QS
718-937-7111 **308**D

Copacabana
617 W 57, MA
212-582-2672 **124**A

Jimmy's Bronx Cafe
281 W Fordham Rd,
BX, 718-329-2000
214B

The Latin Quarter
2551 Broadway, MA
212-864-7600 **136**B

Les Poulets
16 W 22 St, MA
212-229-2000 **117**B

Life
158 Bleecker St, MA
212-420-1999 **113**C

Mother
432 W 14 St, MA
212-366-5680 **112**A

Nell's
246 W 14 St, MA
212-675-1567 **112**E

Pyramid Club
101 Av A, MA
212-473-7184 **114**E

seland
9 W 52 St, MA
2-247-0200 **125A**

e Roxy
5 W 18 St, MA
2-645-5156 **116D**

O.B.'s
ounds of Brazil)
4 Varick St, MA
2-243-4940 **109A**

ca Paradise
5-20 Jamaica Av,
, 718-464-3600
340A

nnel
0 W 12 Av, MA
2-695-4682 **116A**

ebster Hall
5 E 11 St, MA
2-353-1600 **114A**

AZZ &
TANDARDS

gonquin
W 44 St, MA
2-840-6800 **125D**

t.Coffee
9 Av A, MA
2-529-2233 **114B**

e Baggot Inn
W 3 St, MA
2-477-0622 **113C**

ell Cafe
0 Spring St, MA
2-334-2355 **109A**

emelman's Bar
E 76 St, MA
2-744-1600 **134D**

irdland
5 W 44 St, MA
2-581-3080 **125C**

The Blue Note
131 W 3 St, MA
212-475-8592 **113C**

Bowery Bar
40 E 4 St, MA
212-475-2220 **114C**

Bull and Bear
Lex. Av @ 49 St, MA
212-872-4900 **126D**

Café Carlyle
35 E 76 St, MA,
212-744-1600 **134D**

Detour
349 E 13 St, MA
212-533-6212 **114B**

Homefront
236 E 54 St, MA
212-560-2271 **125A**

Iridium
44 W 63 St, MA
212-582-2121 **128D**

Izzy Bar
166 First Av, MA
212-228-0444 **114B**

Internet Cafe
82 E 3 St, MA
212-614-0747 **114C**

The Jazz Standard
116 E 27 St, MA
212-576-2232 **118B**

Jules
65 St Marks Pl, MA
212-477-5560 **114A**

Knitting Factory
74 Leonard St, MA
212-219-3055 **106D**

Lenox Lounge
288 Lenox Av, MA
212-722-9566 **145B**

Michaels Pub
57 E 54 St, MA
212-758-2272 **126B**

Metronome
915 Broadway, MA
212-505-7400 **118C**

Opaline
85 Av A, MA
212-475-5050 **114D**

St Nick's Pub
773 St Nicholas Av,
MA, 212-283-9728
152D

Savoy Lounge
355 W 41 St, MA
212-947-5255 **120B**

Smalls
183 W 10 St, MA
212-929-7565 **113A**

Sweet Basil
88 Seventh Av S, MA
212-242-1785 **113C**

Village Vanguard
178 Seventh Av S,
MA, 212-255-4037
112B

Visiones
125 MacDougal St,
MA, 800-831-BEBOP
113C

Wells
2247 Seventh Av,
MA, 212-234-0700
149A

Zinc Bar
90 W Houston, MA
212-477-8337 **109A**

Zinno
126 W 13 St, MA
212-924-5182 **113A**

LATE NIGHT
EATS

Around the Clock
8 Stuyvesant St, MA
212-598-0402 **114C**

Blue Ribbon
97 Sullivan St, MA
212-274-0404 **109A**

Carnegie Deli
854 Seventh Av, MA
212-757-2245 **125A**

Coffee Shop
26 Union Sq W, MA
212-243-7969 **118C**

Erizo Latino
422 W Broadway, MA
212-941-5811 **109A**

Florent
69 Gansevoort St,
MA, 212-989-5779
112A

NY Noodle Town
28 1/2 Bowery, MA
212-349-0923 **107C**

The Odeon
145 W Broadway. MA
212-233-0507 **106D**

Pravda
281 Lafayette St, MA
212-226-4696 **109B**

Raoul's
180 Prince St, MA
212-966-3518 **109A**

Uncle George's
33-19 Broadway, QS
718-626-0593 **309C**

Wollensky's Grill
205 E 49 St, MA
212-753-0444 **127C**

PUBS & BARS

Ear Inn
326 Spring St, MA
212-226-9060 **108D**

Standard
158 First Av, MA
212-387-0239 **114B**

McSorley's Old Ale
House
15 E 7 St, MA
212-473-9148 **114C**

White Horse Tavern
567 Hudson St, MA
212-243-9260 **112B**

SUPPER CLUBS

Laura Belle
120 W 43 St, MA
212-819-1000 **126C**

The Rainbow Room
30 Rockefeller Plz,
65th floor, MA
212-632-5000 **126A**

Supper Club
240 W 47 St, MA
212-921-1940 **125C**

Tatou
151 E 50 St, MA
212-753-1144 **126B**

TO FIND A TOP 100

simply turn to page
and locate a club or
pub in grids
A,B,C or D.

MA = Manhattan
BX = The Bronx
BK = Brooklyn
QS = Queens
SI = Staten Island

PERFORMING

Aaron Davis Hall
CUNY, W 135 St @
Convent Av, MA
212-650-7100   **148**B

Alice Tully Hall
Lincoln Center, MA
212-875-5000   **128**B
Chamber Music Society

American Opera Projects
463 Broome St, MA
212-431-8102   **109**D

Amato Opera
319 Bowery, MA
212-228-8200   **110**A

Avery Fisher Hall
Lincoln Center, MA
(212) 875-5030   **128**B
NYC Philharmonic

Bargemusic, Ltd
Fulton Ferry
Landing, BK
718-624-4061   **406**B

Belmont Italian American Playhouse
2385 Arthur Av, BX
718-364-4700   **215**B

Billie Holiday Theatre
1368 Fulton St, BK
(718) 636-0918   **416**B

The Bronx County Historical Society
3309 Bainbridge Av
BX, 718-881-8900
209D

Bronx Opera Co.
5 Minerva Pl, BX
718 365-4209   **209**D

Brooklyn Academy of Music (BAM)
30 Lafayette Av, BK
718 636-4100   **407**D

Brooklyn Center for Performing Arts
Campus Rd
@ Hillel Pl, BK
718-951-4500   **429**A

Brooklyn Heritage House
581 Mother Gaston
Bd, BK, 718-385-1111
418B

The Center for Art & Culture of Bedford Stuyvesant
1368 Fulton St, BK
718-636-6948   **416**B

CSC Repertory
136 E 13 St, MA
212-677-4210   **114**A

CAMI Hall
165 W 57 St, MA
212-841-9650   **129**C

Carnegie Hall
881 Seventh Av
@ W 57 St, MA
212-903-9600   **125**A

Circle in the Square
1633 Broadway, MA
212-307-2700   **125**A

City Center
131 W 55 St, MA
212-581-1212   **125**B

Colden Center for the Performing Arts
65-30 Kissena Bd, QS
(718) 793-8080   **329**B

Danspace at St Mark's Church-in-the-Bowery
131 E 10 St, MA
212-674-8194   **114**A

Dance Theater Workshop (DTW)
219 W 19 St, MA
212-924-0077   **117**C

Delacorte Theater Shakespeare in the Park
Central Park, MA
212-861-PAPP   **133**A

Dia Center for the Arts
548 W 22 St, MA
212-989-5912   **116**B

En Foco
32 E Kingsbridge Rd
BX, 718-584-7718
215A

Ensemble Studio
549 W 52 St, MA
212-247-4982   **124**B

FIT, Haft Auditorium
227 W 27 @ 7 Av, MA
212-307-2700   **117**A

Florence Gould Hall
Alliance Française
55 E 59 St, MA
212-355-6160   **130**A

Gowanus Arts Exchange
295 Douglass St, BK
718-596-5250   **415**A

Greek Cultural Center
27-18 Hoyt Av S, QS
718-726-7329   **309**A

Henry Street Settlement
Louis Abrams Arts Center,
466 Grand St, MA
212-598-0400   **111**C

HERE
145 Sixth Av, MA
212-647-0202   **109**A

Historic Richmond Town
441 Clarke Av, SI
718-351-1611   **522**B

Hostos Performing Arts Center
500 Grand
Concourse, BX
718-518-4300   **227**A

Irish Arts Center
553 W 51 St, MA
212-757-3318   **124**B

Jamaica Arts Center
161-04 Jamaica Av
QS, 718-658-7400
337D

The Joseph Papp Public Theater
425 Lafayette St, MA
212-260-2400   **113**D

Joyce Theater
175 Eighth Av, MA
212-242-0800   **117**C

Joyce SoHo
155 Mercer St, MA
212-431-9233   **109**B

The Juilliard School
Lincoln Center, MA
(212) 799-5000   **128**B

The Kitchen
512 W 19 St, MA
212-255-5793   **116**D

Langston Hughes Community Arts Ctr.
102-09 Northern Bd,
QS, 718-651-1100
320A

La MaMa E.T.C.
74 1/2 E 4 St, MA
(212) 475-7710   **114**C

Lehman College Center for the Performing Arts
250 Bedford Park
Bd W, BX
718 960-8232   **209**C

Lincoln Center for the Performing Arts
Lincoln Center, MA
212-875-5400   **128**C

Majestic Theater
651 Fulton St, BK
718-636-4181   **407**C

Manhattan School of Music
120 Claremont Av, MA
212-749-2802   **144**A

Merkin Concert Hall
129 W 67, MA
212-362-8719   **128**E

The Metropolitan Museum of Art
1000 Fifth Av, MA
212-535-7710   **133**E

The Metropolitan Opera House
Lincoln Center, MA
212-362-6000   **128**E
American Ballet Theatre
& Metropolitan Opera

...er Theater–
...umbia Univ
...ay @ 116 St, MA
...-854-1754 **144B**

...zi Newhouse
...coln Center, MA
...W 65, MA
...-362-7600 **128C**

...v Victory Theater
...W 42 St, MA
...-564-4222 **125C**

...w–York
...torical Society
...CPW, MA
...-873-3400 **133C**

... New York
...lic Library for
...Performing Arts
...ay @ 65 St, MA
...-870-1630 **128B**

...w York State
...eater
...coln Center, MA
...-870-5570 **128D**
... Ballet • NYC Opera

...yorican
...ets Cafe
... E 3 St, MA
...-505-8183 **114D**

...ce Downtown
...eater
...pruce St, MA
...-346-1715 **105C**

...n Asian
...pertory Theater
... W 46 St, MA
...-505-5655 **124D**

...rforming Garage
...Wooster St, MA
...-966-3651 **109D**

P.S. 122
150 First Av, MA
212-477-5288 **114B**

**Queens Theater
in the Park**
Flushing Meadows
QS, (718) 760-0064
320D

Regina Opera Co.
65 St @ 12 Av, BK
718-232-3555 **427C**

Riverside Church
490 Riverside Dr, MA
212-222-5900 **145A**

**Radio City
Music Hall**
Sixth Av @ 50 St, MA
212-247-4777 **125B**

**St Ann's Center
for Restoration
and the Arts**
157 Montague St, BK
718-834-8794 **408D**

**St Mark's Church–
in–the–Bowery**
Second Av @ 10 St,
MA, 212-674-8194
114B

**Shakespeare
in the Park–
Delacorte Theater**
Central Park, MA
212-861-PAPP **133A**

**The Spanish
Institute**
684 Park Av, MA
(212) 628-0420 **130B**

**Snug Harbor
Cultural Center**
1000 Richmond Ter, SI
718-448-2500 **506B**

**The Studio Museum
in Harlem**
144 W 125 St, MA
(212) 864-4500 **145A**

**The Sylvia & Danny
Kaye Playhouse–
Hunter College**
Park Av @ 68 St,MA
212-772-4448 **130B**

Symphony Space
2537 Broadway, MA
212-864-5400 **136B**

TADA!
120 W 28 St, MA
212-627-1732 **117B**

**Theatre for the
New City**
155 First Av, MA
212-254-1109 **114B**

**Thelma Hill
Performing Arts
Center**
University Plz, BK
718-488-1051 **409C**

**Thalia Spanish
Theater**
41-17 Greenpoint Av,
Sunnyside, QS
718-279-3880 **317A**

Town Hall
123 W 43 St, MA
212-840-2824 **125C**

**Tribeca Performing
Arts Center**
199 Chambers St, MA
212-346-8510 **104C**

**Vivian Beaumont
Theater**
Lincoln Center
150 W 65 St, MA
212-362-7600 **128B**

**Walter Reade
Theater**
Lincoln Center, MA
212-875-5600 **128C**

Westbeth Theatre
151 Bank St, MA
212-741-0391 **112D**

Winter Garden
1634 Broadway, MA
212-239-6200 **125A**

**Winter Garden at
the WFC**, MA
212-945-0505 **104C**

92nd St Y & YWCA
1395 Lex. Av, MA
212-996-1100 **139A**

FILM

**American Museum
of the Moving Image**
35 Av @ 36 St, QS
718-784-0077 **309C**

**American Museum
of Natural History**
CPW @ 79 St, MA
212-769-5650 **133C**

Angelika Film Center
18 W Houston St, MA
212-995-2000 **113D**

**Anthology Film
Archives**
32 Second Av, MA,
212-505-5110 **114C**

Film Forum
209 W Houston St,
MA, 212-727-8110
109A

French Institute
55 E 59 St, MA
212-355-6160 **130D**

**Museum of Modern
Art (MoMA)**
11 W 53 St, MA
212-708-9400 **125B**

**The New York
Film Academy**
100 E 17 St, MA
212-674-4300 **118D**

**New York
Public Library–
Donnell Library**
20 W 53 St, MA
212-621-0618 **126A**

Sony IMAX
1998 Broadway
@ 68 St, MA
212-336-5000 **128B**

Thalia Theater
250 W 95 St, MA
212-864-7700 **136B**

Walter Reade Theatre
Lincoln Center, MA
212-875-5600 **128B**

The Ziegfeld
141 W 54 St, MA
212-765-7600 **125B**

YMCA Cine-Club
610 Lex. Av, MA
212-755-4500 **126B**

TO FIND A TOP 100

simply turn to page
and locate a cinema
or theater in grids
A,B,**C** or D.

MA = Manhattan
BX = The Bronx
BK = Brooklyn
QS = Queens
SI = Staten Island

SHOPPING

ART & PAPER

Alphabets
115 Av A, MA
212-475-7250 **114**B

The Art Store
1 Bond St, MA
212-533-2444 **113**D

Kate's Paperie
561 Broadway, MA
212-941-9816 **109**B

NY Central Art Supply
62 Third Av, MA
212-473-7705 **114**C

Pearl Paint
308 Canal St, MA
212-431-7932 **106**B

Poster America
138 W 18 St, MA
212-206-0499 **117**D

BOOKS & MUSIC

Argosy
116 E 59 St, MA
212-753-4455 **130**D

Barnes & Noble
33 E 17 St, MA
212-253-0810 **118**B
plus 9 locations
citywide.

Sale Annex
128 Fifth Av, MA
212-253-0810 **118**C

Borders WTC
5 WTC, MA
212-839-8037 **104**D

Coliseum
1771 Broadway, MA
212-757-8381 **129**C

Colony Records
1619 Broadway, MA
212-265-2050 **125**C

Empire State News
Empire State Bldg,
MA, 212-279-9153
121D

HMV
2081 Broadway, MA
212-721-5900 **128**B
Herald Sq Store

Hudson News
Penn Station, MA
212-971-6800 **121**C

Rizzoli International
454 W B'way, MA
212-674-1616 **109**B

St Mark's Book Shop
31 Third Av, MA
212-260-7853 **114**A

Shakespeare & Co.
716 Broadway, MA
212-529-1330 **113**D

The Strand
828 Broadway, MA
212-473-1452 **113**A

Subterranean Records
5 Cornelia St, MA
212-463-8900 **113**B

Tower Records
692 Broadway, MA
212-505-1500 **113**D

Universal News
977 Eighth Av MA
212-459-0932 **129**C

Virgin Megastore
1540 Broadway, MA
212-921-1020 **125**C

DESIGNERS

Agnès B.
116-18 Prince St, MA
212-925-4649 **109**B

Anna Sui
113 Greene St, MA
212-941-8406 **109**B

Armani
760 Madison Av, MA
212-988-9191 **130**B

Betsey Johnson
130 Thompson St,
MA, 212-420-0169
109A

Calvin Klein
654 Madison Av, MA
212-292-9000 **130**D

Comme des Garçons
116 Wooster St, MA
212-219-0660 **109**B

Helmut Lang
80 Greene St, MA
212-925-7214 **109**B

Paul Smith
108 Fifth Av, MA
212-627-9770 **117**D

Ralph Lauren
867 Madison Av
@ 72 St, MA
212-606-2100 **130**B

Todd Oldham
123 Wooster, MA
212-219-3531 **109**B

Tocca
161 Mercer, MA
212-343-3912 **109**D

Yohji Yamamoto
103 Grand St, MA
800-803-4443 **106**B

DEPARTMENT STORES

Barneys NY
660 Madison Av, MA
212-826-8900 **130**D

Bergdorf Goodman
754 Fifth Av, MA
212-753-7300 **130**C

Bloomingdales
1000 Third Av, MA
212-705-2000 **130**D

Brooks Brothers
346 Madison Av, MA
212-682-8800 **126**D

Canal Jean
504 Broadway, MA
212-226-1130 **109**D

Century 21
22 Cortlandt St, MA
212-227-9092 **104**D

Felissimo
10 W 56 St, MA
212-247-5656 **126**A

Lord & Taylor
424 Fifth Av, MA
212-391-3344 **122**A

Macy's–Herald Sq
151 W 34 St, MA
212-695-4400 **121**C

Pearl River
277 Canal St, MA
212-219-8107 **106**B

Saks Fifth Avenue
Fifth Av @ 49 St, MA
212-753-4000 **125**D

Syms
42 Trinity Pl, MA
212-797-1199 **102**C

Takashimaya
693 Fifth Av, MA
212-350-0100 **126**B

Terra Verde
122 Wooster St, MA
212-925-4533 **109**B

F.A.O. Schwarz
767 Fifth Av, MA
212-644-9400 **129**D

ELECTRONICS

Harvey's
888 Broadway, MA
212-228-5354 **118**C

J&R Music World
23 Park Row, MA
212-238-9000 **105**C

Stereo Exchange
627 Broadway, MA
212-505-1111 **113**D

GIFTS & TOYS

Enchanted Forest
85 Mercer St, MA
212-925-6677 **109**C

Forbidden Planet
B'way @ 13 St, MA
212-473-1576 **113**E

Little Rickie
49 1/2 First Av, MA
212-505-6467 **114**E

GOURMET

Astor Wines & Liquors
12 Astor Pl, MA
212-674-7500 **114**C

Balducci's
424 Sixth Av, MA
212-673-2600 **113**C

SHOPPING

Barney Greengrass
541 Amsterdam Av,
MA, 212-724-4707
136D

Bouley Bakery
120 W Broadway, MA
212-964-2525 **106D**

Citarella
2135 Broadway, MA
212-874-0383 **132D**

Dean & DeLuca
560 Broadway, MA
212-431-1691 **109B**

Fairway Market
2127 Broadway, MA
212-595-1888 **132D**

Fairway Market
(Uptown)
2328 Twelfth Av, MA
212-234-3883 **148C**

Green Markets
212-477-3220
Union Sq, MA **118D**
Borough Hall, BK
408D

Sheffield Plaza,
MA **124C**

Gourmet Garage
453 Broome St, MA
212-941-5850 **109D**

Guss's Pickle Products
35 Essex St, MA
212-254-4477 **110D**

Patisserie Lanciani
414 W 14 St, MA
212-989-1213 **112B**

Sherry–Lehmann
679 Madison Av, MA
212-838-7500 **130D**

Yonah Schimmel
137 E Houston St, MA
212-477-2858 **110A**

Zabar's
2245 Broadway, MA
212-787-2000 **132B**

HOME & DESIGN

ABC-Home & Carpet
888 Broadway, MA
212-473-3000 **118C**

Ad Hoc Softwares
410 W B'way, MA
212-925-2652 **106B**

Bed Bath & Beyond
Sixth Av @ 18 St, MA
212-255-3550 **117D**

Crate & Barrel
650 Madison Av, MA
212-308-0011 **130D**

Chelsea Antiques
Market
110 W 25 St, MA
212-929-0909 **117B**

Depression Modern
150 Sullivan St, MA
212-982-5699 **109A**

Henri Bendel
712 Fifth Av, MA
212-247-1100 **126A**

Moss
146 Greene St, MA
212-226-2190 **109B**

Prince Lumber
15 St @ Ninth Av, MA
212-777-1150 **116D**

Shabby Chic
93 Greene St, MA
212-274-9842 **109B**

Smith & Hawken
394 W B'way, MA
212-925-0687 **109C**

Urban Archaeology
285 Lafayette St, MA
212-431-6969 **109B**

**INSTRUMENTS–
MUSICAL**

Sam Ash
160 W 48 St, MA
212-719-2299 **125C**

Manny's
156 W 48 St, MA
212-819-0576 **125C**

The Music Store
44 W 62 St, MA
212-541-6236 **128D**

JEWELRY

Bulgari
730 Fifth Av, MA
212-315-9000 **126A**

Cartier
725 Fifth Av,
Trump Tower, MA
212-308-0843 **126B**

Harry Winston
718 Fifth Av, MA
212-245-2000 **126A**

Tiffany & Co.
727 Fifth Av, MA
212-755-8000 **126A**

Tourneau
12 E 57 St, MA
212-758-7300 **130D**

Van Cleef & Arpels
744 Fifth Av, MA
212-644-9500 **126C**

**PERSONAL
CARE & VANITY**

Astor Place Hair
Designers
2 Astor Pl, MA
212-475-9854 **113B**

Gauntlet
144 Fifth Av, MA
212-229-0180 **117D**

Georgette Klinger
501 Madison Av, MA
212-838-3200 **126B**

Jason Croy
301 W 4 St, MA
212-691-8299 **112B**

Kiehl's
109 Third Av, MA
212-677-3171 **114A**

Elizabeth Arden
691 Fifth Av, MA
212-546-0200 **126A**

Vidal Sassoon
767 Fifth Av, MA
212-535-9200 **129D**

Russian & Turkish
Baths
268 E 10 St, MA
212-505-0665 **114B**

SPORTS

Blades– 6 locations
120 W 72 ST, MA
212-787-3911 **128B**

NikeTown, NY
6 E 57 St, MA
212-891-6453 **130D**

Paragon
867 Broadway, MA
212-255-8036 **118C**

THEME STORES

The Disney Store
711 Fifth Av, MA
212-702-0702 **125C**

Hard Rock Cafe
221 W 57, MA
212-459-9320 **125A**

Warner Bros.
Studio Store
1 E 57 St, MA
800-223-6524 **129D**

WORLD MARKETS

Arthur Av, BX
(Italian) **215B**

Main St. Flushing,
QS, (Chinese) ..**321A**

La Marqueta,
Park Av @ 110-118
Sts, MA **146C**

Fulton Mall, BK ......
(Hip-Hop) **409B**

Harlem USA,
125 St, MA (African
American) **145A**

Hunts Point, BX
(produce) **223C**

74 St & 37 Av, QS
(Indian/Pakistani) ....
..................**319A**

Manhattan Av, BK
(Polish) **402B**

Roosevelt Av @ 74–
110 St, QS (Latino) ..
..................**318A**

149 St
Third Av @ 149 St,
BX (Latino) **227A**

SPORTS 3

ARENAS & STADIUMS

Aqueduct Race Track
Rockaway Bd
@ 110 St, QS
718-641-4700 **343**C

**Belmont Park
Race Track**
Hempstead Tpk @
Plainfield Av, QS
718-641-4700 **341**C

**USTA National
Tennis Center**
Flushing Meadow–
Corona Pk, QS
718-760-6200 **320**B
US OPEN (Sep)

**Continental
Airline Arena**
The Meadowlands,
NJ, 201-935-3900
NY Nets (Nov-Apr) **120**A
NJ Devils (Oct-Apr)

Giants Stadium
The Meadowlands,
NJ, 201-935-8222
Giants (Sep-Jan) **120**A
Jets (Sep-Jan)
Metrostars (Apr-Sep)

Madison Sq Garden
7 Av @ W 32 St, MA
212-465-6741 **121**C
NY Cityhawks (Apr-Jul)
NY Liberty (Jun-Aug)
NY Knicks (Nov-Apr)
NY Rangers (Oct-Apr)
WTA Tennis (Nov)

**Meadowlands
Race Track**
The Meadowlands,
NJ, 201-438-3100
120A

Shea Stadium
Flushing, QS
718-507-8499 **320**B
Mets (Apr-Oct)

Yankee Stadium
161 St & River Av,
BX, 212-760-6200
Yankees (Apr-Oct) **121**C

CITY LINKS
18 Holes
Douglaston
6320 Marathon Pkwy,
QS, 718-428-1617
325C

Dyker Beach
Seventh Av @ 86 St,
BK, 718-836-9722
434B

LaTourette
1000 Richmond Hill
Rd, SI, 718-351-1889
516C

Mosholu
Van Cortlandt Pk, BX
718-655-9164 **209**B

Pelham/Split-Rock
Shore Rd, BX
718-885-1258 **206**A

Bucket of Balls
Chelsea Piers
12 Av @ 23 St, MA
212-336-6400 **116**C

Family Golf Center
Randall's Island, MA
212-427-5689 **302**B

Golden Bear
Alley Pond Park, QS
718-225-9187 **324**A

Turtle Cove
1 City Island Rd, BX
718-885-2646 **206**D

FIELD OF DREAMS
Baseball
Dyker Beach Park
BK **434**B

Alley Pond Park
QS **332**B

Batting Practice
Chelsea Piers
12 Av @ 23 St, MA
212-336-6500 **116**C

**Hackers, Hitters
& Hoops**
123 W 18 St, MA
212-929-7482 **117**D

**Randall's Island
Practice Center**
MA, 212-427-5689
302B

Cricket
Randall's Island
MA **302**B

Softball
**Canarsie Beach
Park,** BK **431**A

GOTHAM GRID IRON
Football Pick Up
Harris Park
BX **209**C

Central Park
MA **133**A

Marine Park
BK **438**A

Hurling
Gaelic Park
BX **208**D

Rugby
Randall's Island
MA **302**B

GYM FOR A DAY
Asphalt Green
555 E 90 St, MA
212-369-8890 **139**D

Club La Raquette
119 W 56 St, MA
212-245-1144 **125**B

Crunch Fitness
54 E 13 St, MA
212-475-2018 **113**B

Eastern Athletic
43 Clark St, BK
718-625-0500 **408**B

**NY Health
& Racquet**
• 20 E 50 St, MA
212-593-1500 **126**B
• 39 Whitehall St, MA
212-269-9800 **103**C
(7 locations in MA)

NY Sports Club
1635 Third Av, MA
212-987-7200 **139**C

**Printing House
Fitness & Racquet**
421 Hudson St, MA
212-243-7600 **108**B

**Sports Center at
Chelsea Piers**
12 Av @ 23 St, MA
212-336-6000 **116**C

World Gym
232 Mercer St, MA
212-780-7407 **113**D

YM & YWCA
• 610 Lex. Av, MA
212-755-4500 **126**B
• 42-07 Parsons Bd,
QS, 718-353-4553
321B

HOOP DREAMS
*There are a number
of courts in NYC
where great
street basketball
can be experienced
indoors and out.
Here's a sampling
of the best:*

Indoors
Gaucho's Gym
478 Gerard Av
@ 149 St, BX **226**B

IS 8
Merrick Bd @
108 Av, QS **338**D

Outdoors
"The Cage"
W 4 St, MA **113**C

Fort Tryon Park
Margaret Corbin Plz
MA **158**D

"The Garden"
Surf Av @ 25 St, BK
442D

**Holcombe
Rucker Park**
155 St @ Eighth Av,
MA **153**A

Kingston Park
Atlantic Av
@ Kingston Av, BK
416B

St Albans Park
Merrick Bd
@ 172 St, QS **345**A

Walker Park
Bard Av @
Livingston Ct, SI
506B

MARATHON MADNESS

NY Road Runners Club Fred Lebow Pl,
E 89 St, MA
212-860-4455 **137**D

The NY Marathon is 30,000 runners coursing through five boroughs on the first weekend in November. Starts on the Verrazano Bridge and ends in Central Park
513D**-129**A

RACQUETS
Tennis

USTA National Tennis Center
Flushing Meadows–
Corona Park, QS
718-760-6200 **320**B

NY Health & Racquet Tennis
Wall St @ Piers 13
& 14, MA
212-422-9300 **103**B

Ma Sports Club
42-02 Vernon Bd, QS
718-937-2381 **308**C

City Courts
Central Park
65 St & West Dr, MA
212-280-0205 **137**A

Prospect Park
Parkside Av
@ Park Cir, BK **422**A

Van Cortland Park
Broadway @ 241 St,
BX **209**A

GLOBAL GOALS
Soccer Pick-Ups
Marine Park
BK **438**A

East River Park, MA
Sunday 11am **111**D

Flushing Meadows
QS, Sunday 11am
320D

Red Hook, BK
Sunday 11am **414**A

SKATING – ICE

Lasker Rink
110 St & Lenox Av,
MA, 212-534-7639
141B

Kate Wollman Rink
Prospect Park, BK
718-965-8904 **422**B

Rockefeller Center
MA, 212-332-7654
125C

Sky Rink
Chelsea Piers, MA
212-336-6100 **116**C

Staten Island War Memorial
Clove Lakes Park, SI
718-720-1010 **511**B

Wollman Rink
S Central Park, MA
212-396-1010 **129**D

World's Fair Rink
Flushing Meadows–
Corona Park, QS
718-271-1996 **320**B

South St Seaport
Seaport Plz, BK
212-732-7678 **105**D

STREET WHEELS
Bikes
119 miles of bike routes exist. today with plans for 781 more miles:

Central Park
MA **129**A

Forest Park Dr
QS **336**A

Mosholu/Pelham Greenway
BX **209**B

Shore & Marine Pkwys
BK **426**A**-439**C

Bay St, SI **507**B

Blades
Empire Skate Club of NY (ESCNY)
212-592-3674

NY Skate Patrol
212-439-1234

Central Park
MA **129**B

Battery Park Esplanade
MA **104**C

Brooklyn Bridge
MA **105**A

Shore & Marine Pkwys
BK **426**A

Boards
Brooklyn Bridge
@ Park Row, MA
105A

Central Park
The Mall, MA **129**B

URBAN HOOVES
Stables
Claremont Riding Academy
175 W 89 St, MA
212-724-5100 **136**D

Jamaica Bay Riding Academy
7000 Belt Pkwy, BK
718-531-8949 **431**A

Lynne's Riding School
88-03 70 Rd, QS
718-261-7679 **336**A

Riverdale Riding Academy
Van Cortland Pk, BX
718-548-4848 **203**C

Pelham Bay Stable
9 Shore Rd, BX
718-885-0551 **206**C

VOLLEYBALL
Big City Volleyball League
212-288-4240

NY Urban Professional Athletic League
212-877-3614

Central Park
on 68 St, MA **129**B

Dalton Gym
E 87 St @ Third Av
MA **139**C

HS Environmental Studies
444 W 56 St, MA
124B

Lost Battalion Hall
Rego Park, QS **328**A

WATER SPORTS
Canoe & Kayak
Metropolitan Canoe & Kayak Club
MA, 212-724-5069

Sebago Canoe Club
Paedergat Basin,
BK, 718-241-3683
431A

Dyckman Marina
W 254 St, BX **208**A

NY Kayak Co
601 W 26 St, MA
116A

Sail
Manhattan Sailing School
North Cove, MA
212-786-0400 **104**C

Great Hudson Sailing Center
Chelsea Piers, MA
212-741-7245 **116**A

Swim
Indoors–

63 St YMCA
5 W 63 St, MA
212-787-1301 **129**C

Asphalt Green
555 E 90 St, MA
212-369-8890 **139**D

Vanderbilt YMCA
224 E 47 St, MA
212-756-9600 **127**C

Outdoors–

Hamilton Fish Pool
128 Pitt St, MA
212-387-7687 **111**A

THEATRE

ON BROADWAY

Ambassador
215 W 49 St, MA
212-239-6200 **125**C

Belasco
111 W 44 St, MA
212-239-6200 **125**D

Booth
222 W 45 St, MA
212-239-6200 **125**C

Broadhurst
235 W 44 St, MA
212-239-6200 **125**C

Broadway
1681 Broadway, MA
212-239-6200 **125**A

Brooks Atkinson
256 W 47 St, MA
212-307-4100 **125**C

Circle in the Square
1633 Broadway, MA
212-239-6200 **125**A

Cort
138 W 48 St, MA
212-239-6200 **125**C

Criterion Center
1530 Broadway, MA
212-764-7903 **125**C

Ethel Barrymore
243 W 47 St, MA
212-239-6200 **125**C

Eugene O'Neill
230 W 49 St, MA
212-239-6200 **125**C

Gershwin
222 W 51 St, MA
212-586-6510 **125**A

Golden
252 W 45 St, MA
212-239-6200 **125**C

Helen Hayes
240 W 44, MA
212-307-4100 **125**C

Imperial
249 W 45 St, MA
212-239-6200 **125**C

Longacre
220 W 48 St, MA
212-239-6200 **125**C

Lunt-Fontanne
205 W 46 St, MA
212-575-9200 **125**C

Lyceum
149 W 45 St, MA
212-239-6200 **125**C

Majestic
247 W 44 St, MA
212-239-6200 **125**C

Marquis
1535 Broadway, MA
212-382-0100 **125**C

Martin Beck
302 W 45 St, MA
212-239-6200 **125**C

Minskoff
200 W 45 St, MA
212-869-0550 **125**C

Music Box
239 W 45 St, MA
212-239-6200 **125**C

Nederlander
208 W 41 St, MA
212-307-4100 **121**A

Neil Simon
250 W 52 St, MA
212-757-8646 **125**A

Palace
1564 Broadway, MA
212-730-8200 **125**C

Plymouth
236 W 45 St, MA
212-239-6200 **125**C

Richard Rodgers
226 W 46 St, MA
212-307-4100 **125**C

Roundabout
1530 Broadway, MA
212-869-8400 **125**C

Royale
242 W 45 St, MA
212-239-6200 **125**C

St James
246 W 44 St, MA
212-239-6200 **125**C

Shubert
225 W 44 St, MA
212-239-6200 **125**C

Virginia
245 W 52 St, MA
212-239-6200 **125**A

Vivian Beaumont
Lincoln Center, MA
212-239-6200 **128**B

Walter Kerr
219 W 48 St, MA
212-239-6200 **125**C

Winter Garden
1634 Broadway, MA
212-239-6200 **125**A

OFF & OFF-OFF

American Jewish
307 W 26 St, MA
212-633-9797 **117**A

American Place
111 W 46 St, MA
212-840-2960 **125**D

Actors Playhouse
100 Seventh Av, MA
212-239-6200 **117**C

Astor Place
434 Lafayette St, MA
212-254-4370 **113**C

Atlantic
336 W 20 St, MA
212-239-6200 **117**C

Beacon
2124 Broadway, MA
212-307-7171 **132**D

Bouwerie Lane
330 Bowery, MA
212-677-0060 **114**C

Castillo Cultural Center
500 Greenwich St,
MA, 212-941-1234
106A

Century
111 E 15 St, MA
212-239-6200 **118**D

Cherry Lane
38 Commerce St, MA
212-239-6200 **113**C

City Center Stage
131 W 55 St, MA
212-581-1212 **125**A

Classic Stage Co
136 E 13 St, MA
212-677-4210 **114**A

Currican
154 W 29 St, MA
212-736-2533 **117**A

Douglas Fairbanks
432 W 42 St, MA
212-239-4321 **120**B

Duffy
1553 Broadway, MA
212-695-3401 **125**C

Duo
62 E 4 St, MA
212-598-4320 **114**C

Ensemble Studio Theatre
549 W 52 St, MA
212-247-3405 **124**E

Ford Center for the Performing Arts
214 W 43 St, MA
212-307-4100 **125**C

Greenwich House
27 Barrow St, MA
212-242-4140 **113**C

Harold Clurman
412 W 42 St, MA
212-594-2370 **120**

Helen Hayes
240 W 44 St, MA
212-944-9450 **125**

Irish Repertory
132 W 22 St, MA
212-727-2737 **117**

THEATRE

**Cocteau
rtory**
Bowery, MA
677-0060 **114C**

ish Repertory
E 91 St, MA
831-2000 **139A**

Houseman
W 42 St, MA
354-2220 **120B**

th Anderson
W 42 St. MA
564-7853 **120B**

MaMa E.T.C.
/2 E 4 St, MA
) 475-7710 **114C**

b's
W 44 St, MA
997-1780 **125C**

king Glass
W 57 St, MA
307-9467 **124B**

ille Lortel
Christopher St,
, 212-239-6200
112D

rtin Kaufmam
W 42 St, MA
239-6200 **120B**

netta Lane
Minetta La, MA
420-8000 **113C**

w Amsterdam
W 42 St, MA
307-4100 **125C**

New Dramatist
424 W 44 St, MA
212-757-6960 **124D**

**New Perspectives
Theater Co**
750 Eighth Av, MA
212-730-2030 **125C**

New Victory
209 W 42 St, MA
212-564-4222 **125C**

NY Theatre Workshop
79 E 4 St, MA
212-460-5475 **114C**

Orpheum
126 Second Av, MA
212-477-2477 **114A**

Pearl Theatre Co
80 St Marks Pl, MA
212-598-9802 **114A**

**Playwrights
Horizons**
416 W 42 St, MA
212-279-4200 **120B**

Promenade
2162 Broadway, MA
212-239-6200 **132D**

The Public Theater
425 Lafayette St, MA
212-239-6200 **113D**

St Luke's Church
308 W 46 St, MA
212-246-3540 **125C**

Samuel Beckett
410 W 42 St, MA
212-594-2370 **120B**

Signature Theater
555 W 42 St, MA
212-244-7529 **120B**

SoHo Playhouse
15 Vandam St, MA
212-691-1555 **109A**

SoHo Repertory
46 Walker St, MA
212-334-0962 **106B**

Stardust
51 St @ B'way, MA
212-239-6200 **125A**

**Sullivan Street
Playhouse**
181 Sullivan St, MA
212-674-3838 **109A**

Synchronicity Space
55 Mercer St, MA
212-343-1181 **109D**

Theatre East
211 E 60 St, MA
212-838-0177 **131C**

**Theater for the
New City**
155 First Av, MA
212-254-1109 **114B**

Theatre Four
424 W 55 St, MA
212-239-6200 **124B**

Theatre Off Park
224 Waverly Pl, MA
212-627-2556 **112B**

Ubu Repertory
15 W 28 St, MA
212-679-7540 **117B**

Union Square
100 E 17 St, MA
212-505-0700 **118D**

Variety Arts
110 Third Av, MA
212-239-6200 **114A**

Westside
407 W 43 St, MA
212-239-6200 **120B**

Westside Repertory
252 W 81 St, MA
212-874-7290 **132B**

Wings
154 Christopher St,
MA, 212-627-2961
112B

WPA
519 W 23 St, MA
212-206-0523 **116B**

13th St Repertory
50 W 13 St, MA
212-675-6677 **113A**

22 West
22 W 135 St, MA
212-862-7770 **149B**

28th St Theatre
120 W 28 St, MA
212-727-7722 **117B**

45 St
354 W 45 St, MA
212-333-7421 **125C**

55 Grove St Cabaret
55 Grove St, MA
212-366-5438 **112D**

ON or OFF?
*Because you are
within a few blocks
of Broadway does
not mean you are
ON Broadway.*

*ON Broadway the-
aters generally
offer 500 seats or
more, and are
under contract to
produce ON
"Broadway plays."*

*TKTS
For half-price
tickets to same day
performances head
to the TKTS booth
@ Broadway &
West 46 St.*

Telecharge
212-239-6200

Teletron
212-340-4171

Ticketmaster
212-307-4100

TO FIND A TOP 100

simply turn to page
and locate the
theatre in grids
A,B,C or D.

MA = Manhattan
BX = The Bronx
BK = Brooklyn
QS = Queens
SI = Staten Island

1898

Amusing the Masses

No Biz Like Show Biz

HARLEM ON MY MIND

GETTING IT UP

To Be Or Not To Bop

1904

1915

1926

1931

1948

We've
you how
here to the
twenty pages, w
got here from t
points in each of
century, New Yor
we look at ours
and how that
has shape
globa

N
10

1998

hown
get from
On the next
how you how we
—how, at crucial
en decades of this
changed the way
as Americans,
ess of change
ntemporary
ure.

TRUTH IS WHAT SELLS

1998

GREED IS GOOD

1986

HOW FAR TO GO TOO FAR?

1976

THE PROMISED LANDSCAPE?

1961

FREEDOM TO DRIP

1951

If, at the end of the 20th Century, New York is becoming a theme park, it is just one more proof that what goes around comes around.

At century's start, New Yorkers built on the innovations of world's fair producers to create the first permanent theme park for mass entertainment. Between 1895 and 1904, in fact, four competing theme parks opened at Coney Island, with Ferris wheels and carousels, freak shows, thrill rides, and recreations of exotic or fantastic worlds (including "Selenian" midgets on a green— cheese moon, a transplanted Inuit tri... Alaska, and a ch... premature babie... not to mention a... unplanned low—... trict for boozing... bling, and whor...

Coney Island & the Inventi...

photo © Brown Brothers

Amusing

(See Lucy, the Colossal Elephant at right.) By the time the subway reached Coney Island in 1920, upwards of a million people jammed the parks and beaches every summer Sunday.

Lucy, the Colossal Elephant of Coney Island

Lucy may have been inspired by Jumbo, the elephant P. T. Barnum brought from London to NYC, an immediate hit with New Yorkers (she stands in comparison, beneath Lucy).
Lucy was a seven-story wooden structure with a tin skin. Though conceived as a hotel, and later an auditorium, rumors have it that Lucy was really a brothel. Customers would enter through a door at the right hind leg.

f the American Theme Park

1904

e Masses

No Biz like Show Biz **1915**

From the 1890s Yiddish theaters and music halls of the Lower East Side, Jewish entertainers, artists, and entrepreneurs moved uptown and created Show Biz.

By 1915, Broadway and Tin Pan Alley had industrialized the production and distribution of the nation's entertainment, using African-American, Jewish, Irish, and Italian immigrant idioms to lampoon, dissect, and ultimately transform American culture.

Talent and content assembled for the Ziegfeld Follies and its competitors, including the Shubert Brothers'

The Passing Show and Jerome Kern's Princess Theater Shows, were dispatched throughout the country via the vaudeville circuit, through which the performers and material became an integral part of the life of heartland America.

In direct lines of succession the system gave rise to the modern Broadway musical (Kern's "Show Boat" in 1927), to Hollywood comedy and musical films, to radio and television variety shows, to the pop music industry, and to the distinct Yiddishization of the American comic sensibility in an unbroken line from the Marx Brothers to Billy Crystal.

"And if anyone, on hearing Jerome Kern say that Irving Berlin IS American music, is then so famous to object on the ground that he was born in Russia, it might be pointed out that if the musical interpreter of American civilization came over in the foul hold of a ship, so did American civilization."

Alexander Woolcott

Comedian Fanny Brice became nationally famous portraying poor Jewish girls from the Lower East Side making their way through life and love in America.

From Second Avenue to the Great White Way

George M. Cohan was a Yankee Doodle Dandy.

Jazz-age Harlem was ground zero for an explosion of creativity among African–Americans, a modernist urban expression of cultural roots in the rural South, the Caribbean, and Africa. The blues and other ancestral forms were made contemporary in the Harlem Renaissance, just as Picasso and other Europeans were drawing inspiration from African art. The poems of Langston Hughes and Countee Cullen, the music of Duke Ellington, the murals of Aaron Douglas, the stories of Zora Neale Hurston, the novels and plays of Claude McKay—all spoke a new language that informed a new political consciousness exemplified by such Harlem-based political figures as Adam Clayton Powell and Marcus Garvey. And white folks had to pay attention.

Langston Hughes
Poet, essayist, playwright, novelist he championed the blues and the language of the common man as literature.

The Weary Blues
"...To the tune o' those Weary Blues.
With his ebony hands and each ivory key
He made that poor piano moan with melody
O Blues!"

I, Too
They'll see how beautiful I am
And be ashamed –
I, too, am America.

BLACK IS BEAUTIFUL

Hoodoo in America

The writer Zora Neale Hurston, like the dancer Katherine Dunham after her, was trained in anthropology. She refused to countenance the notion of race based on skin color, and instead focused on the roots of culture, producing both field studies and literary works based on the folklore of the rural South and African and Caribbean carryovers in the spiritual lives of African Americans, including "hoodoo" (voodoo) traditions in New Orleans.

Civil Rights by Copyright

"Hurston was before her time... Like Billie Holiday and Bessie Smith, she followed her own road, believed in her own gods, pursued her own dreams, and refused to separate herself from 'common' people.. She was a cultural revolutionary simply because she was always herself..." **Alice Walker**

HE FIRST WAVE

Skyscrapers as a Badge of Cityhood

Mies van der Rohe. In the 1990s, after seeing the sterility the glass box had led to, Philip Johnson himself went post-modern

Questioned in 1996, Johnson had this to say: "What do I know that I didn't know before? I didn't know about this wonderful material out there, using concrete."

1931

Is the Skyscraper tolerable?
Lewis Mumford

GETT

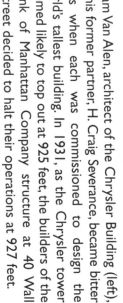

Modern vs Moderne Architecture

Even while the economy sank toward rock bottom in the Great Depression, American architecture was reaching from Manhattan bedrock toward the stars. Ignoring the European modernism that would resurface after World War II as the International Style of glass-and-steel boxes, the New York skyscraper went "moderne," or deco – not just tall and sleek, but goddam glamorous.

William Van Alen, architect of the Chrysler Building (left), and his former partner, H. Craig Severance, became bitter rivals when each was commissioned to design the world's tallest building. In 1931, as the Chrysler tower seemed likely to top out at 925 feet, the builders of the Bank of Manhattan Company structure at 40 Wall Street decided to halt their operations at 927 feet.

Meanwhile, workers were secretly assembling the rustless steel sections of the Chrysler spire which, when lifted through the dome and bolted into place, brought the building to its triumphant height of 1,048 feet. The triumph was short-lived. Lamb's Empire State Building was completed later that year, at 1,250 feet.

But the seeds of minimalist dogma were even then being planted in New York. The young Philip Johnson co-curated a 1932 exhibition at

ING IT UP

To Be or Not to Bop
Jazz goes classic on 52nd St

BOP [bebap, rebop]

America was flush with success from World War II when bebop took 52nd Street by storm. The new music arrived on the street fully formed, complete with its own fashions, manners and attitude.

First developed in the early 40s by Dizzy Gillespie, Charlie Parker, Bud Powell, Theolonius Monk, Kenny Clarke, and Max Roach, bop is shorthand for the syllables bebab and rebop commonly used in scat singing to accompany the distinctive two note rhythm shown here.

bä - o - ä - ü - lä - dä

DIZZYMANIA

These guys were among the best dressed men in America, but Dizzy Gillespie was the kingpin and object of mass adulation.

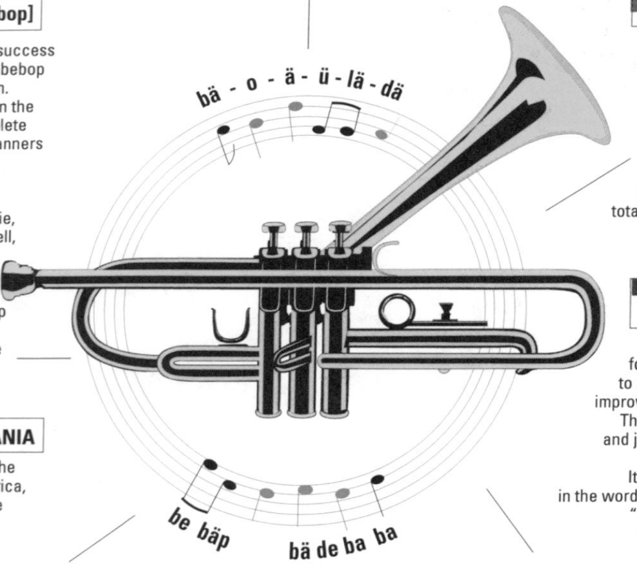

be bäp   bä de ba ba

NY48

THE LATIN CONNECTION

"I thought he (Dizzy) was the greatest thing I had ever heard. The difference was he came with a new approach and confirmations and a different pattern than the old jazz. In it there was the evolution of American music ..."

MARIO BAUZA
The gran'daddy of Latin Jazz

BENDIN' THE HORN

"The truth is it was an accident. I could have pretended that I went into the basement and thought it up, but it wasn't that way. It was an accident ..."

DIZZY GILLESPIE

BIRD & DIZ

"I had never seen anything like it. Charlie would end his solo on a particular note and John [Dizzy] would start with that same note and go with it some totally different place."

BUD JOHNSON

JAZZ AS ART

Bop opened the four-to-the-bar beat to allow the utmost in improvisational freedom. The drummer follows and justifies the soloist.

It was a new music, in the words of Quincy Jones, "like nitroglycerine, sheer electricity."

It took jazz from the dance floor to the concert hall, from entertainment to art.

1951: BYE, BYE, BOP

"Right now it's rough. Everybody wants you to play what they call dance music. What they mean is that ticky-ticky-tick stuff. Man, that ain't dance music!"

DIZZY GILLESPIE

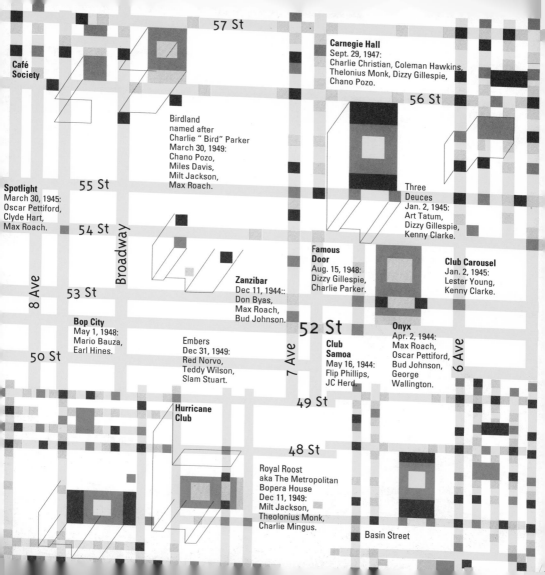

57 St

Café Society

Carnegie Hall
Sept. 29, 1947:
Charlie Christian, Coleman Hawkins,
Thelonius Monk, Dizzy Gillespie,
Chano Pozo.

56 St

Birdland
named after
Charlie " Bird" Parker
March 30, 1949:
Chano Pozo,
Miles Davis,
Milt Jackson,
Max Roach.

**Three
Deuces**
Jan. 2, 1945:
Art Tatum,
Dizzy Gillespie,
Kenny Clarke.

Spotlight
March 30, 1945:
Oscar Pettiford,
Clyde Hart,
Max Roach.

55 St

54 St

Broadway

**Famous
Door**
Aug. 15, 1948:
Dizzy Gillespie,
Charlie Parker.

Club Carousel
Jan. 2, 1945:
Lester Young,
Kenny Clarke.

8 Ave

53 St

Zanzibar
Dec 11, 1944::
Don Byas,
Max Roach,
Bud Johnson.

Bop City
May 1, 1948:
Mario Bauza,
Earl Hines.

50 St

Embers
Dec 31, 1949:
Red Norvo,
Teddy Wilson,
Slam Stuart.

52 St

7 Ave

**Club
Samoa**
May 16, 1944:
Flip Phillips,
JC Herd.

Onyx
Apr. 2, 1944:
Max Roach,
Oscar Pettiford,
Bud Johnson,
George
Wallington.

6 Ave

49 St

**Hurricane
Club**

48 St

Royal Roost
aka The Metropolitan
Bopera House
Dec 11, 1949:
Milt Jackson,
Theolonius Monk,
Charlie Mingus.

Basin Street

FREEDOM TO DRIP **1951**

"How New York Stole the Idea of Modern A...

Cold War Culture Wars

The US Government's need to convince European elites that America was not only a military and economic superpower, but also a cultural one, required an American school of painting. In the freedom of Jackson Pollack's Action Painting and the "all-over-style" Abstract Expressionism, the State Department found a powerful weapon in its Cold War culture war with the Soviet Union.

*Inspired by the ideas of Serge Guilbaut

Action Painting in the Atomic Age

Pollack's drip paintings exemplified the anxiety of the nuclear era and expressed the dreadful power of the unseen. For the avant–garde, abstraction was the only way to deal with a society grown accustomed to the image of the mushroom cloud and children diving under their desks.

"They know themselves better than artists who over–intellectualize their work."
Harold Rosenberg,
Art critic of the New Yorker

"The American Century"
as proclaimed by
Henry Luce,
founder of *Time*.

 **VS**

When Is a Picture Complete?
The New York School was bent
on freeing color and line. If the
ultimate goal of art is to resolve
the differences between form and
content, for the New York School
form became content.

"The conclusion forces itself that
the main premises of western art
have at last migrated to the United
States, along with the center of
gravity of industrial and political
power."
Clement Greenberg,
*Art critic of the Nation, and Author
of "Avant Garde and Kitsch"*

Bigger Is Better
The movement's preference for
dramatically large canvases and
its desire to give spontaneous
expression to the unconscious
was used by liberals of the **Vital
Center** to prove American
superiority in the struggle
between free western democratic
man versus the alleged Eastern
communist drone.

Goodbye Paris
US Government–sponsored
exhibitions skillfully turned
this avowedly apolitcal
movement of pure paint into
a cultural weapon of the Cold
War and virtually assured
New York's place as the
art capital of the world.

The Promised L

The Powerbroker
Robert Moses, city planner, parks commissioner, and mega–builder extraordinaire, parlayed a series of seemingly obscure appointive jobs in city and state government into an empire that overwhelmed mayors and governors.

Moses on Jacobs
Dear Bennett,
  I am returning the book (The Death & Life of Great American Cities by Jane Jacobs) you sent me... Aside from the fact that it is intemperate, and inaccurate, it is also libelous. Sell this junk to someone else. RM

From a letter to Bennett Cerf, co-founder of Random House.

Lincoln C

NY Coliseum, 128

1961: How the Great Moses was wiped out by Jane Jacobs

Bulldozer Diplomacy
Even as Moses created an impressive network of parks, highways, housing projects, beaches, and bridges (see graphic), he destroyed stable neighborhoods (such as the South Bronx) and accelerated middle–class flight to the then undeveloped suburbs. When he proposed "urban renewal" for Greenwich Village, Jane Jacobs took him on.

The Moses Motto:
"If the end doesn't justify the means, what does?"

Javits Center, 120A

Holland Tun, 108C

Brooklyn Battery Tun, 102D

ndscape ?

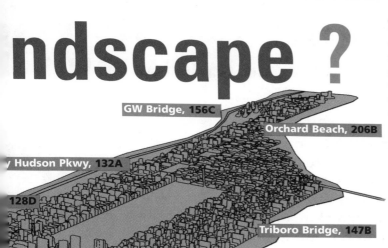

GW Bridge, 156C

Orchard Beach, 206B

y Hudson Pkwy, 132A

128D

Triboro Bridge, 147B

usewife, editor and apostle of cities

United Nations, 127C

Midtown Tun, 127C

The Apostle

Jane Jacobs, housewife and community activist, stood up to Moses and the planning titans who thought the car supreme. With her ground-breaking book, The Death & Life of Great American Cities, Jacobs fought for diverse neighborhoods, and successfully challenged the modernist dogma's claim that planned, geometric urban spaces would improve society. City planning was never quite the same again.

photo © Mayanne Hogbin

Paradigm Shift

"Jane was the first and probably the best and most incisive critic of the plague that modern architecture and urban renewal have visited upon our cities. What a pleasure to salute her." Norman Mailer

"Her common sense was what made her such a radical thinker." Erik Wensberg

On The Death & Life...

It's one of those rare books that make a difference in world history" Rudolf Flesch

"The abattoir for sacred cows" Charles Abrams

"What a dear sweet character she isn't!" Roger Starr

Jacobs on Winning

"...The 2nd time I got arrested I enjoyed the ride...We won it without a filing system. Everything we needed was always near the top!"

If the history of modern Western painting is one of a continuing series of conceptual erasures, of taking away what was heretofore considered the essence of art (nature, beauty, authorship, and paint), as Arthur Danto has argued, then Andy Warhol's Brillo Box may well mark the end of the master narrative that has defined modern Western painting.

Whatever.

Here's what Andy said:

"I like painting on a square, because you don't have to decide whether it should be longer—longer, or shorter-shorter, or longer-**shorter.**"

Andy "Candy" Warhol pr

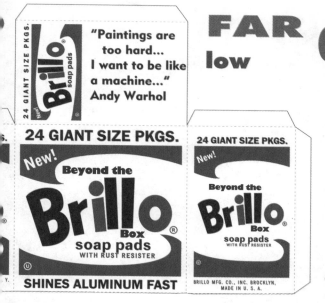

"Paintings are too hard... I want to be like a machine..." Andy Warhol

FAR

low

24 GIANT SIZE PKGS.

New!

Beyond the

Brillo ®

Box

soap pads
WITH RUST RESISTER

SHINES ALUMINUM FAST

24 GIANT SIZE PKGS.

New!

Beyond the

Brillo ®

Box

soap pads
WITH RUST RESISTER

BRILLO MFG. CO., INC. BROCKLYN, MADE IN U. S. A.

ed to sell his semen in a limited edition.

Gee..

"I'm using silkscreens now. I think somebody should be able to do all my paintings for me...

I think it would be so great if more people took up silkscreens so that no one would know whether my picture was mine or somebody else's.

"I'd prefer to remain a mystery. I never like to give my background and, anyway, I make it all up different every time I'm asked."

GREED IS GOOD

'86 –the Age of Milken...

We know, or think we do, when art slides into commerce. But when does commerce itself become art? At what point, does it so infuse and change culture that it can be said to be the dominant aesthetic?

Put it somewhere around 1980, three years after Michael Milken first understood the leverage that could be obtained from debt, making something out of less than nothing, and artists of the deal began to use his insight to redraw the world.

By the end of the decade Milken, Ivan Boesky, Martin Siegel, Dennis Levine, Charles Keating, and others whom Tom Wolfe dubbed "Masters of the Universe" had landed in jail—but from Moscow to Bejiing the whole world now dances to the siren song they sang.

1998: J
Even tho
the secu
million in
recent T
reigns. I
issued in
at the he

Ivan Boesky
sentenced to 3 year
settles SEC charges
$100 million.

Milken is supposedly barred from industry for life (he just paid $48 ...ling a probation violation on the ...Warner–Turner merger), junk still ...$119 billion in junk bonds were ...7, triple the amount sold in 1986 ...of the age of Milken.

Michael Milken is ... a man of pure intellect and virtue, incapable of committing any but the slightest of sins or misdemeanors... **Jude Wanniski**, memo to Frank Rich 12/17/96

Rapid progress is unsettling.. These leaps of progress cause rapid change, and in rapid change there are always people who loose.... **Robert Bartley**, editor of the Wall Street Journal 5/17/92

...ennis Levine
...enced to 2 years,
...1,962.000 in fines
and penalties

Judge Kimba Wood

Michael Milken
sentenced to 10 years, and
$600 million in fines and
restitutions. Barred from the
securities industry for life.

Martin Siegel,
sentenced to 2 months.

TRUTH IS W

"It was a [Bronx] DJ style which helped to create the lifestyle which came to be known as hip-hop." **David Toop,** Author of The Rap Attack

It goes back to Africa...it was the Dillard storyteller that would tell the stories through hand clappin' and congas... at the same time, they would be getting their history and they would be getting the news.
KRS-1, Rap Pioneer

"...Rap is Black People's CNN..."
Chuck D, Public Enemy

"...The revolution will not be televised..."
Gil Scott-Heron

"...Don't push me 'cause I am close the edge. I'm tryin' not to lose my head..."
Grandmaster Flash & the Furious Five

"...I'll wet you like I never met you..." **Lil' Kim**

"You're Nobody (Til Somebody Kills You)
The Notorious B.I.G.

"They are the style—setters"
Betsey Johnson, Fashion designer

---

* the truth as sold by **Stuart Ewen,** author of "All Consuming Images"